ORACLE8 AND UNIX PERFORMANCE TUNING

Ahmed Alomari

Prentice Hall PTR
Upper Saddle River, NJ 07458
http://www.phptr.com

ISBN 0-13-907676-X

9 780139 076763

90000

Library of Congress Catalog-in-Publication Data

```
Alomari, Ahmed
    Oracle8 and UNIX performance tuning / by Ahmed Alomari
        p.   cm.
    Includes index.
    ISBN 0-13-907676-X
    1. Oracle (Computer file)  2. Relational databases.  3. UNIX
(Computer file)
QA76.9.D3A519  1998
005.75'65--dc21                                    98-22873
                                                      CIP
```

Editorial/production supervision: *Maria Molinari*
Interior formatting: *Vanessa Moore*
Cover design director: *Jerry Votta*
Cover design: *Scott Weiss*
Manufacturing manager: *Alexis R. Heydt*
Acquisitions editor: *Mark Taub*
Marketing Manager: *Dan Rush*
Editorial assistant: *AudriAnna Bazlen*

© 1999 Prentice Hall PTR
Prentice-Hall, Inc.
A Simon & Schuster Company
Upper Saddle River, NJ 07458

For more information, contact
        Corporate Sales Department,
        Phone: 800-382-3419; FAX: 201-236-7141
        E-mail (Internet): corpsales@prenhall.com
or write: Prentice Hall PTR
        Corporate Sales Department
        One Lake Street
        Upper Saddle River, NJ 07458

Printed in the United States of America

10   9   8   7   6   5   4   3

ISBN 0-13-907676-X

Prentice-Hall International (UK) Limited, *London*
Prentice-Hall of Australia Pty. Limited, *Sydney*
Prentice-Hall of Canada, Inc., *Toronto*
Prentice-Hall Hispanoamericana S.A., *Mexico*
Prentice-Hall of India Private Limited, *New Delhi*
Prentice-Hall of Japan, Inc., *Tokyo*
Simon & Schuster Asia Pte. Ltd., *Singapore*
Editora Prentice-Hall do Brasil, Ltda., *Rio de Janeiro*

CONTENTS

Contents

LIST OF TABLES

LIST OF FIGURES

PREFACE

The purpose of this book is to share my experiences in the areas of UNIX and Oracle performance and tuning. Although this book may be used as a reference guide for UNIX kernel or Oracle startup parameters, it is intended to be an overall reference for concepts. The chapters of this book provide a tremendous level of detail on the internal workings of the Oracle and UNIX kernels. The purpose of including so much detail is to give the reader a complete understanding of Oracle and UNIX. It is this understanding that will enable the reader to apply these concepts to specific applications and/or user environments, thus enabling the reader to maximize the performance of his or her environment.

It is a key characteristic of this book that only the latest versions of Oracle and UNIX are discussed. The book covers Oracle7 and Oracle8, Sun Solaris 2.4, 2.5, and 2.6, Sequent Dynix 4.1, 4.2, and 4.4, and HP-UX 10 and 11. This will enable the reader to focus on the functionality and enhancements of the new versions, avoiding discussion of old releases.

Another characteristic of this book is that I have organized it into two major areas: decision support and transaction workloads. I felt that rather than focus on areas in the Oracle kernel and discuss each parameter, I would focus instead on the workload and discuss the affected areas of the Oracle kernel per workload.

Recommended prerequisites for this book are a basic understanding of SQL, UNIX shell language, and experience with UNIX system and Oracle database administration.

I have been a user of Oracle and UNIX across many different platforms including Sun, Sequent, HP, VAX/VMS, MS-DOS, Windows, and IBM RT. In this book, I intend to cover in great detail the Sun Solaris, Sequent Dynix/ptx, and HP-UX operating systems.

I hope you enjoy this book and find it useful in mastering the areas of performance and tuning. Good luck, and away we go!

ACKNOWLEDGMENTS

This book is dedicated to my uncle, the late Dr. Muayyad Al-Omari. My uncle was a professor in cardiothorasic surgery and was one of the first surgeons to perform open heart surgery in the Middle East. He was also a member of the American College of Surgeons for his achievements and publications in medicine. He was a great inspiration to me and my family. His family values and lively personality are an example for us to emulate.

Special thanks to my parents, Mukarram Alomari and Dr. Suha Alomari, and to my wife Lana who give true meaning to the words commitment, dedication, and excellence. Their values and encouragement keep me constantly striving to excel.

Thanks to the rest of my family Mustafa, Mohammed, May, Abdullah, and Zina for their support and encouragement.

I would also like to sincerely thank Henry Dai of Oracle and the Oracle engineers and support staff with whom I have had the pleasure of working with. Thanks also to the Sun, HP, and Sequent engineers and support staff. Thanks to Vincent Carbone for his contributions on the Sequent architecture and performance tuning recommendations.

I would also like to thank the reviewers, Nasser Siddiqi, Vincent Carbone, Michael Machowicz, Ross Campbell, and Omar Halaseh. Their diligent and careful review helped me improve the format and organization of the book.

Thanks also to Mark Taub of Prentice Hall and the Prentice Hall staff for the editing and publishing efforts of this book.

Best Regards,

Ahmed Alomari
aalomari@us.oracle.com

INTRODUCTION

TUNING AND SCIENCE

Tuning is by no means a science—meaning that it is not exact. Tuning is, however, similar to science in that tuning should follow the scientific technique. Science calls for defining the problem, followed by the formation of a hypothesis, and finally the performance of a series of tests on the hypothesis. Tuning is, in fact, very similar. Tuning should begin with the system and database administrator not necessarily defining the problem, but defining the goal. Then the system and database administrator must continue to develop test cases until the goal is reasonably achieved. For example, if the goal of a particular application is to achieve 1,000,000 transactions per second as the system throughput, the database administrator should execute as many test cases as necessary until the transactions per second (TPS) rate is achieved. The database administrator and developer should continue to tune the database and the application parameters until the desired TPS rate is achieved.

TUNING BY ITERATION

Tuning is definitely an iterative process that requires precision, analysis, and focus. One key element is that you must tune in a controlled environment. In other words, you should not change 20 different parameters at once and then reexecute the benchmark tests. Although you may have achieved the level of performance you desire, you will not have a concrete analysis as to which parameters directly affected the system performance. During the tuning process, try to minimize the amount of change per test (or benchmark) so that you can quantify each change in terms of its effect on performance. For example, if you are experiencing a low buffer cache hit ratio in the UNIX kernel, do not alter all the parameters associated with the buffer cache and paging at once. Try to increase the size of the buffer cache at a nominal rate at each iteration and measure the performance at each iteration. For example, consider the following system:

```
Iteration:             Parameter:                Performance Metric:
=========================================================================
    1          db_block_buffers=10000      Buffer Cache Hit Ratio=85%
    2          db_block_buffers=12000      Buffer Cache Hit Ratio=96%
```

In this example, increasing the size of the Oracle buffer cache by 20 percent resulted in a 13 percent performance gain in terms of the buffer cache hit ratio. However, tuning is not this simple. The 13 percent buffer cache hit ratio gain may have caused a performance degradation in other areas.

The goal of performance and tuning is twofold: First, the obvious one, is to achieve the desired performance metrics for the system; second, qualify and quantify in detail the environment that helped achieved the desired performance levels. The result of the summarized findings should also help in capacity planning for future projects.

TUNING BY UNDERSTANDING

Another problem with performance and tuning that I have both witnessed and heard from customer sites is that the database and/or system administrator alters system and/or database parameters without a clear understanding of the purpose of the parameters. Each parameter in the UNIX kernel and the Oracle Database Management System (DBMS) has a specific purpose and performance can be seriously affected if care is not taken to understand its purpose before its value is altered.

My advice to you is to gain as much understanding of the details of your environment by learning the concepts and the purpose of the tunable parameters before you embark on your performance tuning efforts. For example, if you are running Oracle8 on an HP-UX Version 11 V2200 server, you should first learn the V2200 architecture so that you can take advantage of your system's architecture, then learn the concepts of the HP-UX Version 11 Operating System (OS), and finally learn all of the Oracle HP specific features.

TUNING AND TRAINING

Similar to performance and tuning, training is also a continuous iterative process. A great philosopher once said that life is simply one large classroom where lessons are taught and learned continuously. If you are going to be the person primarily responsible for system performance, I encourage you to work with your management to seek approval for formal training courses. Do not try to learn everything by yourself. This may result in a painful and time-consuming experience. The trainers who teach the advanced courses of operating system concepts and performance tuning have a tremendous amount of knowledge, expertise, and valuable experience that can help make your efforts more successful. I especially recommend that you take the formal Oracle training courses such as *DBA I, DBA II,* and *Performance and Tuning*. Also, I strongly recommend that you take a course in operating system concepts and hardware architecture from your particular hardware vendor. For example, Sun offers an excellent course on the internals of the Solaris operating system that provides the student with detailed knowledge of the internal workings of the Solaris UNIX operating system. If you are trying to maximize the performance of your particular environment, you will definitely need to learn the details of your specific environment. And who better to learn the details from than the people who engineered the original software and hardware.

GETTING THE MOST FROM YOUR ENVIRONMENT

As you begin tuning on different platforms and environments, you will find that you can increase performance by taking advantage of platform-specific features. Oracle is an excellent example of a single product providing the same functionality on more than 92 different platforms. Oracle provides extensions for each platform in order to take advantage of that platform's capabilities. You must make a serious effort to understand your platform so that you can tune the system accordingly and thus take advantage of your platform's features. For example, some UNIX platforms do not provide asynchronous I/O on file systems (a more detailed discussion on asynchronous I/O will follow in Chapter 3). Sun, however, does provide asynchronous I/O on both raw (character) devices and file systems (block devices). Using this feature can increase your system's performance if you use file systems for your database files.

In Oracle7, you may discover that init.ora parameter files are not straightaway portable to other platforms. For example, you will probably receive some errors when you try to use an init.ora startup file taken from a Sun Solaris platform to a Sequent Dynix platform. This further illustrates Oracle's platform-specific extensions that take advantage of the respective platform. In Oracle8, platform-specific init.ora parameters were made generic. This ensures that the parameter has the same effect regardless of the platform.

TUNING ON THE PROJECT LOG

One of the major problems associated with performance and tuning is that it is usually left as a post-project task rather than a pre-project task. Consequently, the database and system administration staff are left to deal with this issue after the application has been moved into production. This is a difficult task because once the system is serving a production workload, it is nearly impossible to alter system parameters and restart the system. Or, if there is a service window whereby the system can be brought down for maintenance or backups, the window is usually too small to allow for benchmarking or performance testing.

Therefore, it is critical that the effort of tuning the system be made part of the project plan before the project is launched. In other words, the application or database system should not be launched until the level of performance is acceptable and all reasonable workloads have been tested fully. For example, if you plan to launch a decision-support data warehousing system that will support an average of 100 concurrent users, testing the system with a few users running a few queries is far from sufficient. You must test the system by scaling from one user all the way up to as many as 150 users in order to measure contention, scalability, and response time as the user community continues to grow.

THE TEAM

Another major problem associated with tuning is the lack of human resources to perform the tasks associated with tuning. This is due largely to the fact that tuning is viewed as a task of the system and database administrator. Tuning is neither a task for one person nor for one particular group. Tuning must be viewed as a task in which all groups participate and should include the application group, the system test group, the system administration group, the network administration group, the database design group, and the database administration group. All of these groups must act as a team so that the desired level of performance can be achieved in all areas, starting with the desktop all the way through the servers and including all the layers in between.

RESOURCES

In my experience dealing with performance and tuning, I have come to the conclusion that there are two major issues: insufficient time to conduct different test cases, and insufficient resources (people and hardware). As for the first problem—insufficient time to conduct different test cases—I can recommend only that the project members request an appropriate period of time for tuning as part of the project plan. At the majority of sites I have visited, very little (if any) time was dedicated to benchmarking. This book will help eliminate the growing pains that individuals involved in tuning are forced to undergo due to the lack of good reference material.

As for the problem of insufficient resources, it is critical to the success of the project that appropriate resources be both dedicated and available. Do not try to launch a 200-G database in production after testing only on a single CPU system with a 1-G database. It is vital that a test environment exists and that it mirror the production environment. This will help facilitate testing and benchmarking without affecting production. It will also strengthen the value of the tests and the benchmarks because the production environment and test environment will be similar. By similar, I mean that if the production environment consists of a 200-G database, the test environment should be near to that in size.

VERSION CONTROL

Do you remember the times when you have said, "I changed something, but I do not remember what, and now performance is worse"? For this reason, and many more, I seriously encourage you to use a version control system for maintaining changes to the database and OS configuration files. Using a version control system makes performance tuning easier because you can check in and check out configuration files of your choice easily without the pain of maintaining different configuration files manually. Whether you choose PVCS, RCS, or any other version control system, the important thing is that you do choose and use one. A version control system also facilitates ease of communication between teammates because all changes are documented and checked into the version control system. You may also want to consider developing a basic GUI front end for the init.ora parameters using something like Oracle Developer/2000. This would enable you to make changes to the parameter file through a GUI tool and store each revision in the database. The version control system also will help management understand more clearly the efforts involved with performance and tuning and can also act as a documentation repository for system configuration.

THE REPOSITORY

In conjunction with a version control system, you should also use a repository manager such as Oracle Designer/2000. This will help you maintain more specific information regarding your Oracle database, such as database creation scripts, SQL (Structured Query Language) scripts, and user-related information such as tables, indexes, users, and permissions. The repository can be used to maintain sizing information on tablespaces, data files, tables, indexes, and other database objects.

STAYING CURRENT

It is critical that you try to keep your computing environment current. Do not fall behind and find that you are running old and unsupported releases of software. You need to stay current with both the operating system versions and the Oracle software. The Operating System (OS) vendors are continuously enhancing their operating system and fixing bugs.

Oracle also is constantly expanding its products' features and functionality. Both the OS vendors and Oracle continually improve the performance of their products through the inclusion of new features and functionality. Therefore, it is key that you maintain a current environment, thereby enabling you to utilize the new features and performance enhancements. I am amazed at the number of sites that are still running SQL*Net V1 and Oracle 7.0. Some sites are still running Oracle V6. The current release of Oracle8 is 8.0, and Oracle8 release 8.0 provides a tremendous number of new features for DSS and OLTP environments. Part of a system's or database administrator's role is to study the latest versions and maintain a current operating environment. OS versions are also extremely critical because OS patches are periodically released from the OS vendor that fix critical bugs such as memory leaks, and system panics and often correct performance problems.

The task of remaining current is twofold: First, you must study the latest version in detail to determine the functionality and enhancements provided; and second, you must maintain a separate test environment. The test environment should be similar (if not identical) to your production environment. The test environment will enable you to test the new versions of the different products thoroughly. This will facilitate a smoother transition when you upgrade production systems since you will be familiar with any bugs, issues, or problems that the new version may introduce. The test environment will also help you work closely with the product vendor by reporting any bugs or issues that you may encounter during testing. The problems you report may be known already, and fixes might be immediately available; or, you may have to work closely with the vendor and provide them with a reproducible test case if the problem you discover is new. Testing new releases and keeping your environment current is a rather large task. For this reason, it is necessary to distribute the workload. For instance, you may have one person or a few people responsible for testing, and another group of people responsible for studying the new releases in detail before testing begins. When you consider an upgrade to a new release of a product, it is important that you work closely with the vendor and inform the vendor of your plans to upgrade. The vendor may have a migration path document, explaining the recommended approach to the migration, as well as a list of the known bugs and issues. In some cases, the vendor may discover critical problems in the new release and may issue a general warning to customer sites informing them thereof.

If you have a large number of systems, upgrading can be a tedious process. For this reason, you should try to automate the upgrade process as much as possible. Try to have, at a minimum, one NFS server that has all the product releases on at least one system organized by product and version. Using multiple NFS servers reduces the dependency on one system and increases the performance of the installations since not all installations will access only one NFS server. Then, you can simply NFS-mount the necessary partition on the system you want to upgrade. This avoids having to use CDs or tapes to install or upgrade software. Also, using the NFS technique, you can develop scripts to upgrade multiple systems simultaneously. As always, remember to perform a complete system backup before you upgrade to a new version of software. You may need to roll back to the backup in the event that the new version introduces some problems.

Chapter 1

INSIDE THE UNIX KERNEL

Despite the simplicity of the UNIX operating system at its inception, UNIX has evolved into a very complex, versatile, and scalable operating system. This complexity is due to the fact that the kernel manages a wide variety of services including Network File Systems (NFS), Input/Output (I/O), sockets, and process and memory management. The UNIX operating system is highly tunable and supports many different types of configuration. This chapter is not meant to be an introduction to the UNIX operating system. On the contrary, this chapter requires that you have a good working knowledge of the UNIX operating system. If you find this material overwhelming or difficult to understand, please consider reading a book on the fundamentals of the UNIX operating system (see the References section).

1.1 UNIX INTERNALS

The UNIX kernel is the central core of the operating system. It provides an interface to the hardware devices as well as to process, memory, and I/O management. The kernel manages requests from users via system calls that switch the process from user space to kernel space (see Figure 1.1).

Each time a user process makes a system call such as read(), fork(), exec(), open(), and so on, the user process experiences a *context switch*. A context switch is a mechanism by which a process switches from one state to another. The process may be either suspended until the system call is completed (*blocking*), or the

FIGURE 1.1   System calls and the UNIX kernel.

process may continue and later be notified of the system call completion via a signal (*nonblocking*). Figure 1.2 shows an example of a context switch.

Figure 1.2 demonstrates a user process issuing a system call, in this case the `read()`[1] system call. The `read()` system call takes a file descriptor, buffer, and the number of bytes to be read as arguments. The `read()` system call forces the user process to block until the completion or timeout of the `read()` system call. Most UNIX operating system vendors provide a library for performing nonblocking (*asynchronous*) I/O calls since the traditional UNIX I/O calls of `read()` and `write()` are blocking (*synchronous*). See Chapter 3 for a more detailed discussion on the UNIX I/O model.

The UNIX kernel provides services to different system resources including I/O, memory management, process management, and network services. A particular application or user process accesses the system resources and services via system calls. The performance of the application is highly dependent on the type of system calls used, and the number of system calls per application. Kernel resources are expensive and should be regarded as a valuable and limited set of resources. In order to maximize performance, the application should minimize the amount of system calls used, thereby reducing kernel space overhead and maintaining the user process in user space for most of the time. However, certain applications, such as a database management system heavily dependent on I/O, cannot avoid system calls. The goal in this situation is to tune the UNIX kernel and the system to respond as quickly and efficiently as possible so that the kernel

---

1. Refer to the manual pages on the `read()` system call.

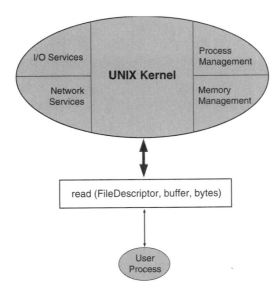

FIGURE 1.2 User process issues `read()` system call.

resources can be freed quickly to service other requests. In other words, the goal of the application should be to minimize the amount of time spent in kernel space while maximizing throughput in the user space.

One of the major system calls central to the UNIX operating system is the `fork()` system call.[2] The `fork()` system call creates another process known as the *child* process, while the process that issued the `fork()` system call becomes the *parent* process. The `fork()` system call duplicates the entire process structure and the process address space of the parent process. The child process inherits the job class characteristics and environment of the parent process. The child process also inherits open file descriptors from the parent process. You can reference the parent process ID of a process using the `ps -ef` command.[3] The `fork()` system call enables one process to create another process either synchronously by waiting on the child process, or asynchronously by continuing the execution of the parent process. The `fork()` system call takes no arguments and returns an integer. The return value can represent one of three distinct values:

1. 0, meaning the `fork()` call successfully created a child process, and 0 refers to the child process within the parent process;
2. −1, meaning the system was unable to create another process. In this case, you can use the `perror()`[4] system call to output the exact error message that caused the `fork()` call to fail; or

---

2. Refer to the manual pages on `fork()` (i.e., man fork) for a detailed description of the `fork()` system call.
3. Refer to the manual pages on `ps` for platform-specific options.
4. Refer to the manual pages on `perror()` for a complete description.

3. A default positive integer greater than 0 that is returned to the parent process which represents the process ID of the child process. The parent process can then wait on this child process, thereby blocking until termination of the child process, or the parent process can continue execution without waiting on the child process. This would be an asynchronous event, and the parent process can be signaled when the child process terminates. The parent process would need to establish a signal handler code segment to trap and interpret the signal from the child process.

The fork() system call is not only used within application programs to create subprocesses and subtasks, but also within the kernel itself to create subprocesses. For example, consider the output in Table 1.1 from the ps -ef command.

TABLE 1.1   Output from the ps -ef command

UID	PID	PPID	TIME CMD
root	0	0	0:01 sched
root	1	0	0:01 /etc/init -
root	2	0	0:00 pageout
root	3	0	3:27 fsflush
root	131	1	0:01 /usr/sbin/inetd -s
root	289	1	0:00 /usr/lib/saf/sac -t 300
root	112	1	0:02 /usr/sbin/rpcbind
root	186	1	0:00 /usr/lib/lpsched
root	104	1	0:12 /usr/sbin/in.routed -q
root	114	1	0:01 /usr/sbin/keyserv
root	122	1	0:00 /usr/sbin/kerbd
root	120	1	0:00 /usr/sbin/nis_cachemgr
root	134	1	0:00 /usr/lib/nfs/statd
root	136	1	0:00 /usr/lib/nfs/lockd
root	155	1	0:00 /usr/lib/autofs/automountd
root	195	1	0:00 /usr/lib/sendmail -bd -q1h
root	159	1	0:00 /usr/sbin/syslogd
root	176	1	0:07 /usr/sbin/nscd
root	169	1	0:13 /usr/sbin/cron

In Table 1.1, the sched process has the Process ID (PID) 0 and a Parent Process ID (PPID) of 0, meaning the sched process is the base process. The init process has a process ID of 1 and a parent process ID of 0, meaning that the init process was inherited by the sched process. The sched process is the scheduler process that is responsible for scheduling processes on the run queue. The inetd daemon has a process ID of 131 and a parent process of 1, meaning the inetd daemon was inherited by the init process. The init process is the system initializer process responsible for spawning and initializing processes with certain defaults.

Therefore, it is apparent that the fork() system call plays a large role in the UNIX operating system and is used frequently in both user applications and system applications. Consider the following program segment that summarizes the fork() system call and its use.

File: sample1.c

```
#define FORK_ERROR     -1

#include <stdio.h>
#include <unistd.h>

main ()
{

   int lpid;

   lpid=fork();   /* fork() issued, return code is checked below for */
   switch(lpid)   /* success or failure. */
   {

       case 0:   /* Child Process section - fork() succeeded, call
                     execl(). */
        execl ("sample2",arg*0,arg*1,....,arg*n, NULL);

       case -1:   /* Unable to create process */
           perror ("Unable to create process");
           exit (FORK_ERROR);

       default:   /* Return to Parent Process */
           /* Either continue or wait on child process. */
           /* Value returned here is process id of child process. */

   }


}
```

The process flow of this program would appear as in Figure 1.3 if compiled and executed.

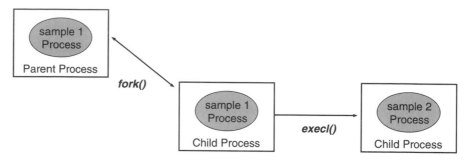

FIGURE 1.3   Process flow.

1.2   UNIX ARCHITECTURE

The UNIX operating system consists of many different layers that manage different resources and services. The basic architecture of the UNIX Operating System (OS) consists of two main layers: the system or kernel layer, and the user layer.

Figure 1.4 illustrates the different layers of the UNIX operating system.

1.2.1   KERNEL LAYER

The kernel layer is the core of the operating system and provides services such as process and memory management, I/O services, device drivers, job scheduling, and

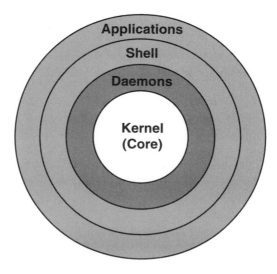

FIGURE 1.4   Layers of the UNIX operating system.

low-level hardware interface routines such as test and set instructions. The kernel layer consists of many different internal routines that process the user requests. Access to the kernel is indirect via system calls. You cannot call the internal kernel routines directly. The system calls provide a mechanism by which a user process via the system call can request a kernel resource or service. The kernel itself is relatively small in terms of its disk and memory storage sizes. On Sequent systems, the kernel is located in the root directory and consists of a single file named unix (/unix). The size of the UNIX kernel on Sequent systems varies depending on the system configuration and the number of device drivers configured. A typical size may range from 1 M–5 M. On Solaris 2.6 systems, the file path for the UNIX kernel is /platform/<platform_type>/kernel/unix. The <platform_type> indicates the type of system architecture such as sun4m or sun4u. It is important to note that when the operating system is installed on the machine, you must allocate enough space for the root file system. If you do not allocate sufficient space, you may not be able to rebuild the kernel because rebuilding the kernel requires a temporary staging area to hold both the new kernel and the previous kernel file. In addition, you may also not be able to install operating system patches if sufficient free space does not exist in the root file system. I recommend that you always leave at least 100 M free in the root file system. Although this may seem high, rebuilding the root file system to increase its space is not an easy task. It is better to have extra space than be short a few megabytes.

The kernel also provides services such as signal handling, synchronization, inter-process communication, file system services, network services, and hardware monitoring. Each time a process is started, the kernel has to initialize the process, assign the process a priority, allocate memory and resources for the process, and schedule the process to run. When the process terminates, the kernel frees any memory and/or resources held by the process. The UNIX process model will be discussed in greater detail later in Section 1.2.5.

1.2.2   FILE SYSTEMS

The UNIX file system is a hierarchical file system that begins with the root (/) file system. Each file system is mounted at a mount-point. For example, the /(root) file system is mounted on the / mount-point. The /usr file system is mounted on the /usr mount-point. Figure 1.5 shows the hierarchical directory structure of the UNIX file system.

In Figure 1.5, the /usr, /var, and /opt directories are subdirectories of the /(root) file system. The /usr, /var, and /opt subdirectories may each be separate file systems from the root file system; however, the hierarchical file structure still applies. In fact, it is recommended that the /(root), /var, /opt, and /usr subdirectories all be separate file systems. This helps prevent the root file system from being filled up with patches, system log files, E-mail, and user software packages. This also increases the performance of the root file system since the overhead of maintaining a larger file system is reduced by separating the Operating System (OS) binaries and executables from user software packages and system log files.

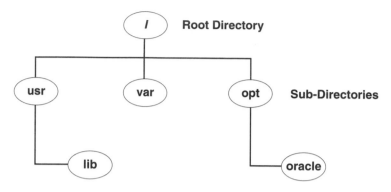

FIGURE 1.5   Directory structure of the UNIX file system.

The UNIX file system has many different file system types such as ufs (UNIX file system), NFS (Network File System), vxfs (Veritas file system), and cdfs (CD-ROM file system). The ufs file system type is the most standard UNIX file system consisting of superblocks, inodes, offsets, and storage blocks. Reads and writes to a ufs file system are done in blocks depending on the size of the file system block size. Block sizes can range from 1K to 8K depending on the file system type selected. NFS is a remote file system that is exported to other client systems. These client systems may mount the remote file system from the server that is exporting the file system. There are system daemons on both sides (NFS server daemons and NFS client daemons) that communicate with each other via RPC (Remote Procedure Call). NFS packets are IP (Internet Protocol) packets that utilize the UDP (User Datagram Protocol) datagram.[5] The vxfs file system type is a file system based on the Veritas Volume Management software.[6] The cdfs file system type is a CD-ROM–based file system, also referred to as hsfs (High Sierra file system) and ISO 9660 CD-ROM file system.

1.2.2.1   ufs

The ufs file system is the most common UNIX file system type and consists of a block-based file system that contains offsets, super-blocks, cylinder groups' maps, inodes, and storage blocks. Figure 1.6 shows the ufs file system type structure.

Each ufs file system consists of multiple cylinder groups with each cylinder group consisting of the structure diagrammed in Figure 1.6. The boot block is contained only in the first cylinder group of the file system (Cylinder Group 0). The boot block is 8K in size and contains the boot strap used during the system boot process. If the file system is not used for booting (i.e., other than the root file system), the boot block is left blank.

---

5. Solaris 2.5 changed the NFS code (NFS Version 3) to utilize TCP/IP instead of UDP which is a more reliable datagram.
6. Veritas provides disk volume management software for UNIX platforms.

Cylinder Group n:

FIGURE 1.6   The `ufs` file system type structure.

The super block consists of information about the file system, such as

- ❑ Status of the file system (used by `fsck`)
- ❑ File system label (name)
- ❑ File system size in logical blocks
- ❑ Date and time stamp of the last update
- ❑ Cylinder group size
- ❑ Number of data blocks per cylinder group
- ❑ Summary data block

     The cylinder group map is a specific feature of the `ufs` file system type and consists of a block of data per cylinder group that maintains block usage within the cylinder. The cylinder group map also maintains the free list of unused blocks, as well as monitors disk fragmentation.

     The inode layer is one of the most important layers within the file system. The inode layer contains most of the information about a file with the exception of the file's name. The name of the file is maintained in a directory. An inode is approximately 128 bytes long. By default, an inode is created for every 2K of storage in the file system. The number of inodes can be specified during the file system creation phase by using the `newfs` or `mkfs` command.[7] See Chapter 3 for more details on tuning file systems. An inode in the `ufs` file system contains the following information:

---

7. Refer to the manual pages on `newfs` and `mkfs` for specific parameters and options.

❑ Mode and type of the file
❑ Number of hard links to the file
❑ User ID of the owner of the file
❑ Group ID of the group to which the file belongs
❑ Number of bytes in the file
❑ Two arrays comprising a total of 15 disk block addresses
❑ Date and time stamp of last access
❑ Date and time stamp of last modification
❑ Date and time stamp of file creation

The core of an inode is two arrays that together consist of 15 disk block addresses. The first array is comprised of 12 direct addresses. These direct addresses map directly to the first 12 storage blocks of the file. If the file size exceeds 12 blocks, the first address of the second array refers to an indirect block. This indirect block consists of direct addresses as opposed to file contents. The second address refers to a double indirect block containing addresses of indirect blocks. The third address references a triple indirect block containing addresses of indirect blocks. Figure 1.7 portrays the ufs addressing scheme.[8]

Table 1.2 shows the maximum number of bytes addressable by each level of indirection.[9]

TABLE 1.2   Maximum addressable size

LOGICAL BLOCK SIZE	DIRECT BLOCKS	SINGLE INDIRECT BLOCKS	DOUBLE INDIRECT BLOCKS
2 K	24 K	1 M	512 M
4 K	48 K	4 M	4 G
8 K	96 K	16 M	32 G

The maximum file size in a ufs file system is 2-G, which is addressable through triple indirection. Triple indirection is a signed 32-bit field, hence the 2 G file limit as most UNIX operating systems are 32-bit.[10] Most UNIX vendors are currently working to convert to a 64-bit–based operating system. The 64-bit operating system will eliminate the 2-G file limit, thus allowing terabyte size files. Although the logical file system block

---

8. Kulihin, Julia, Fox, Mary L., Nester, Joan. *System Administration*, Vol. 2. UNIX SVR4.2 MP, pp. 3–18.
9. Kulihin, Julia, Fox, Mary L., Nester, Joan. *System Administration*, Vol. 2. UNIX SVR4.2 MP, pp. 3–18.
10. Digital has the DEC-Alpha UNIX Servers, which are based on Digital's 64-bit operating system.

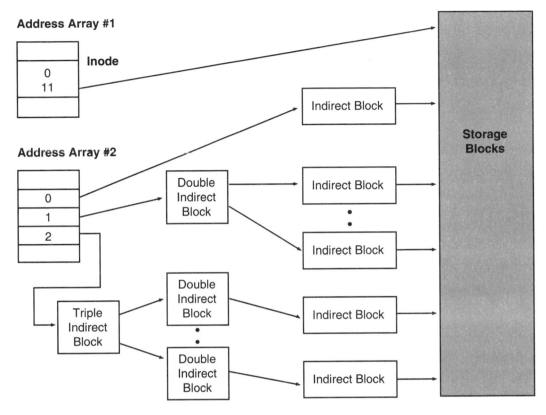

FIGURE 1.7 The ufs addressing scheme.

size ranges from 2K to 8K, ufs provides a smaller subset of a block known as a fragment or chunk. The fragment or chunk is usually 1K in size but can be set to a multiple of the operating system block size of 512 bytes. Fragments are used to accommodate smaller files in order to avoid a wastage of space. The maximum length of a ufs filename is 255 bytes.

Each time a ufs file system is mounted, the state of the file system is checked. If the file system state is stable or clean, the file system is mounted and made available for use. If the file system state is unstable, an fsck is performed on the file system. The fsck utility scans the file system and corrects any discrepancies found between the inode information and data storage blocks. The fsck utility may cause a loss of data if certain inconsistent files are truncated. For large file systems, fsck may take a long time because fsck is a synchronous process and must scan the entire file system. For this reason, you may choose to use a journaled file system such as vxfs.

Super-Block
Object Location Table
Intent Log
Object Location Table Replica
Allocation Unit 0
•   •   •   •
Allocation Unit n

FIGURE 1.8   Structure of the `vxfs` file system.

1.2.2.2   `vxfs`

The `vxfs` file system is based on the Veritas Volume Management software. The `vxfs` file system offers several enhancements over the `ufs`-based file system. It provides extent level allocation and a journal feature. The extent level allocation reduces the allocation workload by allocating an extent (many blocks) at once, as opposed to the `ufs`-based file system which allocates in increments of blocks. The journal feature is similar to the concept of the Oracle redo log. As changes are made to the file system, those changes are recorded in the journal. Therefore, if the system were to crash or panic, an `fsck` would not be necessary since the journals need only to be applied to restore the file system's state of consistency. This significantly reduces the length of recovery time following a system crash or panic. Figure 1.8 details the structure of the `vxfs` file system.[11]

1.2.2.3   NFS

NFS (Network File System) is a remote file system that is accessed by client systems over the network. NFS file system types are extremely common and popular in the UNIX environment. NFS allows multiple client systems access to a common file system from an NFS server. It also provides heterogeneous systems the ability to share files and

---

11. Kulihin, Julia, Fox, Mary L., Nester, Joan. *System Administration*, Vol. 2. UNIX SVR4.2 MP, pp. 3–33.

data. This centralizes system administration since only the NFS server needs to be backed up. This of course also leads to a single point of failure. NFS file systems typically are used for development, home directories, and software distribution. Figure 1.9 shows how an NFS file system works.

In Figure 1.9, the NFS server—that is, the system exporting the file system for remote mounting (access)—is running the NFS server daemons which service NFS client requests. On the client side, the client—a workstation or another server—mounts the file system as an NFS file system and accesses the NFS file system through the NFS client daemons. The NFS client daemons communicate with the NFS server daemons via RPC (Remote Procedure Call). Remote procedure calls enable applications to call procedures (functions) on a remote system. RPC uses the XDR (External Data Representation) protocol for data exchange. For more information on XDR or RPC, refer to the respective manual pages, or refer to a programmer's guide on RPC. A heavily hit NFS server can significantly increase the network traffic. This can affect network and NFS performance. There are many performance issues to consider when using NFS file systems. Performance issues pertaining to NFS are discussed in Chapter 3.

1.2.2.4 cdfs

The cdfs file system is a CD-ROM–based file system that is used to mount CDs for the purposes of installing software and/or data. These file systems are read-only and provide specific options during mounting[12] that control the format of the files on the CD.

● NFS Client Daemons

Network

Client   **RPC**

Exported
File System

● NFS Server Daemons

NFS Server

FIGURE 1.9   The NFS file system concept.

---

12. Refer to the manual pages on the mount command.

1.2.2.5   The vnode

Internally, UNIX manages file systems using *vnodes*. Vnodes are known as virtual nodes and act as a higher-level object to the inode. The UNIX operating system uses the inode object to manage files and file systems. Vnodes are virtual nodes which then map to the specific object type depending on the use of the vnode. For example, for the ufs file system, a vnode consists of an inode. For an NFS file system, the vnode is an rnode (remote node). For more information on the vnode structure, you can browse the vnode header file `/usr/include/sys/vnode.h`. The vnode structure allows for a generic file system implementation regardless of the specific type of file system.

1.2.2.6   Large Files

In the race to provide support for large files (files larger than 2 G in the 32-bit world), operating system vendors have recently provided APIs allowing applications to manage large files. Solaris 2.6, HP-UX 10.2, and Dynix ptx 4.4 provide APIs that support 64-bit file offsets. Many vendors such as Sun, HP, Sequent, Oracle, and Veritas participated in the Large File Summit. The Large File Summit (LFS) is an industry initiative to develop a generic specification for the support of files larger than 2 G. The LFS specification extends the current interfaces to behave differently when dealing with large files. For instance, the `open()` system call will set errno to `EOVERFLOW` if the file is greater than or equal to 2 G.

The LFS draft defines a set of additional 64-bit API functions that provide support for regular size and large size files. In essence, the LFS draft defines a new set of functions named `xxx64()` corresponding to the existing set of functions named `xxx()`. For example, `open64()`, `creat64()`, `lstat64()`, and `lseek64()` are a few of the 64-bit functional interfaces added by the LFS specification. There is also a 64-bit file offset data type, namely `off64_t`.

In Solaris 2.6, setting `_FILE_OFFSET_BITS` to 64 in your application source before including system headers enables the 64-bit interfaces. Setting `_FILE_OFFSET_BITS` to 64 results in `off_t` being type-defined as a `long long` 64-bit data type. In addition, the existing file I/O function calls -`xxx()`- will be mapped to their 64-bit counterpart -`xxx64()`. In order to utilize the large file functionality, refer to your platform specific documentation. Each platform may have a different set of APIs and commands for dealing with large files.

Solaris 2.6 also provides a new mount option which enables or disables large file support. If the file system is mounted with the `largefiles` option, then files larger than 2 G can be created in the file system. The `nolargefiles` mount option disables support for large files. The system administrator can use these mount options on a per file system basis in order to manage large file support.

Large files are useful because they improve system administration and performance. System and database administrators now have the ability to reduce the number of files by utilizing large files. This helps reduce the complexity of backups and restores in dealing with a large number of files. However, large files also reduce the amount of file

I/O parallelism. For example, two 2-G files may be backed up or restored concurrently as opposed to a single 4-G file. Large files may also improve performance by allowing wider stripes. The 2 G file size restriction limited the sizes of disk partitions and thus the width of the stripe. By using the large file feature, more disks can be added to the stripe. For instance, instead of creating a 2-G stripe consisting of three disks, you can create a 4-G stripe consisting of six disks. The large file option has its advantages and disadvantages, but for the most part it is a useful feature enabling UNIX applications to manage large files.

1.2.2.7   UNIX Buffer Cache

UNIX employs a file system buffer cache to cache file system information such as directory name lookups, inodes, and file control block data. The actual file data blocks are part of the virtual memory pages, not the buffer cache. The concept of the UNIX file system cache is simple: data from reads and writes is maintained in the cache in the event that subsequent reads may request data that is already in the cache. This significantly increases performance since access to the cache is in the time order of nanoseconds (memory access speeds), and access to the disk is in the time order of milliseconds (disk access speeds). This is an order of magnitude 100,000 times greater since milliseconds have a base of 10^{-3}, and nanoseconds have a base of 10^{-9}. When a user process issues a read, the kernel first scans through the UNIX file system cache to determine if the data is already in the cache (*cache hit*). A cache hit means that the read request found the data in the cache, thereby avoiding physical disk I/O. If the data is in the cache, the kernel copies the data from the file system cache into the user's workspace. Although this is a memory-to-memory copy, system performance can suffer during periods of high file system activity. This can also lead to increased levels of paging. See Chapter 3 for a discussion of the performance tuning tips for the UNIX file system cache. If the data was not found in the cache (*cache miss*), the kernel issues a physical read to the disk drive(s) containing the data and brings the data into the UNIX file sytem cache. A cache miss means that the data was not found in the cache, and physical I/O was necessary to bring the data into the cache. The kernel then copies the data from the UNIX file system cache into the user's workspace. Figure 1.10 shows a cache hit and Figure 1.11 shows a cache miss.

Each time a user process issues a write to a file system–based file, the data is written to the file system cache and later flushed to disk. Depending on the flags used to open[13] the file, physical writes to the file may be deferred. If the writes are deferred, the data is written only to the cache and is later flushed out to disk by the file system flush daemon. If the file was opened with the flag that requests writes to not be deferred, writes to the file are physically written to the disk. However, all file system reads are always read from the UNIX file system cache, unless specific calls are used to bypass the UNIX file system cache. The size of the UNIX file system cache is controlled by kernel-tunable parameters. On Solaris, the `bufhwm` kernel parameter controls the maximum size of the file system buffer cache. Another related parameter, `npbuf`, controls the

---

13. Refer to the manual pages on the `open()` file system call.

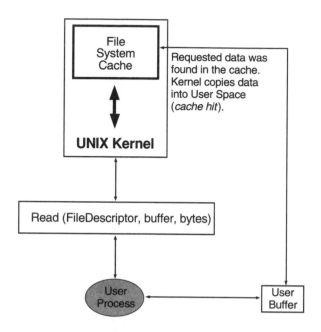

FIGURE 1.10   A cache hit.

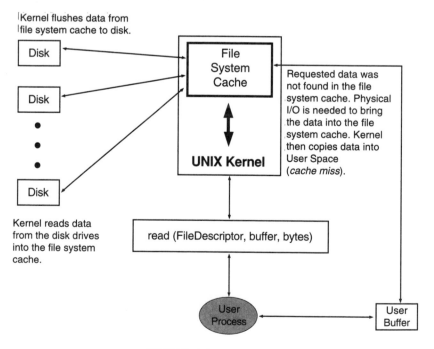

FIGURE 1.11   A cache miss.

number of physical I/O buffers allocated each time more buffers are needed (provided the total amount does not exceed bufhwm). These parameters can be set in the /etc/system file.

The UNIX file system cache uses a least recently used algorithm to age data out of the cache. The file system cache is maintained by a system daemon that is both time-driven and space-driven. The daemon wakes up periodically and scans for dirty pages to be written out. The daemon also ensures that there is sufficient space for reads and writes by flushing dirty disk pages to disk or aging out least recently used data. The file system daemon is tunable, and performance gains can be achieved by tuning the file system daemon appropriately.

1.2.3   VIRTUAL MEMORY

The UNIX operating system is based on the virtual memory model. The virtual memory model allows a process or a system to address more memory than physically exists. The UNIX virtual memory model consists of a set of memory pages, usually 4K each. Older versions of UNIX had page sizes of 8K. You can determine the page size on your platform by using the sysconf() [14] system call. The UNIX operating system uses a swap device in addition to physical memory to manage the allocation and deallocation of memory. For example, a machine with 64 M of physical memory and a 192-M swap device supports a virtual memory size of 256 M. Earlier versions of UNIX did not provide a finer level of memory management than swapping. Swapping is the process by which the system no longer has enough free physical memory available, and processes are completely swapped out (written) to the swap device. Once the process has been completely written out to the swap device (i.e., swapped out), the physical memory occupied by the process can be freed. The swap device can be a single file or series of files, and each swap file can be no larger than 2 G. [15] Therefore, the UNIX kernel virtual memory is based on both the physical memory and swap device. Figure 1.12 on the following page illustrates the virtual memory and swap device.

Because the UNIX operating system is based on the virtual memory model, a translation layer is needed between virtual memory addresses and physical memory addresses. This translation layer is part of the kernel and is usually written in machine language (Assembly) to achieve optimal performance when translating and mapping addresses. Figure 1.13 illustrates the virtual to physical translation layer within the kernel.

In Figure 1.13, each time a user process accesses memory, the kernel uses the address translation layer to map the virtual memory address into a physical memory address. Virtual addressing makes it possible to address larger amounts of memory than physically exist. As long as the virtual memory address scheme supports large memory configurations, adding additional physical memory is straightforward. Most 32-bit UNIX

---

14. Refer to the manual pages on the sysconf() system call.
15. This is due to the limitation that a single file on 32-bit UNIX platforms cannot exceed 2 G. Most OS vendors currently provide large file support.

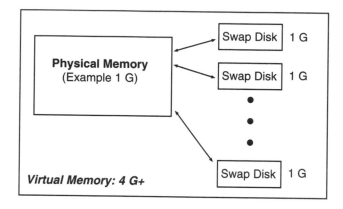

FIGURE 1.12   Virtual memory model.

kernels support a maximum of 4 G of direct addressable memory per process, and extensions are provided to address memory beyond 4 G.

Current versions of UNIX provide a more granular approach to swapping known as *paging*. Paging swaps out various different pages in memory to the swap device rather than the entire process as in swapping. This not only increases performance by minimizing the time needed to load a process into memory, it can also provide more physical memory to other processes. In certain instances, a process might allocate a large section of memory upon process invocation. However, most of this memory may remain unused during the life of the process. For example, declaring a large SGA when only a small

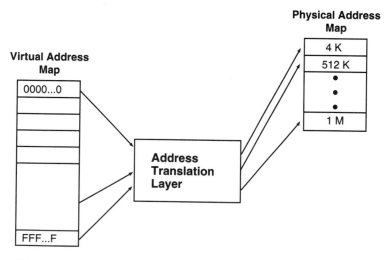

FIGURE 1.13   Virtual to physical memory address translation layer.

section of the SGA is actively used could cause the unused portions of the SGA to be paged back to the free list. This allows other processes access to these physical memory pages. Hence, paging not only minimizes the chances of a complete swapout, it also provides higher availability to memory by utilizing idle memory pages. The UNIX kernel maintains a free list of memory pages and uses a `page` daemon to periodically scan the memory pages for active and idle pages. The `page` daemon uses a clocklike algorithm to maintain pages in memory. Figure 1.14 shows the paging algorithm.[16]

In Figure 1.14, the `page` daemon using the minute hand (fronthand) scans the page list and examines the reference bit. If the reference bit is active, the page's reference bit is set to idle. If the reference bit is marked idle (meaning that no references have been made to this page), the page becomes a candidate for the page free list. During the second phase, the hour hand (backhand) scans the page list. If the reference bit is still idle and was set to idle during the previous scan, the page becomes a candidate for the free list. If the page reference bit is set (meaning that the page is active and has been referenced), the page is left alone. This algorithm's goal is twofold: to ensure that the system has plenty of free memory, and to minimize paging and swapping. There are system thresholds that control the frequency of the `page` daemon. As the available free memory closely approaches these thresholds, the `page` daemon will increase the frequency of its scans in order to increase the amount of free memory. The thresholds include limits such as the amount of memory that is always left free, the desired or ideal amount of free memory, and the amount of free memory before swapping occurs. All of these limits control the activity of the `page` daemon. Higher limits cause an active `page` daemon.

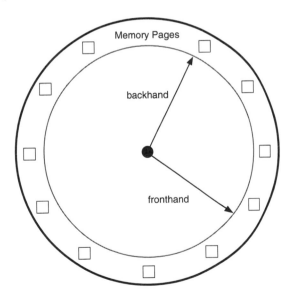

FIGURE 1.14   The paging algorithm.

16. SunService. *SunOS 5.X Internals Guide SP-365*, Revision B.1, September 1993, pp. 5–6.

Lower limits reduce the activity of the page daemon. Tuning the page daemon is discussed in Chapter 2.

Paging and swapping can severely impact the performance of your system, and efforts must be made to ensure that swapping never occurs and that paging activity is minimized. It should be noted that swapping is an act of desperation by the UNIX kernel to free memory immediately. This act of desperation causes processes to be completely swapped out in order to free memory. Thrashing occurs when even swapping was not successful in freeing memory, and memory is needed to service critical processes. This usually results in a system panic, as this is the last action that the kernel can take to free memory. Swapping needs to be avoided at all costs as this is evidence of insufficient memory. You may need to tune your system and/or application to use less memory or you may need to add additional physical memory to accommodate the workload.

1.2.4 SHARED MEMORY

The UNIX System V Release 4 operating system standard provides many different mechanisms for interprocess communication. Interprocess communication is required when multiple distinct processes need to communicate with each other either by sharing data or resources or both. Interprocess communication is also used when processes are dependent on one another. For example, one process may be responsible for updating files while another process is responsible for receiving the updates. Once received and verified, the process that receives the updates may forward the updates on to the other process to process the updates. These two processes need a method to share data. Shared memory is one of the methods of UNIX System V Release 4 interprocess communication. Shared memory, as the term suggests, enables multiple processes to "share" the same memory, in other words, multiple processes mapping into the same virtual address map. Shared memory avoids expensive memory-to-memory copies when processes need to share data in memory. Shared memory also increases application portability because most platforms support shared memory. Figure 1.15 illustrates the concept of shared memory.

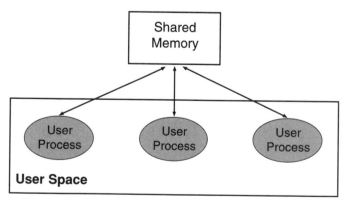

FIGURE 1.15   Shared memory concept.

Many applications use shared memory as a technique for interprocess communication. Oracle uses shared memory to hold the System Global Area (SGA). This enables Oracle processes and Oracle user connections to attach to the same SGA without having to copy the SGA between each process. Having to copy the SGA between processes not only would be time consuming, but memory requirements would also grow at an explosive rate.

1.2.5 PROCESS MODEL

The UNIX operating system uses a priority-based round-robin process scheduling architecture. Processes are dispatched to the run queue based on priority and are placed on the sleep queue based either on the process' completion of its time slice or by waiting on an event or resource. Processes can sometimes result in a deadlock when waiting on a resource. Hence, user applications need to provide deadlock detection to ensure that user processes do not deadlock on resources.

```
machine1% myprogram
```

When a user issues the command `myprogram` at the UNIX prompt, the kernel places the request for myprogram on the dispatch queue with a certain level of priority. The default priority for the particular job class is assigned assuming that no specific priority has been requested either through the `nice`[17] command or `priocntl()`[18] system call. The internal kernel routines scan the dispatch queue and the sleep queue to ensure that processes are not starved from the CPU and that processes do not exceed their time slice. Do not confuse internal kernel routines with system calls. Internal kernel routines are routines that can be used and called only by the kernel. System calls are the user interface to the kernel system services. For example, `fork()` and `read()` are examples of user system calls, while `getpage()` and `putpage()` are examples of internal memory management routines. Figure 1.16 illustrates the process scheduling cycle of the UNIX OS.

Figure 1.16 shows both the dispatch (i.e., run) queue and the sleep queue as containing processes. The dispatch queue contains processes marked as ready to run. Once a process is marked as runable, the process will begin execution on a CPU as soon as a CPU becomes available. In Figure 1.16, three processes are shown on the dispatch queue that then begin execution on the three available CPUs. Once the time slice (time-share job class) of the process is exceeded, the process is migrated to the sleep queue in favor of other processes which have been sleeping and are now marked as ready to run. The process scheduling algorithm in the UNIX kernel tries to balance CPU time collectively with other processes in order to avoid CPU starvation and CPU saturation. Once on the

---

17. The `nice` command enables a user to change the priority of a particular user process. Only the superuser or root account can increase the priority of a process using `nice`.
18. The `priocntl()` system call provides a system call interface to user process priority management.

FIGURE 1.16 Process scheduling cycle of the UNIX OS.

sleep queue, the process with the highest priority will be scheduled to run. The same holds true of the dispatch queue. The kernel may also *preempt* processes by reducing their priority. Preemption is a technique used by the UNIX kernel to stop a currently running process or set of processes and schedule other processes to run. A process can be preempted under many different circumstances, such as when the process exceeded its time slice, a higher priority process needs to be scheduled, a system event or interrupt occurred that needs to be serviced, or the process appears to be waiting on a resource that is busy. The kernel maintains information about processes including the current process state. Using the ps command, you can obtain the process state of a particular process or list of processes. For example, Table 1.3 shows the output listing from the ps command.

TABLE 1.3 Output listing from the ps command

ST	UID	PID	PPID	TIME	CMD
S	root	0	0	0:01	sched
S	root	1	0	0:01	/etc/init -
O	root	2	0	0:00	pageout
R	test	281	280	0:01	xterm
Z	test	282			<defunct>

The process state can be classified as one of the following:

> S — Process is currently sleeping.
>
> O — Process is currently running on a CPU.
>
> R — Process is ready to run.
>
> I — Process is idle; currently being created.
>
> T — Process is being traced.
>
> X — Process is awaiting memory.
>
> Z — Process is a zombie.

In a process state of S, the process is sleeping and is waiting on an event. The event could be waiting on an I/O request completion, waiting for a locked resource, or waiting on some data that is not yet available. A swapped process will also have a state of S (sleeping). Putting a process to sleep and later awakening the process is an expensive operation and can lead to performance problems—especially when a high number of process sleeps occur. A process state of O means the process is active and is running on a CPU. The process state R indicates that the process is ready to run, and as soon as a processor becomes available, the process will run (assuming it is not preempted in favor of a higher priority process). A process state of I indicates that the process is idle and is being created or initialized. A process state of T indicates that the process is being traced. This is common during debugging mode when parent processes trace child processes to detect problems. X refers to the state when the process is awaiting additional memory. Lastly, Z refers to the zombie process state. The zombie process state has two main meanings: the first is that the process (child process) has terminated and has a parent process. The second is that the process is marked to be killed by the UNIX kernel. Each process has a complete process structure associated with it when it is created. This process structure has a link to the address space of the process. During the zombie state, the process structure and address space are removed and freed back to the system. The only information remaining in the kernel for a zombie process is an entry in the process table. The kernel is responsible for cleaning up the process table and removing zombie entries. Figure 1.17 shows the process map within the kernel.

The process structure contains many different fields, including process information and process statistics. Each time a process is created, a separate process structure for the process is created. To learn more about the process structure, I encourage you to read the <proc.h> header file located in the /usr/include/sys directory. This header file is platform-specific, and it provides a complete listing of the process structure.

FIGURE 1.17   Process structure.

1.2.6   THE JOB SCHEDULER

The UNIX operating system job scheduler provides three different types of job classes as listed in Table 1.4. Each class listed in Table 1.4 has a discrete set of global priorities that control the scheduling order of the tasks (processes) within the particular job class. The job classes listed in Table 1.4 are listed in order of increasing priority. It is critical to understand the purpose as well as the properties of each job class. The understanding of the different job classes will enable you to further understand the kernel's job scheduling policy. I must emphasize that extreme care must be taken before altering the job class and/or priority of any particular process. Doing so without a full understanding of the possible effects could cause system instability, possibly forcing the system to panic. Please consult with your hardware and OS vendor before altering job-class parameters. Figure 1.18 summarizes the UNIX job scheduling classes.[19]

TABLE 1.4   Job classes provided by the UNIX operating system job scheduler

JOB CLASS	PRIORITY RANGE
Time-share	0 through 59 (59 being the highest); default job class
System	60 through 99; reserved for system daemon processes
Real-time	100 through 159; highest priority job class

19. SunService. *SunOS 5.X Internals Guide SP-365*, Revision B.1. September 1993, pp. 6-7.

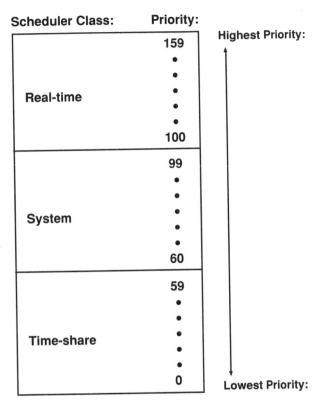

FIGURE 1.18   UNIX job scheduling classes.

1.2.6.1   Time-Share Job Class

The time-share job class is the default job class and has priority 0 through 59, with 59 being the highest priority. In this job class, each process is assigned a time slice (or quantum). The time slice specifies the number of CPU clock ticks that a particular task (or process) can occupy the CPU. Once the process finishes its time slice, the process priority usually is decreased and the process is placed on the sleep queue. Other processes waiting for CPU time may have their priority increased, thereby increasing their likelihood to run. Unless specified through the dispadmin[20] or priocntl command, any time a new process is created, it will be assigned to the time-share job class with a default priority. You can use the ps -c command to list the job class and priority of a process.

---

20. The dispadmin command is the Solaris utility used for process scheduler administration while the system is running. You can use this command to change job classes. Refer to the manual pages on dispadmin for a complete listing. On Sequent, use the priocntl command. On HP, use the rtsched to schedule a real-time job.

For example

```
myhost%> ps -c
  PID   CLS   PRI   COMD
  2403   TS    59   csh
 15231   TS    48   ps
```

In this example, the output from the `ps -c` command shows the Process ID (PID) of the current shell as well as the `ps` command itself. Both processes are in the Time-Share (TS) job class, and have a priority of 59 or less.

1.2.6.2 System Job Class

The system job class is reserved for system daemon processes such as the pageout daemon or the file system daemon. The priority range for the system job class is between 60 and 99. The system job class has a higher priority than the time share job class. This is to ensure that the system can provide services to the time-share job class processes when system services such as memory, and/or file I/O are requested. Although it is possible to alter the job class of a time-share process to real-time, it is not recommended because the process would run at a higher priority than the system daemons. Use extreme care before altering the job class or priority of processes.

1.2.6.3 Real-Time Job Class

The real-time job class is the highest priority job class and has no time slice. Real-time process priorities range between 100 and 159. The fixed-priority job class (real-time) ensures that critical processes always acquire the CPU as soon as the process is scheduled to run—even if processes in other classes are currently running or scheduled to run. Again, use caution when switching priorities or job classes of processes. Consult with your vendor before switching processes into different job classes. There may be some operating system–specific issues when the job class or priority of a process is altered. Because there is no time slice with real-time processes, the number of context switches is reduced significantly, which can increase performance. More discussion on process management as it pertains to performance follows in Chapter 2.

1.2.7 THREADS MODEL

Several UNIX operating system vendors support the threads model either through a vendor-supplied library, or by supporting and supplying the POSIX[21] threads library. Sun Solaris 2.X provides a Solaris threads library as well as the POSIX threads library. HP-UX 10.X provides user threads and HP-UX 11.0 provides both user and kernel threads. The threads model consists of an LWP (Light-Weight Process) structure. A thread is a unit of control or execution within a process. A thread can be thought of as a subtask or

---

21. POSIX is the Portable Operating System for the UNIX Standards Committee.

subprocess. Unlike the process model, which creates a separate process structure for each process, the threads model has substantially less overhead than a process. A thread is part of the process address space; therefore, it is not necessary to duplicate the process address space of the process when a new thread is created. The `fork()` system call creates a new process and duplicates the process address space of the parent process. However, when a thread is created, it is part of its process address space. This significantly reduces memory consumption as well as creation time for the thread. There is an order of magnitude of difference between creating a process versus creating a thread. It takes approximately 1000 times longer to create a full process than it does to create a thread.

Each thread can be bound to a CPU, thereby enabling parallel processing. There are various routines such as `thr_create()`, `thr_suspend()`, `thr_join()`, and `thr_continue()` that create a thread, suspend a thread, block until thread termination, and continue execution of a thread, respectively.[22] Threads are extremely efficient but also are extremely complex. There are many issues such as signals, stacks, and synchronization that have to be considered carefully when using the threads model as opposed to the process model. The threads model calls for high-throughput low-overhead asynchronous processing. By default, threads are asynchronous and careful thought has to be given to the design of a threads application with respect to synchronization. While the concepts of threads and threads programming are certainly beyond the scope of this book, I intend to discuss the basic concepts of threads as well as the performance gains associated with threads. I encourage you to obtain a more detailed text on threads and threads programming.

Prior to the availability of threads, parallelism and asynchronous processing were accomplished by using the `fork()` system call. Using the `fork()` system call, a process created another process allowing both the parent and child process to execute simultaneously (assuming enough CPUs were available to handle multiple processes). The fork technique generates tremendous system overhead because separate process structures must be created and additional memory must be allocated. Solaris 2.X is a multithreaded operating system and most of the system daemons use threads to service requests.

1.2.8 SIGNALS AND INTERRUPTS

Fundamental to any operating system are the concepts of signals and interrupts. Signals are software events and interrupts are hardware events. Signals can be asynchronous or synchronous. Asynchronous signals can occur at any point. Asynchronous signals are things like the QUIT signal (CTRL-\), software interrupt signal (CTRL-C), or hang-up signal. Synchronous signals are caused by an invalid operation such as a floating-point exception, a divide-by-zero error, a segmentation violation, or a bus error. Signals are

---

22. For more information on these Solaris thread system calls, refer to the manual pages on either `thr_create()`, `thr_continue()`, `thr_join()`, or `thr_suspend()`. The POSIX thread calls start with `pthread`, such as `pthread_create()`.

commonly used within applications as a method of communication between processes. Applications also use signals to trap certain events such as a user issuing the kill command on a specific process. The application could trap the kill signal and then shut down cleanly, as opposed to not trapping the signal and immediately aborting due to the kill request. You can use the `signal()`, `sigset()`, or `sigaction()` system calls to establish a signal handler in your application. You may choose to take a certain action upon receiving a certain signal or choose to ignore the signal and allow your application to continue. Certain signals, such as fatal hardware events, cannot be ignored and usually result in a core dump with the application being terminated. You can refer to the manual pages on signals or refer to the `/usr/include/sys/signal.h` file for system-defined signals. You can also define your own application user-specific signals.

Interrupts are kernel events that are used to notify the kernel when an event has occurred. A user application may issue a series of I/O calls and the kernel will pass these I/O calls to the I/O queue. The I/O devices involved will then process the I/O requests and then send an interrupt to the kernel, notifying the kernel that the I/O requests have completed. The kernel may then send a signal to the user process notifying the process that its I/O requests completed. The user process can then check the error code of the I/O system calls to determine if the I/O completed successfully. The kernel also uses interrupts to preempt processes or take a processor off-line.

1.2.9   NETWORK SERVICES AND COMMUNICATION

The kernel provides various network services including remote login, file transfers, *connectionless* connections, and NFS. The kernel provides a system daemon, the `inetd` daemon, to provide network services such as `rlogin`, `rsh`, `ftp`, and many other TCP/IP–based services. The default networking stack protocol for the UNIX kernel is TCP/IP. TCP/IP works in two parts: TCP (Transmission Control Protocol) is responsible for the virtual circuit layer that provides bidirectional data transmission; IP (Internet Protocol) is responsible for packet transmission between the user processes and the networking layer. Figure 1.19 shows the relationship between TCP and IP.

FIGURE 1.19   The networking layers.

When the system is booted in multi-user mode, the `inetd` daemon is started. The `inetd` daemon is the Internet services daemon responsible for `telnet`, `rlogin`, `rsh`, and other types of Internet services. Upon a `login` or `telnet`, the `inetd` daemon forks and execs the appropriate daemon such as `in.telnetd` for a `telnet` session. The `/etc/inet/inetd.conf` file is the configuration file used to configure the `inetd` daemon. You can use this file to restrict certain Internet services such as remote shell (`rsh`) or finger. Upon an Internet service request such as `ftp`, the `inetd` daemon forks and execs the appropriate service daemon such as `in.ftpd` in the case of an `ftp` request. Using the `ps` command, you can verify this as there should be a process for the `ftp` session (`in.ftpd`), and the parent process ID should be the process ID of the `inetd` daemon. Most system administrators disable certain Internet services such as the remote shell and finger in order to increase the security of the system.

The raw IP layer consists of connectionless sockets. Sockets are a low-level method of communication using endpoints. With sockets, you can specify the type of protocol to use within the communication endpoint.

The UNIX kernel also supports other methods of communication such as pipes, named pipes, sockets, and messages. Messages are another method of interprocess communication. Messages typically are used to send special data to processes. A pipe is a unidirectional mechanism used to send streams of data to other processes. Named pipes are also another method of interprocess communication that provide a permanent path, as opposed to the traditional pipe. Sockets are bidirectional and are generally used for network communication between clients and servers. The client opens the communication endpoint via a socket, and the server listens on the socket to receive the communication.

1.2.10 I/O SERVICES

The UNIX kernel provides many different types of I/O including the standard synchronous I/O that consists of the `read()` and `write()` system calls, asynchronous I/O, streams I/O, and network I/O. Network I/O consists of the various different network services such as `ftp`, `telnet`, and other TCP/IP or other protocol-driven I/O services. Stream I/O is a mechanism for character-based I/O between the kernel and user processes. Examples of a stream are network connections, tape media, and other character devices. Asynchronous I/O is an enhancement to the standard synchronous I/O that allows non-blocking reads and writes. The kernel performs the asynchronous reads and writes and returns control to the calling program immediately following the asynchronous I/O system call. In the synchronous model, calling the system call `read()` or `write()` would not return control to the calling program until the completion of the `read()` or `write()` call. With asynchronous I/O, calls to `aioread()` or `aiowrite()` return immediately following the call.[23] If a signal handler has been established, the user process is later signaled when an outstanding asynchronous I/O call completes. Solaris 2.X provides a user

---

23. The `aioread()` and `aiowrite()` calls are provided by the Solaris asynchronous I/O library (`libaio.so`). For more information on the calls, you can refer to the manual pages on `aioread()` and `aiowrite()`.

library for writing applications using asynchronous I/O. The full path of the library is `/usr/lib/libaio.so` (shared library). Sequent also provides the library `/usr/lib/libseq.a` that contains the asynchronous I/O system calls.

The Sun Solaris library provides the `aioread()` and `aiowrite()` system calls for initiating asynchronous reads and writes, respectively. Sequent's library, `libseq.a`, provides `DIO_Read()` and `DIO_Write()` which, in addition to asynchronous I/O, provide direct I/O to file systems. Direct I/O bypasses the file system cache and accesses the disks directly.

1.2.11 SYNCHRONIZATION

The UNIX kernel provides several different methods of synchronization. Synchronization is the process of locking a resource to ensure consistency so that two or more processes do not invalidate each other's modifications. Although multiple processes can execute concurrently, locks are needed when a process wants to protect a resource such as a file, data block, and/or section of memory. For instance, consider the standard banking transaction: An individual is withdrawing money from his or her account, while another relative is depositing funds into the same account simultaneously. Without synchronization (locking), the end balance may not be reflected correctly.

The Solaris kernel provides the following methods of synchronization:[24]

1. mutex locks
2. condition variables
3. semaphores
4. multiple-reader single-writer locks

Mutex locks are mutual exclusion locks and can be used at the process level or at the individual thread level. Mutex locks are simple and efficient low-level locks. Condition variables are used in conjunction with mutex locks to verify or wait on a particular condition. Semaphores are a standard method of synchronization and are part of the System V Release 4 interprocess communication kit. A semaphore is a nonnegative integer count of available resources. The integer count is either incremented or decremented as resources are freed or obtained, respectively. A semaphore count of zero indicates that no more resources are available. Multiple-reader single-writer locks are more complex than the other three types of synchronization as they provide multiple-reader locks as well as a writer lock. Multiple-reader single-writer locks are primarily used for data that is queried more often than updated. No reader locks can be obtained while a writer lock is held. Writer lock requests are favored over readers.

1.2.12   SYSTEM DAEMON LAYER

The concept of daemons is fundamental to the UNIX OS. A daemon is simply, as the term suggests, a task acting on behalf of another task or entity. In other words, a daemon is nothing more than a background job or process responsible for a certain task or set of tasks. The UNIX kernel consists of numerous system daemons that are responsible for memory management, file system management, printer jobs, network connections, and several other services. For example, consider the output shown in Table 1.5 from the ps command.

The listing in Table 1.5 from the ps command shows some of the system daemons that are running.[25] The pageout daemon (in Table 1.5 with process ID=2) is responsible for writing modified (i.e., dirty) pages to the file system. The page daemon, under certain conditions, will scan the memory page list and determine if the page is currently in use or has been recently referenced. Depending on the paging algorithm used[26], the page daemon either will skip the memory page or return the page to the free list.

TABLE 1.5   Output from the ps command

UID	PID	PPID	TIME	CMD
root	0	0	0:01	sched
root	1	0	0:01	/etc/init -
root	2	0	0:00	pageout
root	3	0	3:27	fsflush
root	131	1	0:01	/usr/sbin/inetd -s
root	289	1	0:00	/usr/lib/saf/sac -t 300
root	112	1	0:02	/usr/sbin/rpcbind
root	186	1	0:00	/usr/lib/lpsched
root	104	1	0:12	/usr/sbin/in.routed -q
root	114	1	0:01	/usr/sbin/keyserv
root	122	1	0:00	/usr/sbin/kerbd
root	120	1	0:00	/usr/sbin/nis_cachemgr
root	134	1	0:00	/usr/lib/nfs/statd
root	136	1	0:00	/usr/lib/nfs/lockd
root	155	1	0:00	/usr/lib/autofs/automountd
root	195	1	0:00	/usr/lib/sendmail -bd -q1h
root	159	1	0:00	/usr/sbin/syslogd
root	169	1	0:13	/usr/sbin/cron
root	194	186	0:00	lpNet

---

25. The preceding output from ps was generated from a Sun Server running Solaris 2.5.
26. Paging algorithms are discussed in detail in Chapter 2.

The main goal of the `page` daemon is to ensure that the system does not run out of memory. After the page has been flushed out to disk by the `pageout` daemon, the page is placed on the page free list. The `pageout` daemon continues to run as long as there are pages to be written out to disk.

Another system daemon is the `fsflush` daemon. This daemon is responsible for flushing *dirty* disk pages from memory to disk. A dirty page is a page that has changed and has been marked as dirty, meaning that the page should be written out to disk upon the next write-out scan. The UNIX kernel employs a UNIX file system cache for managing file systems. All writes to a file system–based file are first written to the file system cache, assuming the writes do not explicitly bypass the UNIX file system cache. The goal of the `fsflush` daemon is to ensure that dirty file system pages are written to disk.

System daemons are critical to the operating system and service requests both from the kernel and from the user. The goal of these daemons is to satisfy these requests while maintaining the integrity of the system. System daemons generally close the standard files `stdin`, `stdout`, and `stderr`.[27] The file descriptor values for `stdin`, `stdout`, and `stderr` are 0, 1, and 2, respectively. Output from system daemons is usually directed to the system console or specific system administration files.

1.2.13 SHELL LAYER

The UNIX operating system also provides different types of shells that act as a command interpreter and an interface to the OS. UNIX provides three standard types of shells: The Bourne shell (`sh`), the Korn shell (`ksh`), and the C-shell (`csh`). The Bourne shell and C-shell seem to be the most common. You may use the shell of your choice and customize it accordingly using the dot (.) files such as `.login`, `.cshrc`, and `.logout` for the C-shell. The `.cshrc` is the C-shell resource file invoked each time a C-shell is created. You can set objects such as environment variables, aliases, and file locations. You can also use your shell to invoke specific startup scripts or programs. Your default shell can be set by the UNIX system administrator in the `/etc/passwd` file or equivalent namespace in NIS or NIS+. Some UNIX vendors also provide a restricted shell (`/usr/lib/rsh`). This should not be confused with the standard remote shell (`rsh`), which is a remote login facility. The restricted shell is a special shell that restricts the user from changing environment variables and from changing directory locations. Under a restricted shell, the user may execute only commands found in the $PATH environment variable. This shell is often useful for secured accounts that need to run certain applications only. The system administrator can use a restricted shell to increase system security, permitting the user to run only certain commands and applications.

1.2.14 APPLICATION LAYER

The application layer within the UNIX architecture consists of user-level programs or scripts that are written in some sort of programming or script language. These programs

---

27. `Stdin`, `stdout`, and `stderr` are the default file descriptors associated with each process. `Stdin` refers to standard input. `Stdout` refers to standard output, and `stderr` refers to standard error.

or scripts tend to be executable or binary files used within an application. If a programming language such as C or C++ is used, the source code for the application is compiled using the C or C++ compiler. The compiler then generates object code specific to the platform and architecture. For example, compiling C code on a Sequent machine using DYNIX/ptx 4.4 generates object code based on the Intel architecture and the DYNIX/ptx operating system. Linking the object code produces a DYNIX/ptx format executable.

The application layer is an important layer within the UNIX architecture as it is responsible for running applications such as Oracle8, business-specific applications, graphics tools, and development and debugging tools. It is important that you understand this layer and all the layers beneath. This solid understanding will help you understand the Oracle architecture, thereby maximizing your ability to successfully tune your Oracle and UNIX environment.

Chapter 2

MEMORY AND PROCESSOR TUNING

The previous chapter explained the fundamentals of the UNIX operating system. This chapter covers the performance issues associated with memory and multiple processors. This chapter covers the Symmetrical Multiprocessor (SMP), and the Nonuniform Memory Access (NUMA) architectures.

Memory and processors are expensive system resources and should be regarded as such when tuning a system. Although systems can often become memory- or processor-bound, the answer is not always to add more hardware. The application may not be scalable or may not be using memory efficiently; therefore, additional hardware upgrades may not offer any gain.

There are two methods of tuning memory and processors: the *poor man's technique* and the *right-sizing technique*. The poor man's technique assumes that no additional hardware can be purchased or allocated, and the system administrator must use all means necessary to tune with what is available. In other words, adding memory or adding processors is not an option. For this technique, a conservationist approach must be taken to utilize memory as efficiently as possible while minimizing an application's CPU time. In this way, processes will be short transactions that occupy the CPU for a minimal period of time. Because the processes are short transactions, the system can handle multiple processes since each process occupies the CPU for only a small amount of time. The right-sizing technique, on the other hand, requires a greater effort in capacity planning. Right-sizing requires the collection of a tremendous range of statistics detailing scalability, performance metrics, application and database workload, and growth rates. Collectively, these statistics will help size a system accordingly with respect to the amount of physical memory, number of processors, number of disk drives and controllers, and number of media backup devices (tape drives).

2.1 UNIX MEMORY MODEL

The UNIX memory model is based on the virtual memory model which combines physical memory as primary storage and physical disk as secondary storage. This combination of primary and secondary storage represents the total virtual memory available to the system. Figure 2.1 demonstrates the concept of the virtual memory model.

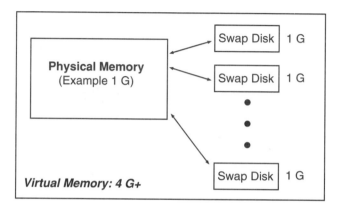

FIGURE 2.1   The virtual memory model.

In Figure 2.1, the total amount of memory available to the system is the total amount of virtual memory. Therefore, virtual memory = physical memory + swap device(s). In this example, the total amount of virtual memory available is 4G. The virtual memory consists of memory pages, usually 4K in size. The memory pages are managed by the `page` daemon, and a free list of free memory pages is maintained. The goal of the `page` daemon is to maintain a certain level of free memory as specified by the tunable thresholds and to maximize memory performance by maintaining active memory pages in physical memory for as long as possible.

2.1.1 PAGING

As discussed in Chapter 1, paging is the mechanism by which memory is divided into memory pages, typically 4K in size. The memory pages are then managed by the `page` daemon. The best way to think of the `page` daemon is as a cache manager for the virtual memory pool. Before a discussion on the page daemon commences, a review of some common terminology is in order. Table 2.1 defines these terms.

The `page` daemon is responsible for scanning the memory page reference bit to determine whether a page is active or idle. The `page` daemon uses a clocklike algorithm. Figure 2.2 details the clocklike algorithm of the `page` daemon.

In Figure 2.2, the total system memory is divided into smaller memory units known as pages. The `page` daemon scans through the memory pages periodically to

TABLE 2.1   Common paging terminology

TERM	DEFINITION
Page-in	Means that a page was requested and was subsequently brought into main memory.
Page-out	Occurs when a page is written out to disk (handled by the `pageout` daemon).
Page fault	Occurs when a page that has been requested had been returned to the free list, and the reference to the page forced the page to be reclaimed and brought back into main memory. There are two types of page faults: *minor page faults* and *major page faults*.
	Minor page fault–occurs when a page request was made for a page that has been returned to the free list. The minor fault indicates that although the page has been returned to the free list, it has not yet been reused. Hence, the page is brought back into the address space of the requesting process.
	Major page fault—occurs when a page request was made for a page that has been returned to the free list, but the page has been already reused by another process. This means that a new page would have to be allocated and the page data would have to be restored from the swap device, translating into physical I/O from the swap device.
Page attach	Occurs when a request for a page determines that the page is already in memory, and the process simply attaches to the page and increments the reference count by one. A large number of attaches is common during shared library usage and/or the use of shared memory by different programs.

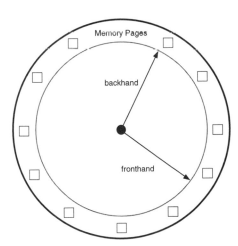

FIGURE 2.2   The clocklike algorithm of the `page` daemon.

determine the activity of the pages. The clocklike algorithm uses a two-phase scan. Upon the first scan, the memory page's reference bit is checked. If found to be idle, the page becomes a candidate for the free list. If found to be active, meaning the page is currently being accessed, the page reference bit is set to idle. Upon the second scan, if the page's reference bit is still found to be idle and its reference bit was set to idle during the first phase scan, the page becomes a candidate for the free list, possibly resulting in a *page-out*. If, however, the page reference bit is set to active, meaning the page has been referenced, the page is left untouched.

There are several paging parameters that control both the action and the frequency of the `page` daemon. The paging parameters are `lotsfree`, `desfree`, `minfree`, `slowscan`, `fastscan`, and `handspreadpages`.[1] In Solaris, you can set these parameters in the `/etc/system` kernel configuration file. You must reboot the system for your changes to take effect.

The `lotsfree` parameter specifies (in number of pages) the upper-bound threshold of the amount of free system memory. If the available free memory is maintained above this upper bound, the `page` daemon will be idle until the available free memory falls below this parameter. To set this parameter on Solaris, edit the `/etc/system` file and enter the following line:

```
                    set lotsfree=<# of pages desired>
Example:            set lotsfree=256
```

In order for the change to take effect, you must reboot the system. You can verify that the change took effect by issuing the following command:

```
mysystem# adb -k /dev/ksyms/dev/mem   * must be executed as root

physmem 3e09                 * Output from adb
lotsfree/D                   * enter lotsfree/D
lotsfree:
lotsfree:    256             * value displayed in decimal
```

The adb utility is the Solaris general debugger and can be used to attach to the kernel to obtain kernel parameter values. The `/dev/ksyms` device is the kernel symbol table driver. The `/dev/mem` is the device that maps to the system's physical memory. After you issue the adb command, adb outputs the total physical memory being used.[2] Output from adb defaults to hexadecimal, but you can request decimal values by placing the `/D` switch after the respective kernel parameter. For example, `lotsfree/D` reports the value of the `lotsfree` parameter in decimal. For more information on the use of adb, refer to the manual pages on adb.

---

1. The kernel paging parameters are operating system–specific, and you should refer to the system administration manual for your specific platform.
2. You can decrease the amount of physical memory by setting the kernel parameter physmem. Although this is not recommended, you can use this feature for benchmarking or testing.

In Solaris 2.4 the default value for `lotsfree` is 256 pages for the sun4d architecture.[3] Solaris 2.5.1 sets the default value of `lotsfree` to `physmem/64`, and improves the overall algorithm. In Solaris 2.6, the default for `lotsfree` is 1.5% of physical memory. When the available free system memory is equal to `lotsfree`, then the `page` daemon uses the `slowscan` rate. The kernel checks to see if the available free system memory is less than `lotsfree` four times per second during the 100-Hz clock routine. If so, the `pageout` daemon is signaled.

The `desfree` parameter specifies (in number of pages) the middle bound value for the `page` daemon. If the available free system memory falls below `desfree` when pages are grabbed from the page free list, the `pageout` daemon is awakened. If the available free system memory remains below `desfree` for an average of 30 seconds, processes will selectively be swapped out to the swap device. The default for `desfree` is half the value of `lotsfree`.

The `minfree` parameter specifies (in number of pages) the absolute minimum amount of free system available memory. On Solaris, if the free system available memory is lower than `minfree` for an average of five seconds, the swapping out of processes will begin until the amount of free memory is restored to at least `minfree`. If the free available system memory falls below `minfree`, the *swapper* will continue to work aggressively until the minimum amount of free memory exists. The default for `minfree` is half the value of `desfree`.

The `slowscan` parameter defines the number of pages scanned per second by the `paging` algorithm when the available free memory is equal to `lotsfree`. The default for `slowscan` is 100. The frequency of the `page` daemon increases linearly from `slowscan` to `fastscan` as the available system memory drops from `lotsfree` to zero.

`Fastscan`, similar to `slowscan`, specifies the number of pages scanned per second when the available free memory is near zero. In other words, as the available memory drops from `lotsfree` to zero, the frequency of the `page` daemon in terms of pages scanned per second will increase from `slowscan` to `fastscan`. Since Solaris 2.4, the default for `fastscan` is `physmem/4` with a maximum limit of 16384.

`Handspreadpages` specifies the distance (in pages) between the page daemon's `fronthand` scan and `backhand` scan. Higher values for `handspreadpages` increase the likelihood of pages remaining in main memory. Smaller values will result in the `fronthand` scan and `backhand` scan being closer to each other. This will increase paging activity and possibly increase the occurrence of page faults. On Solaris, you can set the `handspreadpages` kernel parameter in the `/etc/system` file. The default value for `handspreadpages` is typically set to the value of `fastscan`.

On Solaris, the `page` daemon is awakened by the `page_create()` routine when insufficient memory exists to satisfy the `page_create()` request. The `page` daemon can also be awakened by the `page_create()` routine if, after satisfying the memory request, the available free system memory falls below the value of `desfree`. The `page` daemon is also signaled by the `schedpaging()` routine, which calculates

---

3. You can determine the architecture of your Sun system by using the `uname -a` command.

the number of pages to be scanned in the current scan cycle. The `schedpaging()` routine is scheduled via the `callout_thread()` routine. The two-handed paging clock algorithm is implemented by the `pageout_scanner()` routine. The `pageout_scanner()` routine initializes the clock hands and then sleeps until the amount of available free system memory falls below the value of `lotsfree`. The `pageout_scanner()` maintains two key variable counters: pushes and count.

The pushes variable contains the number of pages needed to be flushed out to disk. The count variable indicates the number of times that the `pageout_scanner()` routine completed an entire clock cycle without freeing any memory pages. If the value of count exceeds two, `pageout_scanner()` sleeps. The count variable is used to prevent the `pageout_scanner()` from occupying CPU time when no work is being performed by the `pageout_scanner()`. The `pageout_scanner()` will continue to scan until either enough free memory exists or the number of pages to be scanned is completed. The internal routine used by the `pageout_scanner()` routine to determine whether or not a page should be placed on the free list is the `checkpage()` routine. The `page_free()` routine places a page on the free list.

On Dynix/ptx 4.4, the header file `/usr/include/sys/mc_vmprvpm.h` defines the default values for the `minfree` and `desfree` paging parameters. You can also use the `/etc/vmtune` utility to set the value of `desfree` or `minfree`. The `/etc/vmtune` utility is described in greater detail in Section 2.4.

Figure 2.3 summarizes paging parameters and `page` daemon scan rates.[4]

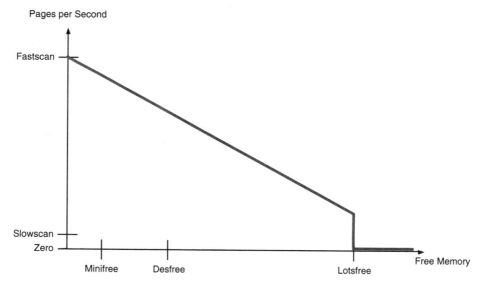

FIGURE 2.3   Paging parameters and the `page` daemon scan rates.

4. Cockcroft, Adrian. *Sun Performance and Tuning*. Prentice Hall. 1995. p. 204.

2.1.2 SWAPPING

Swapping is the process by which all of the memory pages of a given process are written out to the swap device (swapped out). Swapping is generally an act of desperation by the operating system to free memory if the `page` daemon has failed to do so during its normal scanning process. The swapper process is activated by the `sched` system daemon when the free available memory falls below `desfree` and `minfree` for a specific time quantum. For instance, in Solaris 2.4, the time quantum is five seconds. Figure 2.4 illustrates the concept of swapping.

FIGURE 2.4   The concept of swapping.

In Figure 2.4, process 3485 is swapped out, meaning that all memory pages used by process 3485 are written out to the swap device. The kernel then returns all the memory used by the process to the free list. The kernel will continue swapping out processes until the available free system memory is at least equal to `minfree`. The swapper process is also invoked whenever a thread that is not currently loaded in memory is added to the dispatch queue.[5] Each scheduling class has its own swapping routines. When a swap-out takes place, the swapper calls the job class specific swap-out routine. The swap-out routine nominates a thread to be swapped out from each respective job class. The swap-out routine then swaps out the process structure and associated kernel stack of the thread with the lowest priority.

---

5. SunService. *SunOS 5.X Internals Guide SP-365*, Revision B.1. September 1993, pp. 5–15.

In Solaris, the two routines responsible for swap-outs are `ts_swapout()`, and `rt_swapout()` for the time-share job class (`ts`) and real-time job class (`rt`), respectively. The `ts_swapout()` routine does not consider threads that have any of the following conditions:

❑ The thread is in the process of being created.
❑ The thread is not currently loaded into memory.
❑ The thread's `t_schedflag` `TS_DONT_SWAP` is set.
❑ The thread's `t_proc_flag` `TP_LWPEXIT` is set
❑ The thread was recently swapped in.

Real-time threads are never swapped out. Real-time processes and their associated kernel stack are locked in memory. Because real-time threads are not swapped out, the `rt_swapin()` routine simply indicates whether or not there are currently runable threads in the real-time scheduling class that are loadable into memory.

2.2 PROCESS MEMORY MODEL

The UNIX operating system process memory model is based on the virtual memory model. In addition to the address space of a given process consisting of memory pages, the kernel also provides an *anonymous* memory layer. The anonymous memory layer is used to manage anonymous memory pages by using anonymous structures that map to the anonymous pages by means of hash tables.

Figure 2.5 shows the different segments that are associated with a process such as the user stack segment, hole segment, data segment, and text segment. The kernel, of course, is separate from the user process and contains two main stacks: the kernel stack and the interrupt stack. The user stack segment is used to store local variables and is also used during function calls. The user stack is dynamically allocated and dynamically adjusted. The typical default for a user stack for a process is 8 M.[6] The hole segment is where the local memory storage is managed. Calls like `malloc()` and `mmap()` are serviced through the hole segment. The data segment contains items such as global variables and static variables. A static variable maintains its last value. A nonstatic variable is not exported to the linker. The text segment contains the actual code of the process. Each segment is responsible for managing its respective memory pages. Within the stack segment, there are four different types of stacks:

1. User stack
2. Kernel stack

---

6. You can use the `sbrk()` routine to alter the size of the stack. For more information on the call, refer to the manual pages on `sbrk()`.

3. Alternate signal stack
4. Interrupt stack

The data and stack segments' pages consist of *anonymous* memory. Anonymous memory is used for the uninitialized section (bss) of the data segment, the stack segment, and a Copy-on-Write (COW). A copy-on-write occurs when a change to a private page is made, causing a private copy of the page to be created and leaving the original page intact. The change then is made to the private copy of the page. This is done for reasons of consistency when pages are mapped as private. If the page is mapped as shared, the change is made to the original page. Anonymous memory can exist either in the main memory or on the swap device. However, anonymous memory is not identifiable through the file system. Anonymous memory is located using the anonymous memory structures

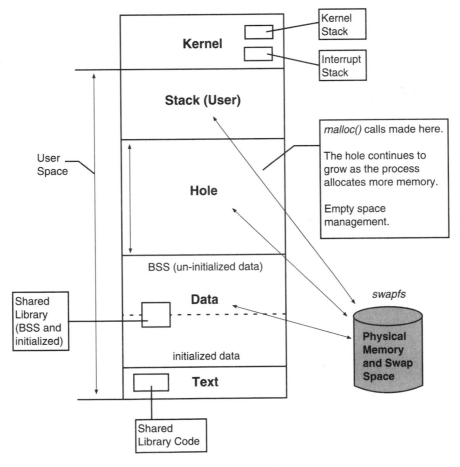

FIGURE 2.5 Segments of a process.

that in turn use hash tables. Each memory page consists of a `vnode` and an offset. Memory pages are located using hash tables and the offsets. Anonymous pages must first reserve permanent backing store via the swap device, even if the backing store is not used. This is to guarantee that upon a `fork()` and/or `exec()`, sufficient memory exists up front to successfully complete the `fork()` and/or `exec()`, avoiding situations in which the `exec()` call fails at some point later in the execution due to insufficient memory and/or swap space. The `tmpfs` file system provides a file system layer for anonymous pages. Upon process termination, all anonymous memory pages are zeroed out using the `/dev/zero` device before the pages are returned to the free list. This is done for security reasons to prevent data from being read from the anonymous pages.

When the `fork()` system call is issued, the address space of the parent process [the process issuing the `fork()`] is duplicated for the newly created child process. The data pages are marked as Copy-on-Write (COW). Figure 2.6 illustrates the duplication of the parent process address space for the child process that results from the `fork()` call.

Typically following a `fork()`, an `exec()` is performed to make the child process execute another program. The `exec()` system call takes an executable as its first argument as well as any arguments passed to the executable. When the `exec()` call is issued following the `fork()`, the child process' stack, data, and text segment layers are overlaid with the new executable as passed in to the `exec()` call. Only data pages and stack pages are saved to memory. Shared libraries (text and data segments) are also a part of the process structure address space. Shared libraries are paged in dynamically from the file system. Program text and file data are also paged in from the file system.

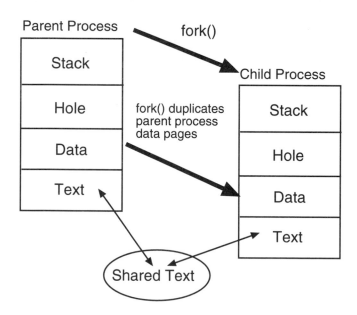

FIGURE 2.6   The `fork()` system call.

File data can also be paged out as well. Because text pages are not modified (meaning the executable does not modify itself while running), the loaded executable's text segment will not generate any dirty file system pages. Text segments are not backed by swap as opposed to data and stack segments. Hence, executable text segments avoid the flushing of dirty file system pages to disk because no dirty pages exist for a text segment. Shared libraries provide a significant performance gain as well as a substantial reduction in memory requirements. When a program that uses shared libraries is executed, the OS will mmap() the shared library into the user's process address space. The mmap() system call maps a file system–based file directly into user space without the overhead of first copying the file into the UNIX file system cache, followed by another copy into the user's address space. The mmap() call eliminates copy overhead by directly mapping the file into the user's address space. This not only saves CPU cycles but also reduces memory requirements by eliminating buffer copies. Shared libraries also allow multiple processes to share the same code (functions and modules). If an executable were statically linked (meaning that the executable contains, as part of the executable, all the referencing objects and libraries), multiple processes running the same executable may have to allocate the memory address space necessary to hold the objects and libraries that were invoked by the main executable. If, on the other hand, the executable were linked dynamically (or shared), each process that invoked the library would simply mmap() to the address where the library is loaded. This means that the shared library needs only to be loaded into memory once. For a large shared library, this can result in significant memory savings. If you are developing a large application that will serve many users, the libraries that you develop should be developed as shared libraries.

2.3 MONITORING PAGING AND SWAPPING

By now, you should be familiar with the basic concepts of paging and swapping. In order to maximize the performance of your system, you should monitor the paging and swapping activity by using sar or vmstat. The sar utility is a generic reporting utility available on UNIX platforms. The vmstat utility is available with Solaris. You can monitor paging activity by using the sar -p command. For example, on a Sequent system,

```
myhost> sar -p 1 5

DYNIX/ptx myhost 4.0 V4.1.3 i386

vflt/s   pflt/s   pgfil/s   rclm/s
51.24    0.00     0.00      0.00
 4.96    0.00     0.00      0.00
 7.56    0.00     0.00      0.00
 2.50    0.00     0.00      0.00
 5.83    0.00     0.00      0.00
```

In this example, the `sar -p` (paging) option is used to collect paging activity statistics. The first parameter following the `-p` option is the polling interval, in seconds. In this case, sar reports paging statistics every second. The second parameter following the `-p` option is the number of iterations of particular statistics that sar reports. Therefore, in this case, sar reports paging statistics every second for five iterations. The `vflt/s` column reports the number of virtual faults per second. A virtual fault is the result of an address translation page fault, meaning that a virtual address no longer maps to a valid physical page. The `pflt/s` column reports the number of page faults per second. The `pgfil/s` is the number of virtual faults per second that were handled by pages being paged in from the file system. The `rclm/s` column reports the number of page reclaims per second. A page reclaim occurs when a page that was *stolen* has to be brought back into main memory after being placed on the page free list. You can also use the `/etc/monitor` utility on Sequent to monitor paging and swapping. For example,

```
myhost> /etc/monitor
```

usr %	389	pgdrec	80	semops	552
sys %	320	pgin	0		
tot %	709	ppgin	0		
procs	1339	pgout	0		
on p	5	ppgout	0		
runq	0	sw in	0		
wait	6	pswin	0		
sleep	1328	sw out	0		
swapped	0	pswout	0		
fs io	2	fs brd	8		
phys io	4	fs bwt	0		
sysc	13414	fs rdh	100		
csw	1068	fs wth	100		
intr	754	raw rd	294		
traps	63369	raw wt	72		
fork	1	raw rKB	1591		
vfork	1	raw wKB	289		
exec	3	lckcnt	12		
dk xf	542	%locks	0		
dk KB	2882	deficit	0		
ttyin	0	free	512418		
ttyout	0	dirty	18		
pf	796	tot vm	52280584		
pg rec	127	msgops	1		

On Sequent, the `/etc/monitor` utility also reports paging statistics such as page ins, page outs, the amount of free memory, and the number of dirty pages. For more information on the /etc/monitor utility, refer to the manual pages on /etc/moni-tor (i.e., man monitor). The /etc/monitor utility reports free memory in units of 1K (1 kilobyte). You can also use the sar -r command on Sequent systems to deter-mine the number of free memory pages available for user processes (freemem), and number of free disk blocks available from the swap device for swapping (freeswap).

In Solaris, you can use the sar -p command to monitor paging.

```
myhost> sar -p 1 5

SunOS myhost 5.5 generic sun4m

        atch/s   pgin/s ppgin/s  pflt/s  vflt/s slock/s
        0.00     1.00    2.00     5.00   10.00   0.00
        0.00     2.00    4.00     0.00    7.00   0.00
        0.00     1.00    2.00     0.00    0.00   0.00
        0.00     1.00    2.00     0.00    0.00   0.00
        0.00     0.00    0.00     0.00    0.00   0.00

Average 0.00     1.00    2.00     1.00    3.40   0.00
```

In this example, the atch/s column indicates the number of times per second that processes attached to shared pages already in memory. The pgin/s column indicates the number of page-in requests per second. The ppgin/s column is the number of page-ins per second. The pflt/s column reports the number of page faults per second. The vflt/s column reports the number of virtual faults per second. Virtual faults occur when a translation from a virtual page to its corresponding physical memory page deter-mines that the physical page is no longer in memory. The slock/s column reports the number of page faults incurred per second as a result of software locks that require phys-ical I/O.

In Solaris, you can also use the vmstat utility to monitor paging and/or swap-ping. For example,

```
myhost> vmstat 1

procs    memory     ————— page ————— disk        faults         cpu
r b w    swap  free re  mf pi po fr de sr s3 s6 — — in  sy   cs us sy  id
0 0 0    3556  7788  0   0  2  1  2  0  0  0  0  0 38 568  68  9  3  88
0 0 0 123784   892  0  12  0  0  0  0  0  0  0  0 53 333  99  0  2  98
0 0 0 123784   892  0   0  0  0  0  0  0  0  0  0 63 276  82  0  0 100
0 0 0 123784   892  0   0  0  0  0  0  0  0  0  0 53 327  93  0  0 100
0 0 0 123784   892  0   0  0  0  0  0  0  0  0  0 49 283  88  0  0 100
0 0 0 123784   892  0   0  0  0  0  0  0  0  0  0 72 369  97  0  2  98
```

The `vmstat` utility, similar to `sar`, reports the number of page reclaims (`re`), minor page faults (`mf`), page-ins (`pi`), page-outs (`po`), kilobytes freed (`fr`), the anticipated amount of short-term memory shortfall (`de`), and the number of pages scanned (`sr`).

To monitor swapping, use the following `sar` command:

```
myhost> sar -w 1 5

SunOS myhost 5.5 generic sun4d

swpin/s bswin/s swpot/s bswot/s pswch/s
  0.00     0.0     0.00     0.0     107
  0.00     0.0     0.00     0.0      90
  0.00     0.0     0.00     0.0      92
  0.00     0.0     0.00     0.0      88
  0.00     0.0     0.00     0.0      97

Average   0.00     0.0     0.00     0.0      95
```

The `sar` command shows the number of swap-ins per second (`swpin/s`) and swap-outs per second (`swpot/s`). You can also use the Solaris `vmstat` command with the `-S` option (`vmstat -S 1`) to monitor swapping activity. On Sequent, you can use the `/etc/monitor` utility to monitor swapping as well as paging. In the `/etc/monitor` example given previously, swap-ins and swap-outs are reported along with paging statistics. On HP, you can use `sar` or the HP Glance Plus tools to monitor paging and/or swapping.

To adequately tune paging and swapping on your system, you should use the `sar` and/or `vmstat` utilities to monitor paging and swapping. There are also Graphical User Interface (GUI) tools from Sun, HP, LandMark, and BMC Software[7] that provide graphical displays of paging and swapping. These tools provide additional performance monitoring features that are extremely useful. I strongly encourage you to purchase a complete and concise set of GUI performance monitoring tools. If you administer a mixed environment such as a combination of Sun, Sequent, and HP, you may want to consider purchasing a cross-platform tool. This will provide you with a consistent level of administration and monitoring tools for your heterogeneous environment. While `sar` and `vmstat` can provide useful information, they are less user friendly than GUI monitoring tools. And, as the old saying goes, "a picture is worth a thousand words." In this case, a GUI graph of your system's performance makes a magnitude of difference over character-mode tools that require you to compute percentages and/or conversions manually. The majority of the GUI monitoring tools also provide client and server agents that enable you to monitor all of your systems from a single console.

---

7. BMC Software offers the Patrol (GUI) Software Suite.

2.4   TUNING PAGING

2.4.1   PHYSMEM

The physmem kernel parameter sets the total amount of physical memory in the system. This value is set automatically when the kernel boots. You should not need to set this parameter. Many kernel variables are dependent on physmem, and if physmem is set inappropriately, it may cause abnormal system behavior. However, if you are bench-marking an application or a system, you may want to set this value to reduce the amount of memory available. You can then increase the value of physmem for each iteration at some nominal rate and document the performance gains of increasing system memory. For example, suppose your system has 1 G of memory. You may want to set physmem to the equivalent of 128 M and run the application. Then, you can continue to increase the value of physmem in increments of 128 M until you finally reach 1 G. At each itera-tion, you will be able to measure the effects of adding memory to the system. You may find that little if any gain is offered by increasing the memory. This tends to indicate that either the application utilizes a very small amount of memory, or that the application may be heavily dependent on other resources such as disk I/O and/or the CPU. Before you launch your application, you should thoroughly review the complete application memory requirements with the application staff and system administration staff. You can do this by examining the different data structures within the application and any dynamic memory allocations. Be especially careful when looking for dynamic memory allocation routines. Programmers often use elegant techniques to allocate memory, and it may not be directly obvious to the reader. In Solaris, you can set physmem by placing a line in the /etc/system file as follows:

```
set phsymem=262144
```

Remember that physmem (as are most other Solaris kernel paging parameters) is represented in pages, not in bytes. The preceding example sets the physmem to 262,144 pages, each 4K in size.[8] This translates into 1 G of available memory. For your change to take effect, you must reboot the system. Following the reboot, you can verify that your change took effect by using the adb command.

2.4.2   LOTSFREE

The lotsfree kernel parameter sets the upper bound of free memory that the system tries to maintain. If the available free memory is always above lotsfree, the page daemon will remain idle until the amount of free memory falls below lotsfree. If your system has plenty of memory, such as 1 G or higher, you may want to consider set-ting lotsfree to a low value to avoid unnecessary paging. However, on systems

---

8. The sun4u architecture (Ultra series) uses an 8K page size. This increases the performance of large memory allocations.

where memory is scarce you may want to set `lotsfree` to a higher value than the default. This will cause the `page` daemon to be much more active and will help ensure that processes are not starved of memory. This also means that cache hit rates will be much lower since the `page` daemon will more than likely continue to return pages to the free list until the system has sufficient free memory.

2.4.3 DESFREE

The `desfree` kernel parameter sets the middle bound of free memory that the system tries to maintain. The value of `desfree` also causes the system to choose between paging and swapping. If the available free memory falls below `desfree` and remains below `desfree` for more than a certain period of time, swapping is employed in place of paging. Again, if your system has plenty of free memory, you should set the value of `desfree` to a low value to prevent an overactive `page` daemon. If your system has a limited amount of memory, using the default or increasing `desfree` helps avert memory deprivation.

On Sequent systems, `desfree` is the amount of free memory (expressed in kilobytes) that the swapper would like maintained on average. The default of `desfree` is 2 percent of the real memory available following the system boot. You can use the `/etc/vmtune` utility on Sequent to set or to view the paging kernel parameters. For example, to set `desfree` to 10 M on your Sequent system, issue the following command as root:

```
myhost {root}-> /etc/vmtune -desfree 10240
```

The `/etc/vmtune` utility then shows all the values of the paging parameters, including your recent change, and asks you to confirm the change. For more information on the `/etc/vmtune` utility, refer to the manual pages (i.e., man `vmtune`).

```
myhost{root}->  /etc/vmtune -desfree 10240

    128 minRS
1902808 maxRS
     20 RSexecslop
      4 RSexecmult
      5 RSexecdiv
    100 dirtylow
    200 dirtyhigh
    128 klout_look
    100 PFFvtime
      8 PFFdecr
      2 PFFlow
     20 PFFincr
```

```
  15 PFFhigh
1088 minfree
10240 desfree    * (new desfree value)
 400 maxdirty
Ok? y
```

2.4.4 MINFREE

The `minfree` kernel parameter sets the absolute lower limit of free available memory. If free memory drops below `minfree`, swapping of processes begins until the amount of free memory is at least equal to or greater than `minfree`. After that point, the `page` daemon resumes its normal algorithm. Be extremely careful when you set `minfree`, as this represents the lowest limit. For large-scale systems with an abundance of memory, set `minfree` to a low value such as 1 M or 2 M. The default is usually lower than this value. Nevertheless, setting the value of `minfree` to a reasonable value reduces the likelihood of the system swapping and possibly thrashing. If your system has 4 G of memory or more, 1 M–2 M is relatively small compared to the total amount of available memory. Allowing the amount of free memory to approach `minfree` when `minfree` is very small, such as 512K, is quite dangerous and can lead to excessive swapping. `Minfree` needs to be set reasonably so that swapping is avoided, and so the system always has a legitimate amount of free memory available. On Solaris, you can set the value of `minfree` in the `/etc/system` file.

On Sequent, `minfree` is expressed in kilobytes and represents the lowest amount of free memory maintained on the average before desperation mode swapping is initiated. Desperation mode swapping sorts the list of processes by resident size and by the amount of time the process spent sleeping and then swaps out the selected processes accordingly. The resident size is the amount of memory pages of a process that are resident in real memory. It is important to note that a process may not necessarily be entirely resident in real memory. You can tune additional parameters using `vmtune`, such as the minimum resident set size (`minRS`), as well as the maximum resident size (`maxRS`). If you are not able to lock the SGA, you may want to consider setting the `maxRS` parameter to the maximum size of the Oracle SGA in order to ensure that the entire SGA is resident in real memory. Never set `maxRS` to an amount larger than the amount of physical memory. A larger `maxRS` reduces paging activity and page faults by maintaining more of processes' memory pages in real memory. Use caution when setting maxRS as it is a global setting and can cause excessive paging if many processes are allocating large amounts of memory. Sequent provides the flag SHM_HARDLOCK to the `shmget()` system call which allows shared memory segments to be hardlocked. This prevents the shared memory segment from being swapped out or paged out. Using this feature alleviates the need of having to set maxRS to achieve the goal of maintaining the SGA memory pages in real memory.

The `PFFvtime` is the number of CPU clock ticks between page fault frequency checks. The default is usually 100 clock ticks (or one second). The `PFFlow` parameter is the minimum page faulting rate per second before the resident set decreases. The PFFdecr parameter is the number of kilobytes to decrease the resident set size. PFFhigh is the maximum page faulting rate per second before the resident set increases. PFFincr is the number of kilobytes to increase the resident size. The dirtyhigh and dirtylow parameters specify the maximum and minimum size (in kilobytes), respectively, of the dirty memory list. The maxdirty parameter specifies the maximum size of the dirty memory list (in kilobytes) before aggressive swapping begins. You can set the value of minfree using the /etc/vmtune utility. For example, the following command (which must be executed as root) sets minfree to 1 M:

```
myhost {root}-> /etc/vmtune -minfree 1024
```

2.4.5 MAXPGIO

The maxpgio parameter regulates the number of page-out I/O operations per second that are scheduled by the system. On Solaris, the default is 40 pages per second on older systems and 60 pages per second for Sun4d systems. The default is based on the 3600 rpm disk drive. However, most new disk drives are either 7200 or 10000 rpm. Therefore, you can increase the value of maxpgio in accordance with your disk drive speeds. Avoid setting maxpgio too high so that the disk is not saturated with page I/O requests. On Solaris, the formula for maxpgio is disk rate (in revolutions per second) x 2/3. If your swap disk drives are 7200 rpm, set maxpgio = 120 rps x 2/3 = 80.

When tuning the kernel paging parameters, you must maintain the following range check:

$$LOTSFREE > DESFREE > MINFREE$$

It is extremely important that your settings meet the above constraint check. Otherwise, the system might experience atypical paging behavior. Improperly setting the paging parameters might also cause the system to panic. Use care before altering the values of the kernel paging parameters. You should also maintain a reasonable multiplying factor between the kernel paging parameters. In other words, LOTSFREE should be a positive multiplier of DESFREE, and DESFREE also should be a positive multiplier of MINFREE. This ensures that the values of each are not so close to each other that swapping is triggered by a hairline memory allocation. The value of the multiplier depends on the amount of physical memory available on the system. For systems with large amounts of memory (i.e., 2 G or more), you may want to use a higher multiplier. For a system with a small-to-medium amount of memory, use a smaller multiplier. For example, on a system with 2 G of physical memory, if MINFREE is set to the equivalent of 1 M, you may want to set DESFREE to 2 M or a higher multiple of 1 M, and LOTSFREE to 4 M or a higher multiple. Avoid using large multipliers, otherwise you may have too large a gap between idle paging and swapping.

I would suggest that before altering the paging parameters you review your settings with your hardware vendor's OS engineers. They will help you verify the settings and review in detail any associated implications. When tuning paging parameters, make sure you study the system default values, as well as examine any additional parameters that are dependent on the paging parameters. Default values often change between OS versions as the OS becomes more and more efficient. Parameters often become obsolete and are replaced with new parameters. Therefore, you should always study the new OS version in detail before you apply settings from an older OS release.

2.5 SWAPPING

The swapper is run by the sched daemon. A process or thread is not considered swappable if the process or thread

- ❏ is part of the system scheduling class;
- ❏ is part of a process being forked;
- ❏ is in the zombie state; or
- ❏ has its address space in the kernel's address space.

Swapping is triggered when the average amount of free memory (avefree) is less than desfree or minfree. There are two types of swapping: leisure and desperate swapping. Leisure swapping begins when the amount of free memory falls below desfree. The swapper selects the processes to be swapped out. Usually the most idle processes (sleeping) are selected for swap-out. Desperate swapping begins when the amount of free memory falls below minfree (the absolute minimum). Processes are selected for swap-out based on the resident size, idle time, and priority. Desperate swapping is much more aggressive than leisure swapping because the swapper must restore the amount of free memory to at least minfree. Although processes may reserve swap space upon startup, a page of swap is not generally allocated until the page has to be flushed out. Also, some of the UNIX kernels allow swap space to be part of the physical memory pool because the kernel considers the physical memory and swap space as one large virtual memory pool (physical plus swap device). For example, Solaris allows reserved swap space to be part of physical memory. This improves the speed of swap reservation since the reservation may be done in physical memory rather than on physical disk. Swapping can severely impact performance.

Excessive swapping can also cause the system to appear unstable and can result in a panic. Recall that swapping is an act of desperation by the operating system to free memory immediately. Hence, the system selects processes to be swapped out, subsequently flushing these selected processes out to the swap device. The memory used by these processes can then be returned to the free list. Although swapping is commonly an outcome of a system lacking sufficient memory, swapping is often caused by *runaway* programs. Programs sometimes cause memory leaks due to improper process cleanup or by forgetting to free memory structures during the life of a process. Memory leaks are generally difficult to detect, especially in daemon programs that run continuously and `fork()` children to parallelize requests. There are numerous tools available on the market that help detect memory leaks and memory access violations. Rational Software offers the purify tool, which detects memory leaks and access violations. Bounds Checker is another tool that also provides similar functionality. I cannot overemphasize the importance of such tools. These tools save programmers days and weeks of searching through code to find memory leaks. The time and effort saved by these tools well outweigh the cost of these tools. There are also regression testing tools such as SQA Team Test that thoroughly test the application. Testing tools may not pinpoint the exact location in the code that is causing the memory leak. However, through continued regression tests, you stand a higher chance of reproducing the memory leaks and locating the cause. Testing tools, coupled with the memory leak detection tools such as Purify, provide a robust and proper development environment.

On Sequent, you can tune the swap allocation policy. The kernel parameter `SWAP_ALLOC_POLICY` controls the swap allocation policy. If set to 0 (the default), swap space is allocated at process startup. If insufficient swap space exists to invoke the process, the process is terminated. If `SWAP_ALLOC_POLICY` is set to 1, swap space is allocated for processes upon startup except for paged incarnation virtual segments, `mmap()` or anonymous map objects, address space page tables, and the U-block of a process. If `SWAP_ALLOC_POLICY` is set to 2, no swap space is allocated at process startup except for shared pagable kernel objects. Setting `SWAP_ALLOC_POLICY` to 2 could lead to termination of a process throughout the execution of the process due to insufficient swap space. A value of 0 ensures that enough swap space exists to start the process. You should set the value of `SWAP_ALLOC_POLICY` to 0. This guarantees that if sufficient swap space exists, the process will start successfully. Although a value of 0 may increase process startup time, it is a much safer setting, and the time needed to reserve swap space during process startup is extremely minimal.

In order to avoid high paging and swapping, you should study in complete detail the applications that will be running on the system. Items of concern are the lifetime of the process, memory requirements of the application, allocation and de-allocation routines, and process termination mechanisms. The more detailed information you have about the applications that will be running on your system, the easier it will be to tune your system in accordance with its requirements. I am constantly surprised by the reply that a system administrator receives after asking a developer, "how much memory does your application need?" The surprising reply is that a developer is often not sure how much memory is being used in the application. However, as the system administrator, you must work closely with the development staff to find the answers to the items of concern listed in this paragraph. The tuning advice with regard to swapping is: *avoid it at all costs.*

2.5.1 CONFIGURING SWAP

The UNIX operating system generally reserves (not allocates) swap space when processes are invoked. This ensures that the process can be swapped in and swapped out. The rule of thumb for configuring swap space is two to three times the amount of physical memory. I recommend that you create a swap device three to four times the amount of physical memory. For example, if you have a system that has 512 M of memory, you should have a swap device of 1.5 G–2 G in size. This helps reduce the likelihood of your system's running out of swap space. Although the physical swap device should not be used frequently, since the goal is to keep processes in real (physical) memory, it is a good idea to have a more than sufficient amount of swap space in the event that it is needed. Also, some installer programs and applications require a generous amount of swap space upon startup. I also recommend that you distribute your swap files across different disk drives and controllers. You should create many smaller swap devices rather than one large swap device. For instance, in the previous example, do not create a swap device on only one disk drive of 2 G in size. Create at least four different swap files on different disk drives to distribute the swap I/O. This will also improve the performance of the `page` and the `pageout` daemons when pages need to be brought in from the swap device or written out to the swap device (a more detailed discussion on I/O tuning follows in Chapter 3). To list the currently configured swap devices, use the `swap -l` command:

```
myhost>  swap -l

path                 dev       swaplo    blocks
/dev/dsk/qd0s1       101,1     0         204800
/dev/vol/v_swap01    121,60    0         204800
/dev/vol/v_swap02    121,225   0         204800
/dev/vol/v_swap03    121,69    0         204800
/dev/vol/v_swap04    121,78    0         204800
/dev/vol/v_swap05    121,58    0         204800
/dev/vol/v_swap06    121,67    0         204800
/dev/vol/v_swap07    121,76    0         204800
```

In this example, eight swap devices of 100 M each are configured. Try to keep swap disks separate from other disk drives. In other words, try to dedicate at least several disk drives to swap. To add swap devices, use the `swap -a` command, and update the necessary files so that the swap devices are brought online when the system boots. For example, to add an entire partition to the swap device, issue the following command as root:

```
myhost{root}->  swap -a /dev/dsk/c1t1d0s4
```

For systems with large amounts of physical memory, such as 32 G or 64 G, a relatively small amount of swap space, such as 3 G or 4 G, should suffice. Configuring the amount of swap space is dependent on the amount of physical memory. In essence, create a reasonable amount of swap space and be sure to distribute the swap files.

2.6 MEMORY SHORTAGES

The virtual memory model allows processes to allocate more memory than physically exists. While this may be possible, it is certainly not optimal. It is important that the development and administration staffs completely understand both the memory requirements of the application(s) being deployed, and the memory availability of the systems running the application(s). Using `sar`, `vmstat`, and/or other performance monitoring tools, you can determine whether or not the system is experiencing high amounts of paging and/or swapping. High amounts of paging and swapping indicate either that the system lacks sufficient memory to accommodate the memory allocation requests of the application(s), or that the kernel paging parameters need to be tuned. If the former case, you may need to consider adding additional physical memory, or reducing the amount of memory used in the application. If the latter case, you can tune the kernel paging parameters by following the guidelines listed above. When you monitor paging and swapping, do not be alarmed by high rates in the areas of page faults, virtual faults, page-ins, and/or attaches if they occur only for a brief moment. This is usually a result of application startup latency in which memory structures are allocated and initialized. Only be concerned with high rates that continue for a reasonable amount of time. You should try to monitor the paging and swapping activity throughout the entire lifetime of the application, inclusive of startup and shutdown. For an application that runs in nonstop mode, try to choose several periods of low, medium, and high usage to monitor the paging and swapping activity. For a system running the Oracle7 or Oracle8 DBMS, monitor paging and swapping while user applications are in progress. You should also monitor paging and swapping during peak periods to determine if adding more users increases the paging and/or swapping activity.

2.7 MEMORY SURPLUS

On systems where memory is abundant, it is important that this memory be utilized efficiently, and thus to its full potential. Applications should not be developed on the premise of "do not worry about memory allocation and de-allocation, the system has plenty of memory." This premise often leads to memory leaks and the inefficient use of a precious and expensive resource like memory. The application should never take for granted that plenty of memory will always exist, and therefore the application will always be able to run. There may be other applications running concurrently that also use large amounts of memory that may preclude your application from running. You should avoid using static memory declarations for application structures. Always allocate the memory dynamically, and free the memory once the structure is no longer needed. You can use the `malloc()` system call, or `shmop()` system call to allocate memory within your process.[9] Statically allocating an array in a program assumes that the structure is created and allocated. If for some reason the array could not be allocated upon execution, you may receive all sorts of strange errors ranging from segmentation violations and bus errors to arithmetic errors when you try to manipulate a nonexistent array. Using the `malloc()` or `shmop()` system calls to allocate the memory as soon as it is needed ensures that if the object could not be allocated due to insufficient memory, the application can trap the allocation error and terminate the application gracefully. Remember to use the `free()` system call to free memory when it is no longer needed. Consider memory as a resource similar to energy. You turn on lights when needed, and you increase the degree of lighting until it is suitable. Similarly, use memory when it is needed, and free it when it is no longer needed just as you turn off lights when leaving a room. There is no benefit to allocating memory that is never used. In fact, it may impede other users from obtaining the memory that their application needs.

2.8   KERNEL MEMORY ALLOCATOR

The kernel memory allocator (`kma`) is responsible for servicing all memory allocation and de-allocation requests. The `kma` is also responsible for maintaining the memory free list. On Solaris, you can monitor the activity of the `kma` using the `kma` command. Using `sar -k`, you can monitor the workload of the `kma` by observing the amount of allocations for small and large requests for memory as well as the number of memory requests that failed. You can also obtain statistics on the amount of memory allocated for oversize requests, and the number of failures for oversize requests. You should monitor `kma` activity in conjunction with paging and swapping activity in order to determine the occurrence of memory shortages. Solaris 2.4 implemented a new and more efficient algorithm for kernel memory allocation. The algorithm improves the cache hit rates and reduces CPU overhead. Solaris 2.4 also improved upon Solaris 2.3 by replacing internal kernel lookup tables with hash lookup tables. This improves the speed of kernel table lookups.

2.9   LARGE MEMORY MODEL

Hardware vendors continue to make major advancements to enterprise servers including the ability to support larger amounts of memory and larger disk farm configurations. In order to utilize more server memory effectively, operating system vendors have provided

---

9. The `malloc()` call is the generic memory allocation system call. The `shmop()` system call allows the caller to perform shared memory operations such as creating a shared memory segment, attaching to the segment, or removing the segment. For more information, refer to the manual pages on `malloc()` or `shmop()`.

extensions for large memory support in a 32-bit world. This allows applications such as Oracle to create an SGA larger than 4 G and maintain more data in memory, thereby reducing physical I/O. In the 32-bit virtual memory model, a user process's address space is limited to a maximum of 4 G minus the kernel overhead. For those system architectures employing a 32-bit chip, OS vendors need to provide extensions for an extended cache in order to work around the 32-bit virtual address limit.

Depending on the platform-specific implementation, the concept of an extended cache model on a 32-bit architecture centers around the ability to map in memory pages to the user process during use and unmap the memory pages when they are no longer needed by the process. This essentially takes the burden of having to deal with extended caches off the application and places it on the OS. The application simply makes a system call to map the memory page in and unmaps the page when no longer needed. The overhead of mapping and unmapping buffers is relatively trivial when compared with the overall gain of extended caches. In most cases, mapping a buffer is an inexpensive operation involving mostly L2 cache page table translations from virtual to physical addresses. Until chip manufacturers and OS vendors migrate to a 64-bit environment, the extended cache feature is critical to large-system performance. This allows large-scale size databases to utilize a large extended cache and reduce physical I/O by maintaining more data in the cache.

Solaris 2.7 provides 64-bit capabilities and a 64-bit development environment. The 64-bit option of Solaris 2.7 requires a 64-bit chip architecture such as the UltraSPARC. For Intel platforms, the Solaris 2.7 64-bit option will require Intel's new generation IA-64 (64-bit) microprocessors.

Sequent provides extended cache functionality via the `virtwin()` and `shmatvw()` system calls to handle mapping extended cache buffers into the user process address space. Oracle8 on the Sequent NUMA-Q systems has been optimized to take advantage of the extended cache feature. Oracle8's extended cache feature allows the SGA buffer pool layer to reside outside the process' virtual address space. Buffers are mapped, only when needed, into a set of *window panes*.

HP-UX 11.0 also provides 64-bit OS functionality including features such as large memory segments, and large files. HP-UX 11.0 allows a shared memory size of 8 Tb, a maximum file system and file size of 128 G, and a 4 Tb process data space. The V2200 HP Enterprise server supports 64-bit HP-UX 11.0 and provides a significant performance increase over the T-Class servers. HP is also working jointly with Intel and also helped design the Intel IA-64 architecture.

Oracle8 Release 8.0.4S will be a 64-bit version available on platforms providing 64-bit support such as Solaris 2.7 (SPARC) and HP-UX 11.0. Oracle 8.0.4S allows you to increase performance and scalabilty by taking advantage of your 64-bit platform, such as allowing larger memory configurations, more users, and more processes. Oracle8 Release 8.0.5, as well as future releases of Oracle8, will also provide the 64-bit option. This allows for larger database configurations as well as larger memory pools.

2.10   LARGE PAGE SIZES

Another useful feature that helps increase the performance of large SGAs is the large page size feature. This allows a page size of 1 M or 4 M for example, rather than the default page size of 4K or 8K depending on the platform. Using the large page size feature reduces the work on the kernel memory allocator, page daemon, and results in improved efficiency of virtual memory. The large page size feature is most useful for large SGAs.

In Solaris 2.6, a large page size of 4 M is used when a large shared memory segment is created. When attaching to the shared memory segment via the `shmat()` call, you should set the SHM_SHARE_MMU flag. In addition, the virtual address you specify should be 4 M aligned and ISM (Intimate Shared Memory) should be enabled.

HP-UX 11.0 provides a variable page size option which allows you to specify the size of the page depending on the type of workload. Large page sizes may be used for process text, process data, process heap, shared memory, and shared libraries. Using the `chatr` command, you can specify the text or data page size. The kernel also chooses the page size transparently for executables with a *default* page size. The kernel uses the size of the object at the time of creation to determine the optimal page size. In order to use the large page size, the virtual address must be aligned with the page size being specified. HP-UX 11.0 provides large page size tunables including `vps_pagesize`, `vps_ceiling`, and `vps_chatr_celing`. The `vps_pagesize` parameter specifies the default page size to use for all objects created. The `vps_ceiling` parameter specifies the maximum size allowed for transparently selected pages. The `vps_chatr_ceiling` specifies the maximum page size that can be set for an executable via the `chatr` command.

2.11   SHARED MEMORY PARAMETERS

As stated previously, shared memory is a System V Release 4 method of interprocess communication. It allows multiple processes to attach to the same memory segment and allows the sharing of data. This avoids having to perform memory-to-memory copies from one process to another in order to share data. This reduces the kma workload as well as CPU cycles of copying data. Shared memory is no different than regular memory in the sense that it still consists of memory pages and is also managed by the page daemon in the same manner that regular memory is managed. When you start the Oracle8 instance, the Oracle kernel creates at least one shared memory segment to hold the SGA. Then, when users connect to the database, the user's respective server process attaches to the shared memory segment to access the SGA. Shared memory pages can be locked in memory upon creation by using the lock flag in the `shmget()` or `shmctl()` system call. The `mlock()` system call locks the memory pages specified in the `mlock()` call in main memory. This prevents the pages from being swapped or paged out.

Using the `mlock()` call can have dangerous repercussions unless used properly. Preventing memory from being paged out may cause the system to become unstable if the amount of free memory available to the system drops below the specified paging limits. Sequent Dynix 4.2 provides a mechanism by which a shared memory segment can be locked into memory thereby increasing performance. This also increases the performance of Oracle by pinning the SGA into main memory, and preventing it from being paged out. In order to enable shared memory use on your system, you must set several kernel parameters. The kernel parameters associated with shared memory are `SHMMAX`, `SHMMIN`, `SHMNI`, and `SHMSEG`. The `SHMMAX` kernel parameter controls the maximum size, in bytes, of a single shared memory segment. The `SHMMIN` kernel parameter specifies the minimum size of a shared memory segment in bytes. The `SHMNI` kernel parameter specifies the number of shared memory identifiers. The `SHMSEG` kernel parameter specifies the number of shared memory segments per process. Set the value of `SHMMAX` to the maximum size of your SGA so that the SGA can fit into one contiguous shared memory segment. This ensures that the SGA is held in one shared memory segment. Otherwise, if your SGA is larger than `SHMMAX`, multiple shared memory segments will need to be allocated. Do not set `SHMMAX` to an amount larger than the amount of physical memory existent on the system. On HP, use the SAM tool to set the shared memory kernel parameters and reboot the system. On Sequent, use the menu tool to configure the kernel and set the shared memory kernel parameters. The menu tool also prompts if you want to rebuild the kernel and reboot the system for the changes to take effect. On Solaris, you can set these parameters by editing the `/etc/system` file and placing the entries that follow in the file. You must reboot your Solaris system for the changes to take effect.

Example /etc/system file

```
set  shmsys:shminfo_shmmax=104857600
set  shmsys:shminfo_shmmin=1
set  shmsys:shminfo_shmni=100
set  shmsys:shminfo_shmseg=10
```

On Sequent, you can set the following parameters to enable shared memory locking: `SHM_LOCK_OK`, `SHM_LOCK_UID`, `SHM_LOCK_MIN`, and `SHM_LOCK_MAX`.

2.12 SEMAPHORE PARAMETERS

Semaphores are also one of the System V Release 4 mechanisms of interprocess communication. Semaphores are used to protect resources. As resources are allocated, the semaphore counter is decremented. As resources are freed, the counter is incremented. A count of zero indicates that no resources are available. By default, the Oracle8 Server uses semaphores. There are also kernel parameters associated with semaphores that you may need to set. The semaphore kernel parameters—SEMMAP, SEMMNI, SEMMNS, SEMMNU, SEMMSL, SEMOPM, SEMUME, SEMUSZ, SEMVMX, and SEMAEM—are defined in Table 2.2.

TABLE 2.2   Semaphore kernel parameters

PARAMETER	FUNCTION
SEMMAP	Defines the number of entries in the semaphore map.
SEMMNI	Defines the number of semaphore identifiers.
SEMMNS	Defines the number of semaphores in the system.
SEMMNU	Specifies the number of undo structures in the system.
SEMMSL	Defines the maximum number of semaphores per user ID.
SEMOPM	Defines the maximum number of operations per semop call.
SEMUME	Specifies the number of undo entries per process.
SEMUSZ	Defines the size of the undo structure, in bytes.
SEMVMX	The maximum value of the semaphore.
SEMAEM	The amount used to adjust the maximum value of the semaphore upon exit.

On HP, use the SAM tool to set the semaphore kernel parameters and reboot the system. On Sequent, use the menu tool to set the semaphore kernel parameters. The menu tool will also prompt if you want to rebuild the kernel and reboot the system for the changes to take effect. You can monitor semaphore activity by using the sar -m command. On Solaris, you can set these parameters by editing the /etc/system file and placing the entries that follow in the file. You must reboot your Solaris system for the changes to take effect.

Example /etc/system file

```
set semsys:seminfo_semmap=10
set semsys:seminfo_semmni=10
set semsys:seminfo_semmns=60
set semsys:seminfo_semmnu=30
set semsys:seminfo_semmsl=25
set semsys:seminfo_semopm=10
set semsys:seminfo_semume=10
set semsys:seminfo_semusz=96
set semsys:seminfo_semvmx=32767
set semsys:seminfo_semaem=16384
```

2.13 PROCESSOR ARCHITECTURE

The processor and memory architecture of a symmetrical multiprocessing system relies on the *shared everything* architecture. In the shared everything architecture, a single system runs a single operating system consisting of processors, memory, and disk that are shared among the users and processes. Figure 2.7 highlights the shared everything architecture.

In Figure 2.7, the total system memory is shared between the processors and processes. The shared everything architecture requires an *affinity* algorithm. The affinity algorithm, sometimes referred to as the loose affinity algorithm, is responsible for transferring processes and/or threads from one CPU to another. For example, suppose a process is running on CPU 1 and then goes to sleep. When the process is later awakened, another process may be occupying CPU 1. Therefore, the process will have to be assigned to another CPU. On a uniprocessor system, affinity and cache coherency are not an issue since there can be only one active process or thread at any one moment. On a multiprocessor system, however, this is an issue that the OS has to deal with. For example, suppose a process running on CPU 1 requires data from memory or disk that is already in another CPU's cache. Rather than requesting the data from memory, it can request the data from the other CPU's cache. This is significantly faster because cache chips typically use SRAM (Static Random Access Memory). SRAM speeds range from 10 to 50 nanoseconds. Main memory typically uses DRAM (Dynamic Random Access Memory). DRAM speeds generally range from 60 to several hundred nanoseconds.

2.13.1 CACHE CONCEPTS

The concept of the cache is to substantially accelerate successive access to the same data. In other words, the very first access to data requires physical I/O (assuming the data is stored on some sort of physical media device) to bring the data into main memory. If the process accessing the data is currently running on a processor, the most recently accessed

FIGURE 2.7 The shared everything architecture.

data may be in the CPU's cache. Therefore, subsequent access to the data will not require physical I/O because the data is in either the CPU's cache or the main memory. This significantly reduces physical I/O and increases overall performance.

Cache memory has several characteristics. First, cache memory is expensive relative to regular DRAM memory. For this reason, you will not find huge amounts of on-chip cache memory on the CPU versus off-chip cache. A typical size for an on-chip cache is 20K. Typical off-chip cache sizes range from 512K to 4 M, depending on the hardware vendor of the processor. Second, cache memory requires more physical space and expends more power than DRAM chips. Finally, there is a point of diminishing return. The point of diminishing return occurs when adding additional cache memory provides little, if any, gain. In some cases, adding additional cache memory may actually reduce system performance.

The *cache hit ratio* is the number of times the data was found in the cache versus having to read the data from outside the cache (main memory or physical I/O to the disk). A higher cache hit ratio is always desirable and increases system performance. A cache miss results when the data requested was not found in the cache and had to be read either from main memory or disk. On the Sun SuperSPARC processor, the on-chip cache incurs a ten cycle cost for a cache miss. If your SuperSPARC processor contains SuperCache, data can be transferred from the SuperCache to the on-chip cache in five CPU cycles. Hence, it is apparent that cache misses can increase the CPU workload by a tangible factor.

There are two main types of caches: a *direct-mapped* cache, and a *set-associative* cache. A direct-mapped cache maps each memory location to a single cache line. Off-chip caches (secondary caches) often use a direct-mapped cache algorithm. A cache line consists of a cache tag and data. The cache tag identifies the process ownership of the cache data. The cache is flushed upon the occurrence of a context switch. In a set-associative cache, a line can exist in the cache in many different locations. The cache lookup must search all possible locations in parallel to find the data. Because the data can be in numerous places in the cache, contention for the cache resource is reduced. However, because the data can be located in several different locations, the logic to manage a set-associative cache is much more complex than that of a direct-mapped cache. Set-associative caches are generally used for on-chip caches. The degree of the set-associative cache is determined by the number of possible locations for the cache line. For example, if there are three possible locations for a cache line, then this cache would be referred to as a three-way set-associative cache. The Sequent Symmetry systems use a two-way set-associative secondary cache for each CPU.

In addition to the mapping styles of the cache, there are also two main cache write algorithms: *write-through-cache*, and *write-back-cache*. In a write-through-cache, a write to main memory is always initiated simultaneously with a write to the cache. In a write-back-cache, the write is written only to the cache. The write-through cache ensures consistency between main memory and the cache. However, write-through caches can reduce performance by issuing many writes to main memory. The advantage of a write-back cache is that subsequent cache writes need not wait on previous cache writes to update main memory.

2.13.2   CACHE COHERENCY

In a multiprocessor system, it is necessary to synchronize data among processors. For example, if a process on CPU 2 modifies some data resident in CPU 2's cache, and another process on CPU 3 needs to read the same data, CPU 3 would need to read the latest change from CPU 2's cache in order to maintain consistency. In order to accomplish cache coherency, the OS kernel employs a cache snooping algorithm. Typically, each CPU module has a *snooping cache*. The snooping cache listens for cache data across the bus. If a CPU writes to a shared cache block, the CPU can choose one of two actions: force every other CPU to nullify their entries pertaining to this cache data, known as the *write-invalidate protocol*; or, another alternative is to force the other CPUs sharing the cache block to update the CPU's copy of the cache block with the new data. This technique is known as the *write-update* protocol.

2.13.3   CENTRAL BUS

In the shared everything architecture, there is a central bus linking the system's processors, memory, and I/O subsystems. The Sequent Symmetry Server uses the Symmetry System Bus (SSB) or the Symmetry Highly Scalable Bus (HSB). The SSB is a synchronous, pipelined, and packet-switched bus. The bus clock rate is 10 Mhz for the SSB, and 30 Mhz for the HSB. The peak data transfer rates are 80 M/second for the SSB, and 240 M/second for the HSB. SSB devices use a 32- or 64-bit data path with a 32-bit address path, thereby yielding a sustained data transfer rate of up to 64 M/second. HSB devices use a 32- or 64-bit data path and a 32-bit address path as well. The sustained data transfer rate for HSB devices can be up to 107 M/second. Because operations are pipelined, the bus can service other transactions following a read or write request, even before the system memory issues its response. Sequent announced the new NUMA-Q (Non-Unified Memory Access) Server series, which introduces a new system architecture that permits substantially larger system configurations (up to 256 processors) and larger transfer rates.

The Sun SPARC Server 1000 and SPARC Center 2000 use the XDBus as the primary system bus. The XDBus is also a packet-switched bus and has a peak data transfer rate of 320 M/second with a 40 Mhz system bus speed. The SPARC Center 2000E increased the system bus speed to 50 Mhz. A typical sustained transfer rate is 250 M/second on the SPARC Center 2000. The SPARC Center 2000 uses a dual XDBus as opposed to the single XDBus in the SPARC Server 1000. The speed of the Sun SPARC processors typically range from 40 Mhz–60 Mhz. The new Sun Enterprise Servers use the *gigaplane* bus as the main system bus. The gigaplane bus allows transfers of up to 2.6 G/second. This is a major improvement over the XDBus. Sun continues to improve the performance of the UltraSPARC processor. The 300-Mhz UltraSPARC-II processor is yet another improvement of the clock speed over the other UltraSPARC processors which were 167 Mhz, 200 Mhz, or 250 Mhz.

2.13.4 NUMA-Q ARCHITECTURE

NUMA-Q is Sequent's implementation of the Nonuniform Memory Access (NUMA) architecture. Figure 2.8 illustrates the NUMA-Q architecture which consists of a series of quads linked together using a high-speed interconnect. The high-speed interconnect, IQ-Link, connects the quads and allows data transfers between the quads at a rate of 1 G/second. IQ-Link also maintains the cache coherency for the system. The IQ-Link is not a backplane, rather a daisy chain connection between quads. When an application requests some data, the IQ-Link scans its own cache (L3) to determine if the data is present. If the data is not found in the IQ-Link's cache, IQ-Link sends a request to the other quads. The NUMA-Q architecture helps overcome the single large backplane bus bottleneck that typically occurs in large SMP systems. NUMA-Q allows hardware vendors to build large-scale SMP systems by adding more quads to the system. However, as more quads are added, more work is placed on the SCI-based interconnect (IQ-Link). Therefore, it is important that continual improvements be made to the interconnect in order to prevent the interconnect from becoming a bottleneck, thereby allowing high-performance and scalable NUMA-Q systems. The idea of NUMA-Q is to offer a model with low latency and high throughput. NUMA-Q offers low latency and high bandwidth by positioning groups of distributed memory in proximity to each processor, referred to as quad local memory. Quad local memory is a significant improvement over the traditional SMP model in which memory access must travel over the shared central bus. Also, data residing in remote memory that is frequently accessed is cached in the local quad in order to improve performance and maintain a high bandwidth.

Oracle and Sequent continue to work together to optimize Oracle8 for NUMA-Q systems, including such things as the placement of SGA memory and Oracle processes and extended cache capabilities. Since the design goal of NUMA-Q is to localize operations per quad, it is important that applications avoid remote operations, if possible. This

FIGURE 2.8 NUMA-Q Architecture.

requires a sophisticated binding between the application and its data access methods. On Sequent NUMA-Q systems, Oracle8 distributes the SGA shared memory segment across the quads in order to balance memory usage and access. Using the ipcs command, you can see the different shared memory segments across the different quads after starting the Oracle instance. Sequent provides the shmgetq() [10] system call which extends the functionality of the standard shmget() system call by allowing you to distribute shared memory segments across the quads.

2.13.5 NEXT GENERATION PROCESSORS

Hardware vendors are working vigorously to deliver 64-bit processors to the marketplace in order to couple the chip with the 64-bit operating systems. Sun currently offers the 64-bit UltraSPARC processor in its Enterprise servers and recently announced the UltraSPARC-III 600 Mhz processor which includes the VIS instruction set and 2.4GB/s memory bandwidth. Intel has developed the IA-64 processor architecture and plans to release Merced™ as the first IA-64 processor in 1999. Sun and HP are working with Intel to deliver IA-64 based systems. Intel also plans to release the Katmai and Deschutes processors in 1998. The Deschutes processor enhances the Pentium II processor by taking the Pentium II processor to 0.25u process technology and much higher frequencies. Deschutes will move the Pentium II processor into new market segments such as the mobile segment. Katmai will offer new MMX instructions and possible support for 3D geometry and dual floating-point operations. In addition to much higher frequencies, the Deschutes, Katmai, and Merced™ processors will also increase the size of the L2 cache over the standard Pentium size of 512K or 1 M. This will help increase application performance by reducing data cache misses.

2.14 THREADS MODEL

The threads model enhances the process model by defining further granular levels within a process known as a thread, and an LWP. A thread is a unit of control, or execution sequence. A thread can also be thought of as an abstraction of the processor. There are several threads standards organizations. UNIX International Threads (UI threads) was an organization formed by Sun and AT&T. The Sun Solaris threads library (libthread.so) is based on UI threads. There is also the OSF DCE (Open Software Foundation Distributed Computing Environment) threads standard. POSIX also developed threads standards, and most vendors are moving toward adopting the POSIX threads. POSIX has released formal threads standards for platforms such as UNIX and Windows NT.

---

10. For more information on the shmgetq() system call, refer to the man pages on shmgetq().

Threads are used to increase the level of concurrency and parallelism and at the same time reduce the process overhead. Prior to threads, parallelism and concurrency were achieved through creating multiple processes [i.e., `fork()`]. Creating multiple processes introduces substantial overhead relative to the threads model as separate stack, data, and text segments must be maintained for each process. Threads share the same address space as the process creating the thread. This significantly reduces memory and CPU overhead. A process consists of a Process Control Block (PCB) as well as its address space. A thread consists of a Thread Control Block (TCB), a stack, operating system control state, and a Kernel Thread Control Block (KTCB). Creating a thread is substantially quicker than creating a process, since the process already exists during thread creation. The time it takes to create a thread is on the order of 1000 times less than the time it takes to create a process. Threads also help reduce context switch overhead and kernel system call overhead because the majority of threads tend to remain in user space. Switching between threads does not involve the switching of address spaces as with the switching between processes. Interthread communication is much easier than interprocess communication because threads share the same address space.

The kernel provides support for threads via the threads library. As part of the kernel support for threads, the kernel provides virtual processors known as LWPs, or Lightweight Processes. By default, there is no fixed assignment of threads to the LWPs. Figure 2.9 diagrams the threads model.

Figure 2.9 illustrates that user threads (application threads) are part of the user space and use no kernel resources. Application threads are therefore extremely lightweight. User threads are managed by the application threads library. The LWP can be

FIGURE 2.9   The threads model.

thought of as a virtual CPU. Application threads are scheduled onto the LWPs via the threads library. If an application thread is bound to an LWP, the LWP is not available for use by other application threads. The kernel thread is the central scheduling object, and a kernel thread is associated with each LWP. Figure 2.9 shows a kernel thread with no corresponding LWP. This kernel thread is referred to as a *system thread* (or `system` daemon), meaning that no corresponding LWP exists. Examples of such daemons are the `pageout` daemon and the clock daemon. Every process consists of at least one kernel thread.

On Solaris, you can set the level of concurrency in your multithreaded application by using the `thr_setconcurrency()` system call. For example, `thr_setconcurrency(10)` sets the level of concurrency to ten by allocating ten LWPs. To maximize parallelism in this example, 10 threads would be created, with each one being bound to a separate LWP.

Threads programming can offer significant performance gains over the traditional UNIX process model. Threads have less overhead and share the same address space as the process creating the thread. Creating a thread is approximately 1000 times faster than creating a process.

2.14.1   THREADS SAFETY

In order to develop a threads application, it is essential that the application be thread-safe. Since most of the libraries and applications were developed using the single-threaded model, care must be taken when calling library calls and system calls from a threaded application. There are four main issues with threaded programming versus the single-threaded model:

1. Global variables
2. Static storage
3. Synchronization
4. Signals

Global variables pose the biggest problem for threaded applications because multiple threads can modify the global variable. Therefore, the integrity of the variable is not guaranteed. Take for example the `errno` global variable. This global variable is used to set the error code following a system call. Suppose that several threads are concurrently issuing system calls. The value of `errno` could be set by any one of the threads issuing system calls. Therefore, synchronization is needed to lock the global variable before it is modified. This protects the variable from being modified from other threads. The same problem of global variables applies to static storage in a threaded application.

Synchronization also poses a problem. For example, many system calls return pointers to standard structures and objects. The application then usually manipulates these structures and objects throughout the course of the application. In a single-threaded process model, this is not an issue since the address space is local per process. However, when multiple subprocesses (threads) share the same address space and run concurrently, the likelihood of these common structures being overwritten by each other is extremely high. For this reason, many of the OS libraries have been rewritten to be thread-safe. On Solaris, you can determine if a system call is thread-safe by viewing the manual pages of the system call. Under the section titled MT-LEVEL, the system call will be labeled as either safe or unsafe. It is important that you determine whether the system call you are using in your threaded application is thread-safe. If not, you will either have to use another equivalent system call that is thread-safe or provide some sort of locking mechanism to prevent one thread from interfering with another.

Signals also must be dealt with carefully in a threaded application. In the process model, signals are process-wide. In other words, if you trap the <CONTROL><C> termination signal anywhere in the process and choose the default signal action for the termination, the entire process will terminate. For a single-threaded process this is not an issue, since signal handlers are established at the process level. However, with threads, each thread has its own signal mask. Remember, receiving signals at the single-threaded process level is quite simple, since the process has only one thread. However, in a multithreaded application, any one of the threads can receive the signal. If the thread receiving the signal does not deal with the signal properly by establishing a per thread signal handler, the entire process may be terminated causing termination of all threads. Therefore, it is important that each thread establish a separate signal mask. This allows each thread to deal with signals appropriate to the particular thread. For example, there is no sense in a thread waiting for I/O signals if no I/O is done by the thread.

2.14.2   THREADS PROGRAMMING

This section on threads is extremely brief and is not intended to be a programmer's guide to threads. For more detail on programming using threads, you should seek out additional text on threads programming.

You should try to use POSIX threads in order to increase the portability of your application. Solaris threads run only on Solaris. Many platforms now support POSIX threads. The threads section is intended to provide you with the basic architecture and concept of threads. I sincerely encourage you to consider threaded programming in any new application design. Some applications are better suited as a single-threaded process. However, the majority of business applications requiring high scalability and high throughput could definitely benefit from a threaded implementation. I do not want to imply that threaded programming is by any means simple and straightforward. On the contrary, threaded programming is probably the most complex method of user-level programming—requiring precision, accuracy, expertise, and extreme care. There are several texts available on threads programming that provide examples and detail the relevant thread system calls. For a developer who likes a challenge, threaded programming will definitely keep you challenged and excited. Many software vendors have projects underway to make use of threads within their software products in order to increase performance and throughput. The Oracle Server on NT uses a multithreaded model via NT threads.

One other key element to threads programming is testing and debugging. Debugging and fully testing a threaded program is quite difficult. Debuggers are now providing the ability to trace threads. However, because threads can execute in a different order each time the application is executed, it may not be easy or obvious to reproduce or detect a bug. Regression testing tools help by constantly running regression tests on the application. If you are developing a multithreaded application, you should obtain a complete set of debugging and regression testing tools that support threads. Maintaining proper threading coding practices and thorough testing will help foster a high-performance bug-free application. Threaded programming is elegant and challenging, and I encourage you to consider using threads for applications that require a high level of performance.

2.15   PROCESSOR TUNING

Hardware vendors are constantly improving processor technology. Sun has introduced a new series of servers called the Ultra Enterprise Series. These systems use the Ultra 167-Mhz, 250-Mhz, 300-Mhz, or 600-Mhz CPU for the 3000, 4000, 5000, 6000, and 10000 (Starfire) Series Servers. This is an enormous improvement over the Sun SPARC 1000 Server and SPARC Center 2000 Series Servers. Not only has Sun increased the processor speed by a factor of almost ten, the backplane bus has also been expanded to sustain larger transfers at higher speeds. HP has also recently announced the V-Class Enterprise server series. Sequent has also introduced the NUMA-Q systems and continues to enhance performance and scalability. HP and Sequent both plan to move to the new high-end Intel processors for their next generation of servers. Processor architectures and speeds will continue to improve, and it is critical that the software systems utilize these high-powered systems as efficiently as possible. For example, if an application does not scale, or does not make use of parallel processing, there will be little gained by adding additional CPUs. Processors are an expensive and vital resource and need to be utilized to their full capacity. The Oracle8 DBMS is one good example of a large-scale application (in this case a database management system) that not only scales but also benefits enormously from the addition of processors.

Right-sizing a system with the proper number of CPUs and memory requires legitimate performance metrics. The application that the system will be serving must be thoroughly benchmarked. CPU utilization statistics must be gathered, and scalability must be measured in terms of adding users and increasing the system workload. Do not rely on industry standard benchmarks or processor benchmarks such as SPECInt. While these benchmarks are useful as a generic baseline measurement, they cannot measure the scalability or performance of a custom application effectively. You must benchmark your application(s) extensively in your environment to determine scalability and performance.

To determine the CPU utilization of an application, use the `sar -u` command. For example,

```
myhost> sar -u 1 5

SunOS myhost 5.5 generic sun4m
    %usr      %sys      %wio      %idle
     0         6         0        94
     1         0         2        97
     0         1         0        99
     0         1         0        99
     0         1         0        99

Average   0         2         0        98
```

The `sar` command (`-u` option) reports CPU utilization. The `%usr` column reports the percentage that the processor was running in user time; `%sys` is the percentage of the processor running in system time; `%wio` is the percentage the processor spent waiting on I/O requests; and `%idle` reports the percentage that the processor was idle. On Sequent, you can also use the `/etc/monitor` utility to monitor CPU utilization. The `/etc/monitor` utility provides a line graph format of CPU utilization per processor. On Sun Solaris, you can also use the `mpstat` command. For instance,

```
myhost> mpstat 1 3

CPU minf mjf xcal  intr ithr  csw icsw migr smtx srw syscl usr sys wt idl
 0   0    0   0    143  42   74  13   0    0    0   518   7   3   0   90
 0   11   0   0    160  60   95   1   0    0    0   299   1   0   0   99
 0   0    0   0    154  54   91   2   0    0    0   332   0   0   0  100
```

The `mpstat` command is similar to the `sar` command in that the arguments to `mpstat` are the time in seconds at which `mpstat` should poll, and the second argument to `mpstat` is the number of iterations `mpstat` should report statistics. The `mpstat` utility reports the statistics per processor, as shown in Table 2.3.

TABLE 2.3   Statistics per processor, as reported by the `mpstat` utility

STATISTIC	DEFINITION
CPU	the processor ID
minf	the number of minor faults
mjf	the number of major faults
xcal	the number of interprocessor cross calls

(continued)

TABLE 2.3 continued

STATISTIC	DEFINITION
`intr`	the number of interrupts
`ithr`	the number of interrupts as threads
`csw`	the number of context switches
`icsw`	the number of involuntary context switches
`migr`	the number of thread migrations to another processor
`smtx`	the number of spins for a mutex lock, meaning the lock was not obtained on the first attempt
`srw`	the number of spins on reader-writer lock, meaning the lock was not obtained on the first attempt
`syscl`	the number of system calls
`usr`	the percentages that the processor spent in user time
`sys`	the percentages that the processor spent in system time
`wt`	the percentages that the processor spent in wait time (waiting on an event)
`idle`	the percentages that the processor spent in idle time

In conjunction with monitoring CPU utilization (**sar -u** or `mpstat`), you should also monitor the run queue to determine if processes are waiting for an available processor. You can use the `sar -q` command to monitor the run queue. For example,

```
myhost> sar -q 1 5

DYNIX/ptx myhost 4.0 V4.1.3 i386

runq-sz %runocc swpq-sz %swpocc
    9.0      82
    7.0      83
    8.0     161
    9.0      83
    8.0      83

Average     8.2      99
```

The `runq-sz` column is the length of the run queue (processes waiting for CPU), and `%runocc` is the percentage of time occupied. The `swpq-sz` column is the number of processes that have been swapped out but are now ready to run, and the `%swpocc` column is the percentage of time occupied. In the preceding output from `sar`, it is obvious that additional CPUs are needed in the system in order to service the amount of processes. The run queue average length is 8.2 and the percentage occupied is 99. This indicates that, on the average, at least eight processes are waiting for CPU. If the run queue in your system consistently shows many processes waiting for CPU, you will need to add additional processors or reduce the amount of concurrent processes on the system.

On Sequent NUMA-Q systems, you can create user run queues to help balance process workload and improve processor utilization. You can use the `/etc/monitor` command to monitor processor and quad utilization. The `/etc/rqcreat` command can be used to create additional run queues. You can specify the processors to be included in the run queue. Use the `/etc/showquads` command to list the quads and processors on your system. The OS scheduler typically balances the workload optimally across quads. However, you may want to consider using the run queues option to improve application processor utilization. As a general rule of thumb when deciding to use run queues, you should create a run queue per quad and not per processor. Then assign your process or set of processes to the specific run queue by using the `/etc/rqadmin` (-assign option). You can use the `/etc/rqstat` command to monitor run queue statistics such as the number of processes active, number of pending processes, and priority of the run queue which can range from –32 to 31. The statistics reported by `rqstat` will help you determine if the run queues are balanced.

You can also use the GUI performance monitoring tools to monitor CPU utilization. These tools will usually display GUI charts and graphs of CPU utilization per processor. You should watch for high WIO percentages. This tends to indicate that I/O is a bottleneck, and processors are spending the majority of their time waiting for I/O completion. Refer to Chapter 3 for more information about tuning I/O. You should also look for high percentages in system time or idle time. High system percentages mean that the processor is spending a large amount of time in kernel space and therefore less in user space. High idle percentages may indicate that the application itself does not make use of multiple processors, and therefore the remaining CPUs on the system may be idle. You may have to consider redesigning the application to parallelize the work either by forking child processes or by creating threads. In general, the ideal goal is to have the application spend most of its time in user space. If the application performs a lot of system calls, then the system mode utilization may also be high. However, if the application is well written and utilizes multiple processors effectively, there should be a minimal amount of contention. User time percentages should range anywhere from 60 percent for applications that issue a large number of system calls to 95 percent for an application with a minimal number of system calls. Anything less than 60 percent is reason for concern and should be reviewed. When tuning an application with respect to its processor utilization, the goal is to maximize user time. This goal allows the processor to spend the majority of its time running the application in user space. System time and certainly I/O wait time need to be minimal so as to not result in an application bottleneck. You must also monitor the run queue to ensure processes are not waiting for CPU.

In order to maximize user time during application execution, several things must be considered. If the application is an I/O-intensive application, then I/O must be configured and tuned appropriately. I/O tuning is discussed in Chapter 3. It is important that you conclude that I/O is not a bottleneck before you begin to tune the CPU utilization of your application. To rule out I/O as a bottleneck, follow the guidelines laid out in

Chapter 3. Once you have determined that I/O is configured and tuned appropriately and that the statistics from the I/O subsystem indicate relatively good performance, you must tune your application to maximize CPU utilization while in user space. In order to maximize user time, you should try to minimize the amount of system calls made in the application. System calls require kernel resources to service the system calls and can result in high system time percentages. In some applications, the system calls cannot be avoided. For example, an I/O-intensive application cannot avoid I/O. However, if the I/O system is tuned properly, the application should see little wait I/O due to the proper I/O distribution. However, there are things that an application can do to reduce system call overhead and user space overhead as well. For example, a typical I/O application that reads and writes randomly to files can make use of new system calls. Consider the following example:

```
lseek (File Descriptor, offset, whence)

write (File Descriptor, buffer, nbytes)
```

OR

```
lseek (File Descriptor, offset, whence)

read (File Descriptor, buffer, nbytes)
```

This example is typical of an application performing file I/O. The application will usually issue an `lseek()` call to position the file pointer to a specific offset within the file and then issue the write to that location in the file. The same strategy is taken when reading from the file. The `lseek()` call is used to position the file pointer to the specified offset, and then the `read()` call is issued from that offset location. This means that for random file I/O, a minimum of two system calls need to be made. A new set of system calls, now available on several UNIX platforms, eliminates the need for two system calls to perform offset-based reads and writes. You can use the `pread()` and `pwrite()` system calls which combine the `lseek()` call and `read()` or `write()` call into one system call, respectively. For instance,

```
pread(File Descriptor, buffer, nbytes, offset);
```

OR

```
pwrite(File Descriptor, buffer, nbytes, offset);
```

Using `pread()` and `pwrite()`, you can reduce the amount of I/O system calls by eliminating the `lseek()` call. This reduces context switch overhead and kernel system call overhead. There are many other similar techniques that can be pursued to reduce system call overhead within an application.

Other common methods of reducing overhead in the application are the C string processing routines such as `strcpy()` and `strcmp()`. A more efficient set of routines is provided that operate on areas of memory. These routines include such calls as `memcpy()` and `memcmp()`. Since a string is simply an array of bytes, the memory-based routines are much more efficient than the string routines.

Applications periodically require certain shared resources. These shared resources in turn require synchronization objects (i.e., locking) such as semaphores to protect the resources. For example, a process may be trying to read from a section of shared memory, while another process is currently writing to that same section. This means that the process that is reading may have to wait until the process that is writing is complete and releases the lock. A typical implementation includes the use of the `sleep()` system call to put processes to `sleep()` when an attempt to acquire a resource fails. Putting a process to sleep and later awakening the process is an expensive operation. If your system has many high-speed processors, you may obtain better performance by implementing a *spin lock* mechanism. A spin lock is a lock that, upon failure to acquire the lock, spins (takes CPU cycles) until the resource becomes available or spins for a specific amount of cycles. The logic is that after spinning some CPU cycles, the process may be able to obtain the lock. Spinning a few CPU cycles on a multiprocessor machine is faster than forcing a process to sleep and later awakening it.

Applications that require interprocess communication often use files or buffer copies to share data. A more appropriate implementation is to utilize one of the System V Release 4 methods of interprocess communication such as shared memory. The application can declare a shared memory segment upon startup, and then each process can attach to the shared memory segment to exchange data. This reduces memory-to-memory copies between processes, thereby increasing memory utilization efficiency.

2.15.1 PREEMPTION CONTROL

Solaris 2.6 provides a new service known as *preemption control* that allows an application to prevent preemption while holding a critical resource. The kernel cannot maintain state information of a user land lock object. Preemption control services addresses this problem by notifying the kernel when the process is holding a critical resource. The preemption control services are implemented as macros instead of library or system calls in order to minimize the performance overhead. The following are the preemption control macros:

- *schedctl_init (void)*
- *schedctl_start (schedctl_t *sched_p)*
- *schedctl_stop (schedctl_t *sched_p)*
- *schedctl_exit (void)*

An application that manages concurrent access to shared resources via locks can be enhanced to take advantage of this feature. By calling the preemption control macros in the application shared resource locking layer, the performance of critical sections in the application can be increased by minimizing the chances of preemption. This translates into the application holding locks for fewer periods of time which in turn increases concurrency throughput. Preemption control uses a set of memory pages shared between the kernel and the user address spaces. The `schedctl_init()` macro allocates the kernel data structures necessary for process preemption control and returns a descriptor to be used with the `schedctl_start()` and `schedctl_stop()` macros. The `schedctl_start()` macro informs the Solaris scheduler that the user process is entering a critical section and that the process should not be preempted. The `schedctl_stop()` macro informs the kernel that the process can be preempted because it is no longer in a critical section of code. The `schedctl_exit()` macro should be called when the process no longer requires preemption control services. The `schedctl_exit()` macro removes the kernel data structures used by the process for preemption control services. Preemption control applies to processes running in the Timeshare (TS) or Interactive (IA) job classes. Preemption control macros have no effect on processes running in the Realtime (RT) job class.

On Sequent, you can enable user-level process dynamic preemption services by setting the value of `root_nopreempt` to zero in the PTX kernel source file `/usr/conf/uts/kernel/i386_space/param_space.c`, and subsequently rebuilding the PTX kernel.

For example, make the following change to the `/usr/conf/uts/kernel/i386_space/param_space.c` file:

```
--> bool_t root_nopreempt=1;   /*must be root to do NOPREEMPT*/
```

change to:

```
--> bool_t root_nopreempt=0;   /*must be root to do NOPREEMPT*/
```

After making the above change, applications can then use the `proc_ctl()` system call to alter process attributes, including preemption control. To enable preemption control in Oracle on your Sequent system, set the `init.ora` parameter `_no_preempt` =TRUE. This can help improve performance by not preempting an Oracle process while it is holding a critical resource such as a latch.

2.15.2 PROCESSOR-RELATED KERNEL PARAMETERS

There are several kernel-tunable parameters that pertain to a multiprocessor system. Some of the key parameters are `maxuprc`, `maxusers`, `maxup`, and `nproc`.[11] The `maxusers` kernel parameter originally was used in UNIX to configure the number of users that could log into the system. The `maxusers` kernel parameter has changed since

---

11. These parameters are operating system-specific, and you should refer to your platform's system administration documentation.

then and is now used to determine the size of the internal kernel tables and process tables upon system boot. A higher number for `maxusers` allocates larger kernel and process tables under the assumption that there will be more users and processes. On Solaris, the default for `maxusers` is set to `physmem`—the amount of available physical memory on the system. For example, on a Sun Solaris system with 2 G of memory, `maxusers` would be set to 2048. If you do not intend to have a lot of users, you may want to consider reducing the size of `maxusers`, thereby reducing the size of the kernel and process tables. On Solaris, you can set this parameter in the `/etc/system` file. The default for `maxusers` on Sequent is usually 64, and you can set this parameter through the `menu` utility. On HP, you can use the SAM utility to set the value of `maxusers`. On Solaris and HP, the maxuprc is the number of concurrent processes per user. On Solaris, you can increase or decrease this value by setting `maxuprc` in the `/etc/system` file. If you have many processes running per user, you may need to increase the value of `maxuprc` on your system. On HP, you can set the value of `maxuprc` by using the SAM utility. On Sequent, the equivalent to `maxuprc` is `MAXUP` which is also the maximum number of processes per user. You can set this parameter by using the menu utility.

The `nproc` kernel parameter is the maximum total number of processes systemwide. This parameter controls the size of the kernel process tables. Therefore, if your system will not have a lot of processes running concurrently, reduce the size of `nproc` to reduce the size of the kernel tables. If, however, your system will be running a large amount of processes, you must set `nproc` to the total amount of processes that will run concurrently on the system. The equivalent to `nproc` in Solaris is `max_nprocs`, which is the maximum number of processes. The default for `max_nprocs` is (10 + 16*maxusers). For example, if you will have no more than 1,000 concurrent processes running on the system, set `nproc` to `1000`. When setting `nproc` or `max_nprocs`, remember to account for the daemon processes and their children. Daemon programs often `fork()` child processes to service requests. If the maximum number of processes is not set appropriately, the daemons may not be able to create subprocesses.

On Solaris, set `max_nprocs=1000` in the `/etc/system` file if your system will have no more than 1,000 concurrent processes. You can set `nproc` through either the SAM utility, or the menu utilities for HP and Sequent, respectively.

2.15.3 THINK PARALLEL

Hardware vendors like Sun, HP, and Sequent provide extremely high-speed high-throughput systems. These systems are constantly being improved and enhanced. Therefore, it is critical that applications deployed on these systems make full use of the multitasking nature of these systems. If you are designing or deploying an application on a multiprocessor system, you need to *think in parallel*. In other words, do not design a synchronous application in which the bulk of the processing resides in one process. You need to parallelize the tasks by creating subtasks either through the use of threads (preferably) or through the use of `fork()` and `exec()` for systems that possibly do not support threads. For example, if you are writing a PRO*C application to load 10 million rows on a ten-processor system, design the program so that you can run at least ten of these processes in parallel with each process operating on a smaller batch size than the total. This will be much faster than waiting for one process that has to do all the work of loading 10 million rows. If you are designing a new application, avoid synchronous bottlenecks such as obtaining an exclusive lock on an object for an extended period of time. Exclusive locks prevent other processes from modifying the object concurrently, even if the other processes modify a different section of the object. Try to parallelize large requests as much as possible by subdividing the tasks into smaller tasks. The hardware that the vendors are releasing nowadays is quite impressive in terms of parallel computing power. However, this power is useless unless the application can push the system to its limit by maximizing the parallelism of the application. An analogy would be a house with a 100-gallon water heater. If only one person lives in this house and uses less than 5 gallons of hot water, the majority of the hot water is being wasted.

One other key footnote: when thinking in parallel, try to involve the vendors as much as possible when designing a large-scale application. The vendors will provide hardware and software engineers who can help explain the architecture of the system, and advise you on how you can utilize the system's features in your application. The vendors will also provide you with benchmark information that you can use to baseline scalability. Many times people complain that their system does not scale, but this may not be due to the hardware and OS itself. Rather, the configuration of the system and architecture of the application are the major contributing factors to scalability.

2.15.4   RIGHT-SIZING THE NUMBER OF PROCESSORS

The million dollar question of *how many processors should I buy for my system* is one that deserves an entire text dedicated to this topic. Indeed, capacity planning is not a simple task. Capacity planning requires prior experience with the platform that you are considering for deployment, as well as a firm understanding of the application(s) being deployed. If you are responsible for capacity planning, you should work closely with your hardware vendor. Your hardware vendor will provide the necessary technical staff that can help you right-size your environment. The hardware vendors also have a significant degree of experience in benchmarking and testing their products. They can advise you as to the number of processors, quantity of memory, and disk I/O subsystems needed to ensure a high-performance system and/or application.

In addition to the advice of the hardware vendors, you should conduct your own research as to the scalability of your application. You will need to spend a serious amount of time gathering detailed statistics using either sar, vmstat, mpstat, or other GUI performance monitoring tools about the performance of your system and application. These statistics will help you determine if you are CPU-bound, memory-bound, or I/O–bound. If you see high percentages of CPU idle time, then obviously, you are not processor-bound. In this case, adding CPUs will not offer any gain as the existing processors are not being utilized fully. If, however, you are seeing close to zero percentages for CPU idle and high user time percentages, this is an indication that you are either processor-bound, or wait-bound. The wait could be due either to the application waiting for I/O requests to complete, or waiting on busy resources. To determine if you are pure processor-bound, you need to ensure that I/O is not a bottleneck, and that system time is minimized. After tuning I/O and monitoring to see that I/O wait percentages are minimal, you should monitor CPU idle time and user time. If wait I/O time and system time are minimal, and CPU idle time is zero or close thereto, and user times are high, you are more than likely processor-bound. High run queue lengths contribute to the fact that not enough processors exist to service all the running processes. Therefore, the OS must time-slice each process to ensure that each process is getting adequate CPU time. If your application is processor-bound, try reducing the number of processes. This should improve user throughput. Continue reducing the number of processes until the user time percentage reaches its peak, the run queue length is near zero, and CPU idle time is minimal. After monitoring the CPU utilization and the run queue, you should have a clear idea as to the number of processors needed to achieve ideal performance. Once you have collected these statistics and tuned the number of running processes, you will have a good feel as to the number of processors and processes needed to achieve the best performance.

2.15.5 AFFINITY BINDING ON MULTIPROCESSOR SYSTEMS

Binding certain processes to a processor can considerably increase performance on a multiprocessor machine. Solaris provides the `pbind` command to bind particular processes to a specific processor. Sequent provides the `tmp_affinity()` system call to bind a process to a processor, as well as the ability to create user run queues. The core advantages of processor binding include providing higher priority and additional CPU time for critical applications, preventing context switching of processes, the symmetric distribution of application workload across multiple processors, and an increased cache hit ratio. Processor binding is not automatic in Solaris. On a multiprocessor system you must explicitly issue the `pbind` command (refer to the manual pages on `pbind`). Either the superuser (i.e., root) or the process' owner can bind a process to a particular processor. Child processes inherit processor binding. Therefore, any spawned processes from a process that is bound to a particular CPU will be bound to the same CPU as the spawning process.

It is recommended that before binding processes you consult with your hardware and OS vendor to discuss possible issues in more detail. In cases where processes are experiencing an imbalance in processor utilization, it is recommended to bind the various Oracle background processes, with the exception of DBWR and LGWR, to different processors. You should leave at least one processor free to service DBWR and other processes. DBWR should not be bound to one particular CPU because this means that only that CPU can service I/O requests. Binding DBWR to a CPU may result in an I/O bottleneck because all DBWR I/O requests would be serviced by only one CPU. LGWR, for the same reason as DBWR, also should not be bound. Oracle8 introduces the concept of I/O slaves which allows for multiple DBWR, LGWR, ARCH, and BACKUP slaves. The I/O slaves can be used to parallelize I/O requests for those platforms that may not provide asynchronous I/O. Avoid binding I/O slaves to specific processors for the same reason as not binding DBWR and LGWR. Keep in mind that binding a process or set of processes to a specific processor does not guarantee exclusive use of the CPU by the binding set of processes. The CPU can still service requests from other nonbounded processes. Study your system and application in detail before you consider processor binding. An application may become CPU-bound under processor binding even if additional processors are available and idle. The performance gain seen by processor binding ranges from 0–15 percent. System scalability could also increase by 20 percent – 30 percent on systems with many processors and an intense workload.

In a multiprocessor system, the UNIX OS scheduler handles the scheduling of processes and ensures that each processor run queue is balanced, thereby avoiding CPU starvation and/or CPU gluttony of certain processes. Use `sar -q`, `sar -u`, and/or `mpstat` to monitor CPU utilization and the run queue. The resulting statistics indicate if processor binding will offer any gains.

2.15.6 PROCESSOR SETS

Solaris 2.6 offers the ability to create processor sets and bind processes to a set of processors rather than just a single processor. There are two types of processor sets: user-created processor sets and system processor sets. User processor sets can be created and managed by using the `psrset` command or `pset_create()` [12] system call. Processors that are assigned to user-created processor sets will only service LWPs that have been bound to that processor set. System-created processor sets may service other LWPs. System processor sets may not always exist on a particular system. System processor sets can be useful in situations where certain processors can communicate more efficiently with each other than with other processors in the system. System-created processor sets can neither be modified nor removed, but you may bind processes to them.

2.15.7 BENCHMARKING PROCESSORS

Once you have tuned your application, you should test your system for scalability in terms of processor scalability. This can be done on Solaris by using the `psradm` command. The `psradm` command must be executed as the root user (`psradm` can be made a `set-uid` program). For example,

```
* takes CPU ID=2 offline
myhost{root}->  /usr/sbin/psradm -f  2

* brings CPU ID=2 online
myhost{root}->  /usr/sbin/psradm -n  2
```

---

12. For more information on the processor set commands, please refer to the man pages on the `psrset` command and the `pset_create()` system call.

On Sequent, you can take a processor off-line or bring the processor on-line by issuing the following commands:

```
* takes CPU ID=3 offline
myhost{root}-> /etc/offline 3

* brings CPU ID=3 online
myhost{root}-> /etc/online 3
```

My recommendation is that you use the respective platform commands to online and offline the system processors. For example, if you have an eight-processor Sun Ultra Enterprise Server 6000, you should turn all but CPU ID=0 off.[13] Then, with at least one processor on-line, run the application and gather the performance metrics. Then, at each iteration, turn on one additional CPU and continue to run the application at each iteration until finally all processors are back on-line. At each interval you can measure the speedup factor of an additional CPU. For example, if running on two CPUs doubled your performance from that of running on one CPU, then you know that adding an additional CPU scaled linearly.

If, however, you begin to notice that after, say four CPUs, there is no performance gain, you can diagnose the problem further by examining the performance metrics from each successive run. This will allow you to measure not only the scalability of your application but the scalability of your system as well. I strongly recommend that you run your application by off-lining and on-lining CPUs to determine the speedup factor. Do not assume that because you only tested with all processors on-line that your application cannot run any faster. You may find that your application performs the same with four processors as it does with eight processors. You can automate the benchmark by creating a script that off-lines all the processors except CPU 0 and then runs the application, and at each iteration brings on-line one additional CPU. Then, you can review the performance metrics gathered by the benchmark script. If you suspect that additional processors are not yielding any gain, you can submit the output of the benchmark to the hardware or OS vendor for review. The performance metrics, specifically the speedup factor, will give you a reliable indication as to how the system will scale if you were to add additional processors. If you start to see that the speedup factor is decreasing or remains the same as more processors are brought on-tline during the benchmark, your application may not benefit from additional processors. You may need to consider redesigning certain portions of the application in order to increase the application's scalability.

Memory and processor tuning are iterative processes that require precision and expertise. This chapter presented the processor and memory model of the UNIX operating system. Using the guidelines presented in this chapter, you should be able to monitor and tune your system and application(s) to maximize memory and processor utilization.

---

13. You should never take processor 0 (CPU ID=0) off-line. The system must always have at least one CPU on-line. On some systems, CPU ID=0 is the base OS processor, and attempting to take it off-line may cause the system to hang or panic.

In Chapter 3 I discuss I/O tuning in a format similar to this chapter. Other than the base system itself, processors and memory are the most expensive and most vital components. You need to utilize these valuable resources as effectively as possible, thereby maximizing your investment and system throughput.

CONFIGURING AND TUNING I/O

This chapter discusses the UNIX I/O model as well as techniques to tune I/O. Disk I/O is probably the most frequent bottleneck and performance issue reported by customer sites. I/O is one of the major contributors to performance for database applications. It is imperative that your I/O system be tuned so that I/O contention is minimal and that the system scales as more users are added to it.

3.1 UNIX I/O MODEL

In traditional UNIX, the I/O model consists of two main system calls: `read()` and `write()`. Both `read()` and `write()` take a file descriptor—either a buffer into which to read the data or a buffer that contains the data to be written—and the number of bytes that are to be read or written as arguments. These two system calls form the basis of the UNIX I/O model. The `read()` and `write()` calls are synchronous, which means that control is not returned to the calling process or program until completion of the `read()` or `write()` call. Both `read()` and `write()` return the number of bytes either written or read. If the `read()` or `write()` call fails, a `-1` call is returned and `errno` is set to the error code that indicates why the `read()` or `write()` call failed. Figure 3.1 illustrates the UNIX I/O model.

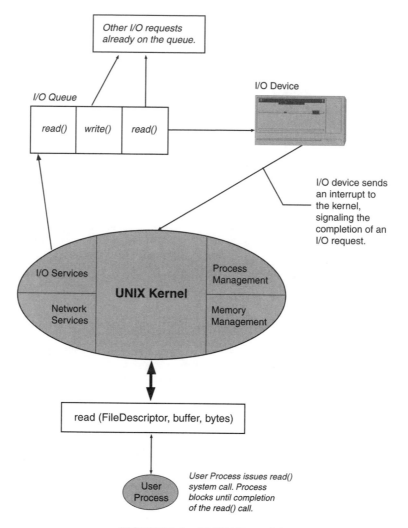

FIGURE 3.1   UNIX I/O model.

In Figure 3.1, a user process issues an I/O request via a system call. The kernel then forwards the I/O request on to the I/O queue. The I/O device then services the request from the queue and sends an interrupt to the kernel once the I/O request is complete. After processing the interrupt and completing the read() request, the kernel then returns control to the calling process and sets the I/O request error code appropriately. The user process can then check the error code to determine if the I/O call completed successfully. If the I/O queue is consistently long, it is an indication that a particular device is being saturated with I/O. This may lead to poor service times. The UNIX I/O model diagram shown in Figure 3.1 is a simplified diagram meant to illustrate the concept of the UNIX I/O model. In actuality, there are many more hardware and software layers involved when performing I/O. The importance is not necessarily to memorize all the different layers, but to be familiar with the basic concepts of I/O in UNIX.

For a system experiencing a tremendous amount of I/O, the synchronous read() and write() calls can cause an I/O bottleneck. Even if the data is distributed across multiple drives and spindles, there may be little benefit, since all read() and write() calls force the user process to block. For this reason, most UNIX vendors provide an asynchronous I/O interface layer. The asynchronous I/O interface layer enables processes to submit nonblocking I/O requests, allowing multiple reads and writes to be issued concurrently. In conjunction with asynchronous I/O, a volume manager can be used to distribute the data across multiple disk drives and controllers. The combination of a volume manager and asynchronous I/O maximizes I/O parallelism and I/O distribution.

3.2 LOGICAL VOLUME MANAGER

A Logical Volume Manager (LVM) provides a tremendous amount of functionality and performance features that substantially increase system throughput and I/O performance. The logical volume manager provides the capability to create and manage striped, mirrored, and RAID (Redundant Arrays of Inexpensive Disks) devices. The logical volume manager provides an interface between the physical devices and kernel I/O services. This interface provides for ease of system administration as well as load balancing in terms of I/O. Stripes and mirrored devices can help to greatly reduce the load on particular disks by employing a round-robin balancing algorithm.

The logical volume manager also allows reads and writes to proceed in parallel, thereby increasing I/O throughput. It also alleviates the need for manual striping, which is a tedious and complex process. The LVM offers tremendous benefits for system administration, performance, scalability, and reliability (mirroring and RAID devices). Figure 3.2 illustrates the use of a logical volume manager.

Figure 3.3 illustrates the relationship between the Oracle Server and the logical volume manager.

3.2.1 STRIPING

Striping—also known as RAID 0 (meaning no redundancy)—is the process of spreading the data across multiple disk spindles. The goal of striping is to distribute disk reads and writes, avoiding *hot areas* and disk I/O saturation. Figure 3.4 illustrates the concept of striping.

FIGURE 3.2 Logical volume manager.

FIGURE 3.3 Logical volume manager and the Oracle Server.

Figure 3.4 shows the shaded area as the stripe across all the disk drives in the diagram. In a stripe, the data is spread across multiple spindles and controllers. A striped device consists of multiple partitions and an interleave. The stripe interleave value specifies the *hunt* size of the data. The hunt size is the number of bytes written to each partition. In other words, if you define a striped device that consists of three disk drives and

FIGURE 3.4   Striping.

the interleave value is defined to be 64K, then the first 64K of data is written to the first partition (or disk) in the stripe. The second 64K of data is written to the second partition (or disk), and finally the third 64K of data is written to the third partition (or disk) in the stripe. Then, the next 64K of data hunts back to the first partition and continues the round-robin algorithm, hunting to the next device as an interleave has been written. Figure 3.5 illustrates the stripe interleave.

Figure 3.5 shows a striped device that consists of three disk partitions with an interleave of 64K. The logical block addresses show the hunting (round-robin) nature of the stripe. The first 64K is stored on the first disk, the second 64K is stored on the second disk, the third 64K is stored on the third disk, and then the data hunts back to the first disk and continues to round robin. The stripe interleave plays a major role in the performance of the stripe. Tuning the stripe interleave is discussed in Section 3.4.

Striping improves performance by distributing the data across multiple disk drives and multiple controllers. Hence, if an I/O operation takes m time units to complete on one of the disks, then an I/O operation on the striped device should take m/n time units, where n represents the number of disjoint and distinct disk drives in the stripe.

FIGURE 3.5   Striping interleave.

Striping not only increases I/O throughput by *n* times, it also sustains a larger I/O workload as more users are added to the system. Striping, also known as RAID 0, offers the best performance over any other type of RAID. However, because striping is RAID 0, meaning no redundancy, most customer sites tend to choose a different level of RAID in order to maintain a higher fault tolerance during a media failure. In a striped device, only one disk drive failure is needed to invalidate the stripe. If a disk drive (or multiple disk drives) in a striped device fails, the data on the stripe is no longer available, and you will need to restore all stripes that contained partitions on the failed disk drive.

Although nothing surpasses the performance of a pure stripe (RAID 0), you must develop a robust backup and recovery strategy in order to avoid losing critical data. Media recovery performance and tuning are discussed in Chapter 7. If you run a mission-critical On-Line Transaction Processing (OLTP) application, you should consider either full mirroring (RAID 1), or some level of redundancy to protect against data loss. You will also need to make frequent backups in the event of a large-scale failure, or in the event that data is unintentionally deleted. If you are running a Decision Support System (DSS) that is primarily read-only, I recommend that you use full striping and schedule periodic backups. Since the data is primarily read-only, data redundancy is not as critical as it is in an OLTP mission-critical system. Whichever level of RAID you choose, try to distribute the data across as many spindles and controllers as possible. And, as always, schedule frequent backups and develop a legitimate and thorough backup strategy.

3.2.2 STRIPING ON SEQUENT

To take advantage of striping on Sequent, it is important that you understand the I/O subsystem in your Sequent Server. On Sequent Symmetry servers specifically, disks are organized in the manner shown in Figure 3.6.

In Figure 3.6, the QCIC (Quad-Channel I/O Controller) board is the main I/O controller and provides four SCSI-2 channels. Each channel is a fast-narrow (8-bit) SCSI providing a transfer rate of up to 10 M/second. The QCIC-W (Wide Quad-Channel I/O Controller) board provides four-wide SCSI-2 channels. Each channel on a QCIC-W board is a wide channel (16 bits) that provides a fast-wide data transfer rate of up to 20 M/second.

Both the QCIC and QCIC-W support the on-line replacement of disk and tape drives. This means that disks and tapes can be added and removed while the system is running without any disruption to the users. You should use the QCIC-W controller board in order to maximize your data transfer rate at up to 20 M/second as opposed to the 10 M/second offered by the QCIC. You can install up to eight QCIC or QCIC-W boards in the S2000 or SE60 system. The QCIC and QCIC-W use the Intel 80960CA microprocessor for on-board function control and coordination. An NCR SCSI controller is used for each SCSI channel on the QCIC and QCIC-W boards. Each SCSI channel on the QCIC-W or QCIC board connects to a SCSI peripheral bay (Pbay). The Pbay can be installed in an expansion cabinet or in the base system cabinet. Each Pbay can contain either six or twelve SCSI devices.

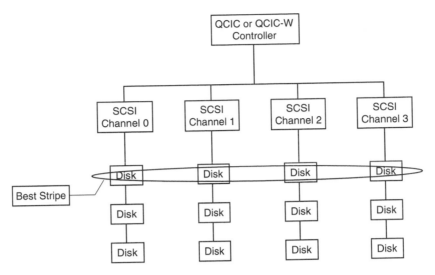

FIGURE 3.6   Sequent Symmetry system controller and disk architecture.

Although Figure 3.6 shows only three disks per SCSI channel, you can have up to twelve drives per SCSI channel. However, you should not have more than six. If you have more than six drives per SCSI channel, the SCSI channel controller may become saturated during concurrent access to the disks that are attached to that controller. Try to distribute the disks across many controllers, setting a limit of six disks per SCSI controller. This will distribute the I/O much more effectively than would having too many disks on one controller.

On Sequent NUMA-Q systems, disks are organized somewhat differently than the symmetry servers. Sequent NUMA-Q systems employ a full-speed (100 M/s) fibre channel host connection to the disk I/O subsystem. Figure 3.7 illustrates a typical configuration.

In Figure 3.7, a single-connect/dual-fabric fibre channel configuration is shown. The configuration consists of a fibre channel PCI card on each quad, 100 M/s-capable fibre optic link, 800 M/s-capable fibre channel switch, and the Fibre Channel (FC) Storage Subsystem. In addition to the I/O subsystem itself, the FC Storage Subsystem consists of one or more fibre channel to SCSI bridges. Each switch connects to every FC Storage Subsystem in the Resource Domain. This allows each quad to have a direct path to every FC Storage Subsystem. If a direct path is not available, Dynix/ptx uses a *multipathing* technique, which routes an I/O request through the IQ Link and then through an available path. The direct path approach results in better performance than the the multipathing technique. Nevertheless, each quad requires a direct path to every I/O device.

The logical volume manager on Sequent is known as the SVM (Sequent Volume Manager). The current version of SVM is Version 2. I strongly suggest that you use

FIGURE 3.7   NUMA-Q fibre I/O subsystem architecture.

the SVM volume manager to manage the disk subsystems in your Sequent system. Do not try to manage the disk partitions manually. Managing the disks manually is a tedious effort that will reduce your overall performance. Without the volume manager, striping has to be done manually, which will not avoid *hot files*. Hot files are data files that are being accessed concurrently by a large number of users. The manual stripe method would place Oracle data files on different disks. However, if a large number of users are querying the same data file, a hot file situation can occur, and disk I/O performance can suffer. With striping, you eliminate hot files because the data is interleaved and striped across multiple disks and controllers. This permits a single Oracle data file to be spread across multiple disks, as opposed to manual striping in which an Oracle data file maps to a single-disk partition. Configuring the SVM requires some basic knowledge of the SVM and its architecture. The SVM has three main object layers: subdisks, plexes, and volumes.

SVM objects are managed in terms of disk groups. A disk group is simply a collection of SVM disks. Disk groups allow you to group disks into logical collections for administrative convenience. For example, disks containing database applications could be placed together in a disk group. SVM requires the existence of at least one disk group, *rootdg* (root disk group). The rootdg disk group is created when SVM is configured for the first time. The rootdg disk group must contain only *bootable* local storage, including the root file system and the primary swap. The remaining SVM disks (i.e., not bootable local storage) must be placed into disk groups other than the rootdg disk group. Furthermore, a disk can only be in one disk group.

Disks in a disk group contain two regions: private and public. The private region contains the SVM configuration database, which is used to manage all the objects within a disk group. The public region contains the remainder of the disk, which contains the actual subdisk storage allocations. Public and private regions are allocated on each disk by disk type. There are three disk types:

- **Sliced**—The public and private regions of these SVM disks are on different disk partitions. The private region of the disk must be located on a type-8 partition. When you attempt to place a partition under SVM control, the software counts the total number of type-8 partitions on the entire disk and matches the type-8 partition with partitions that are neither type-9, type-8, nor type-3 (usually only type-1 partitions remain), in numerical slice order. If there are no type-8 partitions on the disk but the disk is partitioned, SVM labels the disk as type *nopriv* (described below).

- **Simple**—The public and private regions of these SVM disks are on the same partition. SVM automatically designates disks that are nonpartitioned as simple disks. The first part of the disk is private. The remainder of the disk is public.

- **Nopriv**—No private region exists on these SVM disks; therefore, the disks do not contain database configuration information.

Sliced and nopriv disk types are available mostly for compatibility with older versions of SVM. In general, simple disk types should be used. To create a disk group, you must first place the disks under SVM control. To create a simple disk, the disk's Volume Table of Contents (VTOC) partition map must first be removed using the /etc/devdestroy command. Then, using the vxdisk command, the disk can be placed under SVM control. For example:

```
myhost{root}-> /etc/devdestroy    /dev/rdsk/sd8
myhost{root}-> vxdisk -f init sd8 privlen=6000
```

The privlen=6000 option, specifies that 6,000 disk blocks are to be allocated for the configuration database. The size of the private area can be estimated using the following formula:

```
private area size = (nobjects * .68) * 1.20
```

The value for the number of objects (nobjects) includes the estimated number of disks, subdisks, plexes, and volumes in the disk group. The additional 20 percent accounts for future growth. Once the disks are placed under SVM control, the disk group can be created as follows:

```
myhost{root)-> # vxdg -s init db01_dg sd8 sd9 sd10 \
                            sd11 sd12 sd13 sd14 \
                            sd15 sd16 sd17 sd18 sd19
```

The above statement creates the disk group db01_dg which includes disks sd8 through sd19. Note that each simple disk has a private region reserved for the disk group's configuration database. The entire configuration database is contained within a private region. For redundancy purposes, multiple copies are maintained, however it is not necessary to maintain a copy on each disk. SVM, by default, maintains one copy of the configuration database for each SCSI bus of the disk group, with a minimum of four copies. For large systems with many SCSI buses, the default behavior may not be practical. In this case, the *nconfig* option of the vxdg command can be used to specify the number of configuration database copies. In general, four copies of the configuration database should be sufficient (*nconfig=4*).

A description file can be created with all the statements necessary to create subdisks, plexes, and volumes to be used as input into the vxmake command. The following is a description file that creates 8 subdisks of 600 M each, a striped plex using a stripe width of 64K, and the corresponding volume. The ownership of the volume is set to the Oracle user and the dba group. The vxmake command then uses the description fIle to create the subdisks, plex, and volume.

```
File: db01 dg.desc

sd sd8-0 disk=sd10 offset=0 len=12288
sd sd9-0 disk=sd10 offset=0 len=12288
sd sd10-0 disk=sd10 offset=0 len=12288
sd sd11-0 disk=sd11 offset=0 len=12288
sd sd12-0 disk=sd12 offset=0 len=12288
sd sd13-0 disk=sd13 offset=0 len=12288
sd sd14-0 disk=sd14 offset=0 len=12288
sd sd15-0 disk=sd15 offset=0 len=12288
plex item1-01 layout=STRIPE st_width=64 sd=sd8-0,\
        sd9-0,sd10-0,sd11-0,sd12-0,sd13-0, \
        sd14-0, sd15-0
vol item use_type=gen plex=item1-01 \
        user=oracle group=dba
```

The command vxmake is then executed to create the subdisks, plex, and volume.

```
myhost(root)-> vxmake -g db01_dg -d db01_dg.desc
```

3.2.3 STRIPING ON SUN

The Sun Solaris Servers have two main types of disk I/O subsystems: the standard disk trays and the SPARC Storage Array. The standard disk trays consist of fast differential SCSI (10 M/second) or fast-wide differential SCSI (20 M/second). Typically, each tray consists of six disk drives. Each disk tray is connected to a fast differential or fast-wide differential SCSI SBus controller. Figure 3.8 shows the layout of the disk trays.

In Figure 3.8, the disk trays are connected to SCSI SBus cards (either fast or fast-wide). The SCSI SBus cards plug into the SBus slots on the system board. Each system board on a SPARC Center 2000 provides up to four SBus slots. The clock speed of the SBus on the SPARC Server 1000 and SPARC Center 2000 is 20 Mhz. The peak data transfer rates for the SBus range between 45 M/second and 50 M/second. If your system uses the fast SCSI-2 SBus device, the typical transfer rate is 4 M/second, and the peak transfer rate is 11 M/second. If your system uses the fast-wide SCSI-2 SBus device, the typical transfer rate is 8–10 M/second with a peak transfer rate of 22 M/second.[1]

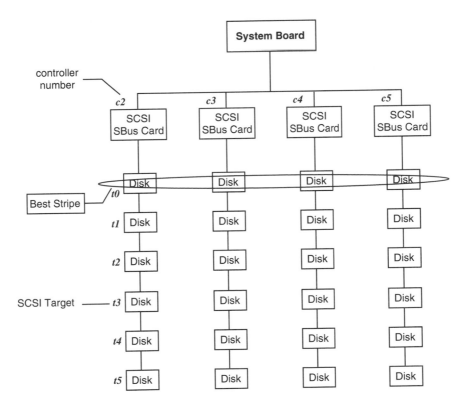

FIGURE 3.8 Sun disk tray architecture.

---

1. Sun SMCC Technical Product Marketing. *Configuration and Capacity Planning for Sun Servers*, Third Edition, Revision A. January 1994, p. 153.

If your system uses the SPARC Storage Array, disks are configured as in Figure 3.9. Figure 3.10 shows the controller and disk configuration for a SPARC storage array.

The SPARC Storage Array is Sun's new line of disk subsystems. The storage arrays replace the older disk tray technology. The storage array consists of six fast-wide internal SCSI controllers that each provide maximum transfer rates of 20 M/second. Each fast-wide controller has five disks connected to it at most. This means that the storage array can hold a maximum of 30 disk drives. The storage array consists of three trays. Each tray has 10 slots, and each slot can hold a disk drive. Within each tray, the first five consecutive disks connect to a separate fast-wide SCSI controller. The second set of five consecutive disks within the tray connect to another fast-wide SCSI controller. The connection between the storage array and the host computer is via a FDDI (Fiber Distributed Data Interface). The FDDI connection increases performance over the standard differential SCSI cable. The SPARC storage array supports up to two FDDI connections. This allows up to two systems to attach to a single storage array. The storage array is also used in the Sun SMP Cluster and Oracle Parallel Server (SMP) environment. The Oracle Parallel Server for the SMP clusters requires that each node in the cluster share the same disks.

In differential SCSI, the data signal (between −5.0 V and +5.0 V) is transmitted along with its inverse signal. A one or zero state is determined by comparing the signal with its inverse. In single-ended SCSI, the host adapter transmits data and ground signals. The one state is determined by the difference between the ground and data signals. Single-ended SCSI limits the physical length that the data can be transmitted, subsequently limiting the length of the single-ended SCSI bus to 6 meters. Single-ended SCSI cannot carry signals as far as differential SCSI. Differential SCSI can carry SCSI signals up to 25 meters. One important footnote is that the length limit of the SCSI bus (6 meters

FIGURE 3.9   Sun storage array.

FIGURE 3.10   Sun storage array architecture.

for single-ended, and 25 meters for differential) includes the cable from the host adapter to the terminator and all the cabling connecting the peripherals. Attempting to exceed the physical length limits of the single-ended or differential SCSI bus may cause data unreliability and SCSI bus resets and/or timeouts.

The fiber channel on the SPARC Storage Array consists of two fibers that allow signals to be carried in opposite directions. As opposed to SCSI, which uses the same set of wires for both directions, the fiber channel allows concurrent transfers of data in both directions. This increases I/O throughput and allows the SPARC storage array to sustain more than 2000 I/Os per second.

In order to create a striped device on the Sun storage arrays or on Sun disk trays, you can use the Sun Solstice Online DiskSuite tool (ODS). The ODS tool enables you to create striped, mirrored, concatenated, and RAID-5 devices. ODS Version 4.0 introduced the GUI Metatool that enables the user to manage ODS *metadevices* via the GUI tool. Prior to ODS 4.0, manual commands were required in order to create and manage metadevices. Metadevices are ODS' logical devices. ODS' main configuration file is the `md.tab` file located in the `/usr/opt/SUNWmd/etc` directory. The `md.tab` file contains entries for each metadevice, as well as the complete definition of the device.

ODS is an easy-to-use tool that enables the quick configuration of logical devices. Figure 3.11 shows the metadevice layer.

To create metadevices, you must first install the ODS software package. I recommend that you upgrade to the latest release of ODS (currently 4.1) if you are currently running ODS. ODS 4.1 provides additional performance enhancements as well as bug fixes to known problems. Once ODS is installed, you can create the database replicas by using the metadb command. For example,

```
myhost{root}-> metadb -a -f /dev/dsk/c1t1d0s7 \
                            /dev/dsk/c2t1d0s7 \
                            /dev/dsk/c3t1d0s7
```

In this example, the metadb command is used to create the metadevice database. The metadevice database is stored on the disk partitions listed in the preceding example. Each partition holds a replica of the metadevice database. In the case of the failure of a disk that contains a metadevice database replica, ODS will read the database information from the other replicas. Placing the database replicas on different disks and different controllers minimizes ODS downtime. Also, you should allocate 3 M of disk space for each metadevice database replica. ODS 4.0 increased the size of the replica database from prior versions of ODS that used less than 1 M. Therefore, when you upgrade to ODS 4.X, you may need to resize your database replica partitions. For this reason, allocate plenty of space upfront so that in the future if new versions of ODS require more space for database replicas, your partition size can handle the growth. I recommend that you allocate 3 M for each ODS replica partition. Although this is more than is necessary now, it will foster a smoother migration to future versions that may require larger replica partition sizes. This avoids the nightmare scenario in which your disk partitions may have to be resized only because of the growth in the metadevice database replica size require-

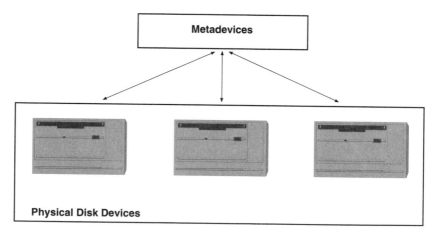

FIGURE 3.11 ODS architecture.

ment. Once the metadevice database is created, you can start to create metadevices. You can do this either by editing the `md.tab` file or by using the GUI metatool that is provided with ODS 4.X. For example, to create a striped metadevice on a Sun Server using the disk trays, edit the `md.tab` file, and place the following entry:

Example md.tab file

```
d1 1 4 /dev/dsk/c2t0d0s3 \
        /dev/dsk/c3t0d0s3 \
        /dev/dsk/c4t0d0s3 \
        /dev/dsk/c5t0d0s3 -i 64k
```

Then save the changes, and exit the file. Now you can use the following ODS commands to create the metadevice:

```
myhost{root}-> metainit -n d1
myhost{root}-> metainit d1
```

The `metainit` command creates and initializes the metadevice by reading the corresponding entry from the `md.tab` file. The first `metainit` (-n option) example verifies the `d1` entry in the `md.tab` file but does not create a `d1` metadevice. The `metainit -n` option is frequently used to validate a metadevice entry without actually creating it. The second `metainit` command creates the metadevice `d1` as defined in the `md.tab` file. The `d1` metadevice is a striped device that consists of four separate disks on four separate controllers with a stripe interlace of 64K. This striped device offers the best performance because all disks in the stripe are on separate controllers.

If your system uses the SPARC storage array, you can use the same commands to create a striped metadevice. The only difference is found in the device naming convention. In the traditional device naming convention of `/dev/dsk/cNtMdRsP`, N represents the controller number, M represents the SCSI target number, R represents the device number on the target, and P represents the slice or partition number. Therefore, `/dev/dsk/c2t3d0s1` refers to controller 2, SCSI target 3, device 0 on SCSI target 3, and slice or partition 1 on device 0, target 3. The storage arrays use a slightly different device naming convention since the base controller is the FDDI SBus slot in the host, and the storage array itself has six internal fast-wide differential SCSI controllers. In the storage array, N represents the base controller number of the FDDI SBus slot, M represents the internal controller number within the array, R represents the SCSI target of the device connected to the internal controller, and P represents the slice or partition number. For instance, `/dev/dsk/c2t3d3s2` refers to controller 2 as the FDDI SBus controller; `t3` is the fourth internal SPARC storage array fast-wide SCSI controller, `d3` is the fourth disk drive off of the `t3` internal controller, and `s2` represents slice 2. To create a stripe within a storage array, edit the `md.tab` file, and place the following entry into the `md.tab` file:

Example md.tab file

```
d1 1 6 /dev/dsk/c2t0d0s3 \
        /dev/dsk/c2t1d0s3 \
        /dev/dsk/c2t2d0s3 \
        /dev/dsk/c2t3d0s3 \
        /dev/dsk/c2t4d0s3 \
        /dev/dsk/c2t5d0s3 -i 64k
```

In this example, a stripe is created that consists of a disk drive (d0) from each internal storage array fast-wide SCSI controller using an interleave value of 64K. The stripe is a six-device stripe spread across the six internal fast-wide SCSI controllers. There are two things you should avoid when striping. The first is never to create a stripe that consists of disks on the same controller. For instance,

Example md.tab file: <AVOID THIS KIND OF STRIPING>

```
d1 1 5 /dev/dsk/c2t0d0s3 \
        /dev/dsk/c2t0d1s3 \
        /dev/dsk/c2t0d2s3 \
        /dev/dsk/c2t0d3s3 \
        /dev/dsk/c2t0d4s3 -i 64k
```

In this example, a stripe device is created that consists of five disk drives on the same controller. This significantly reduces performance by saturating one controller. This example not only prevents parallel disk I/O, it also defeats the whole purpose of striping—to parallelize I/O across multiple controllers and disk drives. The second thing you should never do when striping is to stripe across storage arrays. For instance,

Example md.tab file: <AVOID THIS KIND OF STRIPING>

```
d1 1 5 /dev/dsk/c2t0d0s3 \
        /dev/dsk/c3t0d0s3 \
        /dev/dsk/c4t0d0s3 \
        /dev/dsk/c5t0d0s3 \
        /dev/dsk/c6t0d0s3 -i 64k
```

Assume that c2, c3, c4, c5, and c6 are each separate FDDI SBus controller cards for the five storage arrays. This creates a striped device across five storage arrays. Although this may seem optimal, it is not. The storage arrays are quite different from traditional SCSI controllers. In a traditional SCSI controller environment, this stripe is quite efficient. The storage array uses a fiber connection between the storage array and the host computer. The host computer communicates to the storage array using SSA (SPARC Storage Array) firmware drivers.[2] Each time an I/O request is issued to a storage array, the firmware drivers service the request by sending the I/O request down to the storage array across the fiber connection. Therefore, accessing a single striped device that consists of several storage arrays forces the I/O to the striped device to be broken down over several fiber buses. The latency overhead in this case severely impacts the performance of the stripe because the I/O has to be broken down over several SBuses. A much better approach is to define striped devices within each storage array and then separate I/O by using multiple striped devices from different storage arrays. However, no single striped device should span a storage array. For instance,

Example md.tab file: <Ideal Striping for Storage Array>

```
d1 1 6 /dev/dsk/c2t0d0s3 \
        /dev/dsk/c2t1d0s3 \
        /dev/dsk/c2t2d0s3 \
        /dev/dsk/c2t3d0s3 \
        /dev/dsk/c2t4d0s3 \
        /dev/dsk/c2t5d0s3 -i 64k


d2 1 6 /dev/dsk/c3t0d0s3 \
        /dev/dsk/c3t1d0s3 \
        /dev/dsk/c3t2d0s3 \
        /dev/dsk/c3t3d0s3 \
        /dev/dsk/c3t4d0s3 \
        /dev/dsk/c3t5d0s3 -i 64k
```

This example creates two separate striped devices, each of which stripes within a single storage array. You can then add these two data files to the Oracle database. This parallelizes Oracle writes to the d1 and d2 metadevices when written to simultaneously, thus maximizing I/O parallelism by distributing the I/O.

If your Sun system uses the disk trays, you should stripe across different SCSI controllers. For example, if your system has ten fast or fast-wide SCSI SBus controllers, you can define striped devices to stripe across the ten controllers.

---

2. The SPARC storage array jumbo patch provides the latest firmware release. You should obtain this patch from Sun for your respective OS version if you are using the storage arrays. The jumbo patch fixes many bugs, performance problems, and on-line and off-line errors during heavy storage array I/O.

Example md.tab file: <Ideal Striping for Disk Trays>

```
d1 1 5 /dev/dsk/c2t0d0s3 \
        /dev/dsk/c3t1d0s3 \
        /dev/dsk/c4t2d0s3 \
        /dev/dsk/c5t3d0s3 \
        /dev/dsk/c6t4d0s3 -i 64k

d2 1 5 /dev/dsk/c7t0d0s3 \
        /dev/dsk/c8t1d0s3 \
        /dev/dsk/c9t2d0s3 \
        /dev/dsk/c10t3d0s3 \
        /dev/dsk/c11t4d0s3 -i 64k
```

This example creates two separate striped devices, with each stripe spanning five different disks and five different controllers. Again, if d1 and d2 were Oracle data files, this parallelizes Oracle writes to the d1 and d2 metadevices, thus minimizing contention. Another important consideration when striping is organizing the hardware SCSI controllers in such a way that no more than three fast-wide SCSI SBus controllers are installed per system board. The maximum SBus transfer rate is 50 M/second. If each SCSI SBus controller is a fast-wide SCSI controller with a 20-M/second maximum transfer rate capability, the third fast-wide controller on the same SBus will cause SBus saturation. For fast (single-ended) SCSI, you may use up to the maximum number of fast SCSI SBus slots on the system board (four on the SPARC Center 2000) since each fast SCSI will have a maximum transfer rate of 10 M/second. With fast SCSI, it would take more than five fast SCSI controllers on the same SBus to induce saturation. If you have open slots on other system boards, try to balance the I/O by distributing the number of controllers across different system boards evenly. For example, if you have four system boards with four SCSI controllers or FDDI controllers all on only one board, place a controller on each system board. This avoids SBus and system board bus saturation and distributes I/O much more effectively.

3.2.4 STRIPING ON HP

On HP, the Logical Volume Manager is known as LVM. You can use the lvextend and lvcreate commands to create stripes and logical volume groups. For more information refer to the HP system administration manuals on LVM or to the manual pages on LVM (man lvm). Use the same tuning guidelines on HP as Sequent and Sun. Try to spread your data across multiple spindles and controllers.

3.2.5 MAXIMIZING THE PERFORMANCE OF THE STRIPE

To maximize performance when striping, you should define a striped device that concatenates disk drives with each disk drive being part of a different SCSI controller (i.e., channel). This avoids excessive I/O on one or a few controllers and allows for full parallelism by distributing I/O across multiple controllers. For example, if you create a striped device that consists of three disks on the same SCSI controller, reads and writes cannot proceed in parallel because disks in the striped device are on the same controller. Ensure that each SCSI controller has the same configuration in terms of hardware, software, and data transfer rates. Having different SCSI controllers each with different transfer rates would cause the stripe to operate at the slowest speed because the reads and writes are issued to the stripe. Therefore, try to balance the I/O as best as possible by creating stripes on different controllers and different disks per controller.

One other important footnote is that a single data file may not be able to exceed 2 G in size on certain UNIX platforms due to the hard limit. Therefore, take this fact into account when you design and plan for stripes. However, Solaris 2.6, HP-UX 10.2, and Dynix/ptx 4.4 provide 64-bit interfaces to manage large files allowing you to create files larger than 2 G. Make sure that when you partition the slices on the disk drives that each partition used in a striped device is of equal size; otherwise the striped device will be the size of the smallest partition multiplied by the number of partitions in the stripe. For example, if you were concatenating three devices of 10 M, 500 M, and 500 M, the stripe device would be only 30 M as opposed to 1010 M. The common rule is to make the size of each partition in the stripe equal to the total desired size of the stripe divided by the number of partitions in the stripe. For example, if you are configuring a 2-G stripe device, and you are striping over four disks, each of the four partitions should be sized at 512 M.

3.3 PARTITIONING THE DISKS

On Solaris, you can have at most seven user-defined slices (0 . . . 8). On Solaris, slice2 (`/dev/dsk/c2t1d0s2`) represents the entire disk. Therefore, take this into consideration when you create stripes. For example, if you want to create 2-G striped devices on a storage array, and each disk is 9 G, if you stripe across all six controllers in the array, each partition on the disk will be approximately 341 M. This means that with seven user slices, only 2387 M will be used if each partition is 341 M to be striped across six controllers not exceeding 2 G. Therefore, a large portion of the disk space will be wasted. You can deal with this problem two ways: request smaller disk drives from your disk vendor (2.1 G or 4.5 G are ideal disk sizes for a database server), or reduce the number of controllers that the stripe spans and increase the size of the individual slices. Sequent allows a maximum of 255 partitions or slices on a single disk. Therefore, you should not run into this problem on Sequent.

One important note is that if you intend to use raw devices, you must preserve cylinder 0 manually. Cylinder 0 holds the VTOC information, and if this is not preserved, the VTOC information will be overwritten when writes are performed to the raw device. You can use the format utility on Solaris or the `fmthard` utility to partition the disks. When you partition the disks, allocate one cylinder (the first cylinder—cylinder 0) to the first partition (slice 0). Then, you can partition the remaining slices, leaving you with up to six user-definable slices. Protecting the VTOC is necessary only if you are using raw devices. If you are using file systems, the OS protects the VTOC from being overwritten.

3.4   SETTING THE STRIPE WIDTH

The stripe interleave is an important factor in determining the I/O performance. In general, most sites have seen good performance with 34K or 64K interleaves. However, it is important to note that the interleave can drive the performance based on the following factors: the Oracle block size, the number of devices (partitions) in the stripe, and the DBMS and server workload. For example, a heavily hit OLTP system should use a different interleave size than a pure DSS (read-only) environment. Suppose, for example, the Oracle block size is 4K, and the stripe interleave is 32K. This information of itself is not sufficient to determine performance. More information is required about the physical layout of the disk drives. Suppose further that a striped device is made up of three disks. That means, in order to have full I/O parallelism (in this case three-way parallelism), a read or write request would have to be batched at a size of (stripe-size) × (number of members in the stripe). Or in this case, (32K) × (3) = 96K. This means that Oracle would have to read or write 24 data blocks in order to achieve full parallelism. If the workload were such that a small number of rows were requested, the read requests would consist of small batch sizes. This would not make full use of the stripe itself.

For an OLTP system, there will be many random reads and writes as transactions are inserted, updated, or deleted. The goal here is to spread the I/O across so transactions are not competing with each other in terms of I/O. For an Oracle block size on UNIX, I recommend 2K or 4K for a pure OLTP system. Then, to calculate the ideal stripe width, use a multiplier of the Oracle block size. Also, set _db_block_write_batch=<Oracle block size> × <number of members in stripe>. This helps set the optimal DBWR batch size. For an OLTP system, an Oracle block size of 2K or 4K with a stripe interleave of 32K resulted in optimal performance. Performance gains of up to 100 percent have been observed when using a volume manager with an OLTP system.

For a DSS system, there will most likely be a tremendous amount of sequential large-scale reads. Items such as full-table scans and parallel queries are extremely common. Large joins and sorts are also common in a DSS workload. Therefore, the Oracle block size should be as large as possible, allowing more data to be read in per block. Oracle 7.3 allows for a maximum database block size of 16K (db_block_size=16384). In addition to the block size, set db_file_multiblock_read_count=<block_size / 1024> × <number of members in the stripe>. The Oracle server enforces several constraints pertaining to the maximum setting for db_file_multiblock_read_count such as the maximum I/O size. The maximum I/O size is platform specific and controls the maximum amount of bytes that can be read or written in a single I/O call. On Solaris, the maximum I/O size is 1 M. On Sequent the maximum I/O size is 128K. On HP, the maximum I/O size in Oracle8 is 2 M. This means that db_file_multiblock_read_count cannot exceed 64 on a Sun Solaris system with a database block size of 16K. On a Sequent system with a 16K database block size, db_file_multiblock_read_count cannot exceed 8. Determining the optimal stripe width for a DSS system is a little more complicated than in an OLTP system. In a DSS system, you have two main choices: either parallelize an individual I/O request or parallelize a group of I/O requests. Parallelizing an individual I/O request involves selecting a small stripe width such as 32K or 64K, thereby causing a single I/O to span several spindles. Parallelizing a group of I/O requests involves selecting a large stripe width such as 128K, 512K or 1 M. This results in a single I/O being serviced by a single spindle but collectively servicing disjoint I/Os in parallel across different spindles. For example, suppose on a Sequent system that the stripe width is 128K, and `db_file_multiblock_read_count=8` and `db_block_size=16k`. During a parallel query, each I/O would be serviced by a single disk. However, because parallel query issues several asynchronous I/Os concurrently, many spindles would be servicing I/O in parallel. If the stripe width is 64K, a single I/O during a parallel query would span two spindles. The general rule of thumb is that if you plan to support a high number of concurrent users each running complex and parallel queries, you should choose a smaller stripe size such as 64K so that individual I/O requests are parallelized. If you plan to support only a few concurrent users then typically a larger stripe size is more efficient. There is some overhead associated with striping when an I/O larger than the stripe interleave size is issued. In this case, the I/O needs to be broken into multiple I/Os of the interleave size. Therefore, you should measure and consider this overhead when choosing the stripe size. Performance gains of 500 percent have been observed when using volume management software to optimally stripe the database files in a DSS system.

On Solaris, if you are using ODS with file systems, you should set the stripe interleave to 56K or equal to the file system cluster write size for optimal performance. Solaris uses a memory stride when it writes to file systems so that blocks are written to contiguously before a rotational delay. For example, in a file system with an 8K block size, the default maximum number of contiguous blocks allocated for a file is seven. Therefore, I/O to the file is grouped into seven contiguous blocks, of 8K each. The memory stride used for such a write would be 56K. Therefore, your stripe width should be in sync with the memory stride. This allows contiguous one-pass I/O without having to break the stripe into smaller 56K fragments if your stripe is larger than 56K. You can set the maximum number of contiguous blocks allocated for a file before a rotational delay is inserted by using the `newfs` command (`-C` option) or `tunefs` command (`-a` option). For an 8K file system block size, the default of seven is fine. Setting the stripe width to 56K offers optimal performance within file systems.

3.5 MIRRORING

Mirroring, also known as RAID 1 (meaning full redundancy), consists of complete data duplication. In a striped device, a single loss of a disk within a stripe causes all files that are part of that stripe to become unavailable. Any data on the stripe is lost. In a mirrored device, an exact duplicate of the data is available on another device (the mirrored device). A mirrored device consists of at least two submirrors. The first submirror becomes the primary device, and the second submirror represents the secondary device, and so on. You can use the volume manager to create a mirrored device that has at least two submirrors. For example, using the Sun ODS tool, you can create a mirrored device.

Example md.tab file: <Mirrored Device>

```
d1 1 5 /dev/dsk/c2t0d0s3 \
        /dev/dsk/c3t1d0s3 \
        /dev/dsk/c4t2d0s3 \
        /dev/dsk/c5t3d0s3 \
        /dev/dsk/c6t4d0s3 -i 64k

d2 1 5 /dev/dsk/c7t0d0s3 \
        /dev/dsk/c8t1d0s3 \
        /dev/dsk/c9t2d0s3 \
        /dev/dsk/c10t3d0s3 \
        /dev/dsk/c11t4d0s3 -i 64k

d3 -m d1 d2
```

In this example, two striped devices, d1 and d2, are defined, and d3 is the mirrored device. The d1 device is the primary device of the d3 mirror, and d2 is the secondary device of the mirror. Once you create the mirror by issuing the metainit command, you will no longer be able to use the d1 and d2 devices because they are now part of the mirror. All reads and writes must be performed to the d3 device. The kernel ODS driver handles the duplication of the writes on d1 and d2 when writes are issued to d3. When you create mirrored devices, be sure that the devices that make up the mirror are configured equivalently in terms of size and I/O distribution. For example, do not mirror two metadevices in which one metadevice is striped across four controllers and the second metadevice is striped across two controllers. This reduces the performance of writes because a write to the second submirror may take longer than a write to the first submirror. When mirroring, ensure that the stripes that make up the mirror are configured equivalently. Also, be sure that the stripe widths of the mirrored devices are all equal in order to prevent unbalanced I/O. On Sequent, you can use the volplex utility to build mirrors by attaching a plex to an existing volume. The same logic applies, and you should build the striped plexes first, then build the volume, and attach the striped plexes that you want to act as the mirror to the existing volume. For more information on the Sequent SVM and mirroring, refer to the SVM system administration manuals or the manual pages on volplex. Since the theme of this text is performance and tuning, I assume most readers have a good background with the volume manager of the respective platform. If not, I recommend that you read the SVM (Sequent), ODS (Sun), and LVM (HP) administration and user guides to familiarize yourself with the respective local volume manager.

Mirroring degrades I/O performance due to the fact that each write I/O needs to be duplicated for each submirror. For this reason, you should create a mirror with each submirror striped. Also, each submirror should be on a different controller and on different disks than the other submirrors in order to minimize the performance degradation caused by mirroring. This also provides higher system availability in the event of a controller failure because the data is spread across multiple controllers. In a two-way mirrored device, the performance loss caused by mirroring is approximately 15 percent.

If you are configuring mirrored devices on the Sun storage array, you should configure them so that the striped devices that make up the mirror are not part of the same tray. The Sun SPARC storage array has three trays. If your mirrored device consists of striped devices that are part of the same tray, you will not be able to replace the defective disk during a media failure on the mirror without having to shut the system down. If the submirrors in a mirrored device are part of the same tray, pulling the tray out while the system is running causes the entire mirror to be unavailable. You will certainly not be able to pull the tray if the mirror is in use. Therefore, by distributing the submirrors across different trays, you can pull the tray that contains the defective disk drive without disrupting the mirror because the functional submirror is on another tray. Ideally each submirror metadevice should be on a separate storage array to maximize mirroring performance. However, if this not possible due to a limited amount of storage arrays, spread the submirrors across different trays. Before you pull the tray, be sure to off-line the submirror that contains the defective disk. After you replace the failed disk drive with a new drive, you must issue a sync to the off-line submirror to force all the data from the on-line submirrors to the off-line submirror. The sync process can take a long time for a large mirror device, especially in an active system. However, if your submirrors are distributed properly, the sync time can be minimized by parallelizing I/O. In ODS, use the `metaonline` or `metasync` command to on-line the submirror and sync the mirror after the failed media problem has been corrected. `Metaonline` automatically issues a resync. `Metaonline` should be used in conjunction with `metaoffline`. On HP, use the `lvsync` command to sync the mirror.

Although mirroring decreases write performance, you can use mirroring to your advantage in a DSS (read-only) environment. Some volume managers support geometric reads, meaning that when data is needed from the mirrored device, the volume manager driver reads from whichever submirror is geometrically closer. For example, if the disk read/write heads on submirror 1 are positioned at cylinder 10, and the disk read/write heads on submirror 2 are positioned at cylinder 2200, and data needs to be read from cylinder 11, the geometric read option would use submirror 1 since it is geometrically closer. Geometric reads divide read operations among the submirrors by logical block addresses. For instance, in a two-way mirrored device, the disk space on the mirror is divided into two equally sized logical address ranges. Each submirror can then perform separate reads. Reads to the first section are handled by the first submirror, and reads to the second region are handled by the second submirror. In ODS, you can enable geometric reads through the `metatool` or `md.tab` file when defining the mirror. For example,

Example md.tab file: <Mirrored Device - Geometric Reads>

```
d1 1 5 /dev/dsk/c2t0d0s3 \
         /dev/dsk/c3t1d0s3 \
         /dev/dsk/c4t2d0s3 \
         /dev/dsk/c5t3d0s3 \
         /dev/dsk/c6t4d0s3 -i 64k

d2 1 5 /dev/dsk/c7t0d0s3 \
         /dev/dsk/c8t1d0s3 \
         /dev/dsk/c9t2d0s3 \
         /dev/dsk/c10t3d0s3 \
         /dev/dsk/c11t4d0s3 -i 64k

d3 -m d1 d2 -g
```

This example enables geometric reads for the mirrored metadevice d3. The performance gain offered by geometric reads is 5–10 percent. Geometric reads increase performance for sequential reads. For a DSS application, sequential reads occur frequently, and geometric reads can help increase performance. However, in a DSS environment, mirroring typically is not used because the data in a DSS environment is primarily read-only.

When you create a mirrored device, there are generally two write options: parallel writes and serial writes. On ODS, parallel writes are the default for mirrors. Parallel writes mean that writes to the submirrors are issued in parallel. The serial write option issues a write to each submirror in a serial fashion, waiting for each write to complete before the next write to the next submirror is issued. For best performance, use the parallel write option. This enables writes to the mirror to proceed in parallel, thus minimizing mirroring degradation.

3.6 RAID LEVELS

3.6.1 RAID-5

RAID-5 (Redundant Arrays of Inexpensive Disks) stripes data and parity across several disk drives. This eliminates the parity bottleneck introduced by previous types of RAID that stored the parity data on a single disk drive. RAID-5 treats multiple partitions as one large contiguous slice, which can contain data or parity information. No one single physical partition contains all the parity information—it is distributed across the multiple physical sections. If a disk drive were to fail, data is reconstructed dynamically by performing an XOR on the data and the parity bit. RAID-5 improves sequential read performance, but it may have an impact on overall write performance due to its inefficiency on small writes and the overhead of the parity-bit calculation. The main performance bottleneck of RAID-5 is due to the *read-write-modify* cycle in which a small write request involves two parity calculations and four disk I/Os: one I/O to write the new data, two I/Os to read the old data and old parity in order to compute the new parity, and one I/O to write the new parity. For small write requests, the parity is computed by comparing the new data with the old data and applying the differences to the parity block. For large write requests that involve many disks, parity is computed by performing an XOR on the new data on each disk. Therefore, RAID-5 can seriously reduce performance for frequent small write requests such as redo log writes. RAID-5 can be useful in a data warehousing environment where the majority of I/Os are reads and updates are minimal. RAID-5 offers good random I/O read performance and can also offer good sequential performance if the block sizes in the stripe are smaller than the average size of the I/O request.

In the case of a disk failure, reconstructing the data dynamically can seriously degrade performance, and a synchronization of the data once the defective drive is replaced is a lengthy and expensive operation. However, because the parity information is distributed, the dynamic reconstruction of the data will not be bottlenecked by a single drive. RAID-5 offers several advantages, including its ability to recover from a single disk failure, and it is more cost-effective than mirroring.

3.6.2 RAID-6

RAID-6 enhances the error recovering ability of RAID-5 in the case of multiple drive failures. RAID-5 recovers data from a failed disk by essentially reading the data and parity information from the remaining (available) disks in the stripe set. It is possible that additional disks in the RAID-5 stripe set may fail during the recovery phase, resulting in data loss. Hence, mission-critical applications may require stricter reliability in order to reduce system downtime. RAID-6 employs Reed-Solomon encoding on another drive to protect against any two disk failures. This improves the recoverability of the standard RAID-5 configuration. For small writes, RAID-6 offers less performance than RAID-5 due to the update of the additional parity information. The RAID-6 read-modify-write sequence for small writes requires six disk I/Os in order to update both sets of parity information.

3.6.3 RAID-7

RAID-7[3] is yet another improvement of the standard RAID configurations. RAID-7 provides asynchronous I/O access by utilizing a real-time event operating system local to the RAID-7 array known as the Array Management OS Software. The Array Management OS Software utilizes the CPU and memory buffer resources local to the array to process I/O requests in parallel. This enables I/Os to be queued to the RAID-7 array, thereby allowing the host application to continue processing without having to block on I/Os. The independent channel buffers, real-time OS, and separate control buses are critical to

---

3. RAID-7 products are available from the Storage Computer Corporation (www.storage.com).

the asynchronous and independent nature of RAID-7. RAID-7 offers a high level of I/O throughput over the traditional RAID due to its ability to utilize an independent OS and hardware array resources to process I/O requests.

3.6.4 RAID-S

RAID-S[4], another level of RAID, reduces the overhead of the parity computation by performing the operation via the hardware on the disk drive rather than the controller microcode. RAID-S requires XOR capable disk drives. RAID-S does not stripe data across different disks as is done in a RAID-5 configuration. Instead, RAID-S allows standard I/O performance tuning techniques to be used to distribute the data. RAID-S increases I/O parallelism by performing the XOR operation on the disk drive itself, subsequently reducing the performance penalty associated with small writes.

3.7 HARDWARE VOLUME MANAGEMENT

The software logical volume manager (LVM) such as Veritas, ODS, or SVM adds overhead to I/O operations by consuming additional processor cycles for operations such as logical to physical disk address translations. In the case of mirroring, the LVM needs to propagate the write to the submirrors. In order to improve performance and reduce the server overhead introduced by the software LVM, many disk array vendors have provided hardware RAID functionality through the storage array itself. Typically, the storage array is configured with at least one processor and some local cache memory. This allows the storage array to handle the RAID functionality, off-loading the RAID work from the server. This is referred to as hardware-level RAID. In general, hardware-level RAID is faster and more efficient than the software equivalent. The hardware RAID functionality implemented in the storage array allows the server to focus on application processing rather than RAID operations. Software volume managers are typically used in place of hardware level RAID where the hardware level RAID functionality is limited and cannot meet the performance requirements of the application. Therefore, when evaluating storage arrays, make sure you investigate the configuration details, such as the amount of cache, number and type of processor, and level of RAID functionality provided.

In order to optimally configure your I/O subsystem, you should also benchmark your software LVM against the hardware level RAID provided in your storage array to determine which is more optimal. In some cases, a combination of both offers superior performance. For example, you may configure your system such that the storage array handles the hardware level RAID-1 for mirroring, and the software LVM is used for striping. As storage array technology continues to improve reliability, performance, and functionality, applications can reap the benefits of hardware level performance and powerful RAID functionality.

---

4. RAID-S products are available from the EMC Corporation (www.emc.com).

3.8   NEW STORAGE ARRAY TECHNOLOGIES

Disk array vendors are constantly making major advancements in storage array technology in the areas of performance, reliability, administration, capacity, and interoperability. Customer database sizes continue to grow at explosive rates, raising the need for large-capacity, high-performance, reliable I/O subsystems. Disk drive vendors are also developing faster drives as well as using higher throughput interfaces such as Fibre Channel and Ultra2 SCSI. Coupling the disk drive technology breakthroughs with the storage array progression enables customers to build large-scale databases using the new array technologies yielding impressive I/O rates.

Seagate offers the new high-performance Cheetah and Barracuda drives with the super-fast Ultra2 SCSI (LVD) Low Voltage Differential Parallel SCSI Interface.The Ultra2 SCSI (LVD) interface is part of the SCSI-3 specification and is backward compatible. Ultra2 SCSI (LVD) increases I/O bandwidth, reliability, and cable lengths. Ultra2 SCSI (LVD) is a massive improvement over the previous SCSI rates of 3 M/second, providing SCSI bus data rates of 80 M/second. The increased bandwidth translates into optimal server performance for random access environments requiring swift response times. CAD/CAM engineering and multimedia applications also benefit from the ameliorated drive speeds. Ultra2 SCSI (LVD) increases the bus data rates to 80 M/second and ensures differential data integrity. Ultra2 SCSI (LVD) also allows the SCSI bus cable lengths to be extended to 12 meters. The Barracuda 9LP and Barracuda 18 are 7200-rpm drives with a formatted capacity of 4.5, 9, or 18 G. They offer a 4.17-ms average latency, 7.1-ms seek, and support several different interfaces including the Ultra2 SCSI LVD and Fibre Channel-Arbitrated Loop (FC-AL) interfaces. The new Cheetah drive rotates at 10,000 rpm and accesses data at a rate of 5 ms. The Cheetah drives are available in a 4.5, 9, or 18 G capacity. The Cheetah 18/9LP is capable of data transfer rates of 18 M/second. The average latency time for a Cheetah drive is approximately 2.99 ms. The programmable multisegmented cache employed by the Cheetah family of drives enables substantial I/O throughput in multitasking environments. The 1-M RAM buffer (4 M buffer is optional) can also be divided into 16 equal segments for independent read and write caching.

Sun has made major breakthroughs in improving the SPARC storage array technology. The new storage arrays from Sun offer significant performance gains as well as improved administration and reliability. Sun offers the SPARC Storage Array, the RSM Array 2000, and the Network Enterprise A5000 array. The new SPARC Storage arrays can sustain over 3300 I/Os Per Second (IOPS), thereby enabling high-performance transaction and transfer rates. The RSM Array 2000 is capable of over 4600 IOPS and can sustain a 60-M/second data transfer rate. The RSM Array 2000 can also be configured with up to 128 M of NVRAM (nonvolatile cache) which considerably increases I/O performance. In addition, the RSM Array 2000 provides added reliability and performance by utilizing dual active redundant controllers. The RSM Array 2000 provides a RAID Software Manager that allows you to manage and configure different levels of RAID such as RAID-1, RAID-0+1, and RAID-5. The RSM Array 2000 is designed for applications requiring superior RAID performance and high availability. The A5000 Enterprise

Network Array represents Sun's second-generation fibre channel disk array. The A5000 array supports hot-pluggable power supplies, fans, interface boards, and disk drives. The A5000 array uses a 100-M/sec fibre connection to the host and consists of dual fibre channel loops. The A5000 increases the transfer rate performance of the fibre connection over the original SPARC storage arrays. The A5000 also supports fully redundant RAID configurations. The Sun Enterprise Volume Manager can also be used to configure and manage different RAID level configurations. The Dynamic Multi-pathing (DMP) feature of the A5000 array increases availability via the auto loop failover and load balancing. The new storage arrays from Sun significantly improve performance, reliability, administration, and connectivity.

3.9 ASYNCHRONOUS I/O

The asynchronous I/O model provides system calls [for example, `aioread()` and `aiowrite()`] that perform nonblocking reads and writes. These system calls return immediately following the call itself. If a signal handler has been established, the calling process is later signaled[5] notifying the calling process of the completion of the asynchronous I/O request. Using asynchronous I/O can improve the I/O performance of the Oracle Server drastically. Another way to think of asynchronous I/O is as parallel reads and parallel writes. If enabled, asynchronous I/O allows multiple reads and writes to proceed in parallel, thereby reducing I/O wait time. Using asynchronous I/O in conjunction with the volume manager (striping) maximizes I/O throughput by parallelizing reads and writes and avoids disk I/O saturation through the proper data distribution via the volume manager.

3.9.1 ASYNCHRONOUS I/O IN SOLARIS

To enable asynchronous I/O in the Oracle7 Server on Solaris, set the `init.ora` parameters `async_write=true` and `async_read=true`. In Oracle8, set the init.ora parameter `disk_asynch_io=TRUE`. On Solaris, asynchronous I/O is supported on both file systems and raw devices. Asynchronous I/O on Solaris is handled by the asynchronous I/O library (`libaio.so`). To initiate asynchronous I/O calls on Solaris, you can call the `aioread()` and `aiowrite()` functions that are provided with the Solaris asynchronous I/O library (`libaio.so`). The Solaris asynchronous I/O library uses threads to issue nonblocking reads and writes. Solaris 2.5 and 2.6 made major improvements in the asynchronous I/O layer. Solaris 2.6 provides support for the POSIX asynchronous I/O calls `aio_read()` and `aio_write()`. Using the POSIX asynchronous I/O calls increases application portability. The POSIX `aio_read()` and `aio_write()` calls are provided by the `libposix4.so` shared library. On Solaris, the Oracle Server uses the Solaris asynchronous I/O calls.

---

5. Depending on the specific platform, typically the SIGIO or SIGAIO signal is used to signal a process when an asynchronous I/O request completed.

Solaris 2.5.1 provides asynchronous I/O on files larger than 2 G on the Sun Ultra systems (sun4u). Solaris 2.6 provides the ability to create files larger than 2 G by providing large file support via 64-bit file offsets. The standard Solaris asynchronous I/O calls of `aioread()` and `aiowrite()` support asynchronous I/O on files no larger than 2 G. This is due to the fact that the `libaio.so` shared library used the `lseek()` system call to position the file offset. The `lseek()` call supports only 32-bit file offsets, meaning that a file cannot be larger than 2 G. The `llseek()` system call extends the `lseek()` system call by allowing 64-bit file offsets. In Solaris 2.5.1, the `libaio.so` library uses the `llseek()` system call. Two new asynchronous I/O calls provided with Solaris 2.5.1 and Solaris 2.6 extend large file support to asynchronous I/O. The `aioread64()` and `aiowrite64()` system calls support asynchronous I/O for large files based on 64-bit file offsets via the `llseek()` call for file offset positioning. This not only allows larger size data files in Oracle, it allows asynchronous I/O on files larger than 2 G. Oracle 7.3 and Oracle8 on Solaris support asynchronous I/O on large files.

3.9.2 ASYNCHRONOUS I/O IN HP-UX

To enable asynchronous I/O on HP, set the init.ora parameter `use_async_io=TRUE` in Oracle7 and `disk_asynch_io=TRUE` in Oracle8. On HP, you must configure the async disk driver in the Drivers Area using the SAM tool. Following this you must regenerate the kernel and reboot the system. Use the SAM tool to regenerate the kernel. The new kernel will be located in `/stand/build/vmunix_test`, and the location of the corresponding configuration file used to create the kernel is `/stand/build/SYSTEM.SAM`.

To enable the new kernel changes to take effect, move the `/stand/build/vmunix_test` to the `/stand` directory using the `mv` command, and move the configuration file `/stand/build/SYSTEM.SAM` to `/stand/system`. Remember to back up the old kernel and the old configuration file before you move the newly generated kernel into the `/stand` directory. Once you have moved the newly generated kernel and corresponding system configuration file into the `/stand` directory, reboot the system to force the asynchronous I/O changes to take effect. Asynchronous I/O on HP will be used only when accessing raw (character) devices. This means that if your database consists of file system–based files, asynchronous I/O will not be used. Also, if using asynchronous I/O with raw devices, ensure that the `/dev/async` device is owned by the Oracle software owner and belongs to the dba group. If the `/dev/async` device driver does not exist, create the device driver by using the following command:

```
myhost{root}-> /sbin/mknod /dev/async c 101 0x0
```

The permissions on the `/dev/async` device should be read and write by the Oracle software owner. For example,

```
myhost%> ls -al /dev/async
```

```
crw-rw—    oracle    dba    /dev/async
```

If the file permissions are different than those listed in the preceding example, use the following commands to set the proper permissions:

```
myhost{root}> chown oracle /dev/async

myhost{root}> chgrp dba /dev/async

myhost{root}> chmod 660 /dev/async
```

In addition to creating the /dev/async device driver, you should also set the kernel parameter max_async_ports which specifies the maximum number of processes that can simultaneously open the /dev/async device driver. A low setting for max_async_ports may cause Oracle processes to fail when trying to open the asynchronous I/O device driver.

3.9.3   ASYNCHRONOUS I/O ON SEQUENT

To enable asynchronous I/O on Sequent, set async_write=TRUE in Oracle7 and disk_asynch_io=TRUE in Oracle8. Asynchronous I/O is supported only on raw character devices on Sequent. Asynchronous I/O is handled by the /usr/lib/libseq.a library through the DIO interface layer, which provides several routines that can perform direct I/O and asynchronous I/O. The DIO_Read() and DIO_Write() system calls are used to perform asynchronous I/O on raw devices. Sequent also provides large file asynchronous I/O support via the DIO_Read64() and DIO_Write64() system calls. If you plan to use asynchronous I/O, you should also set some kernel parameters that pertain to asynchronous I/O. The MAXAIO and NABUF kernel parameters specify the maximum number of concurrent asynchronous I/O requests, and the number of asynchronous I/O buffers, respectively. Set MAXAIO to the maximum number of asynchronous I/O requests. For a heavy I/O system, set MAXAIO to 512, and NABUF to 1024. Remember that asynchronous I/O requests hold the data memory image for the asynchronous I/O request resident until the request is completed or canceled. Hence, memory can diminish rather quickly when a large number of asynchronous I/O requests are issued. Make sure you have enough free memory when setting high values for NABUF and MAXAIO.

3.9.4   ASYNCHRONOUS I/O IN ORACLE

The Oracle Server provides asynchronous I/O on most UNIX platforms. Asynchronous I/O increases DBMS performance by performing nonblocking I/O. It also yields a high throughput DBWR by avoiding the standard (synchronous) I/O calls that block DBWR until each I/O is completed. The concept of asynchronous I/O is quite simple. In synchronous I/O, each write or read call would block (meaning not return) until the completion of the call itself. This means that each time LGWR and DBWR issue writes to log files and data files, each respective process must wait (block) until the completion of each write call. This can cause a bottleneck for LGWR and DBWR, and can also cause other Oracle user processes to wait on space in the SGA because LGWR and DBWR have not yet completed their *dirty* writes. If you configure your Oracle Server to use asynchronous I/O, set the Oracle7 `init.ora` parameter `db_writers=1`. In Oracle8 (8.0.4), set the `init.ora` parameter `db_writer_processes=1`. Since asynchronous I/O is enabled, DBWR and LGWR will not block on writes. Therefore, there is no need to have multiple DBWR processes. Using asynchronous I/O and setting `db_writers=1` (Oracle7) or `db_writer_processes=1` (Oracle8) reduces the overhead of having multiple Oracle background processes. It also eliminates the amount of interprocess communication between the master DBWR and its slaves since there only will be one DBWR process when `db_writers=1`.

3.10   I/O SLAVES IN ORACLE8

Oracle8 provides the ability to utilize I/O slaves for those platforms that do not support asynchronous I/O. I/O slaves can also be used with asynchronous I/O. Several new init.ora parameters have been added to control the behavior of I/O slaves. The `init.ora` parameters `arch_io_slaves backup_disk_io_slaves`, `backup_tape_io_slaves`, `dbwr_io_slaves`, and `lgwr_io_slaves` specify the number of I/O slave processes to be used for archives, disk backups, tape backups, database file writes (DBWR), and log file writes (LGWR), respectively. If you enable `dbwr_io_slaves`, only one DBWR process is used, regardless of the setting of `db_writer_processes`. I/O slaves can be used to increase database I/O throughput by parallelizing I/O requests. This helps improve archiving and log write throughput by allowing the slaves to parallelize I/O requests as opposed to Oracle7 which used only a single archiver process (ARCH) and a single log writer process (LGWR). I/O slaves can also improve backup and restore performance for those platforms that do not support asynchronous I/O to tape devices. I/O slaves are dynamically allocated on an as needed basis. This reduces the overhead of spawning processes that are never used. The format of the process name for an I/O slave is as follows: `ora_iNnn_<SID>`, where "i" identifies the process as an I/O slave, "N" is the I/O adapter number, "nn" is the I/O slave number, and "SID" refers to the ORACLE_SID.

In order to determine whether or not you should configure your system to use I/O slaves, monitor the file I/O, DBWR, and LGWR statistics to determine if DBWR or LGWR are falling behind. I/O slaves use shared memory for the I/O buffers. Therefore ensure that your system can afford the memory and processor overhead of the additional processes. To choose an optimal number of I/O slaves, monitor processor, memory, and disk I/O utilization in conjunction with the Oracle I/O statistics. Query the views `v$sesstat` and `v$sysstat` and examine the statistics `physical writes`, `physical reads`, `logical reads`, and `write requests` to determine the I/O rates. You should also correlate the I/O statistics from the `v$sesstat` and `v$sysstat` views with the statistics from the `v$sess_io` and `v$filestat` views. The performance of the I/O slaves is also highly dependent on the data distribution. In order to maximize the performance of the I/O slaves, ensure that your Oracle data files and log files are optimally distributed and sized.

3.11 DIRECT I/O (DIO)

Direct I/O, as the term suggests, bypasses the UNIX file system cache and copies the file system-based file data directly into user space. Direct I/O on file systems is similar to raw devices. However, direct I/O on file systems is synchronous. If asynchronous I/O is not used, Oracle uses the `read()` system call to read from file system-based files. To force Oracle to use direct I/O on your Sequent system, set the Oracle7 `init.ora` parameter `_direct_read=TRUE`. Direct I/O reduces the file system overhead by eliminating file buffering. If your Sequent database uses file system files, you can use Direct I/O to improve file system performance over the traditional `read()` call.

Solaris 2.6 provides the ability to perform direct I/O via the `directio()` system call. Using the `directio()` system call, an application can perform direct I/O on a file thereby bypassing the UNIX file system cache. The mount command also provides the options `noforcedirectio` and `forcedirectio` which control whether or not direct I/O to the file system is forced. Direct I/O can improve large sequential I/O performance. If you are using UNIX file systems for your database files, you can take advantage of the direct I/O feature by mounting the file systems containing the Oracle database files with the `forcedirectio` mount option.

3.11.1 DIRECT I/O IN ORACLE

Oracle uses direct I/O for such operations as backup, restore, and parallel query execution. During parallel query execution, Oracle can read the data blocks directly into the PGA as opposed to the SGA. Oracle can also write data blocks directly to disk when performing large joins or sorts. This is known as direct I/O since Oracle reads and writes directly from and to the disk into the user buffers. The Oracle8 init.ora parameter `db_file_direct_io_count` specifies the number of blocks to be used for direct I/O operations. The size of the direct I/O buffer is a product of `db_file_direct_io_count` and `db_block_size`. The direct I/O buffer cannot exceed the maximum I/O size for your platform. You should set such `db_file_direct_io_count` to a multiple of the data file stripe size so as to maximize I/O throughput. For maximum performance, set `db_file_direct_io_count` such that the direct I/O buffer is equal to the maximum I/O size for your platform. This reduces the amount of I/Os needed since more data can be stored in the direct I/O buffer. This also reduces the number of system calls and reduces context switch overhead.

3.12 KERNELIZED ASYNCHRONOUS I/O (KAIO)

Solaris 2.4 provides a further enhancement to asynchronous I/O (AIO), known as KAIO (Kernelized AIO). KAIO reduces the context switch overhead between kernel and user space by maintaining the AIO layer in the kernel itself. Traditional AIO is performed through a shared library API in which user calls (from Oracle) are made to the AIO API.

These calls must then switch from user space to kernel space in order to perform kernel I/O services. KAIO eliminates this need by incorporating the AIO API services into the kernel itself. During AIO calls, the kernel can lock memory for AIO, thereby making the locked database buffers unswappable. Hence, be sure your system has sufficient free memory to hold the entire SGA and to service AIO requests. KAIO is enabled in Solaris 2.4 by default. Solaris 2.5 further enhanced KAIO, reducing kernel overhead and improving the speed of the KAIO services.

Solaris 2.6 dramatically improved the performance of raw device I/O by optimizing the low level I/O routines and rewriting the SPARC Storage array device driver. If you are running ODS 4.0 and Solaris 2.4 or Solaris 2.5, you will need to install the latest ODS 4.0 jumbo patch 102580. The ODS 4.0 jumbo patch (102580) fixes KAIO errors. Without this patch, KAIO calls to ODS raw metadevices fail, thereby reducing performance. This patch corrects this problem and allows KAIO to be used on ODS raw devices. KAIO is supported on raw devices only. In benchmarks, KAIO has increased performance 30 percent over the standard asynchronous I/O. It also allows asynchronous I/O to tape drive devices. KAIO allocates internal buffers to service asynchronous I/O requests. Hence, make sure your system is not short of memory, otherwise KAIO requests may fail.

3.13 LIST I/O (LIO)

List I/O (LIO), as the term suggests, builds a list of I/O requests and submits the list, asynchronously, to the kernel for processing. In the traditional asynchronous I/O model, a separate I/O call had to be made for each I/O request. For a heavy I/O database server, the traditional method generates significant process, system call, and context switch overhead. List I/O can alleviate this overhead by building a list of I/O requests and submitting the list to the kernel.

On HP-UX, LIO is supported only for database files created on raw devices. LIO is usually performed through a shared library in which user processes call the system call `lio_listio()`. Solaris 2.6, HP-UX, IBM AIX, UnixWare, and SGI all provide list I/O. Refer to the installation and configuration guide of your specific platform to enable LIO.

3.14 READV()

The `readv()` system call performs the same action as read but places the input data into the user buffers that are specified in the call to `readv`. Using `readv` (meaning vector read) reduces the CPU overhead of copying buffers from kernel space (UNIX file system cache) to user space (Oracle buffers). Although `readv()` reduces CPU overhead, the I/O workload is increased by the degree of the buffering (vector). For sequential access of UNIX file system-based files, readv() can increase I/O performance. On raw devices, readv() has shown a performance degradation on Solaris. Therefore, use caution when enabling readv() in the Oracle7 Server. The default value of use_readv is disabled. To enable readv(), set the Oracle7 init.ora parameter use_readv=TRUE. If your Oracle7 database uses raw devices, and asynchronous I/O is enabled, set use_readv=FALSE.

3.15 DB_FILE_MULTIBLOCK_READ_COUNT

The init.ora parameter db_file_multiblock_read_count controls the number of Oracle data blocks read at each I/O read during a sequential (i.e., full-table) scan. For example, setting this parameter to 8 would cause Oracle to read eight blocks at each read request during the sequential scan. Therefore, this parameter can control the performance of sequential scans. A larger value of db_file_multiblock_read_count reduces the number of I/O calls needed to scan the object. For example, if set to 32, and the Oracle block size = 8K, then a sequential scan of a table of size 256K can be read in one pass. If you are using a volume manager, this parameter should be set so that <db_block_size> × <db_file_multiblock_read_count> is a multiple of the stripe size. For example, if your stripe width is 32K, and your block size is 8K, setting db_file_multiblock_read_count=32 results in multiple spindles being accessed in parallel to satisfy the I/O read request.

The values for db_file_multiblock_read_count are operating system specific and cannot be larger than (db_block_buffers/4). The default value for db_file_multiblock_read_count is also operating system dependent. Typically on UNIX platforms, db_file_multiblock_read_count defaults to (max_IO_size/db_block_size). The max_IO_size is the maximum size of a single I/O request. The max_IO_size is also operating system dependent. Oracle 7.3 enforces several constraints when setting db_file_multiblock_read_count. If the user-specified value exceeds the values of the internal constraint checks, db_file_multiblock_read_count defaults to (max_IO_size/ db_block_size). Therefore, when upgrading to Oracle 7.3, you may notice that user-specified values for db_file_multiblock_read_count are being over-ridden. This is due to the enforcement of the constraint checks. For example, if max_IO_size is set to 128K and db_block_size=8192 (8 K), then db_file_ multiblock_read_count cannot exceed 16. A patch that increases max_IO_size to 1 M is available for Oracle 7.3 on Sun Solaris. To obtain the patch, contact Oracle Customer Support, and refer to bug 433762. This patch allows a maximum setting for db_file_multiblock_read_count=128 when db_block_size=8K. However, even though the patch increases max_IO_size to 1 M, db_file_multiblock_read_count is still restricted by (db_block_buffers/4). The patch can help increase the performance of large full table scans and parallel queries.

3.16   FILE SYSTEMS VERSUS RAW DEVICES

The debate over using raw devices instead of file systems is a popular one. The overall consensus seems to be performance versus ease of administration. Although file system technology constantly improves through vendor innovations, raw devices remain the leader in terms of performance and scalability. Figure 3.12 outlines the I/O cycle of raw devices and file systems.

3.16.1   UNIX FILE SYSTEMS

In Figure 3.12, any reads issued to a UNIX file system-based file cause the file metadata to be brought into the UNIX buffer cache, and the file data to be brought into virtual memory. The file data is then copied into the user space (in this case, the Oracle buffers). Therefore, each read translates into a read followed by a copy from kernel space to user space. Also, the UNIX kernel allocates file system buffers for data from the virtual memory pages. The UNIX buffer cache holds information such as inodes, indirect blocks, superblocks, and cylinder group data. File data pages and directory block data are part of the virtual memory pages, not the buffer cache. Hence, a file system-based database server with a tremendous amount of I/O may experience a high amount of paging. The UNIX file system cache employs a least recently used algorithm to maintain the contents of the cache.

File systems have several advantages over raw devices, including sequential read performance, buffering, and ease of administration. The UNIX file system provides look-ahead read for sequential scans. This can help a DSS database when most queries result in full-table scans. Also, the data from the sequential scan, depending on the access frequency, may remain in the cache, and subsequent queries on the data will observe quicker execution times. File system-based files are also much easier to administer in terms of sizing, growth, and backups and restores. There are many backup and restore tools that

FIGURE 3.12   Raw device and file system I/O cycle.

do not yet support raw devices and that offer effortless automated backups and restores of file systems. The block size of the file system can be made to match that of the Oracle block size to minimize I/O during reads and writes. The `readv()` feature can also be enabled to take advantage of file system sequential reads.

Solaris and HP-UX support the Veritas file system (`vxfs`).[6] The Veritas file system (`vxfs`) provides additional features over the standard UNIX file system (`ufs`). The `vxfs` file system uses extent-level allocation rather than block-level allocation by grouping multiple blocks into a single extent. It also provides faster recovery following a system crash by providing journaling. The journaling feature avoids having to `fsck` the entire file system by applying the changes from the journals. On a large file system, this provides tremendous time savings following a system crash. It also provides a higher level of availability because the chance of losing the entire file system is minimal. If you are using file systems, it is recommended that you set the file system block size to the Oracle block size, but not smaller than 4K. The 4K lower limit is due to the fact that the virtual memory page size is 4K. A block size smaller than the page size forces a memory page to be broken down into the size of the file system block size during a write-out. For example, having a 2K Veritas block size would force a 4K memory page to be broken into two writes of 2K each. This would decrease I/O performance.

If you choose to use file systems on a large database, I recommend that you either create a Veritas-based file system, or use the equivalent file system journal feature provided in Sun's ODS 4.X product. This eliminates the need to perform an `fsck` on your file system since the journals only need to be applied to restore the consistency state of the file system. Using the journal feature of Veritas or ODS can considerably reduce the time required to make a file system consistent. It also increases reliability because `fsck` may truncate files, thereby losing data.

3.16.1.1 Tuning the `fsflush` System Daemon

In Solaris, two kernel parameters control the rate of the `fsflush` system daemon: `autoup` and `tune_t_fsflushr`. Recall that the `fsflush` system daemon is responsible for flushing dirty file system pages to disk. If your database uses file systems, `fsflush` can use a considerable amount of CPU time. You can check the amount of CPU time being used by the `fsflush` daemon by using the `ps` command. For example,

```
myhost> /bin/ps -p 3    * fsflush always has PID=3

PID TTY       TIME   COMMAND
  3   ?       62:02  fsflush

myhost> uptime

        2:55pm  up 5 day(s), 21:17 users,
        load average: 0.01, 0.02, 0.02
```

---

6. Using the Veritas Volume Manager, you can create a Veritas file system (`vxfs`).

In this example, fsflush has used over an hour of CPU time since the system was last rebooted. According to the uptime output, the system has been up for 508,620 seconds. Therefore, fsflush used 3,722 seconds of CPU time over a total elapsed system uptime of 508,620 seconds. This represents less than 1 percent of over-all CPU utilization by the fsflush system daemon. If your system experiences high CPU usage times for the fsflush daemon, you may want to decrease the rate at which the daemon wakes up. The autoup kernel parameter controls the maximum age of any dirty memory resident file system page. The default for autoup is 30 seconds. You should set autoup to a larger value, such as five minutes (300 seconds). This reduces the fsflush workload and also increases the cache hit rate since dirty file system pages are more likely to remain in memory longer. The tune_t_fsflushr kernel parameter specifies how often the fsflush daemon wakes up. The default for tune_t_fsflushr is 5 seconds. Set tune_t_fsflushr to a higher value such as 60 seconds to reduce the overhead of fsflush. If your database server uses all raw devices, and file system activity is extremely minimal, increase autoup and tune_t_fsflushr to high values since file system activity is minimal. You can also disable page flushing by setting the kernel parameter dopageflush to zero.

3.16.1.2   Tuning the UNIX Buffer Cache

The UNIX buffer cache is used to cache the file metadata such as file headers, inodes, and indirect block addresses. The cache can significantly increase the perfor-mance of reads and writes as data may be held in virtual memory, thus avoiding physical disk I/O. Access time to the cache is in the order of nanoseconds (typical memory speeds) while physical disk I/O access time is in the order of milliseconds. If you are using file system-based files for your database, you need to tune the UNIX buffer cache to achieve a high read and write hit ratio. You can use sar -b to monitor the hit ratio of the buffer cache. Examine the %rcache and %wcache columns from the sar -b output to determine the cache hit ratios. If the percentages are low, you need to tune the buffer cache parameters if you are using file systems. Determine the hit ratio before modifying the size of the file system buffer cache. If sar -b reports poor hit ratios, increase the size of the file system buffer cache nominally until a hit ratio of 90 percent or higher is achieved. The kernel parameters that can be tuned to achieve a high-perfor-mance buffer cache are NBUF, NHBUF, NPBUF, and BUFHWM. The two main parameters that affect the buffer cache are NBUF and BUFHWM. The NBUF parameter controls the amount of block I/O buffers that are allocated dynamically at each interval when buffer headers are needed. NHBUF is the size of the hash table used to locate a buffer. NPBUF is the number of physical I/O buffers allocated. One I/O buffer is needed for each physical read or write. Increasing this parameter for a system with heavy reads and writes may yield tremendous improvements. BUFHWM is the buffer cache high-water mark that spec-ifies the maximum amount of memory that can be used for block I/O buffers. If you use raw devices for your database files, decrease the size of the buffer cache in order to make more memory available for Oracle and user processes.

In Solaris, bufhwm controls the high-water mark for the size of the buffer cache, expressed in kilobytes. The default for bufhwm on Solaris is 2 percent of physical memory.

You can set the bufhwm parameter by placing a line the /etc/system file as follows:

```
set bufhwm=4096
```

This example sets the buffer cache high-water mark to 4 M. If you are using raw devices and your system has a lot of memory, the 2 percent default can translate into a tangible amount. Therefore, if you use raw devices, reduce the size of bufhwm to 1 M or less. The buffer cache grows dynamically up to the high-water mark. You can also set nbuf and p_nbuf in the /etc/system file. The p_nbpuf parameter specifies the amount of nbuf buffers to allocate in a single allocation.

On Sequent, the BUFPCT kernel parameter specifies the percentage of free memory that is available for the buffer cache. Again, if you use file systems, monitor the cache hit ratio through sar -b. If the hit ratios are low, increase BUFPCT at a nominal rate.

If you use file systems, tuning the buffer cache can increase performance. However, it is important that you balance the buffer cache with the Oracle SGA and user processes. If you increase the buffer cache, there will be less memory available for the SGA and user processes. It is key that you maintain a balance. When tuning the buffer cache, you should monitor paging and swapping in conjunction with monitoring the buffer cache (sar -b). Increasing the buffer cache too much may reduce performance due to increased levels of paging. Review the material that pertains to buffer cache kernel parameters of your respective platform in detail before you alter the buffer cache-related kernel parameters. Parameters and defaults often change with new releases.

3.16.1.3 Tuning the Inode Cache

The ufs file system uses inodes to manage files. The inodes reside on physical disk. When an operation is performed on a ufs-based file, the inode for the file is read into the inode memory cache. The idea is that if the inode is needed again, it will be found in the cache versus the inode having to be read from physical disk. You can increase your system's performance by tuning the inode cache. Use sar -a to monitor the inode cache. If iget/s, which is the number of inodes read per second, is high, it is an indication that the inode cache is too small. On Solaris, you can increase the size of the inode cache by setting the kernel parameter ufs_ninode in the /etc/system file. If the statistics from sar -a show a poor inode cache hit ratio, increase the value of ufs_ninode. On Sequent, the parameter NINODE sets the maximum number of inodes in the file system.

3.16.1.4 Tuning the Directory Name Lookup Cache

Each time a file is opened, the Directory NameLookup Cache (DNLC) is scanned to determine if the file is in the DNLC cache. The DNLC associates a vnode with the name of a file. Typically, short file names are cached and file names that are too long to be cached are looked up by reading the directory. In Solaris 2, file names longer than 30 characters are not cached.

A cache miss translates into more CPU cycles, and possibly more physical I/O, in order to read the directory. In Solaris, you can set `ncsize` in the `/etc/system` file to set the size of the directory name lookup cache. Use the `sar -a` command to monitor the DNLC. The column `namei/s` reports the number of name lookups per second, and the `dirbk/s` reports the number of directory blocks read per second. To make use of the DNLC cache, you should try to minimize the length of file names to less than 30 characters. On HP and Sequent, use the SAM tool or MENU tool to set the `NCSIZE` kernel parameter.

3.16.2   RAW DEVICES

Raw devices bypass the UNIX file system cache, thus eliminating the overhead of copying the data from kernel file system I/O buffers to user buffers. Using raw devices also reduces the workload of the `fsflush` daemon which flushes out file system dirty pages to disk. By using raw devices, less memory is used for the file system cache and file I/O buffers. This reduces system paging, and also makes more memory available for user and Oracle processes, thereby reducing the chances of swapping. Raw devices provide the advantage of utilizing AIO and KAIO.[7] Currently, AIO and KAIO are not supported against file systems.[8] By using asynchronous I/O and KAIO, raw devices can provide a significant performance increase. For an OLTP system where transactions usually result in random I/O, raw devices further increases performance.

There are a number of backup and restore tools that provide full support for raw devices. Consult with your OS vendor to obtain a list of backup and restore tool vendors. If you are not able to obtain a backup and restore tool, you can utilize the `dd` utility to backup raw devices. In nonarchive mode, shut down the database, and issue the following command:

```
myhost%> dd if=<raw device db file name> \
          of=<backup device name> bs=32k
```

I strongly recommend that you use raw devices for your database in order to maximize performance. You should also use a volume manager to configure and to size your raw partitions appropriately. Make sure that you do not waste space when you create raw device partitions. Refer to the *Oracle Server Administration Guide* for exact sizing of database objects. If you are switching from file system files to raw devices, you may use the `dd` utility to do so—assuming you have enough space for the file system data and raw device data.

```
myhost%> dd if=/my_old_FS_file \
          of=/dev/rdsk/my_new_RAW_device bs=32k
```

---

7. Kernelized Asynchronous I/O (KAIO) is available on Solaris 2.4 or higher.
8. Sun provides asynchronous I/O on both file systems and raw devices. Sequent and HP provide asynchronous I/O on only raw devices.

Before you issue this command, be sure that the raw device is at least the same size as the UNIX file system file. The database must also be shut down. The permissions on the raw device file must be owned by the Oracle software owner, with read and write permissions granted to the owner. It is also recommended that you use symbolic links to reference the actual raw device names. This allows the symbolic links to be easily manipulated if the raw device names change during a reconfiguration, and/or OS upgrade. Please refer to the *Oracle Installation and Configuration Guide (ICG)* for your specific platform for more information on the operational issues involved in using raw devices.

3.16.2.1   Maximum Physical I/O Size

The maximum physical I/O size limits the size of a single I/O that can be issued to a device driver. The maximum physical I/O size is platform and driver dependent. For a DSS system in which large size I/Os are being issued, it is important that you set the OS kernel parameter accordingly. Generally, I/Os larger than the size of the maximum physical I/O size are broken down into several segments of the maximum physical I/O size. In Solaris, you can set the `maxphys` kernel parameter in the `/etc/system` OS kernel configuration file. For example, you can set `maxphys` to 1 M to ensure that Oracle multiblock I/Os to raw devices are not broken down into several I/Os. This helps increase I/O throughput and overall performance.

```
set maxphys=1048576        *** ( 1M raw I/O)
```

The Veritas Volume Management software also allows you to specify the maximum I/O size. For Veritas logical devices, the equivalent to `maxphys` is the `vol_maxio` parameter. The `vol_maxio` parameter is specified in units of 512-byte sectors. For example, to set `vol_maxio` to 1 M, place the following entry in your `/etc/system` configuration file:

```
set vxio:vol_maxio=2048    *** (Veritas 1 MB I/O)
```

3.17   SEPARATE SEQUENTIAL AND RANDOM I/O

In order to achieve the best disk I/O performance, consider the following when laying out the data files and redo log files: Redo log file access is completely sequential. Redo log files should be separated from the other database files. If possible, it is a good idea to dedicate a few disks to redo log files. If the same disks are used for both database and redo log files, the disk read and write heads may be constantly moving around the disk to satisfy random I/O requests. If you dedicate a few disks to the redo log files, the reads and writes can continue sequentially since redo log file access is purely sequential. This increases the performance of log writes by reducing the I/O service time.

The redo log files should also be mirrored to avoid loss of the database if a redo log file becomes unavailable due to a hardware failure. Preferably, the mirroring of the redo log file should be at either the hardware or OS level through the volume manager. Mirroring the redo files through multiple Oracle redo log members will cause Oracle extra overhead by issuing I/O to all members within the group. Mirroring at the hardware and/or OS level eliminates the Oracle mirroring overhead by handling the mirroring at the kernel or hardware level. However, keep in mind that with hardware or OS mirroring, any corruption to the Oracle log files will be propagated to the mirror. Therefore, it is a good idea to have at least one Oracle redo log member mirror per redo log group to help guard against redo log file corruption.

Access to data files is often random, and therefore the data files should be spread among the controllers and disk drives as best as possible. Refer to Section 3.2.1 in this guide for helpful hints on striping. Proper data distribution and efficient use of the volume manager can ensure high I/O throughput. Avoid overloading any single disk drive with random I/Os. For a 4-G or 9-G disk drive, random I/Os should not exceed 60–70 I/Os per second. Disk drive manufacturers continue to enhance disk drive technology by improving disk drive spindle speeds, and I/O transfer rates as well as increasing the size of the disk drive cache.

3.18 TABLESPACE OPTIMIZATION

There are various items that need to be considered when optimizing the performance of a tablespace such as the size of the extents, life expectancy of the extents, size of I/O requests, read and write rates, media recovery time requirements, level of concurrency, Oracle Parallel Server (OPS) traffic, I/O workload, and size of the tablespace. Segments that have different size extents should be placed in different tablespaces in order to improve space management and administration. Segments that are periodically dropped and re-created should be separated from other tablespaces so as to minimize tablespace fragmentation. This is the main reason for separating index and data segments since indexes are frequently rebuilt. Oracle 7.3 allows you to rebuild an index by using the following command:

```
SQL> alter index <index name> rebuild;
```

You can also rebuild the index in parallel and choose the `unrecoverable` or `recoverable` option in Oracle7 and the `nologging` or `logging` option in Oracle8 when rebuilding the index. The index rebuild feature is extremely useful for fragmented indexes and avoids your having to first drop and then re-create the index.

Tablespace performance can also be optimized by separating segments that experience different size I/O requests and setting the stripe interleave based on the size of the I/O request and level of concurrency. Read-only segments should be placed in read-only tablespaces. Also, read-only tablespaces can be placed on less expensive media devices such as CD-ROM or RAID-5. In order to improve free list management, place tables that experience a high degree of inserts in different tablespaces than tables that are update and delete intensive.

The level of concurrency should also be considered when designing and configuring tablespaces. For example, in Oracle7, the redo log files have a low level of write concurrency since only LGWR handles redo log file writes. Hence, a more granular level of striping can be used with redo log files. In Oracle8, LGWR I/O slaves can be configured which may require you to stripe your redo log files differently than in Oracle7 since multiple I/O slaves can be issuing concurrent log writes. In addition, LGWR often performs group commits which groups many redo writes together into a single-batch write. Therefore, you may want to set the stripe width for the redo log files according to the average redo write size which is based on your workload. You can calculate the average redo write size by looking at the ratio of `redo size/redo writes` from the `v$sysstat` view. Tablespaces experiencing a high degree of concurrency should be distributed across multiple disks and multiple controllers so as to minimize hot areas. In an OPS environment, it is important that tablespaces and segments be configured such that contention for the same data blocks is minimized. It is also key that you maintain reasonably sized tablespaces in conjunction with the recovery time requirements. Very large tablespaces may preclude you from being able to restore the entire tablespace in a reasonable time window.

3.19 SETTING THE DATABASE BLOCK SIZE

The Oracle database block size can be optimally configured to achieve high I/O throughput. In UNIX, the logical block size of the file system depends on the file system type and the method of access. File system block sizes can be 1K, 2K, 4K, or 8K. If you use file systems, your database block size should be a multiple of the file system block size. Currently, the Oracle Server for UNIX-based platforms allows `db_block_size` to be set to either 2K, 4K, 8K, or 16K (maximum in 8.0). There are some platforms that allow 32K block sizes. If you are using raw devices, set `db_block_size` to a multiple of the OS physical block size (512 bytes). For an OLTP system, set `db_block_size` to either 2K or 4K. In an OLTP environment, the idea is to minimize block contention and free buffer waits. Therefore, a smaller block size such as 2K or 4K results in having more blocks in the buffer cache which helps reduce block-level contention. For a DSS workload, set `db_block_size` to 16K. In a DSS environment, typically large size reads and writes are occurring through complex queries, batch updates, or bulk data loads. Therefore, more rows (data) per block reduces the amount of I/O required because more data is read or written per block. For a mixed workload, set `db_block_size` to either 4K or 8K.

3.20 MONITORING I/O ACTIVITY

You should regularly monitor disk I/O statistics by using utilities such as `sar -d`, and/or `iostat`.[9] In Solaris 2.6, `iostat` provides an option (`iostat -n`) that displays the descriptive disk device name rather than the *sdnnn* format. This allows you to immediately identify the particular controller and disk for which the statistics are being reported. These utilities report useful performance statistics, such as percent busy, average queue length, reads and writes per second, blocks per second, average wait, and average service time. The most important items of focus are average service time and average wait. The average service time is the average elapsed time (in milliseconds) that the disk drive takes to complete an I/O request. The average wait is the average amount of time requests were left outstanding. High averages for these two items indicates an I/O bottleneck. Average service times longer than 50 milliseconds are reason for concern if it continues over a long time. Do not be concerned with service times of 50 ms or less for small intervals of time. This means simply that the system received a large I/O request at that point in time. Be concerned with high average service times that are continuously high. You may have to repartition the data and redo log files to eliminate the I/O contention. The following is an example of the `sar -d` command:

```
myhost> sar -d 1 1

DYNIX/ptx myhost 4.0 V4.1.3 i386

device %busy avque r+w/s blks/s avwait avserv

  qd3     8    1.0     5      79    0.0    16.0
  qd15    8    1.0     5      79    0.0    16.0
  qd24    2    1.0     3      13    0.0     6.5
  qd29    5    1.0    13     436    0.0     3.4
  qd30    6    1.0    14     483    0.0     4.0
  qd31    5    1.0    12     417    0.0     3.7
  qd43    1    1.0     1       7    0.0    14.6
  qd50    1    1.0     1       7    0.0    16.4
  qd57    1    1.0     1       7    0.0    13.9
  qd77    5    1.0    13     417    0.0     3.9
  qd78    6    1.0    14     430    0.0     4.0
  qd79    5    1.0    14     476    0.0     3.6
```

The above `sar` output shows proper I/O distribution. The average service times show good performance. The average wait is 0, meaning that disks are not being saturated. If you see high average service times and high waits, you may need to redistribute I/O

---

9. The `iostat` utility is available on Solaris, and reports disk utilization statistics.

to eliminate the bottlenecks. You can also use the GUI performance monitoring tools to monitor disk and I/O utilization. Whichever utility you use, it is important that you monitor the I/O subsystem periodically to ensure that I/O is not a bottleneck. Using the volume manager and raw devices with proper data distribution can help you avoid disk contention.

3.21 TUNING NFS

NFS file systems are extremely common, and performance can suffer during heavy NFS use. My first recommendation for tuning NFS is to ensure that the back-end file system (the file system being exported as an NFS file system) is striped across multiple disks and controllers. Follow the guidelines in Section 3.2.1 to tune the file system itself. If the file system is not distributed properly, performance of local access and remote access (NFS) of the file system will suffer. Therefore, before you export the file system, use a volume manager to stripe the file system.

In addition, tune the inode cache and DNLC. For heavy NFS activity, you should set the DNLC and NCSIZE to larger values to accommodate the NFS traffic. NFS uses RPC to communicate between the client and the server. NFS packets use the UDP datagram, and client machines manage NFS inodes as an rnode (remote node). Solaris 2.5 introduced NFS Version 3, which increased NFS performance and also switched from UDP to TCP/IP packets. Most other vendors' NFS utilities are still based on version 2.0. For an NFS server experiencing a lot of NFS traffic, increase the number of NFS server daemons (nfsd). This allows more NFS client requests to be serviced in parallel. On Solaris, the nfsd daemon uses kernel threads to service requests. The kernel threads do not experience context switches between user space and kernel space because NFS remains in kernel space. This allows the nfsd daemon to achieve high throughput. On Solaris and HP, you can use the nfsstat utility to monitor NFS performance.

On the NFS server, use nfsstat -s, and on the NFS client, use nfsstat -c. On the server, the calls column (output from nfsstat -s) reports the total number of RPC calls received. The badcalls column reports the total number of RPC calls rejected. The rejects could be due to security or to attempts to access an NFS file system for which the client has no permission. The nullrecv column reports the number of empty RPC packets received. The badlen column reports the number of packets received that were too short to be considered valid. The xdrcall column reports the number of RPC packets received that were poorly formatted, subsequently preventing the packet from being decoded.

On the NFS client, use nfsstat -c to monitor NFS performance. The retrans column (output from nfsstat -c) reports the number of retransmissions. The timeout column reports the number of calls that timed out after awaiting a reply from the NFS server. The wait column shows the number of times a call had to wait due to the unavailability of a client handle. The badxid reports the number of times that a reply received from the NFS server did not correspond to any outstanding call. If you are seeing a high number of retransmissions and `badxids`, your network may be dropping packets, thereby forcing the packet to be resubmitted. You should monitor your network traffic to determine if a lot of collisions or packet drops are occurring. If the value of timeout or wait is high, it is likely that there is a server bottleneck. Monitor the disk statistics on the NFS server to check for I/O bottlenecks.

3.21.1   NFS VERSION 3

Solaris 2.5 and HP-UX 11.0 include NFS Version 3. NFS Version 3 offers several performance enhancements over NFS Version 2 and increases read and write throughput. NFS Version 3 also improves local client cache utilization and reduces server lookup and write requests.

NFS Version 2 has a maximum buffer size limitation of 8K, subsequently limiting the amount of NFS data that can be transferred over the network at one time. NFS Version 3 relaxed this limitation improving NFS transmission efficiency by transmitting larger amounts of data. This also helps NFS to more effectively utilize high-bandwidth network communication such as FDDI and Fast Ethernet.

NFS Version 3 improves NFS performance by improving the client-side cache utilization, using the TCP/IP protocol instead of UDP, improving read and write throughput, and relaxing the network bandwidth restriction. Caching the NFS file data including pages, attributes and directory information on the client helps reduce the NFS overhead of transferring data across the network. The process can read and write to the local cache and avoid network lookups. This helps reduce the call frequency of popular NFS call procedures such as `read`, `readdir`, `readlink`, and `lookup`. Caching significantly increases NFS client performance and enhances server scalability. This translates into clients getting faster access to file data via a fast local cache. Also, the *read-ahead* feature helps NFS clients that are reading files sequentially. NFS detects that the file is being read sequentially and brings the data into the local client cache. Hence, when the process requests the next set of data, it is already present in the local cache. This increases the performance of sequential reads.

NFS Version 3 increases write throughput by eliminating the synchronous writes requirement while maintaining the advantages of the *close-to-open* semantics. The close-to-open semantics refers to when an application closes a file, all the outstanding data is written to the file on the server before the close can complete. This is done to ensure file data consistency. The NFS Version 3 client significantly reduces the number of write requests to the server by grouping multiple requests and then writing the batch through to the server's cache. A commit is then subsequently issued which causes the server to write all the data to stable storage simultaneously. This is known as *safe asynchronous writes*. Safe asynchronous writes considerably reduce the number of server write requests, thereby improving write throughput. The writes are considered safe because status information on the data is maintained which indicates whether or not the data has been stored successfully. The client can query the status information to determine if the server crashed before the commit request once the server is restored.

3.22 NFS AND DATABASE

The NFS service is a kernel service and has a higher priority than user processes. Avoid mixing NFS servers with database servers. In other words, do not set up your database server to act also as an NFS server. NFS requests always take priority over user processes (in this case Oracle). Therefore, Oracle processes may see longer wait times due to NFS requests. In some cases, when NFS experiences timeouts and messages such as "NFS server not responding" appear on the client systems, it can cause the NFS server to halt all other processing until NFS services are restored. For this reason, you should not set up your database server as an NFS server. Separate your database servers from NFS servers.

Do not use NFS file systems to create Oracle data files or redo log files. Oracle issues nondeferred writes to guarantee data consistency once data is written to Oracle files. NFS cannot guarantee this same level of consistency. Therefore, do not use NFS file system-based files within your Oracle database.

3.23 USING THE AUTOMOUNTER

The automounter is a daemon that handles the mounting and unmounting of NFS file systems. The automounter mounts the file system upon use, and unmounts the file system if it is idle for a period of time. This can increase performance by reducing the overhead of mounted file systems that are infrequently used and are idle most of the time. On Solaris, to set up the automounter, you need to configure the /etc/auto_master file to include the /etc/auto_direct file as a search path. Then, place your mount entries in the /etc/auto_direct file. The automounter scans the /etc/auto_direct file and mounts and unmounts the specified file systems. You can also use the automounter equivalent namespace maps in the YP, NIS, or NIS+ naming service. On HP, you can configure the /etc/auto.direct file to set up the automounter. On HP, the automounter unmounts the file system if the file system is not accessed within the default five-minute interval. Using the automounter can reduce kernel resources and file system overhead by mounting the file system only upon use.

3.24 CONFIGURING AND SIZING THE DISK I/O SUBSYSTEMS

There are a tremendous number of disk I/O subsystem vendors, and it is often difficult to determine the appropriate vendor. Before you choose a vendor, it is important that you set some requirements for consideration.

First, the disk I/O subsystem vendor must support a volume manager. If the vendor does not support a volume manager, do not consider this vendor. Without a volume manager, striping and disk administration will be extremely difficult.

Second, for a database application, do not consider any vendor that insists on selling you large disk drives such as 18-G drives. For a database application, the best performance is obtained by distributing I/O across multiple spindles and controllers. The larger the size of the disk, the smaller number of disks you will have to distribute I/O. As far as optimal size, the Seagate Cheetah 4.5-G or 9.1-G 10,000 RPM disks are optimal disk drives for database applications. Try to avoid disk drives larger than 9 G for a database application. Realizing that database sizes are growing at an exponential rate and disk drive and disk array vendors are focusing on capacity, small disk drives such as the 2 G or even 4 G may no longer be available. However, the logic is that the more spindles you have, the better your I/O performance since you will have more disks to spread your data across. For example, four 4.5-G disks are better than having one 18-G disk. Larger disks such as the 18-G drives have their appropriate use, but a database server is not one of them. Larger disk drives work well for NFS servers, Web servers, file system staging areas, operating system binaries, software packages, and documentation.

Third, make sure that, whatever disk vendor you choose, your system's hardware vendor (if different than the disk vendor) supports the configuration fully. If you intend to run Oracle, you should contact Oracle to verify that Oracle supports the disk vendor you are considering.

Fourth, avoid any nonopen proprietary disk I/O subsystem vendors at all costs. Not doing so may impede your future ability to migrate to newer server technologies. It may also hinder your ability to migrate the disk subsystems to different platforms. For example, avoid disk I/O subsystems that do not allow you to turn off certain options, such as mirroring or RAID. The disk I/O subsystem you purchase should allow you to configure the disk in many different ways. This enables you to configure the disks appropriately to an application's requirements.

Lastly, choose a disk vendor that has an extremely reliable product and an excellent track record for customer service. A reliable product will help foster a high system up-time percentage. The excellent customer service track record will help minimize downtime during media failures as the vendor will take all efforts to rush on-site to correct the problem. As a customer, the last thing you want is to sit idle and wait several hours for a service engineer to come and replace a disk, while your system remains down.

These are the five basic rules you should keep in mind when considering a disk I/O subsystem vendor. If you use Sun Servers, you should use the SPARC Storage arrays. The new storage arrays are much more stable and provide tremendous functionality. The new storage arrays use a fast 100-M/second fiber optic connection between the server and the storage array. The storage arrays also allow you to easily migrate to the Sun Cluster environment should you decide to use Oracle Parallel Server in the future. If you use HP Servers, you can use either HP disk or EMC disk. EMC has a close partnership with HP. The EMC Symmetrix disk I/O subsystem uses a large cache (between 1 G and 4 G, depending on the configuration), which can increase database performance by reducing physical I/O. On Sequent, you can use the pbay disk drives, the EMC Symmetrix Unit, or the Clariion Disk Arrays.

Choosing a disk I/O subsystem vendor can be difficult. Following the five guidelines listed previously can help make the decision quicker and clearer. For a database server, the core component is the disk I/O subsystem. An unreliable and poorly performing disk I/O subsystem can wreak havoc on your environment. If you are considering multiple disk I/O subsystem vendors, you may want to request that each vendor provide a loaner unit for benchmarking and testing. This will assist you in making the selection because you will have had hands-on experience in testing reliability, performance, openness, functionality, and scalability.

Chapter 4

APPLICATION TUNING: ELIMINATING THE SQL BOTTLENECK

The application is a core component of any system. It is critical that the application obtain a high level of performance. A poorly designed application can hinder overall performance regardless of the computing power running the application. If the application does not scale or does not make use of parallel processing, adding more hardware provides little, if any, gain. It is important that the application be designed properly, and that it be implemented in such a way that it is permitted to scale and to maintain a high level of performance. In this chapter, I intend to offer recommendations on how to tune an application with the goal of maximizing scalability and performance.

4.1   APPLICATION ARCHITECTURE

When an application is designed, it is critical that its architecture be robust and solid. The architecture must allow the application to scale as more users are added. For example, designing a database application for which the majority of the processing is in one process hinders the application's scalability. You should distribute the application architecture as much as possible to allow for a more modular design. This also aids in debugging. If you are designing a multiplatform application, you may want to consider using a virtual layer and then allowing the virtual layer to call the platform-specific routines. A virtual layer helps isolate the application from the platform-specific issues by providing a consistent generic layer (virtual layer) on top of the platform-specific extensions. See Figure 4.1.

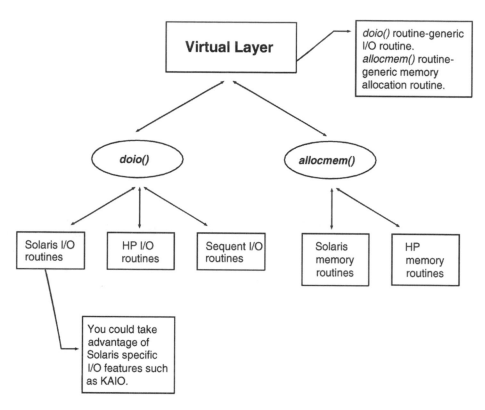

FIGURE 4.1   Virtual layer model.

The virtual layer not only allows you to take advantage of specific features of the platform, but it also provides for a very modular application in which specific platform layers can be modified without also changing the other layers. Although designing a virtual layer can be extremely complex, if you are designing a large-scale platform-independent application, it is well worth the effort.

The virtual layer should also be extended to error handling. Avoid hard-coding specific error numbers in the code. Use header files to store platform-specific error codes, or preferably store the error codes and descriptions in the database. This will allow you to change the error codes and descriptions easily by simply updating the database without recompiling code .

The performance of an application is highly dependent on its design and architecture. You need to spend a legitimate amount of time designing the application, and you must give careful thought to implementation issues, such as security, process management, memory management, error handling, and concurrency. You should also consider platform-specific issues, such as platform-specific performance features. The virtual layer enables your application to take advantage of platform-specific functionality while still maintaining the overall integrity of the application.

When you design the application, especially if it is a large-scale application, you need to think in parallel and asynchronously. Avoid coding practices in which routines wait a long time on processing or resources and thereby cause an application bottleneck. Divide larger tasks into many smaller tasks, and try to execute those tasks in parallel. For example, if you need to read data from two separate and independent tables, do not execute the queries serially. Execute the queries in parallel. For example, if writing a PRO*C program, you could either `fork()` and `exec()` multiple processes, thus allowing the queries to execute concurrently. Or, a more preferred method is to create multiple threads within the PRO*C program itself. Oracle 7.3 provides PRO*C 2.2, which allows for the use of threads within a PRO*C program. If you use threads, you can create multiple threads and then have each thread execute a separate query.

4.2 DEVELOPMENT ENVIRONMENT

You should use a source version control system, such as PVCS or RCS, and a project management and methodology tool during application design and development. The source control system allows for version control maintenance of source code, as well as permitting multiple team members to work on the same application. The source code control system helps to prevent team members from overwriting one another's changes. The project management system helps the project leader track dates and deliverables. It also helps manage the workload by distributing modules of the application to the team members. The methodology tool helps foster a modular design by documenting the individual components and modules of the application. The methodology allows you to observe the dependencies between the modules.

In addition to the source control system and methodology tool, you also must have a complete set of GUI debugging and regression testing tools. These tools will allow you to debug your application as well as perform regression testing on the application. The regression testing helps you catch bugs before the application is moved into production. It can also help you measure scalability by simulating multiple users.

4.3 TUNING PRO*C APPLICATIONS

PRO*C is Oracle's precompiler for the C language. As of Oracle 7.2/ PRO*C 2.1, Oracle has provided support for C++, which allows you to code your application using C++ as well as C. The pre-compiler enables you to embed SQL statements as well as invoke PL/SQL statements that include stored procedures. The precompiler offers you SQL and PL/SQL functionality as well as the power of the host language itself. The flow of a PRO*C program is shown in Figure 4.2.

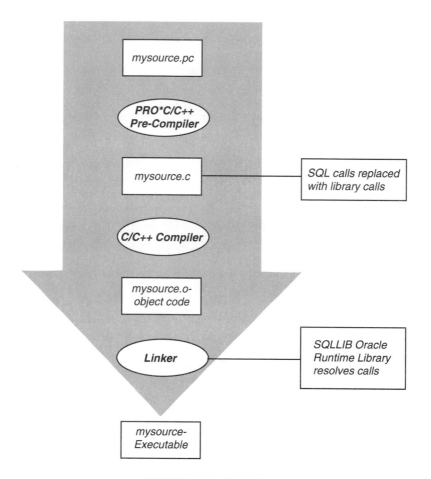

FIGURE 4.2 PRO*C process flow.

In Figure 4.2, the source code file (`mysource.pc`) is passed through the PRO*C precompiler, generating a modified source program file. The modified source program file contains library calls in place of the SQL statements. The modified source program then is passed through the compiler and/or linker, and an executable is produced. The linker uses the SQLLIB run-time library to resolve the calls.

There are several techniques to increase performance that you can use to tune a PRO*C application, which include using the array interface, client-shared library, and reducing the SQL call overhead.

4.3.1 USING ARRAYS IN PRO*C

You should use the array processing feature of PRO*C when processing transactions. The array interface allows you to declare a local C array and populate it with values. Then the array can be used to perform an insert, update, or delete. You can also use arrays to fetch data from Oracle. The array interface increases performance by reducing the SQL calls from the number of records to be processed to a single call. For example, if you wanted to read 1,000 rows from the database, the traditional method is to open a cursor and loop through each fetch until all 1,000 rows are retrieved. This results in 1,000 SQL Fetch calls. If you are running in a networked environment in which the application runs on a server other than the database server, this can increase the network traffic and reduce overall performance. Using an array of 1,000 elements results in only one SQL fetch call. The following is an example of array processing within PRO*C:

Example: *batch_array.pc*

```
#define BATCH_SIZE    1000
#define ORACLE_SUCCESS (sqlca.sqlcode == 0)
#define ORACLE_NUM_ROWS_PROCESSED (sqlca.sqlerrd[2])
#define ORACLE_CODE (sqlca.sqlcode)
#define PRODUCT_DESC_LEN   30

#define SUCCESS 0
#define FAILURE -1


int open_cursor (............)
{

        EXEC SQL DECLARE lpcursor CURSOR FOR
            SELECT PRODUCT_NUM, PRODUCT_DESC
            FROM PRODUCT
            WHERE product_num = :lproduct_num;

        if (!ORACLE_SUCCESS)
        {
         fprintf (stderr,"Unable to Declare Cursor, Oracle Error#:
                %d\n",ORACLE_CODE);
         return (FAILURE);
        }


        EXEC SQL OPEN lpcursor;

        if (!ORACLE_SUCCESS)
        {
         fprintf (stderr,"Unable to Open Cursor, Oracle Error#:
                %d\n",ORACLE_CODE);
         return (FAILURE);
        }
        return (SUCCESS);
```

(continued)

```
}


int fetch_cursor (............................)
{

        /**** Declare the batch arrays and batch size variable  ****/

        int batch_size;
#ifdef PROC8

        /** In PRO*C 8, we can take advantage of the array of
            structures feature.  **/

        struct sproduct
                {
                    int product_num;
                    char product_desc[PRODUCT_DESC_LEN];
                } asproduct[BATCH_SIZE];
#else

    int product_num[BATCH_SIZE];
    char product_desc[BATCH_SIZE][PRODUCT_DESC_LEN];

#endif /* PROC8 */

    /**** this routine assumes a database connection has been
          established *****/

    if (open_cursor() == SUCCESS)
    {

    batch_size=BATCH_SIZE;
    do
    {

#ifdef PROC8

        /* Fetch into the array of structures */

            EXEC SQL FOR :batch_size
                    FETCH lpcursor INTO :asproduct;

#else

        /* If not using PRO*C 8, fetch into the individual
           arrays */
```

```
                    EXEC SQL FOR :batch_size
                         FETCH lpcursor INTO :product_num,
                                              :product_desc;

        #endif  /* PROC8 */


          /****** Code to Process the Array/Batch  ********/


          }
          while (ORACLE_SUCCESS)


        }



}


int update_batch (…………………….)
{


        int batch_size;
        int product_num[BATCH_SIZE];
        char product_desc[BATCH_SIZE][PRODUCT_DESC_LEN];



        /**** this routine assumes a database connection has been
             established *****/

        batch_size=BATCH_SIZE;      /** Set batch size **/

        EXEC SQL FOR :batch_size    /** Update Batch **/
             UPDATE PRODUCT
             SET PRICE = PRICE * 1.10
             WHERE PRODUCT_NUM = :product_num;


        if (!ORACLE_SUCCESS)
        {
          fprintf (stderr,"Unable to Update Batch, Oracle Error#:
                %d\n",ORACLE_CODE);
          return (FAILURE);
        }



}
```

Using arrays to perform SQL operations can considerably reduce SQL call overhead as well as network overhead if running in a distributed environment. There are a few things to remember when using arrays in PRO*C. The first is that with PRO*C releases prior to PRO*C release 8, you cannot use an array of structures within PRO*C. You can, however, use arrays within a single structure to perform batch operations. PRO*C 8.0 does allow you to utilize an array of structures to perform batch SQL and other object-type operations. Using an array of structures allows for more elegant programming and also offers the application developer more flexibility in organizing the data structures. If you use array processing, remember to declare the same length for each array if you are using multiple items within a single batch operation. Therefore, declare a standard batch size, declare all arrays based on the batch size, and use the `FOR :batch_size` clause when you perform SQL operations to specify explicitly the number of rows to be processed. The second thing to remember is that for insert, update, delete, and select statements, `sqlca.sqlerrd[2]` reports the number of rows processed. For batch fetches, `sqlca.sqlerrd[2]` reports the cumulative sum of rows processed. In some cases, using the array interface increased performance 1000 percent. For more information on array processing in PRO*C, refer to the *Pro*C/C++ Precompiler Programmer's Guide* (Using Host Arrays section).

4.3.1.1   Selecting the Batch Size

The maximum batch size is currently 32K. However, in some cases, large batch sizes can reduce performance. If running in a networked environment, larger batch sizes greatly increase the amount of network traffic between the application and the Oracle server process. For networks with heavy traffic or networks experiencing performance problems, using a large batch size can have a negative effect on performance. A large number of columns, especially those with long row lengths, can cause a slow batch operation. Therefore, choose an ideal batch size operation by making the batch size parameter dynamically configurable upon execution, either through some startup configuration file or a pass-in parameter. My recommendation is that you start small, such as 500 for a batch size, and increment this figure nominally until you achieve the best performance. You may find that smaller numbers provide the best performance; however, larger batch sizes generally offer better performance for small SQL-size operations with a minimal number of columns.

When you use batch arrays to process SQL statements in your PRO*C application, do not statically allocate arrays or structures. Always allocate the arrays or structures dynamically by using a memory allocation routine such as `malloc()`. This enables you to free the batch array or structure once it is no longer needed. This also reduces application startup overhead by allocating only the amount of memory needed. The previously provided example statically allocates the arrays. However, this example is to show only the use of arrays in PRO*C. You should always allocate and de-allocate the arrays or structures dynamically to ensure that sufficient memory exists. Also, use the `FOR :batch_size` clause when you perform SQL operations to specify explicitly the number of rows to be processed.

4.3.2 LINKING WITH THE SHARED LIBRARY

The PRO*C compiler version 2.1 and above (Oracle7 release 7.2 and above) added support for C++ as well as a client-shared library. In previous releases of PRO*C, all PRO*C executables were statically linked and subsequently resulted in executables of 2–3 M in size on the average. In PRO*C releases 2.1 and above, a client-shared library, libclntsh.so, was provided so that PRO*C applications could be linked with this shared library. Linking with the shared library significantly reduces the size of PRO*C executables from 2–3 M to 50K–100K on the average. This results not only in massive disk storage savings but also saves compile time and execution time. Since the executables are linked with the shared library, only functions that are called are paged in, which increases the performance of the executable since the memory requirements drop significantly. Also, because it is now a shared library, multiple users running PRO*C and OCI applications will benefit since the shared library enables multiple users to share the memory pages without having to separately reload the library in memory. In order to make use of the client-shared library, relink your PRO*C and OCI programs with the libclntsh.so library (-lclntsh) or libclntsh.sl on HP.

On UNIX platforms, use the proc.mk make file provided in $ORACLE_HOME/precomp/demo/proc directory for Oracle 7.3. For Oracle 8.0, use the demo_proc.mk file provided in $ORACLE_HOME/precomp/demo/proc to build the sample PRO*C programs or as a template make file for your application. Oracle8/PRO*C 8 links with the client-shared library by default. For Oracle 7.2, the proc.mk file is located in $ORACLE_HOME/proc/demo. Set the environment variable ORA_CLIENT_LIB to shared before compiling. For example,

```
myhost> setenv ORA_CLIENT_LIB shared   (C-Shell)
myhost> make -f proc.mk EXE=mysample \    *** 7.2/7.3
          OBJS=mysample.o

myhost> make -f demo_proc.mk build   \   *** 8.0
          EXE=mysample OBJS=mysample.o
```

4.3.3 PRO*C COMPILE OPTIONS

There are several PRO*C compiler options that can increase cursor management performance. The HOLD_CURSOR compile option, when set to YES, causes Oracle to hold the cursor handle that is associated with the SQL statement in the cursor cache. This helps eliminate reparsing should the SQL statement be executed again later in the PRO*C application. This can increase performance by eliminating the need to reparse the SQL statement since the cursor can be reused. HOLD_CURSOR set to NO causes the cursor handle to be reused following the execution of the SQL statement and the closing of the cursor. Set HOLD_CURSOR=YES to increase the cursor cache hit ratio.

The RELEASE_CURSOR compile option, when set to YES, releases the private SQL area associated with the SQL statement cursor. This means that the parsed statement for the SQL statement is removed. If the SQL statement is reexecuted later, the SQL statement must be parsed again, and a private SQL area must be allocated. When RELEASE_CURSOR=NO, the cursor handle and the private SQL area are not reused unless the number of open cursors exceeds MAXOPENCURSORS. Set RELEASE_CURSOR=NO and HOLD_CURSOR=YES to increase the cursor cache hit ratio. Set the MAXOPENCURSORS compile option to the maximum number of cursors used in your application. When setting MAXOPENCURSORS, allow for recursive SQL cursors.

In PRO*C 8, you can increase the performance of the object cache by using the PRO*C compiler DURATION option to specify the duration of pinned objects in the object cache. The default value for DURATION is TRANSACTION which causes the object to be implicitly unpinned upon transaction completion. You can set DURATION=SESSION in order to allow the object to be unpinned following termination of the connection. Setting DURATION=SESSION can improve object cache performance if subsequent transactions need access to the same objects already pinned in the object cache.

4.3.4 PARALLEL PROCESSING USING PRO*C

It is important that you subdivide the tasks in your PRO*C application, allowing them to be parallelized. You can do this by using the fork() and exec() calls to invoke multiple PRO*C applications, or preferably by using the new threads feature provided with PRO*C 2.2/Oracle 7.3. Using the threads feature can help you parallelize your application by creating several threads. For example, you may have several inserter threads that insert data into different tables. You may also have multiple deleter or updater threads.

The new threads option allows a high degree of parallelism by establishing separate contexts via the EXEC SQL CONTEXT ALLOCATE statement, and each thread may use a different context to perform SQL operations. Refer to the section on threads programming in the *Pro*C/C++ Precompiler Programmer's Guide* for more information on the use of threads within PRO*C. Using threads can increase the performance of your PRO*C application significantly by processing SQL statements simultaneously via lightweight threads. Using threads is more efficient and elegant than the fork() and exec() technique that is often used to create multiple processes. Remember that when a fork() is issued from a PRO*C application following an established connection, the child process will not be able to make use of the connection. Although the connection to Oracle is treated as a file descriptor (socket), and fork() duplicates all open file descriptors, the Process ID (PID) of the process that establishes the connection is also used to manage the connection. Therefore, after the fork() and exec(), you may get errors such as ORA-1012 (not logged on) when SQL statements are issued from the child process. If you intend to use fork() and exec() within your PRO*C program, the preferred method is to issue the fork() and exec() before any connection is established, and then establish separate connections in each process (parent and child).

4.3.5 OBJECT CACHE

PRO*C 8 provides an area of client-side memory used to interface to the database objects known as the object cache. The two object interfaces, associative and navigational, are used to manipulate transient copies of the objects and persistent objects, respectively. Objects allocated via the EXEC SQL ALLOCATE statement are transient copies of persistent objects in the Oracle database. Once fetched into the object cache, updates can be made to the transient copies but require explicit SQL statements to make the changes persistent to the database. You can use the EXEC SQL FREE statement to free an object from the object cache. You can also use the EXEC SQL CACHE FREE ALL to free the entire object cache memory. The associative interface is typically used when accessing a large collection of objects or objects that are not referencable, or performing update or insert operations that apply to a set of objects. The navigational interface is generally used when accessing a small set of objects consisting of explicit costly join predicates or performing many small changes to distinct objects. In the navigational interface, the EXEC SQL OBJECT FLUSH statement flushes the persistent changes to the database.

Oracle8 provides two init.ora parameters that control the optimal size of the object cache. The init.ora parameters object_cache_max_size_percent and object_cache_optimal_size specify the maximum size of the object cache and the size that the object cache will be reduced to when it exceeds the maximum size, respectively. The object_cache_max_size_percent specifies the maximum size of the object cache as the allowed percentage of growth beyond the optimal size. When the size of the object cache exceeds the maximum size, it is reduced to the size of object_cache_optimal_size.

4.4 THE MAKE FILE

When you develop applications, always use make files to compile and link code. Do not use manual compile scripts to produce executables. This is especially true of Oracle PRO*C applications. Oracle often provides new make files with new releases that incorporate new functionality. Therefore, if you use manual compile scripts, code that you compiled under a previous release may not link properly under a new release of the Oracle products. If you are developing PRO*C applications, use the sample make files provided by Oracle (proc.mk or demo_proc.mk) to compile and link your application. Make files provide a tremendous amount of functionality by checking and resolving dependencies and reporting errors caused by dependency violation. Make sure you check your make files into your version control system so that you know which make file is needed to build certain applications.

4.5   TUNING SQL

The beauty of the SQL language is that the same SQL statement can semantically be represented syntactically in numerous different ways. In other words, the statement can be rewritten in many different ways but still produce the same results. The key to tuning SQL is to maximize on this principal of the SQL language. Increasing the performance of SQL statements is often done by rewriting the SQL statement more efficiently. Understanding the Oracle optimizer and the SQL execution path can help you tune SQL effectively. The Oracle optimizer provides two methods of optimization: rule-based and cost-based. Each optimization method provides techniques for tuning SQL statements for optimal performance.

4.5.1   RULE-BASED OPTIMIZER

The Rule-Based Optimizer (RBO) chooses the execution plan of a SQL statement with the lowest rank—the idea being that the lowest ranking execution plan should be faster than a higher ranking execution plan. The rule-based optimizer selects execution plans based on a heuristic ranking. The rule-based approach, as the term suggests, uses rules (or ranks) to determine the optimal execution plan for a SQL statement. Table 4.1 summaries the different ranks.[1]

TABLE 4.1   Rule-based optimizer access path rank

RANK	ACCESS PATH
1	single row by ROWID
2	single row by cluster join
3	single row by hash cluster key with unique or primary key
4	single row by unique or primary key
5	cluster join
6	hash cluster key
7	indexed cluster key
8	composite key
9	single-column indexes
10	bounded range search on indexed columns
11	unbounded ranges search on indexed columns
12	sort-merge join
13	MAX or MIN of indexed function
14	ORDER BY on indexed columns
15	full table scan

1. *Oracle7 Server Concepts Manual*, Release 7.3, p. 13.

The rule-based approach uses the ranks of the access paths listed earlier to determine the optimal execution plan for a SQL statement. As can be seen from the table, a full-table scan has the highest rank. This means that Oracle will always consider index scans over full-table scans, even if a full-table scan may be faster than the index scan. To choose rule-based optimization, you can set the init.ora parameter `optimizer_mode=RULE`, or use the alter session command to set `optimizer_goal=RULE`. You can also use the RULE hint as part of the query. A discussion on hints will follow later in Section 4.5.3.

The RBO is best used in an OLTP database where the object structure is relatively static. More specifically, for an OLTP application that will always have a static number of tables with a static number of indexes (primary or other), consistent performance may be guaranteed by using the RBO. If the paths remain the same, meaning that the indexes will always be there, and the type of access is mostly single-row access as in an OLTP application, then the RBO can help foster consistent performance. As opposed to the cost-based optimizer, the RBO does not consider object statistics. Execution plans are determined by order of rank. The RBO can be used in your favor for an OLTP application that remains static in terms of dictionary structure but changes often in terms of space and data. In this case, the cost-based optimizer may use different execution plans based on the statistics, and therefore you may not always obtain the same execution plan with the cost-based optimizer. The RBO is often used by pure OLTP sites to help maintain execution consistency. However, keep in mind that Oracle's direction is to migrate to the cost-based optimizer. Major enhancements and improvements have been made to the cost-based optimizer that have made it much more flexible and efficient than the RBO.

4.5.2 COST-BASED OPTIMIZER

The Cost-Based Optimizer (CBO) uses statistics to help choose the most optimal execution plan. In the case of the CBO, the most optimal plan is the plan that has the lowest estimated cost. The CBO uses object-level statistics to compute the cost required to execute the SQL statement. The statistics can be computed (or refreshed) by using the analyze command. For example to compute statistics on a table, you would use the command

```
SQL> analyze table <table_name> compute statistics;
```

You can also estimate the statistics, as compute statistics will scan the entire object and compute exact statistics on data distribution, size, extents, and additional object-level statistics. If the object is very large, the compute statistics may take a long time—as in hours or even days. In my experience, a 10-G table on a highly tuned multiprocessor server took 23 hours to analyze, and 30 G of temporary tablespace extents. The analyze command does not currently parallelize its work. Hence, large tables can take a long time to analyze as well as plenty of temporary tablespace space. In Oracle 7.2 and 7.3, the estimation of statistics has been improved over previous versions, leading to more accurate statistics. In Oracle8, object statistics can be gathered at the individual partition level. The key to the cost-based optimizer is the *selectivity* and the amount of work needed to execute the statement.

The *selectivity* is the percentage of rows that the query selects from the table. The selectivity is key in determining the execution path. The CBO determines the selectivity by utilizing the statistics. If the statistics are not present, the CBO uses estimated statistics to choose the execution plan. To ensure an optimal CBO execution plan, you should run the analyze statistics command on your objects. The statistics computed by the analyze command allows the CBO to make a much more intelligent decision since the CBO will have a better idea about the data uniqueness and data distribution with the statistics than without.

The CBO chooses the best execution plan based on the least cost. In order to be effective, the CBO needs accurate statistics. Often these statistics are not available due to a dynamic environment in which large amounts of data are being inserted, updated, or deleted. There is also the case of the DSS in which large summary tables are often dropped and rebuilt. Recomputing statistics on these large tables may take too long. For this reason, and many more, Oracle offers SQL hints as an approach to manually tuning SQL. In most cases, you will know far more about your data distribution than will the CBO. This is especially true if the objects you are accessing have no statistics. SQL hints provide the ability to tune SQL statements manually by overriding the default CBO execution plan.

4.5.3 USING HINTS

Hints can increase the performance of your SQL statement substantially. Coupling your intimate knowledge of the data with your knowledge of the Oracle Server, you can use hints to tune your SQL statements to achieve high throughput. Before I discuss the different types of hints, I must make two recommendations: Hints may change between releases, and new hints may be introduced with new releases. For these reasons, avoid hard-coding hints in applications. If a hint is later made obsolete, your application may not perform as expected. This may require you to make changes to the application and force you to redeploy the application following the changes. I recommend that you use views if you choose to use hints. For example, consider the following view:

```
SQL> Create OR Replace VIEW V_PROD
        as select /*+ FULL (p)
                       FULL (c)
                       PARALLEL (p,10)
                       PARALLEL (c,10)
                       USE_HASH (p c) */
          p.product_number,
          p.product_description,
          c.customer_name,
          c.customer_number
        FROM PRODUCT p,
            CUSTOMER c
        WHERE (p.customer_number=c.customer_number);
```

In this example, the view is created with the optimal hints. In this case, the product and customer table are joined with a hash-join using the parallel query option with a degree of 10. Then, your application can simply issue normal SQL operations against this view because the hints are already part of the view. This will allow you to tune the query easily or to change the hints in the future simply by re-creating the view. You will not need to change any application code solely for the purpose of tuning the query since the query is self-contained in the view. You may have to create a lot of views, one for each tuned query. However, this is still a better approach than hard-coding hints in applications.

4.5.4 THE EXPLAIN PLAN

I cannot emphasize enough the importance of the explain plan. Explain plans are crucial to tuning SQL and examining execution plans. The explain plan lists the execution plan that the Oracle optimizer will choose for a given query. This allows you to observe the execution plan before actually submitting the query. You can use the explain plan to analyze your queries, and tune the query before executing it. I am amazed at how often people submit queries (or other SQL statements) that run for hours and days and never run an explain plan on the query until after the fact. Always run an explain plan on every query you intend to use in a production application. This accomplishes two goals: First, it verifies that the query is correct by examining it in detail to ensure that the query returns the desired results. Second, it shows the execution plan of the query. If you feel the execution plan is optimal, then this is simply a confirmation. If the explain plan shows a poor execution plan, then you can tune the SQL statement using hints to obtain a better execution plan. To use the explain plan utility, you must have select permissions on the tables you are attempting to explain, as well as select and insert permissions on the PLAN_TABLE. You can create the explain plan table by running the $ORACLE_HOME/rdbms/admin/utlxplan.sql script. This creates an explain plan table. The following is an example of an explain plan:

```
SQL> explain plan
     set statement_id = 'call pattern'
     into plan_table
     FOR SELECT /*+ RULE */
        * from account a,
             branch b,
             teller t
     where (a.branch_id=b.branch_id) AND
           (b.branch_id=t.branch_id);
```

(continued)

```
ID   EXPLAIN_PLAN                                    POSITION

 0   SELECT STATEMENT
 1      MERGE JOIN                                        1
 2        SORT JOIN                                       1
 3          NESTED LOOPS                                  1
 4            TABLE ACCESS FULL   TELLER                  1
 5            TABLE ACCESS BY ROWID   BRANCH              2
 6              INDEX UNIQUE SCAN   IBRANCH               1
 7        SORT JOIN                                       2
 8          TABLE ACCESS FULL  ACCOUNT                    1
```

The execution path for the preceding query is shown in Figure 4.3. The execution plan shows the individual paths of the execution plan that are needed to execute the query. I strongly urge you to become familiar with explain and execution plans, if you are not

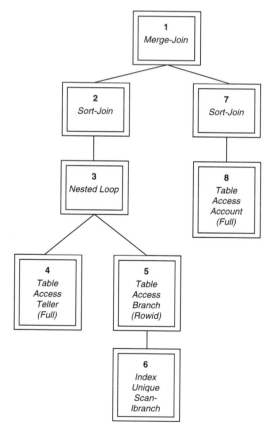

FIGURE 4.3 Query execution path.

already. You should also get into the habit of running explain plans on queries to ensure that the queries are correct and optimally tuned. I have witnessed cases where an explain plan on a query that ran for several hours was used to help tune the query immediately following the explain plan. The explain plan helped to determine the main bottleneck of the query, and the tuning of the query reduced the execution time from hours to seconds. You should not underestimate the power of tuning SQL. Poorly tuned queries that run for hours and days can be made to run in seconds or minutes. Familiarizing yourself with the optimizer execution plan and the explain plan utility will help you analyze and tune SQL statements more effectively.

4.5.5 THE HINTS

The list of hints, and a brief description of how you can make use of these hints when tuning SQL, follow. Again, to use hints, you must embed the hint string explicitly following the keywords select, update, or delete using either the `/*+ HINT */` syntax or `--+ HINT` syntax.

4.5.5.1 ALL_ROWS

The `ALL_ROWS` hint tells the CBO to optimize the statement with the goal of best throughput. The best throughput means that the statement should be executed such that total resource consumption is minimized. For example,

```
SQL> SELECT /*+ ALL_ROWS */
          count(*) from orders;
```

or

```
SQL> SELECT --+ ALL_ROWS
          count(*) from orders;
```

The `ALL_ROWS` hint is often used to tune a SQL statement by optimizing the processing of all the rows.

4.5.5.2 FIRST_ROWS

The `FIRST_ROWS` hint tells the CBO to optimize the statement with the goal of best response time. The best response means that the statement should be executed such that the minimum amount of resources are used to return the first set of rows. The `FIRST_ROWS` hint will always choose an index, if available, over a full-table scan, even if the full-table scan is faster. The `FIRST_ROWS` hint also causes the CBO to use a nested loop join over a sort-merge join whenever the associated table is the inner table of the nested loop. This avoids the overhead of the sort-merge operation. Remember, the goal here is to return the first set of rows the quickest way possible. Therefore, index scans and nested loop joins will be the fastest way to return the first set of rows. For statements using group by, set operators (UNION, INTERSECT, MINUS, UNION ALL), distinct operator, group functions, or FOR UPDATE clause, the CBO ignores the FIRST_ROWS hint because these operations require all the rows to be processed before returning the first row. FIRST_ROWS can be used for applications that need to see the first set of rows immediately and can wait to fetch the remaining set of rows. Prior to Oracle 7.2, the FIRST_ROWS implementation was faulty. Therefore, do not rely on this hint unless running Oracle 7.2 or higher.

4.5.5.3 CHOOSE

The CHOOSE hint tells the optimizer to choose either the CBO or the RBO depending on the availability of statistics. If no statistics are available for any of the tables involved in the statement, the RBO is used. If at least one table has statistics, the CBO is used.

4.5.5.4 RULE

The RULE hint causes the RBO to be used to optimize the statement. The RBO will use the 15-rank access path listed in Table 4.1. The RBO will choose the plan with the lowest ranking. You can use the RULE hint for OLTP applications to guarantee plan consistency. However, keep in mind that Oracle will be phasing out the RBO in future releases in favor of the CBO.

4.5.5.5 FULL

The FULL hint forces a full-table scan on the table specified. The syntax of the FULL hint is FULL (table name), or FULL (table alias name). Even if there is an index on the table, the FULL hint causes a full-table scan to be performed. This hint typically is used in DSS applications in conjunction with the PARALLEL hint.

4.5.5.6 ROWID

The ROWID hint uses ROWID to scan the table. The syntax of the ROWID hint is ROWID (table name), or ROWID (table alias name). You can use this hint in applications where the rowid is available. For example, suppose you fetch some rows from the database and now you want to update those rows. Instead of updating the rows with the standard where clause (selecting those rows of interest), update the rows using the rowids as part of the where clause and use the ROWID hint. When using this technique, you will also need to fetch the rowid values as part of the fetch statement, as well as lock the corresponding rows (to ensure the consistency of the rowids fetched).

4.5.5.7 CLUSTER or HASH

The CLUSTER hint causes a cluster key scan to be performed on the table. The syntax of the CLUSTER hint is CLUSTER (table name). The HASH hint causes a hash key scan to be used. The syntax of the HASH hint is HASH (table name).

4.5.5.8 INDEX or INDEX_COMBINE

The INDEX hint causes the specified index to be used. The INDEX hint forces the optimizer to not consider a full-table scan. The syntax of the INDEX hint is INDEX (table name, index name). This hint is very useful when multiple indexes are used in a query. You can use this hint to specify which index is used. The INDEX hint also works on bitmap indexes (provided in Oracle 7.3). You can also use the new hint provided with Oracle 7.3, INDEX_COMBINE, which has the same syntax as the INDEX hint. The INDEX_COMBINE hint causes the optimizer to use a Boolean combination of the bitmapped indexes specified in the hint.

4.5.5.9 AND_EQUAL

The AND_EQUAL hint causes multiple single-column indexes to be merged. The limit to the number of single-column indexes specified is currently five. The syntax of the AND_EQUAL hint is AND_EQUAL (table index index ...). This hint is very useful when multiple indexes on the same table are used within a query. You can use this hint to specify which indexes to merge. The AND_EQUAL hint is useful when many single-column indexes can be used together to reduce the selectivity of the query as opposed to scanning one index only.

4.5.5.10 USE_CONCAT

The USE_CONCAT hint, introduced in Oracle 7.2, forces combined OR predicates specified in the WHERE clause of the query to be transformed into a compound query via the UNION ALL operator. Without this hint, the transformation would occur only if the cost of the transformation is less than the cost without the transformation. The USE_CONCAT hint can be used with large table queries to help subdivide the larger query into multiple UNION ALL queries. This allows the multiple UNION ALL subqueries to proceed in parallel, which can increase performance over a single large query.

4.5.5.11 ORDERED

The ORDERED hint causes Oracle to join tables in the order the tables are listed in the FROM clause. For example,

```
SQL> SELECT /*+ ORDERED */
     count(*)
     FROM CUSTOMER C,
          ORDERS O,
          PARTS P
     WHERE (C.customer_id=O.customer_id) AND
           (O.partno=P.partno);
```

This causes Oracle first to join the customer table with the orders table and then to join the result of the first join with the parts table. The ORDERED hint can increase performance substantially by specifying small tables first, hopefully causing a reduction in the selectivity when later joined against the larger tables.

4.5.5.12 USE_NL or USE_MERGE or USE_HASH or USE_ANTI or USE_SEMI

The USE_NL hint causes a nested loop join to be used when joining tables. The table specified in the USE_NL hint is the table to be used as the inner table in the nested loop join. The USE_MERGE hint causes a sort-merge join to be used when joining tables. The table specified in the USE_MERGE hint is used to join with the previous resultant sets of a sort-merge join. The USE_HASH hint, introduced in Oracle 7.3, causes a hash join to be used when joining tables. For very large tables that have a good data distribution, hash joins can increase performance significantly. The USE_ANTI hint causes an anti-join to be used for NOT IN subqueries. The USE_SEMI hint causes a semi-join to be used. The syntax for the USE_NL, USE_MERGE, USE_HASH, USE_ANTI, and USE_SEMI hints are as follows: USE_NL (table1 table2 ...), USE_MERGE (table1 table2 ...), USE_HASH (table1 table2), USE_ANTI (table1 table2), and USE_SEMI (table1 table2).

4.5.5.13 PARALLEL or NOPARALLEL

The PARALLEL hint causes Oracle to parallelize a full-table scan or join operation by the degree of parallelization specified in the PARALLEL clause. The syntax for the PARALLEL hint is PARALLEL (table, degree). The NOPARALLEL hint causes the optimizer to disable parallel scanning of the table, even if the table was created with the PARALLEL clause. The syntax of the NOPARALLEL hint is NOPARALLEL (table). The NOPARALLEL hint can be used on small tables where the overhead of using a parallel query increases the time needed to scan the table. The hint can also be used in cases where the table's data is located on one or a few disks and parallelizing the query may have a negative effect.

4.5.5.14 CACHE or NOCACHE

The CACHE hint specifies that the blocks retrieved during a full-table scan for the table specified in the hint are to be placed at the most recently used end of the least recently used (LRU) list in the buffer cache. The CACHE hint can increase the performance of full-table scans for lookup tables that are relatively small by maintaining the table data blocks in the cache. The syntax of the CACHE hint is CACHE (table). The NOCACHE specifies that the blocks retrieved during a full-table scan for the table specified in the hint are to be placed at the least recently used end of the LRU list in the buffer cache. The NOCACHE hint can be used for large tables during a full-table scan so that the overhead of bringing the data blocks into the most recently used section of the buffer cache is reduced. The syntax of the NOCACHE hint is NOCACHE (table).

4.5.5.15 PUSH_SUBQ

The PUSH_SUBQ hint causes the evaluation of nonmerged subqueries to be done at the earliest possible place in the execution plan. This can improve performance by allowing subqueries that reduce the selectivity to be executed first, thereby reducing the number of rows processed upfront rather than near the end.

4.5.5.16 HASH_AJ or MERGE_AJ

The HASH_AJ or MERGE_AJ hints specify the use of an anti-join. An anti-join returns the rows that do not satisfy the predicate, as opposed to a standard join which would return those rows that match the right side and the left side of the join predicate. The anti-join is equivalent to the NOT IN subselect query. However, the NOT IN subselect typically uses a nested loop join to join the subselect with the parent query. The HASH_AJ and MERGE_AJ (introduced in Oracle 7.3) allow you to use a hash or merge-join for a nested subselect query using the NOT IN clause. The HASH_AJ or MERGE_AJ hints need to be specified in the nested subselect following the NOT IN clause to cause Oracle to use a hash or merge-join, respectively. The anti-join feature can increase performance for large subselects.

4.5.5.17 HASH_SJ or MERGE_SJ

Oracle 8.0.4 provides the HASH_SJ or MERGE_SJ hints in order to specify the use of a hash or merge semi-join. A semi-join improves the performance of certain EXISTS subqueries. A semi-join returns the rows that satisfy an EXISTS subquery and avoids the duplication of rows from the left side of the predicate when the subquery criteria can be satisfied by multiple rows on the right side. You can specify the HASH_SJ or MERGE_SJ hints in your query to use a hash or merge semi-join as opposed to using a nested-loop join which is the default for EXISTS subqueries. In order to enable the optimizer to consider semi-join access paths, set the init.ora parameter always_semi_join=HASH or always_semi_join=MERGE.

4.5.5.18 INDEX_FFS

Oracle 7.3.3 and Oracle8 provide a feature known as a fast full scan. The fast full scan feature allows you to perform a full index range scan in parallel. This is useful for data warehousing applications where queries often require scanning the entire table. Using the fast full scan feature, you can scan the index in parallel assuming the index columns satisfy your predicates. A fast full parallel index range scan will likely be faster than scanning the entire table since the index blocks make up less data than the entire data blocks. For example, if your table is 100 G in size, and your index is 10 G, performing a full scan on the index as opposed to the entire table will significantly reduce the amount of I/O needed to complete the query since you will be scanning a 10-G index versus a 100-G table. The syntax of the INDEX_FFS hint is INDEX_FFS (table index). To enable the optimizer to consider fast full scans, set the init.ora parameter fast_full_scan_enabled=TRUE.

4.5.5.19 `PARALLEL_INDEX` or `NOPARALLEL_INDEX`

Oracle8 provides the `PARALLEL_INDEX` or `NOPARALLEL_INDEX` hints that allow you to specify the degree of parallelism for index range scans for partitioned indexes. The syntax for the `PARALLEL_INDEX` hint is `PARALLEL_INDEX` (table index degree). The `NO_PARALLEL_INDEX` hint overrides any parallel settings for the index and its syntax is `NO_PARALLEL_INDEX` (table index).

4.5.5.20 `DRIVING_SITE`

Oracle8 provides a way to speed up distributed join queries by specifying the driving site for the join. The syntax for the `DRIVING_SITE` hint is `DRIVING_SITE` (table). For example, consider the following query:

```
SELECT /*+ DRIVING_SITE (o) */
           o.cust_no
           o.ord_no
FROM customer c,
       orders@reodb o
WHERE (c.cust_no = o.cust_no);
```

Without the `DRIVING_SITE` hint, the rows from the orders table from the remote database will be brought into the local database with the join being executed locally. Using the `DRIVING_SITE` hint, the customer rows will be sent to the remote database and joined with the orders table on the remote database. This will improve distributed query performance since it is likely that there will be fewer customer rows than orders rows. The `DRIVING_SITE` hint is useful for tuning distributed join queries that often join local tables with large-size remote database tables. Using the `DRIVING_SITE` hint, you can choose the driving table that makes the most sense, thereby reducing the data transmission and join workload.

4.5.5.21 `PUSH_PRED` or `NO_PUSH_PRED`

Oracle 8.0.4 provides the `PUSH_PRED` and `NO_PUSH_PRED` hints which allows the optimizer to push the individual join predicates down into the view when the query involves a view with multiple base tables on the right side of an outer join. This enables more efficient execution plans by transforming hash joins into nested loops and full-table scans into index scans. The `NO_PUSH_PRED` hint prevents the join predicates from being pushed into the view. To enable the optimizer to consider pushing the join predicates, set the `init.ora` parameter `push_join_predicate=TRUE`. The syntax for these hints are `PUSH_PRED` (table) and `NO_PUSH_PRED` (table).

4.5.5.22 `MERGE` or `NO_MERGE`

Oracle 8.0.4 provides the `MERGE` and `NO_MERGE` hints which control whether or not a complex view or subquery within a query is evaluated prior to the surrounding query. The `NO_MERGE` hint causes the optimizer not to merge the view. The syntax for these hints are MERGE (table) and NO_MERGE (table). Set the `init.ora` parameter `complex_view_merging=TRUE` to enable the optimizer to consider merging the views.

4.5.5.23 APPEND or NO_APPEND

The Oracle8 hints APPEND and NO_APPEND specify for an insert statement whether or not data is appended to the table and the existing free space in the blocks is used. The APPEND hint causes the data to be appended to the table in the similar fashion as a direct load, and the existing free space in the blocks to not be used. The NO_APPEND hint can be used to override the APPEND mode.

4.5.5.24 STAR or STAR_TRANSFORMATION

The STAR hint causes the optimizer to choose a star diagram execution plan. The star plan places the largest table, usually the fact table, as the last table in the join order and uses a nested loop join on the concatenated index on the fact table to join with the smaller dimension tables. In Oracle8, the STAR_TRANSFORMATION hint provides an alternative method to executing star queries efficiently. The typical method is to perform a Cartesian product on the dimension tables and then join the result via a nested loop index join to the fact table. The Cartesian method works well for a schema with a dense fact table and a small number of dimensions. When there are a large number of dimensions and the fact table is sparse, the star transformation method is a more optimal method. Essentially, the star transformation method transforms the star query into subqueries using bitmap index access paths on the individual constraints without the need of performing a Cartesian product and requiring a concatenated index on the fact table. The various bitmap indexes can then be merged together to complete the query. To enable star transformations you can use the STAR_TRANSFORMATION hint or set the Oracle8 `init.ora` parameter `star_transformation_enabled=TRUE`.

4.5.6 TUNING BY SELECTIVITY

The best way to think of all these different hints is as a large tool box. Selecting the right tools for the right job is what enables you to perform a task adequately. Similarly, selecting the right hints for the right types of queries enables you to maximize your SQL performance. The goal of tuning SQL is first to examine what is being done, how it is being done, and what the selectivity of the query is For example, consider the following query:

```
SQL> SELECT
     count(*)
     FROM CUSTOMER C,
          ADDRESS A,
          ZIP Z
     WHERE (C.ADDRESS_ID=A.ADDRESS_ID) AND
           (A.ZIP_ID = Z.ZIP_ID) AND
           (Z.ZIP_CODE = '94065');
```

This query counts the number of customers who live in the zip code 94065. However, without statistics, it would be difficult to determine the proper execution order of the query. Common sense tells us that starting with the zip table is most optimal, followed by the addresses that reside in the specified zip code, and then followed by the join to the customer table. For example, if you joined the tables in the order listed in the FROM clause, you would scan every customer row and join it with its corresponding address row to determine if the customer's address was in the zip code specified. If the customer and address tables were large tables, this query could take a long time to run. Therefore, a more optimized version of the query is as follows:

```
SQL> SELECT /*+ ORDERED
                INDEX (Z ZIP_CODE_INDEX)
                INDEX (A ZIP_CODE_ID)
                INDEX (C ADDRESS_ID)
                USE_NL (Z A)
                USE_NL (A C) */
        count(*)
     FROM ZIP Z,
          ADDRESS A,
          CUSTOMER C
     WHERE (C.ADDRESS_ID=A.ADDRESS_ID) AND
           (A.ZIP_ID = Z.ZIP_ID) AND
           (Z.ZIP_CODE = '94065');
```

This query is a more optimized version than the original. This query will also return immediately if no addresses exist in the 94065 zip code. The original query would scan all customer rows regardless of which zip code they lived in. Although this may seem like an easy example, all queries (even complex) can be broken down into the individual join layers. Once broken down, you can determine the selectivity of the query by analyzing each subquery layer. The goal is to start with the layer that reduces the selectivity the most. This way you avoid scanning unnecessary rows. Always examine the selectivity of the query and then choose the appropriate set of hints to be used. Additional query tuning tips using hints are offered in Chapter 6.

4.5.7   USING PARALLEL QUERY

In some cases, the selectivity will always be large and cannot be reduced. This is very common with DSS applications that perform full scans and aggregate large amounts of data for the sake of analysis. In this case, use the parallel query option to parallelize the query. The parallel query option, introduced in Oracle 7.1, causes query slave processes to be created, and the base connection is transformed into the query coordinator. The query coordinator is then responsible for dividing the work across the query slaves. Once the query slaves complete their scan, the query coordinator is signaled, and a final merge is done merging the individual slaves. Figure 4.4 illustrates the parallel query option.

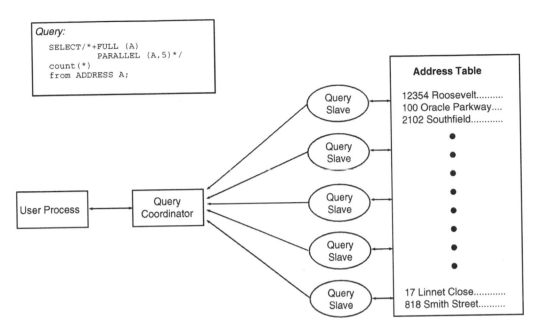

```
Query:
  SELECT/*+FULL (A)
            PARALLEL (A,5)*/
  count(*)
  from ADDRESS A;
```

Address Table

12354 Roosevelt..........
100 Oracle Parkway....
2102 Southfield...........

User Process

Query Coordinator

Query Slave

Query Slave

Query Slave

Query Slave

Query Slave

17 Linnet Close............
818 Smith Street..........

FIGURE 4.4　Parallel query option.

In Figure 4.4, the query uses the parallel query option. In this example, five query slaves (as specified by the degree of parallelism of five in the parallel hint) are spawned by the query coordinator. The query slaves each scan a section of the table and signal the query coordinator when complete. Once all the slaves have completed their scans, the query coordinator merges the query slaves and returns the result to the user process. Parallel query can be used to significantly reduce the time needed to scan a table.

The parallel query option can also be used to parallelize a join. For example, suppose you want to determine the total count of customers broken down by geographic region. The query might look something like this:

```
SQL> SELECT /*+ ORDERED
               FULL ( C)
               FULL (A)
               PARALLEL (C,10)
               PARALLEL (A,10)
               USE_HASH (A C)
               USE_HASH (Z A)  */
       Z.ZIP_CODE, count(*)
       FROM ZIP Z,
            ADDRESS A,
```

(continued)

```
        CUSTOMER C
WHERE (C.ADDRESS_ID=A.ADDRESS_ID) AND
      (A.ZIP_ID = Z.ZIP_ID)
GROUP BY Z.ZIP_CODE
ORDER BY Z.ZIP_CODE
```

There are two types of parallelism when the parallel query option is used: *intraparallelism* and *interparallelism*. The intraoperation parallelism is the degree of parallelism used for a single operation, such as a full-table scan in parallel without any joins or sorts. The interoperation parallelism is the degree of parallelism used between operations, such as a full-table scan and a join. The preceding query demonstrates an example of the interoperation parallelism. The query specifies a degree of parallelism of 10 for the full-table scan. However, once this query is executed, 20 query slaves will be created. Ten of the query slaves will be used to scan the objects, and ten of the slaves will be used to perform the sort and hash join. This not only allows the scan to be parallelized, it also parallelizes the hash join, which can reduce the time of the scan and the join significantly. The parallel query option provides tremendous flexibility and functionality by allowing single scans and joins to be parallelized, thus reducing the elapsed time by an almost linear factor.

The parallel query option uses slave processes to parallelize the query. Each slave process scans a different section of the table. Therefore, it is important that your data be distributed (or striped) across multiple disk drives and controllers. If your data is not distributed properly, using parallel query can have a negative affect by saturating one or a few disks. Distributing your data using the guidelines presented in Chapter 3 can help the query slaves achieve near linear performance by minimizing I/O contention. For more information on the parallel query option, refer to the *Oracle7 Server Tuning Guide* or *Oracle8 Tuning Guide*. Use an explain plan on your query to verify that your hints are being accepted and the query is being executed in parallel. The OBJECT_NODE column of the explain plan table describes the degree of parallelism used for a given query. The OTHER column of the explain plan table shows the text of the query being distributed to each query slave.

The OTHER_TAG column of the explain plan table can be used to determine whether or not a query is being parallelized. If a query is being parallelized, the OTHER_TAG also indicates the stage or event of the parallel query for each operation. The following are the different types of parallel query events:

- PARALLEL_TO_PARALLEL
- PARALLEL_TO_SERIAL
- SERIAL_TO_PARALLEL
- PARALLEL_COMBINED_WITH_PARENT
- PARALELL_COMBINED_WITH_CHILD

The PARALLEL_TO_PARALLEL event indicates that interparallelism is being used and the output of the parallel operation is being sent to another set of parallel slaves for further parallelization. This is usually the case for sorts, hash joins, and merge-joins. The

PARALLEL_TO_SERIAL event indicates that the results of the parallel query execution will be returned to the Query Coordinator (QC) process. The SERIAL_TO_PARALLEL event refers to the step whereby the QC is partitioning the work to the parallel slaves. In the PARALLEL_COMBINED_WITH_PARENT and PARALLEL_COMBINED_WITH_CHILD phases, output from the parallel operation proceeds to the next step within the same parallel process. In this case, no interprocess communication to the parent is required. Using the OTHER_TAG column in addition to the other information from the explain plan allows you to examine the individual steps of your parallel query. The information provided in the explain plan is extremely useful when analyzing complex parallel queries with multiple joins. It is crucial that you become familiar with the explain plan utility in order to understand query execution behavior and tune your queries effectively. More uses of the parallel query option follow in Chapter 6.

4.6 USING PL/SQL

PL/SQL is Oracle's procedural language extension to SQL. PL/SQL has many features above and beyond SQL's capabilities. Using PL/SQL, you can create stored procedures and packages that maximize the power of the server. For example, you can use PL/SQL to invoke stored procedures and packages on the database server. This can help reduce the workload on the client by moving *heavy* processing from the client to the server, where it belongs. This not only reduces network traffic between the client and the server, it also maximizes the use of the server. Database servers tend to be multiprocessor machines with large amounts of memory. Running stored procedures and PL/SQL on the server is much more efficient than duplicating the same code on the client using SQL or some 4th GL language. PL/SQL 2.3 provides a tremendous amount of functionality and can drastically increase performance over the traditional client SQL calls.

Use PL/SQL to process long running SQL operations such as inserts, updates, or deletes that operate on a large number of rows. This avoids the excessive network traffic caused by traditional SQL calls to first fetch the data and then send the data back with its updates. You can accomplish the same task by invoking PL/SQL stored procedures and packages, thereby reducing the network traffic massively. You can call PL/SQL stored procedures and packages from PRO*C and Developer 2000. PowerBuilder also enables you to invoke stored procedures. When you design the application, try to make as much use of server PL/SQL as possible. This not only increases performance, it also maintains business rules and application logic in one central location. If the business rules change, you have to make the change in only one place: the database server. This is a far superior approach over having to change the client application code and redeploy the application to accommodate the change in business rules or logic.

4.6.1 PL/SQL TYPES

PL/SQL 2.3 also provides the ability to create PL/SQL tables (not to be confused with database tables). PL/SQL tables are basically an array of like elements, with the exception that indexing into the array is not done through a consecutive sequential counter as is done with traditional arrays. With PL/SQL tables, you build a table that specifies the data type of the table as well as the index of the table. The index of the table is a binary integer ranging from –2147483647 to +2147483647. This table index option is known as sparsity and allows meaningful index numbers such as customer numbers, employee numbers, or other useful index keys. PL/SQL tables provide an ideal method to process large amounts of data. The PL/SQL tables can be used in PRO*C as well as OCI. This allows you to pass in arrays from PRO*C into PL/SQL stored procedures in order to process large batches of data. PL/SQL tables can increase performance by operating on tables rather than single rows.

Oracle8 expanded PL/SQL to provide the TABLE and VARRAY (variable-size array) collection types. The TABLE collection type is referred to as a nested table. Nested tables are unlimited in size and can be sparse, meaning that elements within the nested table can be deleted using the DELETE procedure. Variable size arrays have a maximum size and maintain their order and subscript when stored in the database. Nested table data is stored in a system table that is associated with the nested table. Variable size arrays are suited for batch operations in which the application processes the data in batch array style. Nested tables make for efficient queries by storing the nested table in a storage table in which each element maps to a row in the storage table. For more information on collection types, refer to the *PL/SQL User's Guide and Reference*.

Oracle8 also extended National Language Support (NLS) for applications by providing the new NLS data types NCHAR and NVARCHAR2. National Language support allows number and date formats to automatically adapt to the language conventions specified by a user's session. This allows native language interaction between Oracle and the application. PL/SQL also supports a national character set that is used for NLS data. The NCHAR and NVARCHAR2 PL/SQL data types enable you to store character strings that are formed from the national character set.

4.6.2   EXTERNAL PROCEDURES

PL/SQL 8.0 introduces a new feature known as external procedures which allow you to call an external host language procedure from PL/SQL. This allows you to utilize the power of the C host language to accomplish certain tasks better suited in a host language like C rather than PL/SQL. For example, you may want to have a PL/SQL procedure invoke an external procedure that performs intense and complex mathematical calculations. The external program is in the form of a Dynamic Link-Library (DLL) which needs to be registered with PL/SQL. The PL/SQL interface then loads the DLL at runtime and calls the routine as if it were a PL/SQL routine. The external procedure feature can be extremely useful for scientific or engineering applications that need the power of the host language.

There are a few steps needed to configure an external procedure. You must identify the DLL, and then register the DLL with PL/SQL. For example, to identify the DLL you would use the following command:

```
SQL> create library banklib as '/apps/lib/banklib.so';

SQL> CREATE FUNCTION getlpaym (
          - Determine the optimal payment
          - plan for a customer loan
          - using a complex financial model.
           irat FLOAT,
           mperd BINARY_INTEGER,
           crsks BINARY_INTEGER,
           lamount FLOAT)
     RETURN BINARY_INTEGER AS EXTERNAL
     LIBRARY banklib
     NAME "getlpaym"  - quotes preserve lower case
     LANGUAGE C;
```

External procedures are ideal for applications performing complex data analysis or modeling allowing the application to benefit from the power of the host language. External procedures should not be used for short-lived functions that are frequently called by the PL/SQL application. For example, using an external procedure to perform simple operations such as adding two numbers and then return the result to PL/SQL is not an optimal use of external procedures. The overhead of performing frequent call-outs to external procedures that are short lived may have a negative effect on overall application performance. Therefore, it is important that you carefully review the application architecture and process flow before deciding to implement application modules as external procedures. When used appropriately, external procedures can provide tangible benefits to certain applications.

4.7 LOCKING CONTENTION

In a distributed application, locking can cause a high number of waits. You can increase the performance of your application by reducing the number of locks held as well as the length of time the lock is held. For example, if you have an application that needs to update rows in a table, lock only those rows and commit the update once it is complete to release the locks. Do not acquire exclusive locks on objects unless they are absolutely needed, and if needed, avoid holding the lock for an extended period of time. One common technique used to lock rows in a PRO*C application is to SELECT the rows for update. The FOR UPDATE clause locks those rows that satisfy the predicate of the query (if no predicate is given, all rows are selected). The FOR UPDATE clause causes the application to wait until the locks are obtained unless the NOWAIT option was specified in the FOR UPDATE clause. This means that the process or application could experience long wait times if another process holds the locks for a long time, or if a number of other users are waiting on the locks. To minimize the contention, use the NOWAIT option when locking rows. If a lock cannot be obtained on the rows, then control is returned to the user with an error indicating that the lock could not be obtained. This will allow the application to continue processing and try for the lock again later.

Another typical PRO*C implementation is when the programmer fetches some rows with the FOR UPDATE clause and then issues an update to those rows following some local processing. To increase concurrency, do not lock the rows upon FETCH; Rather lock the rows as part of the UPDATE statement. This reduces the time that the row locks are held, allowing other users to get the locks on those rows while the application is doing some local processing. If, however, you do not need to lock the rows upon the fetch, then obtain the rowids as part of the fetch, and use the ROWID hint as part of the update. This increases the performance of the update because the update can use the rowids to update the rows.

The beauty of Oracle is that it is centered around the concept of fine-granular-level locking. To take advantage of this feature, design your application so that exclusive locks are avoided unless they are absolutely needed; and distribute the application processing so that data is operated on in smaller batches and in parallel. This avoids one process operating on a large amount of data and possibly preventing others from obtaining locks. Remember, think in parallel and asynchronously when designing an application.

4.8   USING THE SYSTEM PACKAGES

Oracle 7.2 and 7.3 introduced new system packages that allow you to submit jobs, communicate with different sessions, and submit remote procedure calls. The DBMS_PIPE package enables multiple sessions within the same instance to communicate with each other. The DBMS_PIPE package uses named pipes to communicate between sessions. You can use DBMS_PIPE to create public or private pipes. Private pipes allow different sessions of the same user ID to communicate with one another. Any user who has execute permission on DBMS_PIPE and knows the name of the pipe can use a public pipe. The DBMS_PIPE provides a high-performance mechanism for communication between sessions on the same instance by using named pipes. This is much faster than communicating via SQL or PL/SQL to send small messages.

The DBMS_JOB also enables the administrator to schedule jobs. This allows the administrator to schedule jobs such as database maintenance scripts, analyzing tables, space management, or other typical database functions. The DBMS_JOB.SUBMIT procedure submits a job to the job queue. Oracle uses SNP background processes (SNP0 . . . SNP9). Each SNP process executes a job. You can set the number of SNP background processes by setting the init.ora parameter job_queue_processes.

You can also use the DBMS_ALERT package to register alerts. This allows for asynchronous notification of events. Using the DBMS_ALERT, a process could wait on an alert such as an insert into a table. Once the insert commits, the process waiting on the alert is signaled. The process can then continue processing and wait for the next alert following the completion of the processing. This provides a much better approach than sleeping and waking up every so often only to find that no work needs to be done. The DBMS_ALERT package allows a process to receive notification when specific database values change.

The DBMS_DEFER package is used to submit deferred remote procedure calls. The DBMS_DEFER.CALL procedure submits a deferred call to a remote procedure. The remote procedure call is not executed until the deferred call queue is pushed using either the DBMS_DEFER_SYS.SCHEDULE_EXECUTION procedure or the DBMS_DEFER_SYS.EXECUTE procedure. The deferred remote procedure call functionality is provided by the advanced replication option. For more information on the use of deferred remote procedure calls, refer to the *Oracle7 Server Distributed Systems, Volume II: Replicated Data Manual*, or the *Oracle8 Replication Release 8.0 Guide*.

4.8.1 ADVANCED QUEUING

Oracle8 Advanced Queuing (AQ) integrates message queuing functionality into the Oracle8 kernel. Advanced Queuing offers SQL access to messages by storing the messages in a database table. This allows indexes to be utilized to improve message access times. The AQ queues consist of database tables, thus allowing you to manage queues using standard tools. AQ queues can also be imported and exported using the import and export utilities. Since Oracle8 is an object-relational database, messages can be routed based on the content or type of the message. Message contents can also be queried. The integration of messaging services into the database allows messages to be managed in similar fashion as other database objects. Oracle AQ also maintains history information of each message such as the ENQUEUE/DEQUEUE time. Oracle AQ also allows you to manage event journals which helps correlate related messages. Messages can also be prioritized and grouped. Oracle8 AQ allows you to send and receive messages between applications. AQ is integrated into the Oracle8 Server, and is extremely useful for applications that prior to Oracle8 had to develop a complete messaging system or rely on middleware to provide messaging services.

Oracle8 AQ consists of several basic components including the message, queue, queue table, agents, and the queue monitor. The message is the basic unit of information either inserted into or retrieved from a queue. The enqueue and dequeue calls create a message and consume the message, respectively. User queues are used to store messages and exception queues are used to store messages that incurred problems during processing or retrieval. Queue tables are database tables that consist of one or more queues and a default exception queue. Agents are queue users consisting of either consumers or producers of the messages. The queue monitor manages the messages in the queue via a background process. You can also utilize the AQ message queuing functionality from within your PRO*C and OCI applications. This allows your applications to maintain a high level of throughput by avoiding the overhead introduced when using a third-party middleware package to send messages between your applications.

The init.ora parameters aq_tm_processes and job_queue_processes specify the number of queue monitor processes and number of SNP background processes used for snapshots, DBA jobs, and message propagation, respectively. The init.ora parameter `job_queue_interval` specifies the period between wake-ups of the SNP background processes. No queue monitor processes are created if `aq_tm_process-es=0`. The AQ system catalog tables `AQ$_MESSAGE_TYPES` (SYS schema), `AQ$_SCHEDULES` (SYSTEM schema), and `AQ$_QUEUE_STATISTICS` (SYS schema) can be used to monitor the message and queue statistics. The `catqueue.sql` (`$ORACLE_HOME/rdbms/admin`) script creates the AQ related objects.

The Oracle8 AQ option is extremely useful for applications requiring messaging and queuing services. AQ provides a tremendous amount of functionality and flexibility over traditional middleware messaging packages. AQ can increase the performance of your application by utilizing the messaging services incorporated into the Oracle8 Server. For more information on AQ, please refer to the section on AQ in the *Oracle8 Application Developer's Guide*.

4.9 PROFILING AND OPTIMIZATION

I recommend that you profile your application to determine where the majority of processor time is spent. This will allow you to examine the execution path and call graph in greater detail and possibly to identify any bottlenecks. For instance, you may find that your application is spending 40 percent of its time in a certain module or function. You can then analyze the module and/or function to determine if the module or function can be optimized. Profiling is extremely useful, and you should collect profiling statistics on your application before moving it into production. The profiling will also help you identify the source of an application bottleneck (if any). You may find that the bottleneck is in the application space itself, or the network, or the database server, or a combination thereof.

On Intel platforms, there are additional tools such as VTUNE and EMON from Intel that provide a great deal of useful information for application profiling. These tools report application statistics such as call graph profiles and cache utilization. VTUNE can be used to monitor different performance events and can also perform time-based sampling. Coupling these tools with the compiler allows you to study your application flow in detail and optimize accordingly. The statistics gathered from these tools will help you optimize your application in the areas of function flow and data structure design.

Optimization also helps improve the efficiency of object code by optimizing the object code generated. Compiler optimization techniques such as common subexpression elimination, register allocation and utilization, invariant loop hoisting, operation replacement, dead code elimination, loop pipelining, instruction scheduling, code in-lining, code motion frequency, feedback profiling, tail recursion elimination, loop parallelization, cache blocking, and loop inversion are attempts by the compiler to produce high-performance optimized code. Depending on the compiler, you should use the highest level of optimization (`-On` where n represents the level of optimization) when you compile your application. You should also try different levels of optimization to determine which level offers the best performance for your application. You can specify the optimization level as a compiler option through your application's make file. Optimization often increases the performance of the application, and vendors are constantly enhancing and improving the compilers. On Sun Solaris, I recommend that you upgrade to the latest SPARC C Compiler (currently 4.2). The new compiler provides many new features and performance enhancements. It also provides support for the v8plus and v8plusa instruction sets of the V9 Ultra Chip architecture. The V8 SPARC Chip architecture is used in the Sun Server 1000 and Sun SPARC Center 2000 series.

The Sun workshop compiler, such as SC4.2, provides a feedback optimization feature that can be used to optimize the performance of the application binaries. By compiling and linking your application with the -xprofile=collect switch, you can then execute the application in order to generate profile feedback data. You can then use the feedback profile data to recompile and relink your application using the -xprofile=use switch. This helps improve application performance by optimizing the executable based on the profile feedback data. If your compiler supports feedback optimization, you can use this feature to improve the efficiency of the application executables.

Sun also provides an optimized math library that can be used to improve the performance of your application. The optimized math library (libmopt) is provided with the Sun Workshop and can be linked with your application instead of the standard math library (libm). The libmopt routines support only IEEE style treatment of exceptional cases as opposed to libm which can provide ANSI, POSIX, SVID, X/Open, or IEEE. For SPARC systems, the vector math library (libmvec_mt) provides parallel versions of vector functions that rely on multiple processor parallelization.

TUNING AN OLTP SYSTEM

This chapter offers recommendations on performance tuning relating to transaction workloads. It assumes that you are familiar with the basic concepts of the Oracle Server and the standard background processes such as SMON, PMON, DBWR, and LGWR. If you are not familiar with the System Global Area (SGA) and the standard processes, refer to the *Oracle8 Server Concepts Manual*.

The main performance goal of an On-Line Transaction Processing (OLTP) system is the overall transaction processing rate, also referred to as the TPS (transactions per second) rate. The idea is that the individual transactions should be extremely quick and short-lived. Long running transactions are usually submitted in batch. Tuning a system with the primary goal of achieving high TPS rates and high transaction throughput requires that you focus your attention on the relevant areas that can offer the most gain.

The following areas are discussed in this chapter: tuning I/O, latches and locks, DBWR, LGWR, SGA caches, shared pool, redo area, rollback segments, OLTP application-related issues, and object management. These are the key areas that can help to maximize the performance of an OLTP system.

5.1 PERFORMANCE MONITORING

Before I offer tuning recommendations, it is important that you obtain a complete set of database performance monitoring tools for your work environment. I recommend that you use the Oracle Enterprise Manager to monitor your database. The Oracle Enterprise

Manager is an excellent tool that provides GUI graphs and charts of the Oracle Server utilization. This tool is available for Windows NT[1], and helps you avoid using manual SQL scripts to monitor performance. As the saying goes, "a picture is worth a thousand words." The Enterprise Manager can provide you with utilization and performance statistics for the database server much faster than manual SQL scripts. If you are currently using the Server Manager product, you should migrate to the Oracle Enterprise Manager tool.

5.2   TUNING I/O

As stated in Chapter 3, I/O is the single most critical component that pertains to performance in a database system. This section discusses the Oracle I/O-related issues that pertain to the overall performance of an OLTP system, such as the Volume Manager, raw devices, and file systems.

5.2.1   VOLUME MANAGEMENT

It is vital that your I/O subsystem be tuned as best as possible by either using the hardware volume management services or a Logical Volume Manager (LVM). Hardware volume management is generally faster than software volume management. However, if your hardware volume manager is limited in functionality, then you may choose to utilize the software LVM or a combination of both. For example, in an OLTP mission-critical environment, mirroring is typically employed to provide high availability. In this case, using the hardware mirroring may be faster than the software equivalent. The LVM enables you to create stripes, mirrors, or RAID devices. For transaction-intensive systems, try to use striping or mirroring in place of parity-based RAID. Parity-based RAID introduces parity bit calculation overhead, and is often inefficient when performing small writes. Striping or mirroring offers the best performance in terms of I/O throughput. If you use mirroring, make sure your submirrors are separated across different controllers and different disks so that the overhead of mirroring is minimized. If the submirrors are not separated, mirroring can cause an I/O bottleneck by saturating particular disks.

5.2.2   RAW DEVICES

You should also use raw devices for your OLTP database. Raw devices provide the best performance for random reads and writes. Transactions generally result in random I/O as new records are inserted and existing records are updated and deleted. Using raw devices not only helps random I/O, it also reduces the memory and CPU overhead introduced by file systems. For a heavily hit OLTP server, paging levels can be very high when file

---

1. Because the tool is available for Windows NT, you can monitor all your database servers from a single console using SQL*Net or Net8 to connect to the different databases.

systems are used due to the UNIX file system cache. Use the LVM to configure and set up raw devices. Make sure the raw devices are owned by the Oracle software owner and are part of the DBA group. You can do this by using the chown command followed by the chgrp command. The permissions on the raw devices should be 660 (read and write by only the Oracle software owner and the DBA group).

Although file system technology is continually being improved and the performance gap between raw devices and file systems is closing in, raw devices remain the leader in performance. File systems introduce extra overhead including file locking and maintenance of the file system cache and inode control block. Raw devices provide the database administrator with greater flexibility in sizing and database file layout. This allows the DBA to focus on distributing the I/O and sizing the files based on capacity and expected growth.

5.2.3   ASYNCHRONOUS I/O

Another benefit of using raw devices is the capability to use asynchronous I/O.[2] If you are using raw devices, you should enable asynchronous I/O in the Oracle Server. On Solaris, set the async_write=TRUE and async_read=TRUE in Oracle7, and disk_asynch_io=TRUE in Oracle8. On HP, set use_async_io=TRUE in Oracle7, and disk_asynch_io=TRUE in Oracle8. On HP, you must configure the /dev/async asynchronous I/O device driver. Follow the instructions in Chapter 3 to configure the asynchronous I/O driver on HP. On Sequent, set async_write=TRUE in Oracle7 and disk_asynch_io=TRUE in Oracle8 to enable asynchronous I/O if you use raw devices. Also, if you use asynchronous I/O, set the init.ora parameter db_writers=1 in Oracle7 and db_writer_processes=1 in Oracle 8.0.4. In some cases, multiple DBWR processes can improve throughput if a single DBWR begins to fall behind. The combination of asynchronous I/O and raw devices provides high I/O throughput and maximizes scalability as more users are added to the system.

5.2.4   ORACLE WRITES

When Oracle writes to data files or log files through its respective process, DBWR or LGWR, the writes are nondeferred. On most UNIX platforms, Oracle uses the O_SYNC flag when it opens files.[3] The O_SYNC flag causes the data and file control block information to be written physically to the disk (not the cache). The O_SYNC flag is used to guarantee consistency because Oracle must ensure that the data is physically written to the disk. For this reason, it is important that your data be striped and properly distributed in order to avoid I/O bottlenecks during writes. Even if you use file systems and have configured a large UNIX file system cache, writes will still be physically written to disk. The rate at which Oracle writes out is highly dependent on the configuration of the Oracle Server.

---

2. For more information on asynchronous I/O and the use of raw devices, refer to Chapter 3.
3. For more information on the different types of flags, refer to the manual pages on the open() system call.

5.2.5 VERITAS FILE SYSTEM MOUNT OPTIONS

If you choose to use Veritas file systems (vxfs) as opposed to raw devices, make sure that the file system is mounted without the `mincache=closesync` (refer to the `vfstab` options file) option. The `mincache=closesync` option causes the file system cache to write any file updates to disk once the file is closed, thereby reducing the usefulness of the cache. The performance degradation caused by this option is approximately 10 percent.

The vxfs file system type provides additional mount options such as `convosync` and `nolog`. You can mount the file system with either the `convosync=direct` or `dsync` option. The direct option causes reads and writes to bypass the UNIX file system cache and to read and write directly from the disk to the user space. During heavy I/O loads, using direct I/O over traditional file system I/O has seen a 50 percent performance improvement. The `dsync` option, when used in conjunction with the `open()` system call, causes writes to block until the data is physically written to disk, but not the inode information. The inode information is deferred and later written to disk. The `dsync` option can offer a 20–30 percent performance gain if a high degree of file system write concurrency is occurring. If your system and/or application does not benefit from the advantages of the UNIX file system cache, using direct I/O over the `dsync` option can increase I/O performance.

You can also use the `nolog` option which disables file system journaling. This increases performance; however, file system reliability is substantially reduced. With the `nolog` option, you must repair the file system using a full scan via the `fsck` utility. Without the journal logs, the file system may be unrecoverable following a crash.

The following are examples of how to utilize the vxfs mount options:

```
myhost {root}-> mount -F vxfs -o convosync=direct   \
                /dev/vx/dsk/vol1 /mount-point
```

or

```
myhost {root}-> mount -F vxfs -o convosync=dysnc   \
                /dev/vx/dsk/vol1 /mount-point
```

or

```
myhost {root}-> mount -F vxfs -o nolog   \
                /dev/vx/dsk/vol1 /mount-point
```

5.2.6 VERITAS DATABASE EDITION FOR ORACLE

In addition to the Veritas file system, Veritas offers the Database Edition for Oracle and the Quick I/O Database Accelerator, which provide up to a 90 percent performance improvement over the standard UNIX File System (UFS). The Quick I/O Database

Accelerator reduces read/write lock bottlenecks by allowing parallel updates to database files, supports asynchronous I/O, and eliminates double buffering. The Veritas Server Suite Database Edition for Oracle increases performance substantially over the traditional UFS. If you use file systems for your database and do not want to consider raw devices for whatever reason, you should consider using the Veritas Database Edition for Oracle and Quick I/O Database Accelerator to help increase your system's performance.

5.2.7 NUMBER OF DATA FILES

In an OLTP application in which a large number of random reads and random writes are occurring, you can increase performance by having more small-size data files rather than fewer large-size data files when you use file system-based files. This helps reduce the exclusive UNIX file system file write lock bottleneck. Solaris requires an exclusive write lock at the file level to ensure file consistency. The exclusive lock on the file can cause multiple simultaneous writes to the file to be serialized, thereby reducing I/O performance. The workaround is to create many small-size data files, thereby causing writes to be distributed across many different files. If a high degree of write concurrency to a single or a few UFS-based files is occurring, increasing the number of data files by creating many more smaller-size files can increase I/O throughput. For example, instead of creating a single 2 G data file, create four 512-M data files to help reduce contention for the file write exclusive lock.

To help reduce the SGA space taken by file descriptors, you can set the maximum number of open redo log and data files open by the instance to the actual number of redo log files and data files. The `init.ora` parameter `log_files` specifies the maximum number of redo log files that can be opened. Set this parameter to the number of redo log files configured in your database. This more likely than not will be less than the default which helps to reduce SGA space. The `init.ora` parameter `db_files` specifies the maximum number of data files that can be opened during the life of the instance. Set `db_files` to the total number of data files in the database. The default is typically larger than this, and reducing the value of `db_files` preserves space in the SGA.

5.2.8 CHECKPOINTS

A checkpoint occurs when DBWR writes all the dirty database buffers (including committed and uncommitted data) that are in the SGA to the data files. Checkpoints ensure that data blocks in the SGA that are modified frequently are written to disk periodically. DBWR uses a Least Recently Used (LRU) algorithm to age blocks out of the buffer cache. Therefore, an active block that changes frequently may not necessarily be written out to disk if checkpoints are not occurring.

Another advantage of a checkpoint is that, because all database changes up to the checkpoint have been applied to the data files, redo log entries prior to the checkpoint need not be applied in the event of instance recovery. Hence, checkpoints can help reduce the instance recovery time.

Checkpoints always occur during a log switch from one log group to another. When a checkpoint occurs, Oracle updates the headers of all the data files to indicate the occurrence of the checkpoint. The task of updating the headers of the data files is usually handled by the LGWR process. However, if your database has many data files, this can increase the workload of LGWR.

In order to separate the workload of the checkpoint from LGWR's primary work of maintaining the redo log buffer, you can enable the checkpoint process (CKPT) in Oracle7. If the checkpoint process is enabled, it handles updating the header files. To enable the checkpoint process, set the Oracle7 init.ora parameter checkpoint_ process=TRUE. Enabling the checkpoint process can increase performance by allowing a separate process to handle the data file header updates and allowing LGWR to manage the redo buffer. If, however, processors and memory are limited on your system, you may want to consider allowing LGWR to handle the data file header updates. If your system cannot afford the overhead of an additional process, set checkpoint_process=FALSE. In Oracle8, the checkpoint process (CKPT) is enabled by default and the init.ora parameter checkpoint_process has been made obsolete.

You can also set the interval at which checkpoints are started. The init.ora parameter log_checkpoint_interval specifies the number of operating system blocks (usually 512 bytes per block) needed to trigger a checkpoint. If the number of redo log file blocks generated since the last checkpoint exceeds this number, a checkpoint is performed. Regardless of this setting, a checkpoint always occurs after a redo log switch. A redo log switch occurs when LGWR switches from one redo log group to the next, in circular fashion. You can reduce the frequency of checkpoints by setting log_checkpoint_interval to the size of each redo log file. In which case, checkpoints occur only during a log switch. However, keep in mind that this will result in increased recovery times if instance or media recovery is required since the frequency of checkpoints will be reduced. If your application requires swift recovery times, you may want to set log_checkpoint_interval to a smaller value. You should also set the init.ora parameter log_checkpoints_to_alert=TRUE. This will allow you to monitor the frequency of checkpoints by examining the alert_SID.log file located in the background_dump_dest directory.

It is also important that you size your redo log files appropriately so as to avoid constant checkpoints and long redo log I/O waits. The redo size, redo entries, and redo wastage statistics from v$sysstat aid you in properly sizing the redo log files as well as optimally configuring the checkpoint frequency by analyzing the redo workload. The average redo entry size is (redo size / redo entries). The redo wastage statistic reports the number of bytes of unused space in the redo log buffer at the time when the entire redo buffer is written out. Also by setting the init.ora parameter log_check- points_to_alert=TRUE, you can monitor the frequency of checkpoints. Examining the checkpoint frequencies and computing the average redo entry size should give you a good feel as to your system's redo workload, subsequently allowing you to accurately size your redo log files.

5.2.9 DISK CACHE

Storage arrays often contain on-board cache memory to improve the performance of reads and writes. Depending on the size of the cache and the sophistication of the storage array cache manager, reads and writes can generally benefit from the cache thereby increasing overall I/O throughput. If your storage array has cache memory, you should ensure that the cache is enabled in order to improve I/O performance. In certain cases, the storage array cache can be configured to maximize either read or write performance. For an OLTP environment, configuring the cache for maximum write performance improves the performance of transactions and commits. For a data warehousing environment, enabling the cache to maximize read performance helps improve query throughput and may also aid in asynchronous read ahead performance depending on the sophistication of the cache.

If you are using the Sun SPARC storage arrays, you can increase performance by utilizing the NVRAM cache that is provided on the SPARC storage array. The Sun RSM 2000 Array can be configured with 128 M of cache memory. The SPARC storage array models use a 16-M NVRAM cache, which can increase the performance of writes significantly because the data is written to the NVRAM cache (backed up by battery) and later is flushed to disk. To enable the NVRAM fast write cache option, issue the following command

```
myhost{root}-> /usr/sbin/ssaadm  \
              fast_write -e <path>
```

This command enables fast writes to the NVRAM cache. The path parameter is the path to the SPARC storage array. For example, if c5 is the controller number for the SPARC storage array, then issue the following command:

```
myhost{root}-> /usr/sbin/ssaadm  \
              fast_write -e c5

myhost{root}-> /usr/sbin/ssaadm display c5
```

You can use the display option of the ssaadm command to verify that the fast_write option is enabled. Also, if you use the SPARC Storage arrays, make sure you install the SPARC storage array jumbo patch for your specific OS release. Also, the NVRAM cache will not be enabled without the supporting NVRAM batteries. To obtain the NVRAM batteries for your SPARC storage array, contact your Sun representative. The SPARC storage array jumbo patches 103290, 104793, 104708, and 105223 are for Solaris 2.4, Solaris 2.5, Solaris 2.5.1,and Solaris 2.6, respectively.

On the Sun A3000 Storage Array, you can use the raidutil command to enable the NVRAM cache. You can also use the raidutil command to tune several NVRAM cache-related parameters such as the read cache, mirroring, read-ahead prefetch, dynamic flush threshold, and dynamic threshold amount.

It is important that you become familiar with your storage arrays by fully understanding the capabilities and functionality. This allows you to tune your storage I/O subsystem in accordance with the system workload in order to maximize I/O throughput.

5.2.10 MONITORING FILE I/O

You should monitor file I/O periodically to ensure that I/O to the Oracle data files is being distributed properly. You can use the File I/O rate monitor of the Enterprise Manager (Performance Manager) to obtain file I/O statistics. You can also query the v$filestat view. The reported columns and their definitions are listed in Table 5.1.

TABLE 5.1   Reported columns of file I/O statistics

COLUMN	DEFINITION
PHYRDS	Number of physical reads per second since the last sample.
PHYWRTS	Number of physical writes per second since the last sample.
PHYBLKRD	Number of physical blocks read since the last sample.
PHYBLKWRT	Number of physical blocks written since the last sample.
READTIM	Response times per read (in hundredths of a second). *
WRITETIM	Response times per write (in hundredths of a second). *

* Set the init.ora parameter timed_statistics=TRUE.

If you see a high number of read and write requests for a specific data file or limited set of data files, you may need to redistribute your data so that reads and writes are spread out as much as possible across the different data files. If you use a volume manager (hopefully), the file I/O statistics may not give you a clear indication of the back-end disk movement. All file I/O statistics are reported at the database file level. Hence, if you use a volume manager, you should also monitor the I/O using sar -d (or an equivalent tool) to determine if the I/O is being distributed across multiple disks within the single logical volume.

5.2.11 TUNING DBWR

DBWR is responsible for writing dirty blocks from the buffer cache to the data files. It is also responsible for maintaining adequate space in the buffer cache so that the physical I/O is minimized and the buffer cache hit ratio is maximized. Database reads (both logical and physical) are performed by the user shadow process. To maximize the performance of DBWR, ensure that DBWR is not constantly being saturated with write-out requests, and while writing, try to minimize DBWR write time.

In order to minimize DBWR write time, it is critical that your data files be distributed. You should tune I/O following the methods outlined in Chapter 3 to ensure that I/O is properly distributed. If your data is not distributed properly, DBWR may experience high wait times. Therefore, use the volume manager to distribute I/O so that writes can proceed in parallel. Another way to minimize DBWR wait time is to use asynchronous I/O and raw devices. Asynchronous I/O and raw devices provide the best combination for I/O performance. Using asynchronous I/O can reduce the DBWR wait time incurred by the standard synchronous write() system call. Asynchronous I/O allows DBWR to issue multiple writes in parallel without blocking.

If you are not using asynchronous I/O, you should set the Oracle7 `init.ora` parameter `db_writers=n` where n represents the distinct number of disk drives and controllers that your data spans. For example, if most of your data files consist of stripes across five disks, set `db_writers=5`. In addition, try to balance the number of DBWR processes with the number of disks, as well as the number of controllers. This allows high throughput DBWRs by parallelizing writes across controllers. For example, if your data spans ten disks, but only two controllers, setting `db_writers=10` may saturate I/O, causing disk waits, since there are only two controllers to service the I/O requests.

In Oracle8, you can set the init.ora parameter `dbwr_io_slaves` to enable DBWR I/O slaves. In Oracle 8.0.4, you can enable multiple DBWR processes by setting the `init.ora` parameter `db_writer_processes` to the number of DBWR processes desired. If asynchronous I/O is disabled or not supported on your platform, using multiple DBWR processes or I/O slaves can improve database I/O throughput. If you enable I/O slaves or multiple DBWR processes, monitor the `v$filestat` statistics as well as processor utilization to ensure that file I/O is being parallelized and processes are not waiting to run. Configuring too many DBWR processes or I/O slaves may cause a performance degradation if processes spend too much time waiting for processor time or data is not distributed properly.

5.2.11.1 Monitoring DBWR Activity

In order to be sure that DBWR is keeping up with the buffer cache workload, you should monitor the following server statistics that are available through the Enterprise Manager or `v$sysstat` view:

NAME	VALUE
DBWR buffers scanned	104248
DBWR checkpoints	90
DBWR cross instance writes	0
DBWR free buffers found	42069
DBWR lru scans	852
DBWR make free requests	348
DBWR summed scan depth	105038
DBWR timeouts	304495
background checkpoints completed	4
background checkpoints started	5
dirty buffers inspected	0
free buffer inspected	884
free buffer requested	117224
physical writes	14115
summed dirty queue length	644
write requests	2886

The following points summarize the preceding DBWR statistics:

❏ DBWR buffers scanned statistic reports the number of buffers in the Least Recently Used (LRU) section of the buffer cache scanned by DBWR when it searches for dirty buffers to write-out to disk. DBWR buffers scanned includes clean buffers as well as dirty buffers. You should divide DBWR buffers scanned by the value of DBWR lru scans to determine the average number of buffers being scanned.

❏ DBWR checkpoints reports the number of times DBWR was signaled to perform a checkpoint.

❏ DBWR free buffers found is the number of buffers that DBWR found to be clean when requested to make free buffers. Divide DBWR free buffers by the value of DBWR make free requests to determine the average number of free buffers at the end of the LRU.

❏ DBWR make free requests is the number of requests made of DBWR, including requests made by DBWR, to make more buffers free in the LRU section of the buffer cache.

❏ DBWR timeouts is the number of timeouts accumulated by DBWR during idle writes. Idle writes occur when DBWR scanned the buffers but found nothing to write-out. Do not be alarmed by a high number of DBWR timeouts. This simply means that DBWR found nothing to write out during its scan.

❏ Dirty buffers inspected reports the number of dirty or modified buffers found in the cache. If the value of dirty buffers inspected is large or continues to increase, DBWR is not keeping up with the workload.

❏ Physical writes, background checkpoints completed, and background checkpoints started will give you a good indication of the amount of physical I/O occurring. High numbers indicate that too much physical I/O is occurring, and that either DBWR is falling behind and/or the buffer cache is too small.

5.2.11.2   The DBWR Parameters

The three primary init.ora parameters that affect DBWR are db_block_write_batch, db_block_checkpoint_batch, and db_file_simultanenous_writes. The _db_block_write_batch parameter specifies the number of blocks to batch in each DBWR I/O.[4] A larger value for _db_block_write_batch means that more blocks are written out at each batch I/O. This reduces the overall activity of DBWR because when DBWR writes, it will write a larger batch. Smaller values for _db_block_write_batch may increase the activity of DBWR, since DBWR will have to write out many smaller size batches rather than fewer larger size batches.

---

4. db_block_write_batch has been made an underscore parameter (_db_block_write_batch) because Oracle dynamically determines the optimal batch size based on db_file_simultaeous_writes.

To determine if _db_block_write_batch is optimally set, divide the summed dirty queue length by the number of write requests to determine the average length of the dirty list. The summed dirty queue length is the sum of the LRU queue length following the completion of every write request. In the previous example, the summed dirty queue length is 644, and write requests is 2886. Therefore the average size of the dirty queue length is 644/2886=.22. The free buffer inspected is the number of buffers skipped in the buffer cache by user processes attempting to find a free buffer. If the value of free buffer inspected is high, it means that the buffer cache consists of a large number of modified buffers. You should either increase the size of the buffer cache, or increase the _db_block_write_batch to force more dirty buffers to be written out. Free buffer requested is the number of times a free buffer was needed to create and/or load a block. Set _db_block_write_batch=128 and increase it if necessary. Continue to increase _db_block_write_batch until the summed dirty queue length and free buffer inspected are small. However, do not set _db_block_write_batch so high that the I/O subsystem is oversaturated with too many I/Os thereby causing long I/O wait queue lengths.

The db_block_checkpoint_batch specifies the batch size of DBWR checkpoint writes. A high value for db_block_checkpoint_batch allows checkpoints to complete quickly. You should set db_block_checkpoint_batch such that checkpoints always complete before the next checkpoint. This will reduce the wait time between checkpoints.

The db_file_simultaneous_writes specifies the number of simultaneous batches issued by DBWR for each database file. If your operating system does not support multiple writes per device, then you should set db_file_simultaneous_writes=1. If you are using file systems, setting db_file_simultaneous_writes to a high value may have a negative effect due to the exclusive file-write lock that is used to guarantee file consistency. On raw devices with asynchronous I/O, set db_file_simultaneous_writes to at least twice the number of distinct members in the striped volume and to no more than five times the number of members. For example, if your striped data file consists of six distinct disk drives, set db_file_simultaneous_writes=12 (minimum setting) and no more than db_file_simultaneous_writes=30. Use larger values for db_file_simultaneous_writes for wide striped files (numerous members). Monitor the v$filestat view and disk I/O utilization (sar -d) to determine the optimal setting for db_file_simultaneous_writes. Storage arrays with large amounts of cache can typically sustain a large number of concurrent I/Os, therefore larger settings for db_file_simultaneous_writes can often increase database I/O throughput.

5.3 LATCHES AND LOCKS

Latches are internal locks used by Oracle to protect structures in the SGA. Locks are user-level dictionary locks that are placed on user objects such as tables, indexes, and other database objects. There are two main types of locks: *DML locks* and *DDL locks*.

DML locks are data locks that are used to protect data such as tables and rows. DDL locks are used to protect dictionary objects such as table definitions. Oracle uses the enqueue manager to manage concurrent access to objects. For example, multiple Oracle users can request share-level locks on the same table. An enqueue is managed as a First-In, First-Out (FIFO) queue. A latch, on the other hand, has no order. If a process fails to obtain a latch, the process may spin or sleep for a specified period of time and try to obtain the latch later. While the process is spinning or sleeping, another process could have obtained the latch.

5.3.1   LRU LATCHES

The database buffer cache (db_block_buffers) is managed by a Least Recently Used (LRU) algorithm. Entries in the buffer cache are protected by cache latches. The following query shows the relevant buffer cache latches:

```
SQL> select name,
              gets,
              misses,
              sleeps,
              immediate_gets "IMGETS",
              immediate_misses "IMMISSES"
       from v$latch
       where name like '%cache buffer%' or
             name like '%cache protect%'
       order by name;
```

NAME	GETS	MISSES	SLEEPS	IMGETS	IMMISSES	
cache buffer handles	15218	0	0	0	0	
cache buffers chains	9710209	0	0	78715531	2	
cache buffers lru chain	**426086**	**1**	**1**	**4948587**	**0**	(*LRU latches*)
cache protection latch	0	0	0	0	0	

4 rows selected.

The buffer cache latches are used to protect blocks in the buffer cache during simultaneous operation. Oracle 7.3 introduced another tunable init.ora parameter, db_block_lru_latches, that allows you to tune the number of LRU latches. On multiprocessor systems with a large buffer cache and a heavy OLTP user community, contention for the LRU latches can cause a performance degradation.

In the previous example, the misses and sleeps are extremely low (most of them are zero). This allows a high throughput buffer cache minimizing contention during concurrent use. If your latch statistics indicate high misses or sleeps for the buffer cache LRU latches, increase db_block_lru_latches. If you are experiencing buffer cache LRU contention, set db_block_lru_latches=<number of available processors> to reduce the contention for the LRU latches.

5.4 TUNING REDO

For an OLTP system, the redo buffer and the redo log files can be the biggest bottleneck if not tuned properly. It is critical that user processes and Oracle background processes are not waiting constantly on LGWR or space in the redo buffer. If the redo area is not properly tuned, it can cause high user process wait times, waiting on LGWR to make space available in the redo buffer or complete checkpoints.

The LGWR process writes to the redo log files in a circular fashion. Figure 5.1 shows the circular cycle of the LGWR.

The redo log files contain redo entries, which consist of data that is used to reconstruct changes made to the database, including rollback data. Redo entries also contain rollback segments as well as data. They are a low-level mapping of the database changes. The redo entries cannot be used by applications to show the user actions.[5]

5.4.1 CONFIGURING THE REDO LOG FILES

Before you begin to tune the redo buffer in the SGA, it is critical that your redo log files be configured properly. Make sure that each redo log member file within a group is striped across multiple disks and multiple controllers. One thing to remember is that members of a redo log group are written to asynchronously (simultaneously), and redo log groups are written to synchronously. This means that redo log groups can be on the

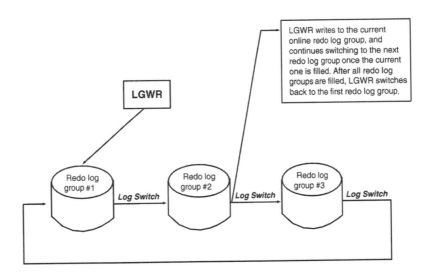

FIGURE 5.1 Circular cycle of the LGWR.

---

5. BMC Software offers the SQL*Trax tool that allows you to examine the Oracle redo log files to show detailed information on changes. For more information on the tool, contact BMC Software Company.

same set of disks as are other redo log groups since LGWR writes only to one active group at a time. Therefore, if you have multiple members within a group (Oracle redo log mirroring), make sure each member is on separate set of disks and controllers so that LGWR writes can proceed in parallel to each member. Figure 5.2 shows how redo log files should be configured.

In Figure 5.2, redo log members are separated across different disks and different controllers to ensure that LGWR writes proceed in parallel. If you are mirroring the Oracle redo members (meaning you have multiple members within a single redo log group), LGWR attempts to write to the members asynchronously (assuming asynchronous I/O is enabled). Therefore, if your members are all on the same disk, contention for the disk is likely to occur. The redo log groups, however, can be on the same set of disks as the other redo log groups because Oracle writes to only one redo log group at a time. As Figure 5.2 shows, redo log members of the same group are separated across different controllers and disks. However, each redo log group is on the same set of disks and controllers as the other groups. You should dedicate at least a few disks for redo log files. Try to avoid mixing redo disks with other data since this will reduce overall I/O performance.

5.4.2 VOLUME MANAGEMENT MIRRORING VERSUS ORACLE MIRRORING

Another tuning technique you can use—if you are using a hardware or software volume manager that supports mirroring—is to use the mirroring functionality that is provided with the hardware or software volume manager. Mirroring by the logical volume manager is done in kernel space, and hardware mirroring is typically handled by the storage array which is much more efficient than user-space mirroring (Oracle issuing multiple writes). However, keep in mind that in the case of corruption, hardware-level or OS-level mirroring will duplicate the corruption across the mirror which may render your database useless if only one redo log member exists per group. Oracle mirroring (meaning multiple

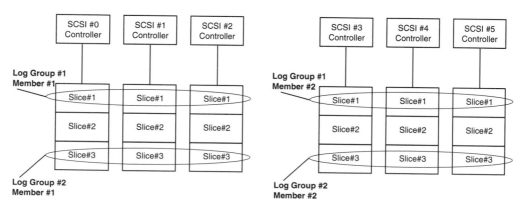

FIGURE 5.2 Ideal redo log file configuration.

redo members exist per redo log group) can add another level of safety by having multiple redo log members. In the case of corruption, Oracle will likely detect the corruption and continue writing to the valid redo log members. Therefore, it is a good idea to have at least two redo log members per redo log group and allow the OS or hardware-level mirroring to handle additional redundancy.

5.4.3 USING PRESTOSERVE FOR THE REDO LOG FILES

Sun offers additional technology to increase the performance of redo log files if you use file systems. *PrestoServe* is high speed static memory that is backed up by lithium batteries. Even during a loss of power, the data in the PrestoServe memory is backed up by battery power that can last up to several years. The batteries are charged during normal system operation. PrestoServe can significantly increase performance on synchronous writes to files. Instead of writing the data to the disk physically, the data can be written to the PrestoServe static memory and flushed out later. This allows a high throughput LGWR by reducing the I/O wait time during LGWR writes. Committing the data to the PrestoServe, as opposed to the physical disk, is approximately 20 times faster. If your redo log files are file system-based, using PrestoServe on your Sun Solaris system can increase the performance of LGWR.

There are a few things to consider when using PrestoServe. If using Solaris 2.4, you must install the PrestoServe patch 103043 and use the PrestoServe release 2.4.2. This patch fixes some bugs and addresses the Solaris 2.4 incompatibility issue. In addition, if you are running ODS 4.0, you need to install the ODS jumbo patch 102580, which addresses the sequencing of PrestoServe and ODS startup upon system boot. If you are using all raw devices and ODS, disable PrestoServe. Also be extremely careful when using PrestoServe with ODS on Solaris 2.4 and above. If the proper patches are not installed and the system is not configured properly, the entire file system can become corrupt, resulting in a file system that needs to be rebuilt and restored. You should contact Sun Service to verify that your system and OS release are compatible with PrestoServe.

Appropriately tuning your redo log files can ensure a high throughput LGWR. For an OLTP system, redo is one of the major contributors to the workload as rows are constantly being inserted, updated, and/or deleted. Remember to use sar or other I/O monitoring utilities to monitor redo disk utilization. Make sure that I/O is being distributed across the different disk drives and controllers. One key footnote is that without a volume manager, you will not be able to set up striping. This means that each redo log file will be on one disk only. This significantly reduces performance by saturating one disk. Hence, use the volume manager to stripe redo log files as manual striping will not be effective.

5.4.4 MONITORING THE REDO BUFFER

The key to tuning the redo buffer is monitoring the `redo log space wait time`. The `redo log space requests` value reports the number of times a user process had to wait for space in the redo log buffer. This indicates that redo buffers are being filled faster than LGWR can write (free buffers). The redo log space requests statistic is incremented when a log switch is forced or a user process had to wait on a log switch. Redo log space requests should be zero, meaning sufficient redo buffer space regularly exists for user processes. In addition to the redo log space requests, you can monitor the value of redo log space wait time, which reports the time spent waiting for log space (in 1/100s of a second). You can monitor redo log space requests and redo log space wait time by querying the v$sysstat table or by using the Oracle Enterprise Manager. The following shows the query against the v$sysstat table reporting the number of redo log space requests:

```
SQL> select  name,value
        from v$sysstat
            where name = 'redo log space requests';
```

If redo log space requests continues to increase, then you should increase the size of the redo buffer by setting the init.ora parameter log_buffer. The log_buffer setting should be a multiple of the database block size (db_block_size). Make sure your system has sufficient memory available before you increase the size of log_buffer. Increasing the size of the log_buffer may cause a higher level of paging if sufficient memory does not exist.

5.4.5 TUNING REDO LOG BUFFER LATCHES

The redo buffer is the area in the SGA that contains the redo entries. The buffer is a synchronous buffer that is flushed periodically by the LGWR process. The LGWR process writes redo entries out to the redo log disk files. Before a redo entry can be written into the redo buffer, space in the redo buffer must be allocated for the redo entry. Allocating space in the redo buffer is controlled by the allocation latch. The redo entry is then copied into the redo buffer using either the redo copy latch or the redo allocation latch. There is only one redo allocation latch per instance; therefore, in order to avoid a redo bottleneck, the time the redo allocation latch is held should be kept to a minimum.

The init.ora parameter log_small_entry_max_size specifies in bytes the maximum redo entry size that can be copied to the log buffers using the redo allocation latch without obtaining the redo copy latch. If the redo entry is larger than log_small_entry_max_size, the redo copy latch must be used to copy the data into the redo buffer. In this case, the allocation latch is released after space is allocated in the redo buffer and a redo copy latch is obtained. If the redo entry is less than or equal to log_small_entry_max_size, the redo entry is copied on the redo allocation latch, and the allocation latch is released following the copy. Therefore, by reducing log_small_entry_max_size, more copies will be done through the redo copy latch as opposed to the allocation latch. You can also increase performance by setting the log_small_entry_max_size=0, significantly reducing the time that the allocation latch is held.

The `init.ora` parameter `log_simultaneous_copies` regulates the number of redo copy latches available for concurrent writes into the redo buffer. For good performance on a multiprocessor system, you can set `log_simultaneous_ copies=<2>` × `<number of CPUs>`. If `log_simultaneous_copies=0`, all writes are considered small and the copies into the redo buffer are made without the copy latch. On a uniprocessor system, redo copy latches are not used since only one process can be actively copying into the redo buffer at a time. By default, `log_simultaneous _copies=`number of CPUs in the system. It is recommended that `log_simultaneous _copies` be set to anywhere between its default value to a maximum of two times the number of CPUs in the system. The performance gain from tuning these two parameters depends on the amount of redo and transaction activity of the system.

To determine the hit and miss ratios for the redo log buffer latches such as the redo allocation latch and the redo copy latch, you can query the `v$latch` view by using the following query:

```
select name,
        sum (gets) "Gets",
        sum (misses) "Misses",
        sum (immediate_gets)"IM_Gets",
        sum (immediate_misses) "IM_Misses"
from  v$latch
where name like '%redo%'
group by name;
```

NAME	Gets	Misses	IM_Gets	IM_Misses	
redo allocation	266829	737	0	0	
redo copy	39592	58	256865	335	
redo writing*	42081	438	0	0	* **Oracle8 latch**

In this example, the redo latch statistics show some misses for both wait and immediate get requests. The redo writing latch (Oracle8) is used to coordinate the writing of the redo log and waiting for redo writes. However, the percentage of misses to gets in the above example is extremely low. Latch misses will normally occur during periods of high-volume concurrent use; however, the percentage of misses to gets should be low. If your statistics show contention (high misses) for the redo latches, you should increase the number of redo copy latches (if running on a multiprocessor system) and set `log_small_entry_max_size=0` to reduce the length of time that the redo allocation latch is held. If you are still experiencing contention in Oracle7, try prebuilding redo log entries before the copy latch is requested. The next section describes how to prebuild redo log entries.

The Oracle7 `init.ora` parameter `log_entry_prebuild_threshold` specifies the maximum number of bytes to group together before copying the redo entry to the redo log buffer. A nonzero value of `log_entry_prebuild_threshold` causes user processes to prebuild redo entries before the redo copy latch is requested. For multiprocessor systems, setting this value can help reduce the time that the redo copy latch is held. On a uniprocessor system, set `log_entry_prebuild_threshold=0`. Do not change the default of `log_entry_prebuild_threshold` (which is zero) if your system is experiencing memory shortages or memory contention. To adequately tune this parameter, review the system statistics (`v$sysstat`) to determine the total number of redo entries generated (`redo entries`) and the total amount of redo generated, expressed in bytes (`redo size`). The `redo entries` and `redo size` statistics will give you a good feel for how much redo is being generated, and therefore how much redo should be grouped together.

5.4.6 VECTOR POSTING

Oracle8 release 8.0.4 provides a performance enhancement to post and wait operations known as vector posting. Vector posting allows a process to post a set (vector) of processes in a single post call. This reduces system call overhead and improves the performance of processes such as LGWR. After writing out redo entries to the redo log files, LGWR may need to post a set of foreground processes. Without the vector post, LGWR would need to separately post each foreground process. By using the vector post feature, LGWR can post the foregrounds in a single post call. For semaphores, enabling vector posting may require you to increase the values of the semaphore kernel parameters such as `SEMOP` (maximum number of operations per `semop()` call). To enable vector posting set the init.ora parameter `_use_vector_post=TRUE`. Vector positing has shown a 3–5 percent performance gain for systems with heavy OLTP workloads.

5.4.7 SHARED LATCHES

Oracle8 improves latch utilization by employing shared latches. Shared latches allow multiple processes concurrent read access to a section of memory by using a low-level synchronization mechanism. In Oracle8, the redo copy latches, both parent and children, can be shared. This helps increase redo throughput since multiple processes can simultaneously acquire a redo copy latch in shared mode. Shared latches may not be supported on all platforms, such as platforms that do not support the ability to perform an atomic compare-and-swap. Shared latches are supported on the Sun Ultra systems (sun4u architecture).

5.5 MONITORING DBWR AND LGWR

In order to maximize the performance of the DBWR and LGWR processes, it is important that DBWR and LGWR keep up with the workload. If DBWR or LGWR fall behind, user processes can experience long wait times. Also, it is important that both DBWR and LGWR keep up with the workload in order to avoid situations of recursive waiting. One of the major reasons that cause a slow DBWR or LGWR is due to I/O contention. If data files and redo log files are not distributed properly, DBWR and LGWR can spend a large majority of their time waiting on I/Os to complete. This is turn causes user foreground processes to wait on events such as checkpoints and buffer flushes. You can query the v$system_event, v$session_event, and v$session_wait views to determine if processes are waiting on I/O. The v$system_event view reports the total number of event waits for all sessions. The v$session_event view reports total number of event waits per session. The v$session_wait view reports the events that sessions have just completed waiting on or are currently waiting on. These views are extremely useful for pinpointing contention. For example, the following query lists the total number of waits and wait times for file I/O events:

```
SQL> select event,
            total_waits,
            time_waited
      from v$system_event
      where event like '%file%'
      order by total_waits desc;
```

EVENT	TOTAL_WAITS	TIME_WAITED
db file sequential read	60650	28315
log file parallel write	6852	2751
log file sync	6797	2630
control file sequential read	103	3
file open	81	1
db file scattered read	79	27
refresh controlfile command	13	0
file identify	11	3
control file parallel write	10	18
log file sequential read	3	1
log file single write	3	1
db file parallel write	2	5

```
12 rows selected.
```

The above query shows that the file I/O events db file sequential read, log file parallel write, and log file sync account for a majority of the process event waits. The db file sequential read event refers to when a foreground process is waiting for a sequential read from the database to complete. The log file parallel write event refers to when redo entries are written from the redo log buffer to the redo log files. If the init.ora parameter timed_statistics=TRUE, the TIME_WAITED column of the v$system_event view can help determine if I/Os are taking too long. You should check the disk utilization statistics to determine if the disks containing the redo log files are being saturated and if disk contention is occurring. If you determine there is redo log disk contention, you may have to relocate your redo log files onto dedicated disks or reconfigure the redo log files to increase the degree of striping. The log file sync event reports the wait time of LGWR writing redo entries for a given user session. When a user session commits a transaction, the redo information for the session is flushed to the redo log file. The user session posts the LGWR process to write the redo buffer entries to the redo log file, and the LGWR process will then post the user session upon completion. Querying the system event views can help you identify the contention for resources. You can further identify the exact file of the I/O event by querying the v$session_wait view as follows:

```
SQL> select event,
            p1,
            p2,
            p3,
            state
    from v$session_wait;
```

Each event listed in v$system_event or v$session_event can be correlated with the v$session_wait view. The v$session_wait view lists the wait event, session id, and wait event parameters for a given session. Therefore, you can use the v$session_wait view to drill down on the wait event while the session and wait events are in progress. The v$session_wait view provides the event parameter columns p1, p2, and p3 that help you further analyze the reason behind the event wait. For example, for the db file sequential read event, the parameters p1, p2, and p3 refer to the file number of the file being read from, block number, and the number of blocks being read, respectively. You can then correlate the file number with the v$datafile view to determine which Oracle file is being read from.

Using the information provided in the v$system_event, v$session_event, and v$session_wait views can help you determine if DBWR or LGWR are waiting on I/O events. If sessions are spending too much time waiting on file I/O events, this indicates that there is an I/O bottleneck. You will also need to correlate the event wait statistics with the disk utilization statistics (e.g., sar -d) in order to determine if I/O is being distributed across multiple disks and multiple controllers. You should strive to eliminate I/O wait events by ensuring that the Oracle data files and redo log files are configured, sized, and distributed optimally. It is key that you identify and resolve disk I/O contention and bottlenecks in order to ensure that DBWR and LGWR are keeping up with the workload.

5.5.1   USING I/O SLAVES AND MULTIPLE DBWR PROCESSES

Oracle8 provides the ability to utilize I/O slaves for platforms that do not provide support for asynchronous I/O, or where the asynchronous I/O provided is inefficient. If the statistics show that DBWR or LGWR is falling behind, subsequently causing bottlenecks, you may want to try configuring I/O slaves in order to increase DBWR or LGWR throughput. The init.ora parameters dbwr_io_slaves, and lgwr_io_slaves specify the number of I/O slave processes to be used for database file writes (DBWR), and log file writes (LGWR), respectively. Oracle 8.0.4 allows you to configure multiple DBWR processes in place of DBWR I/O slaves by setting the init.ora parameter db_writer_processes=<n> where n is the number of DBWR processes. If you enable `dbwr_io_slaves`, only one DBWR process is used, regardless of the setting of `db_writer_processes`. I/O slaves can help increase database I/O throughput by parallelizing I/O requests. I/O slaves are dynamically allocated on an as needed basis. This reduces the overhead of spawning processes that are never used.

In order to choose the optimal number of I/O slaves or DBWR processes, you need to review the I/O statistics `physical writes`, `physical reads`, `logical reads`, and `write requests` from the `v$sesstat` and `v$sysstat` views to determine the I/O rates. In addition, you should compare the I/O statistics from the `v$sesstat` and `v$sysstat` views with the statistics from the `v$sess_io` and `v$filestat` views. Choosing the right number of I/O slaves and/or DBWR processes involves you reviewing the I/O rates and statistics. In a normal situation where your data files and redo log files are optimally striped and disk I/O contention is minimal, I/O slaves will more than likely not be needed when asynchronous I/O is enabled and is fast and efficient. However, if DBWR or LGWR are falling behind, and disk I/O contention has been resolved, you should enable LGWR slaves and multiple DBWR processes to help parallelize the work of LGWR and DBWR. It is important to note that if your disk contention is due to the fact that your database and redo log files are not optimally distributed and striped, starting additional DBWR processes or I/O slaves can have a negative effect on performance since more processes will be issuing I/O. Multiple DBWR processes and I/O slaves are primarily intended for workloads where DBWR and LGWR are not driving the I/O subsystem hard enough. In other words, your I/O subsystem is not being fully utilized. In this case, additional processes can help drive the I/O subsystem harder, thereby increasing I/O throughput.

5.6 TUNING `SPIN_COUNT`

The `init.ora` parameter `spin_count` controls the amount of CPU ticks (cycles) that a process executes after an initial attempt to acquire a busy resource (latch). After the number of `spin_count` ticks, the process makes a second attempt to acquire the resource. If the resource is still unavailable, the process is put to sleep and is later awakened when the resource becomes available.

Putting the process to sleep and later awakening it is an expensive operation. Forcing the process to spin longer before it acquires the resource yields higher performance than putting the process to sleep on a multiprocessor system. A high `spin_count` value on a single processor system may cause CPU starvation of other processes because the spinning process is occupying the only CPU. The default for `spin_count` on most UNIX platforms is 2,000 (on multiprocessor machines), which is adequate for most applications. Increasing `spin_count` generally results in greater CPU utilization.

If you are seeing a high number of latch sleeps and your system has many high-speed processors, increasing `spin_count` may increase your performance over the time spent sleeping. Continue increasing `spin_count` at a nominal rate (increments of 500 or 1,000) until latch sleeps are minimized. Also, when you increase `spin_count`, monitor CPU utilization to ensure that processes are not being starved of CPU time because of the increase in spin_count. You may have eliminated latch sleeps, but process elapsed times may have increased due to their inability to obtain CPU time. You can monitor latch statistics by examining the v$latch table or by using the latch monitor of the Enterprise Manager. Set spin_count to zero (i.e., no spinning) if running Oracle on a single-processor machine.

There are two main types of latch requests: wait and nowait. The *latch monitor* reports the two types of latch requests. The GETS (wait) column reports the number of times a process acquired the latch on its first attempt but had to wait before acquiring the latch. The MISSES (wait) column reports the number of times a process acquired a latch after failing to acquire the latch on the first attempt. The SLEEPS (wait) column reports the number of times a process was put to sleep while waiting for a latch. The GETS (no wait) column reports the number of times a process acquired the latch without waiting. The Misses (no wait) column reports the number of times a process failed to acquire a latch and did not wait after failing to acquire the latch.

The *latch free* event in the v$system_event view reports the wait time on latches. If no latch contention is occurring, the latch free event will not be reported. If the latch free event occurs, you can review the wait times for the latch free event in the v$system_event view to determine the severity of the latch contention. These latch statistics (from the v$system_event and v$latch views) can help you determine if you are experiencing latch contention. The sleeps column in v$latch should be near zero. High sleep latch rates indicate latch contention. There are many different latches used within the Oracle kernel, and minimizing latch contention can help foster a high throughput system with minimal wait time. You can use the following query to identify the latches experiencing contention (misses):

```
select substr (l.name,1,30) name,
               (misses/(gets+.001))*100 "MISS_RATIO",
               (immediate_misses/(immediate_gets+.001))*100
                        "IMMEDIATE_MISS_RATIO"
from v$latch l,
     v$latchname ln
where (l.latch#=ln.latch#) AND
       (((misses/(gets+.001))*100 > .2) OR
       ((immediate_misses/(immediate_gets+.001))*100 > .2))
order by l.name;
```

NAME	MISS_RATIO	IMMEDIATE_MISS_RATIO
redo copy	0.0249938	.041334735

The following query can be used to list the latch statistics:

```
SQL> select name,
            gets,
            misses,
            sleeps,
            immediate_gets "IM_GETS",
            immediate_misses "IM_MISS"
     from v$latch
     order by name;
```

NAME	GETS	MISSES	SLEEPS	IM_GETS	IM_MISS
KCL free list latch	0	0	0	0	0
KCL name table latch	0	0	0	0	0
NLS data objects	0	0	0	0	0
archive control	0	0	0	0	0
cache buffer handles	7	0	0	0	0
cache buffers chains	588477	0	0	3823	0
cache buffers lru chain	1158	0	0	254567	0
cache protection latch	0	0	0	0	0
cached attr list	0	0	0	0	0
cost function	0	0	0	0	0
device information	0	0	0	0	0
dml lock allocation	1402	0	0	0	0
enqueue hash chains	132894	0	0	0	0
enqueues	263882	0	0	0	0
error message lists	0	0	0	0	0
global transaction	0	0	0	0	0
global tx free list	0	0	0	0	0
...	...	...	...	...	...
...	...	...	...	...	...
...	...	...	...	...	...
...	...	...	...	...	...
virtual circuits	0	0	0	0	0

5.6.1   REDUCE_ALARM

You can use the init.ora parameter reduce_alarm (wakeup monitor) to reduce the interprocess alarm traffic. If reduce_alarm=TRUE, an additional background process (WMON) is created to help reduce the alarm interprocess workload and system call and context switch overhead associated with alarms. In certain cases, enabling the wakeup monitor has shown a performance increase of 6 percent. However, this is highly dependent on the nature of the workload and application. Enabling WMON has also resulted in performance degradation for certain application environments. Therefore, set reduce_alarm=TRUE only if it provides a performance gain and only after thoroughly testing your system and application with the wakeup monitor process enabled.

5.7 TUNING ROLLBACK SEGMENTS

Rollback segments store the pre-image of changed data. The rollback segment contains the data as it existed before the change. It is used to restore the data in the event that the transaction aborts, issues a rollback statement, or terminates abnormally. Rollback segments are also used to create read-consistent views of data for transactions that may have started before the data was modified. Transactions (non read-only transactions) are assigned to rollback segments by Oracle from the pool of rollback segments that are specified in the `init.ora` parameter `rollback_segments`. The two `init.ora` parameters `transactions_per_rollback_segment` and `max_rollback _segments` specify the number of rollback segments brought on-line in the rollback cache in the SGA upon instance startup. The two parameters do not limit the number of rollback segments that can be used by transactions. Oracle always maintains the SYSTEM rollback segment in addition to the user private and public rollback segments. The minimum number of rollback segments that will be brought on-line upon instance startup is defined by the value of

```
CEIL (TRANSACTIONS / TRANSACTIONS_PER_ROLLBACK_SEGMENT)
```

The `CEIL` function rounds up to the next integer. For example, if `TRANSACTIONS=100`, and `TRANSCATIONS_PER_ROLLBACK_SEGMENT=1`, Oracle, upon instance startup, attempts to bring at least 100 rollback segments on-line from the pool of available rollback segments.

The approach to tuning rollback segments is twofold: quantity and sizing. The quantity approach ensures that enough rollback segments exist to service the amount of users and transactions without causing high waits or transaction failures. Sizing refers to the storage parameters of the rollback segments that ensure that rollback segments are not constantly extending, shrinking, and/or wrapping.

5.7.1 NUMBER OF ROLLBACK SEGMENTS

As far as quantity, you should create enough rollback segments to serve the transaction workload. Ideally, each concurrent user (session) should have a separate rollback segment to eliminate rollback segment contention. However, not only will this increase the size of the rollback cache, it may also not even be possible due to space availability. Before you create rollback segments, make sure that the underlying tablespaces housing the rollback segments are striped and spread across multiple disk drives and controllers. Start by creating a default set of rollback segments such as 10 or 20. You can then query the `v$waitstat` to determine if user processes are waiting on rollback segments. For example, the following query can be used to list the undo wait statistics:

```
SQL>    select class,count,time
        from v$waitstat
        where class in ('free list',
                'system undo header',
```

```
                              'system undo block',
                              'undo header',
                              'undo block')
              order by class;
```

CLASS	COUNT	TIME
free list	0	0
system undo block	0	0
system undo header	0	0
undo block	0	0
undo header	0	0

```
5 rows selected.
```

From this query, you can see that no user process had to wait for a rollback segment block or header (undo block and undo header). Rollback segments are also referred to as undo segments because they contain the pre-image of the data that allows the transaction to be undone (rolled back).

The following queries report the total number of requests for data as well as the rollback segment hit ratios:

```
SQL> select sum(value) "Total # Requests of Data"
     from v$sysstat
     where name in ('db block gets','consistent gets');
```

```
Total # Requests of Data
```
```
          5295232
```

```
SQL> select name,waits,gets,
            (100-(waits/gets)) "Hit Ratio"
     from v$rollstat a,v$rollname b
     where (a.usn=b.usn);
```

NAME	WAITS	GETS	Hit Ratio
SYSTEM	0	4356	100
RBS1	0	5425	100
RBS2	0	6974	100
RBS3	0	5326	100
RBS4	0	9539	100

If the hit ratios are 95 percent or higher, then the number of existing rollback segments is optimal. If, however, the hit ratios are low and waits are high, you need to add more rollback segments. You can add more rollback segments by issuing the create rollback segment statement and adjusting the relevant init.ora parameters.

5.7.2 SIZING ROLLBACK SEGMENTS

The sizing of the individual rollback segments is critical to the overall performance. If rollback segments are not sized properly, extends and shrinks can occur frequently, thereby reducing the performance of the transaction. To size a rollback segment appropriately, you will need to estimate the amount of data being modified, inserted, or deleted by each transaction. Remember to consider batch size operations that operate on a number of rows simultaneously as opposed to a single row at a time. For large batch transactions, you may want to consider creating separate rollback segments, as discussed in Section 5.7.3. Once you have a good feel for the amount of data being modified, then you should size the initial extents of each rollback segment so that a transaction can always complete by using only the initial extent. This eliminates the need of the transaction to continue extending itself, subsequently resulting in recursive storage management overhead. When a transaction needs another extent, the transaction is extended across another extent within the rollback segment. The number of times a rollback segment extended itself and allocated another extent is reported by the extends column in the v$rollstat view. You can also use the Enterprise Manager to report rollback segment hit and miss ratios. If the number of extends is high, it is an indication that the extent sizes are too small.

A new feature of Oracle7 provides the OPTIMAL storage parameter used within rollback segments. The OPTIMAL parameter specifies the optimal size of the rollback segment when a shrink of the rollback segment occurs. A shrink occurs when multiple rollback segment extents are de-allocated into one large (optimal size) rollback segment extent. The optimal size must be at least larger than (INITIAL + NEXT + ⋯⋯ up to MINEXTENTS). The OPTIMAL setting can be used to cause rollback segments to shrink down to the optimal size. For long-running transactions, the OPTIMAL parameter should be set large so that the frequency of shrinks is reduced. For short-running transactions, set optimal to the minimum value so that rollback segments will tend to be small, increasing the likelihood they will remain in the cache. You should tune the OPTIMAL setting so that the number of shrinks is extremely low, and the average sizes shrunk are high. A high number of shrinks indicates that the OPTIMAL setting is too low.

When you size rollback segments, you should set the INITIAL and NEXT extent values the same. The value for PCTINCREASE for rollback segments is always zero. Setting the INITIAL and NEXT extent to the same value helps prevent fragmentation.

In addition to the rollback statistics columns listed previously, you should also monitor the high-water mark size as well as the number of wraps that occur. The high-water mark reports the maximum space ever used by a rollback segment. The wraps column reports the number of times a transaction continued writing from one extent in a rollback segment to another existing extent. The average active sizes (aveactive) column reports the average number of bytes used by active extents in the rollback segment. These rollback statistics are available through the v$rollstat view. Analyzing the number of wraps, shrinks, extends, and average sizes can help you size your rollback segments more effectively. The goal is to minimize extends and shrinks by maintaining a transaction in a single or few rollback segment extents.

5.7.3   LARGE TRANSACTIONS

If your application consists of long-running transactions that process large amounts of data, you may want to consider creating separate large rollback segments for this purpose. The application can then assign its transaction to the large rollback segment specifically by using the following command:

```
SQL> SET TRANSACTION USE ROLLBACK SEGMENT
          <rollback segment name>;
```

This enables the long transaction to utilize a dedicated rollback segment to ensure that adequate rollback space exists to complete the transaction and to minimize contention with other users issuing small transactions. This technique is also ideal for batch runs that run for an extended period of time (typically overnight).

5.8   THE SHARED POOL

Oracle7 introduced the concept of the shared pool. The shared pool, as the term suggests, allows multiple users to share SQL and PL/SQL areas. This reduces parsing overhead for multiple repeated SQL. The shared pool consists of three main areas: the library cache, the data dictionary cache, and session information. The size of the shared pool is specified by the init.ora parameter shared_pool_size.

5.8.1   LIBRARY CACHE

The library cache consists of the shared SQL and PL/SQL areas. It helps reduce parsing overhead by maintaining parsed SQL and PL/SQL in the library cache. Therefore, any subsequent execution of the same exact SQL or PL/SQL eliminates the need to reparse the statement. This increases performance, especially for OLTP systems that tend to have a custom application issuing the same generic SQL. Using bind variables in your SQL statements also helps increase the utilization of the library cache.

A library cache miss can occur if a user submits a parse call for a SQL statement that does not exist in the library cache or in the shared SQL area. Oracle will parse the SQL statement and allocate a shared SQL area for the statement. You can reduce the library cache miss ratio by ensuring that users maximize the utilization of the shared SQL area. A library cache miss can also occur if a shared SQL statement was aged-out of the shared pool. This causes the SQL statement, once reexecuted, to be reparsed, and Oracle then has to allocate a shared SQL area for the statement and then execute the statement. Maintaining a high library cache hit ratio can increase performance by reducing parsing and shared SQL area allocation overhead. You can monitor the library cache by querying the v$librarycache view. The following query computes the library cache hit ratio:

```
SQL> select sum(pins) "Executions",
            sum(reloads) "Cache Misses",
            100-(round((((sum(reloads)/sum(pins)))),2))
            "Lib. Cache Hit Ratio"
from v$librarycache;
```

The output of the query should look as follows:

Executions	Cache Misses	Lib. Cache Hit Ratio
209041	1096	99.99

The cache hit ratio in this case is 99.99 percent, which is an excellent hit ratio. You can maintain a high library cache hit ratio by ensuring that the shared pool is sized appropriately, that SQL statements are being reused, and that cursors are also being reused. You should set the init.ora parameter open_cursors to the maximum number of concurrent cursors that will be opened by a session.

The library cache is dependent on the fact that SQL statements must be exactly the same, character for character. This means that spaces and case sensitivity will affect whether or not a SQL statement is reused. To maximize the use of the library cache, ensure that SQL statements are exact. Also, use bind variables to specify predicate values in the WHERE clause. This will avoid queries in which WHERE clauses are hard-coded with scalar values. Using bind variables allows the SQL statement to be reused because the statement is exactly the same, only the value of the run-time bind variable is changing. Tools such as Developer/2000 help increase the library cache hit ratio since multiple uses of the same Developer/2000 application will execute the same SQL.

You can also increase the speed of SQL execution by setting the init.ora parameter CURSOR_SPACE_FOR_TIME=TRUE. When set to TRUE, this parameter causes shared SQL areas to be pinned in the shared pool. As long as there is an open cursor that references the shared SQL, the shared SQL is not aged-out of the shared pool. This can increase the performance of SQL execution by maintaining shared SQL in the cache. This parameter, when set to true, also causes the private SQL area allocated for each cursor to be maintained in the library cache. This improves cursor allocation and initialization time as well as overall SQL execution time. If this parameter is set to FALSE, Oracle needs to scan the library cache to determine if the SQL statement is in the shared SQL area. If set to TRUE, this check is not needed since the shared SQL area cannot be aged-out while at least one active cursor references the SQL statement. Only set this parameter to TRUE if your shared pool is large enough.

Another init.ora parameter SESSION_CACHED_CURSORS can be used to cache multiple reuses of a session cursor. If more than three parse requests are issued on the same SQL statement, the session cursor associated with the statement is moved into the session cursor cache. Subsequent parses on the SQL statement by the same session will be faster because the cursor is in the session cursor cache. An LRU algorithm is used to age-out cursor entries from the session cursor cache.

You can set the SESSION_CACHED_CURSORS through the init.ora file or through the following command:

```
SQL> alter session set session_cached_cursors = <value>;
```

By querying the v$syststat view, you can obtain statistics on the use of cached session cursors. For example, consider the following output from v$sysstat:

NAME	VALUE
parse count	4106
session cursor cache count	7
session cursor cache hits	1653

Divide the session cursor cache hits by the parse count to determine the percentage of parses that are being serviced from the session cursor cache. In this case, 1653/4106 is approximately 40 percent. You should increase the value of session_cached_cursors if the percentage is low. You should also monitor the parse count at the session level by querying the v$sesstat view. If little gain is observed after increasing the value of session_cached_cursors, it is an indication that the application is not reexecuting the same SQL statement within the same session enough times to cause the cursor to be migrated to the cursor cache.

You should also query the v$db_object_cache view to list the objects in the library cache. The view maintains statistics such as the number of loads, executions, pins, and locks. The v$db_object_cache view allows you to determine the objects loaded in the library cache as well as corresponding object-level statistics.

5.8.2 DATA DICTIONARY CACHE

The data dictionary cache is also part of the shared pool. The data dictionary cache is used to cache data dictionary objects such as tables, indexes, internal storage management tables, and other data dictionary objects. You can monitor the cache hit ratio of the data dictionary cache by querying the v$rowcache view. The following query is an example that reports v$rowcache statistics.

```
SQL> select sum(gets) "DC. Gets",
            sum(getmisses) "DC. misses",
            round(((1-(sum(getmisses)/
                  sum(gets)))*100),2) "DC.Hit Ratio"
            from v$rowcache;
```

DC. Gets	DC. misses	DC.Hit Ratio
656763	954	99.85

This example shows a high cache hit ratio (99.85%). If you see low cache hit ratios, you need to increase the size of the shared pool. A low data dictionary cache hit ratio can cause a tangible performance degradation because OLTP transactions usually result in *recursive* SQL. Recursive SQL refers to a user SQL statement that requires additional backend SQL, such as storage management, to complete the statement. Insufficient space in the shared pool can cause data dictionary objects to be aged-out quickly, thereby decreasing the cache hit ratio and impacting future accesses to the dictionary objects.

5.8.3   MAXIMIZING THE SHARED POOL UTILIZATION

To size the shared pool adequately, you need to monitor four things: the library cache hit ratio, data dictionary cache hit ratio, session cache hit ratio, and memory used. Monitoring the cache hit ratios has been discussed in previous sections. The memory used is also important. You can query the v$sgastat view to determine if the shared pool is too large and is not being utilized. The following query shows the output from the v$sgastat table showing free memory:

```
SQL> select name,
        bytes/1024/1024 "Size in MB"
        from v$sgastat
        where name='free memory';

NAME            Size in MB
_____

free memory    39.6002884
```

In this example, there is 39 M of free memory in the shared pool, which means that the total size of the shared pool is not being utilized. In this example, the size of the shared pool is approximately 60 M (shared_pool_size=60000000). This means that more than half of the shared pool is not being used. Large amounts of free memory reported by v$sgastat indicate that memory is being wasted, and could be better directed to other areas such as the buffer cache, redo buffer, or other user processes.

5.8.4   FRAGMENTATION IN THE SHARED POOL

Fragmentation is also a problem that can cause performance problems with the shared pool. As objects of different sizes are brought in and aged-out of the shared pool, memory can be fragmented. To correct this problem, Oracle provides parameters that help deal with the problem of fragmentation within the shared pool.

The init.ora parameters SHARED_POOL_RESERVED_SIZE and SHARED_POOL_RESERVED_MIN_ALLOC specify the amount of the shared pool memory to be reserved from the total shared_pool_size for allocations, and the minimum amount of space to be allocated from the shared pool free list. If a shared pool memory allocation is larger than the value of SHARED_POOL_

RESERVED_MIN_ALLOC, space can be allocated from the reserved list if the allocation cannot be satisfied from the free list.

SHARED_POOL_RESERVED_SIZE should be set so that all requests for memory in the shared pool can always be satisfied without having to age objects out of the shared pool. The general rule is to set SHARED_POOL_RESERVED_SIZE equal to 5–10 percent of the total shared_pool_size. Be careful when setting SHARED_POOL_RESERVED_SIZE, because a high value can cause objects to be aged-out so that sufficient free memory is always reserved. A value of zero for SHARED_POOL_RESERVED_SIZE means that no shared pool space is reserved. Set SHARED_POOL_RESERVED_MIN_ALLOC so that allocations do not overallocate space and waste memory that other processes could have used. If you enable the shared pool reserve, you should query the v$shared_pool_reserved view to obtain statistics on the shared pool reserve area. The v$shared_pool_reserved view maintains statistics regarding shared pool reserve usage such as available space, number of requests, misses, request failures, and amount of space used. The statistics from the v$shared_pool_reserved view can also aid in sizing the shared pool reserve area.

5.8.5 PINNING OBJECTS IN THE SHARED POOL

When a large object needs to be loaded into the shared pool, Oracle may age out smaller objects to make memory space available for the large object. Memory fragmentation may occur if objects are frequently loaded into the shared pool and then aged out. Oracle8 improved the SGA cache management by using segmented memory structures. This helps reduce the fragmentation that can occur by the loading and unloading of large objects in the shared pool.

The package DBMS_SHARED_POOL can help you improve response time and reduce fragmentation by pinning large objects in the shared pool. The DBMS_SHARED_POOL package provides the procedures DBMS_SHARED_POOL.KEEP and DBMS_SHARED_POOL.SIZES to pin the specified object in the shared pool and display the shared pool objects of a size larger than the size specified by the parameter in the SIZES procedure call. For example, the following SQL can be used to show the objects in the shared pool larger than 5K:

```
SQL> SET SERVEROUTPUT ON SIZE 5000
SQL> EXECUTE DBMS_SHARED_POOL.SIZES(5000);
```

The procedures DBMS_SHARED_POOL.KEEP and DBMS_SHARED_POOL.UNKEEP can be used to pin objects in the shared pool, and allow objects to be aged out, respectively The syntax for the procedures is

```
DBMS_SHARED_POOL.KEEP (object, object type);
```

```
DBMS_SHARED_POOL.UNKEEP (object, object type);
```

The `object` parameter is the value that is returned from the `DBMS_SHARED_POOL.SIZES` procedure call. If you have large objects such as PL/SQL packages, pinning the object in the shared pool can improve overall response time and shared pool utilization. Pinning certain objects can also help reduce shared pool memory fragmentation. The `DBMS_SHARED_POOL` package is created from the SQL script dbmspool.sql (located in `$ORACLE_HOME/rdbms/admin`).

5.9 SIZING THE SGA

Oracle creates at least one shared memory segment upon instance startup to hold the SGA. The SGA should be in physical memory. Reads and writes to the SGA are significantly faster than physical reads and writes to the disk. Therefore, it is important that the SGA areas be optimally sized in order to reduce physical I/O and maximize memory utilization. The total amount of shared memory required by the Oracle Server for the System Global Area (SGA) can be calculated by the following formula:

```
total shared memory (size of SGA) = Fixed Size +
                                     Variable Size +
                                     Database Buffers +
                                     Redo Buffers.
```

The fixed size is determined by the products that have been installed on the system. The variable size is determined by the majority of the init.ora parameters. The database buffer cache size is determined by the value of <db_block_buffers> × <db_block_size>. The default block size (db_block_size) is 2K. Therefore, if db_block_buffers=10000, the size of the database buffer cache would be 20 M. The redo buffer size is determined by the log_buffer parameter (specified in bytes).

The key to tuning the SGA in terms of obtaining the most optimal values for db_block_buffers, shared_pool_size, log_buffer, and log_archive_buffers is to monitor the utilization and respective hit ratios of each. For example, if you have a 95 percent buffer cache hit ratio and 0 redo log space requests, start decreasing the size of each buffer by 5 percent to see the effects on the buffer cache hit ratio and redo log space requests. If the hit ratio and redo log space requests remain the same, then obviously the buffer areas were unnecessarily large. Conversely, if you experience poor hit ratios, continue to increase the size of each area experiencing the poor hit ratio until the hit ratio is optimal. You should target hit ratios of at least 90 percent to allow for future system scalability. Also, be careful when you increase the size of the SGA to make sure excessive paging or swapping does not occur.

5.9.1 MULTIPLE BUFFER POOLS

Oracle8 allows you to configure multiple buffer pools in order to improve buffer cache utilization. Object access patterns can vary depending on the application. A very large segment that is frequently accessed can cause the data buffers of other segments to be aged out of the cache. This reduces the overall benefits of the cache and results in the large segment consuming a large majority of the buffer cache. Multiple buffer pools can improve buffer cache utilization in situations where large segment reads are not occurring frequently enough to synchronize with the flush cycle of the buffer cache. In this case, you can either relocate the large segment to a separate recycle buffer pool, or place the small segments in the keep buffer pool. This helps separate the segments based on the access frequency, thereby maximizing the utilization of the buffer cache. The recycle buffer pool should be smaller than the default cache and is intended for quick reuse of buffers. The keep buffer pool can be used to improve the response time of SQL statements by ensuring that the small segments are not aged-out of the buffer cache. This in turn helps reduce cache misses and physical I/O.

A recycle buffer pool is beneficial for very large tables that are experiencing random I/O access. The idea behind the recycle buffer pool is to remove the objects from memory once they are no longer needed. A keep buffer pool is useful for small, frequently accessed tables requiring quick response times. Use the following queries to determine the number of cache buffers used by the particular object or segment and total number of database buffers:

```
SQL> SELECT count(*) "Number of Object Buffers"
     FROM x$bh
     WHERE obj in
             (SELECT data_object_id
              FROM dba_objects
              WHERE (object_name = <object name> ) AND
              (object_type = <object type>));

SQL> SELECT value "Total DB Buffers"
     FROM  v$parameter
     WHERE name = 'db_block_buffers';
```

You can divide the number of object buffers by the total number of database buffers to determine the percentage of cache buffers used by a particular segment.

The `init.ora` parameters `buffer_pool_keep` and `buffer_pool_recycle` specify the number of buffers and latches to be allocated for the keep and recycle buffer pools, respectively. The buffers allocated to the keep and recycle buffer pools are allocated from the total amount of database buffers specified by `db_block_buffers`. The latches for each buffer pool are allocated from the total number of LRU latches specified by `db_block_lru_latches`. Therefore, the aggregate number of buffers and latches for all buffer pools cannot exceed the values of `db_block_buffers` and `db_block_lru_latches`. The following is an example setting of the buffer pool `init.ora` parameters:

```
buffer_pool_keep=(buffers:8500, lru_latches:4)

buffer_pool_recycle=(buffers:1000, lru_latches:2)
```

The storage clause of the ALTER or CREATE SQL commands allows you to specify the default buffer pool for the object via the BUFFER_POOL option. You can also query the object definition views such as USER_TABLES and USER_INDEXES to determine the buffer pool for an object.

The V$BUFFER_POOL_STATISTICS view provides buffer pool statistics that will help you tune and size the individual buffer pools based on the application workload. The logic behind the keep buffer pool is to help reduce physical I/O by maintaining objects in memory. Use the following query to monitor the keep buffer pool cache hit ratio:

```
SQL> SELECT round(1-((physical_reads)/
                (db_block_gets+consistent_gets)),2)
                || '%' "Keep Buffer Hit Ratio"
        FROM v$buffer_pool_statistics
        WHERE name='KEEP';
```

In order to effectively measure the keep buffer pool cache hit ratio, you should compute the hit ratio only after the system has been running for some time, thus allowing time for the buffers to be loaded into the buffer pool. It is important that you size the buffer pools appropriately. An object that continues to grow may no longer fit in the keep buffer pool, subsequently losing its blocks from the buffer cache. It is key that you size the buffer pools optimally according to your workload in order to maximize buffer cache utilization.

In addition to monitoring buffer pool utilization, you should also monitor the LRU latch statistics to determine if there is contention for the LRU latches. The following queries can be used to determine the LRU child latches and associated buffer pool name experiencing LRU latch contention:

```
SQL> SELECT child#,
                misses/gets "LRU Latch Miss Ratio",
                sleeps/gets "LRU Latch Sleep Ratio"
        FROM V$LATCH_CHILDREN
        WHERE (name = 'cache buffers lru chain')
        ORDER by child#;
```

Miss and sleep ratios higher than 1 percent indicate LRU latch contention. Using the following query, you can determine which buffer pool is experiencing LRU latch contention by specifying the child# of the LRU latch from the previous query:

```
SQL> SELECT name
        FROM V$BUFFER_POOL
        WHERE (lo_setid <=: child #) AND
                (hi_setid >=: child #);
```

After identifying the child latches and specific pools experiencing the LRU latch contention, you may need to increase the number of LRU latches (`db_block_lru_latches`) or reconfigure the number of latches assigned to each buffer pool.

In Oracle8, if you configure multiple DBWR processes (`db_writer_process-es`) with only one buffer pool, the buffer cache is divided up amongst the DBWR processes by LRU latches; whereby each LRU latch manages an LRU list. Each LRU list consists of database block buffers. In such a case, it is important that each DBWR process receive an equivalent distribution of buffers so as to balance the workload among the DBWR processes. This avoids situations where certain DBWR processes receive a large LRU list to process while others receive very small LRU lists. If you configure multiple buffer pools and multiple DBWR processes, the number of LRU latches per pool should be equal to or a multiple of the number of DBWR processes configured. In the case of multiple buffer pools, each buffer pool may have a different block utilization rate. Buffer blocks in the recycle buffer pool are typically frequently modified whereas buffer blocks in the keep pool may be seldom modified. This translates into more writes for the recycle buffer pool than that of the keep buffer pool. Consequently, in order to achieve an optimal load balance, each DBWR process should receive an equal number of LRU lists per pool. When multiple buffer pools are employed, each buffer pool maintains a contiguous range of LRU latches. It is important that you optimally configure the number of LRU latches based on the number of available processors, number of DBWR processes, and buffer pool configuration. This helps ensure an even workload distribution across the DBWR processes thereby maximizing database I/O throughput.

5.9.2 LARGE POOL

Oracle8 provides the ability to configure a separate memory pool to be used for large memory allocations in Multithreaded Server (MTS) environments. Memory allocated for MTS sessions can reduce the amount of shared pool memory available for the shared SQL cache. This may cause additional parses and loads because of SQL statements that may get aged-out of the cache to make space for MTS session memory allocations. Configuring a separate pool for MTS session memory helps reduce contention for shared pool memory. The large pool can also be used for I/O buffers during backups. The `init.ora` parameters `large_pool_size` and `large_pool_min_alloc` specify the size of the large pool and the minimum allocation size when memory is allocated from the large pool, respectively. You can also examine the POOL column of the `v$sgastat` view to determine in which pool objects reside. The large pool is not managed as a cache, and objects are not aged out of the large memory pool. The large memory pool is a memory allocation heap which can be used for MTS session memory and backup and restore I/O buffers.

In order to size the large pool optimally, you can query the `v$sysstat` view to determine the amount of session memory allocations:

```
SQL> select name,value
     from v$sysstat
     where (name like '%memory%') AND
           (name like '%session%')
   order by name;
```

NAME	VALUE
session pga memory	44924560
session pga memory max	44924560
session uga memory	365168
session uga memory max	29576300

The session memory allocation statistics provided by the v$sysstat view can be used to size the large pool appropriately. You should also query the v$sesstat view in order to obtain the session memory allocations per session rather than a total at the instance level (v$sysstat). The v$sesstat view allows you to determine the amount of session memory allocated per session. You may find that certain sessions are allocating large amounts of memory while other sessions are using very little session memory.

5.10   TUNING SHARED MEMORY

Oracle uses shared memory to hold the SGA. User processes (connections) attach to the shared memory segment via their corresponding shadow process. The shadow process then can access the SGA to perform the client requests.

Solaris provides the *Intimate Shared Memory* (ISM) option. The intimate shared memory option allows processes attaching to the same shared memory address to share the same page table entry, which avoids having to duplicate page table entries for each process, thereby reducing memory consumption. To enable ISM in the Solaris kernel, edit the /etc/system file and place the following entry:

```
set shmsys:share_page_table=1
```

To enable the use of ISM within the Oracle Server, set the init.ora parameter use_ism=TRUE. Enabling the ISM feature can increase performance dramatically on Solaris systems with a large number of concurrent users.

Another init.ora parameter pre_page_sga enables you to increase the performance of the SGA for those platforms that do not support shared memory segment locking. In Solaris, if use_ism=TRUE, the SGA shared memory segments are locked in memory. Sequent also locks shared memory segments. Locking shared memory prevents the shared memory segments (i.e., SGA) from being paged-out. If your platform does not support the locking of shared memory, you can use the `init.ora` parameter `pre_page_sga` to try to keep the SGA memory pages warm. If `pre_page_sga=TRUE`, the SGA memory pages are touched upon connection and instance startup. This increases instance startup time and user connection time but can help reduce the number of page faults thereafter by causing all SGA pages to be brought into memory. This maximizes the performance of the SGA by bringing all the SGA pages into memory upon startup or user login as opposed to incrementally. If your system does not support shared memory locking, set `pre_page_sga=TRUE` to increase the utilization of the SGA.

The maximum amount of shared memory allowed in the system is determined by the kernel parameters SHMMAX, SHMMIN, SHMSEG, and SHMMNI, shown in Table 5.2.

TABLE 5.2   Shared memory kernel parameters

PARAMETER	DEFINITION
SHMMAX	Specifies the maximum size of a single shared memory segment.
SHMMIN	Specifies the minimum size of a shared memory segment.
SHMMNI	The maximum number of shared memory identifiers.
SHMSEG	The maximum number of shared memory segments that can be attached by a process.

On Sequent, there are also memory limits per process that will need to be increased if you are configuring a large SGA. The kernel parameters SVMMLIM and HVMMLIM control the soft and hard limits, respectively, of virtual memory available per process. You should set these parameters to the maximum amount of memory addressable by your system. The maximum amount of shared memory available to a single process is equal to the value of SHMMAX × SHMSEG. Declaring a large SGA may require you to relocate the base address of the SGA. The base address of the SGA is defined in the file `ksms.s` (`$ORACLE_HOME/rdbms/lib`). If you change the base address of the SGA, you will need to relink the Oracle Server executable.[6]

5.11   SIZING THE BUFFER CACHE

The size of the buffer cache is specified by the `init.ora` parameter `db_block_buffers`. The buffer cache is used to cache database blocks in the SGA in order to reduce the amount of physical I/O. Hence, a larger cache can help increase per-

---

6. Check with Oracle support and your OS vendor's support to ensure that the correct base address is selected when remapping the SGA.

formance by maintaining changes in the cache as opposed to on the physical disk. If your system is primarily an OLTP system, you should use a smaller database block size, such as 2K or 4K, allowing more database blocks to be cached in the SGA. To size the buffer cache appropriately, use the following query to query the v$sysstat table to report the buffer cache hit ratio:

```
SQL> select round(((1-(sum(decode(name,
              'physical reads',value,0))/
               (sum(decode(name,'db block gets',value,0))+
               (sum(decode(name,'consistent gets',
               value,0))))))
               *100),2) || '%' "Buffer Cache Hit Ratio"
    from v$sysstat;



    Buffer Cache Hit Ratio
    _____

                   97.63%
```

[Formula:
Hit Ratio = 1 − (`physical reads`/(`db block gets`+`consistent gets`))]

In this example, the buffer cache hit ratio is high (97 percent). You should target a buffer cache hit ratio of at least 90 percent to allow for scalability as more users are added to the system. Monitor the cache hit ratio, and continue to increase db_block_buffers until you achieve a high cache hit ratio such as 90 percent or higher. You should also monitor the buffer cache hit ratio at the session level via the v$sesstat view. The v$sesstat view maintains statistics at the session level while the v$sysstat view maintains statistics at the instance level. Monitoring the buffer cache hit ratio at the session level allows you to identify the offending sessions that are causing large displacements in the overall buffer cache hit ratio. In addition, monitoring the buffer cache hit ratio at the session level may also help you identify those sessions that could benefit most from multiple buffer pools. When you increase the size of the buffer cache, be sure that your system has enough memory to accommodate the increase; otherwise paging may increase and swapping may occur. Also, when you tune the buffer cache, make sure you monitor the other areas in the SGA to ensure that increasing the buffer cache did not offset another area.

In Oracle8, you can use the v$recent_bucket view to estimate the gains of increasing the size of the buffer cache. The init.ora parameter db_block_lru_extended_statistics enables the collection of statistics for the v$recent_bucket view. Setting db_block_lru_extended_statistics=500 collects 500 rows of statistics in the v$recent_bucket view. Each row in the v$recent_bucket view corresponds to the addition of a buffer. When db_block_lru_extended_statistics=500, statistics are collected in order to estimate the potential gain of increasing the buffer cache size by an additional 500 buffers. The following query shows the cache hits per interval of 500 additional buffers:

```
SQL> SELECT 500*TRUNC(ROWNUM/500)+1||
            ' to '||500*(TRUNC(ROWNUM/500)+1)
              "Interval",
          SUM(count) "Buffer Cache Hits"
     FROM V$RECENT_BUCKET
     GROUP BY TRUNC(ROWNUM/500);
```

Interval	Buffer Cache Hits
1 to 500	45320
501 to 1000	17680

The query results show that adding 500 buffers results in 45,320 cache hits. Adding an additional 500 buffers yields 17,680 cache hits in addition to the 45,320 cache hits from the first addition of 500 buffers. This results in a total of 63,000 cache hits when 1,000 buffers are added to the buffer cache. Using the above query can help you optimally size the buffer cache. It will also help you identify the drop-off point of the buffer cache hit ratio whereby adding additional buffers results in minimal (if any) gain.

In Oracle8, you can use the v$current_bucket view to estimate the performance of a reduced size buffer cache. The v$current_bucket view maintains a row for each buffer in the buffer cache and the amount of cache hits thereof. To enable the collection of statistics for the v$current_bucket view, set the init.ora parameter db_block_lru_statistics=TRUE. The v$current_bucket view helps you estimate the number of cache misses that would occur if the buffer cache size were reduced. The following query determines the number of cache hits that occur at each interval set of 1,000 buffers:

```
SQL> SELECT 1000*TRUNC(ROWNUM/1000)+1 ||
             ' to '||1000*(TRUNC(ROWNUM/1000)+1)
               "Interval",
           SUM(count) "Buffer Cache Hits"
     FROM V$CURRENT_BUCKET
     WHERE (ROWNUM > 0)
     GROUP BY TRUNC(ROWNUM/1000);
```

Interval	Buffer Cache Hits
1 to 1000	6370
1001 to 2000	0
2001 to 3000	0
3001 to 4000	0
4001 to 5000	0
5001 to 6000	0
6001 to 7000	0
7001 to 8000	0
8001 to 9000	0
9001 to 10000	0

The above query results show that buffers 9,001–10,000 contribute no cache hits. This query also shows that no cache misses would occur until the buffer cache is reduced to 1,000 or fewer buffers. This indicates that the buffer cache is unnecessarily large and can be reduced significantly in size without incurring cache misses.

Using the buffer cache statistic views v$recent_bucket and v$current_bucket can help you optimally size your buffer cache. The statistics provided by these views can also help you conserve memory by avoiding configuring large size buffer caches that are not fully utilized. Enabling db_block_lru_statistics and db_block_lru_extended_statistics can impact performance due to the overhead of collecting the statistics. Therefore, you should disable these parameters once you have completed tuning the buffer cache size.

5.12   TUNING ARCHIVING

If your database is in archive mode, you may want to increase the size of the archive buffers so as to minimize the amount of time LGWR is blocking, awaiting the ARCH (archiver) process to archive a redo log file. If archiving mode is enabled, LGWR cannot switch back to the log file that is currently being archived until the archiver completes the copy of the redo log file.

The init.ora parameter log_archive_buffer_size specifies the size of each archival buffer in redo log blocks size (i.e., 512 bytes). The init.ora parameter log_archive_buffers specifies the number of buffers to allocate for archiving. The default, which is sufficient for most workloads, is 4. Increasing the value of these parameters increases the speed of the archiver process significantly. However, a faster archiver process at the expense of slower background processes decreases overall system performance. Tune these parameters accordingly with the goal of synchronizing the archival rate with the other background processes, such as LGWR and DBWR.

You can also enable archiving I/O slaves if your platform does not support asynchronous I/O or the implementation of asynchronous I/O is not efficient. The `init.ora` parameter `arch_io_slaves` can be used to configure several I/O slaves for the purposes of parallelizing archive I/O requests. You should also monitor the archive destination disks to determine if disk I/O contention is occurring. Disk I/O contention can cause the ARCH process to wait on I/O completion and may also result in LGWR backing up if LGWR needs to switch back to the redo log file that is currently being archived.

5.13   THE POST-WAIT DRIVER

The Oracle Server, by default, uses semaphores to coordinate shared resource access. One semaphore is used per Oracle process. A process that needs a lock on an already-locked shared resource will suspend and wait until the resource becomes available. When the resource becomes available, the process' semaphore will be incremented when the process is posted. Semaphores can be an expensive operation for post and wait requests, and have resulted in poor scalability on certain platforms.

In an effort to improve scalability, several platforms provide a post-wait driver as an alternative to expensive semaphore operations for interprocess communication. To enable the post-wait driver in the Oracle Server, set the `init.ora` parameters `use_post_wait_driver=TRUE` and `post_wait_device=<post wait device name>`. Once enabled, Oracle will no longer use semaphores. You can verify this through the `ipcs` command while the Oracle Server is running. The post-wait driver is not available on all platforms. Check with the *Oracle Installation and Configuration Guide* for your specific platform for instructions on enabling the post-wait driver. You can use the post-wait driver to increase performance on certain platforms. If you are running Oracle on a Sequent system, you can choose between the post-wait driver and semaphores. On Sequent, the performance gain offered by the post-wait driver versus semaphores is approximately 5 percent. On Solaris, Oracle uses semaphores because of their demonstrated scalability and high performance.

5.14   TUNING TCP/IP

The default packet size used by SQL*Net V2 and Net8 is 2K for the Session Data Unit (SDU). The packet size utilized by the TCP/IP stack and underlying network layer is 1K for most platforms. The SDU should be equal to, or a multiple of, the underlying TCP/IP packet size. Extra network overhead may be needed if the packet size is smaller than the SDU size since each SDU packet would be broken down into smaller packet sizes. Some platforms allow to you increase the OS TCP/IP packet size. Increasing the OS packet size to 2K allows SQL*Net/Net8 packets and OS TCP/IP packets to be the same size.

5.14.1   SESSION DATA UNIT (SDU)

The Oracle networking layer places data in buffers and then sends the buffers when full or when the data is requested. The Session Data Unit (SDU) is the buffer that is used to send data across the network. By adjusting the SDU unit size from the default of 2K, you may be able to increase performance by reducing the number of networking round trips. You should only modify the SDU size if large amounts of data are being transmitted, a Wide Area Network (WAN) is being used where latency is critical, or the packet sizes are consistently the same size. The Transport Data Unit (TDU) is the block used to transmit the data to the underlying protocol adapter. TDU and SDU can be set to different sizes; however, in most cases there is little advantage in doing so.

Before adjusting the sizes of SDU and TDU, you should examine the amount of network traffic by querying the v$sysstat view:

```
SQL> select name,
            value
     from v$sysstat
     where upper(name) like '%NET%';
```

NAME	VALUE
bytes sent via SQL*Net to client	2385783
bytes received via SQL*Net from client	1655637
SQL*Net roundtrips to/from client	6587
bytes sent via SQL*Net to dblink	0
bytes received via SQL*Net from dblink	0
SQL*Net roundtrips to/from dblink	0

This query reports the amount of bytes of SQL*Net/Net8 traffic as well as the number of round trips. This information can help you size the SDU and TDU buffers more effectively based on the network traffic. You should also query the v$system_event view to determine if users are waiting on networking events:

```
SQL> select event,
            total_waits,
            time_waited,
            average_wait
     from v$system_event
     where upper(event) like '%NET%';
```

EVENT	TOTAL_WAITS	TIME_WAITED	AVERAGE_WAIT
SQL*Net message to client	6665	6	.000900225
SQL*Net more data to client	343	7	.020408163
SQL*Net message from client	6662	76648	11.5052537
SQL*Net more data from client	45	1	.022222222
SQL*Net break/reset to client	24	0	0.0

After determining the amount of networking traffic and whether users are experiencing waits on networking events, you can adjust the size of SDU and TDU by modifying the `tnsnames.ora` and `listener.ora` files on both the client and the server. In general, performance has increased when setting SDU to a multiple of the database block size. In addition to reviewing the networking statistics and events, you should test your application thoroughly in order to determine the optimal settings for SDU/TDU.

```
TNSNAMES.ORA:

sales- (DESCRIPTION=
        (SDU=8192)   ***** session data unit buffer size
        (TDU=8192)   ***** transport data unit size
        (ADDRESS= (PROTOCOL=tcp)
        (PORT=1521)
        (HOST=myhost))
        (CONNECT_DATA= (SID=prods))
    )
```

```
LISTENER.ORA: The parameters need to appear in the SID_DESC
clause.
```

```
SID_LIST_LISTENER =
   (SID_LIST =
      (SID_DESC =
          (SDU = 8192) ***** Connects to this SID
          (TDU = 8192) ***** using an 8k packet size.
          (SID_NAME = prods)
          (ORACLE_HOME = /myhost/unix/oracle)
       )
    )
```

5.14.2 NO DELAY FLAG

TCP often coalesces packets together before transmitting in order to reduce round trips and group small numbers of requests into a single packet. This function of grouping requests may cause delays for a small number of clients requiring immediate responses. If using the TCP/IP protocol adapter with SQL*Net V2 or Net8, you can enable the no delay flag by setting the parameter `tcp.nodelay=yes` in the `protocol.ora` file.

5.15 TUNING THE ORACLE NETWORKING LAYER

Whether you are using SQL*Net V2 or Net8, it is important that you configure the Oracle networking layer optimally in order to improve network utilization and throughput. By utilizing the different options of SQL*Net V2 and Net8, you can maximize the utilization of network resources and improve network transmission efficiency.

5.15.1 OUT-OF-BAND BREAKS

The UNIX TCP/IP stack supports the mechanism utilized by SQL*Net and Net8 TCP/IP for out-of-band breaks. The Net8 and SQL*Net V2 listener process negotiates out-of-band breaks by default. Performance can increase up to 20 percent by using out-of-band breaks over using in-band breaks. For those platforms that do not support out-of-band breaks, the Oracle server process polls periodically to check for client-side interrupts. You can also increase the interval between checks for client-side interrupts by setting the parameter BREAK_POLL_SKIP in the sqlnet.ora file on the server side. You can set BREAK_POLL_SKIP to a very large number to reduce the number of polls that are done (i.e., BREAK_POLL_SKIP=10000000). The performance gain offered by tuning BREAK_POLL_SKIP is minimal, but it can help reduce system calls and context switches.

5.15.2 DEADMAN ALERT

SQL*Net V2 uses the TNS (Transparent Name Substrate) interface, allowing multiple different stacks to connect to the Oracle Server. SQL*Net V2.1 and above offer an extremely useful feature known as *deadman alert*. Deadman alert probes for dead or invalid connections and terminates the corresponding server processes, thereby freeing up system resources (memory, locks, etc.). Deadman alert is extremely useful for situations where client PCs are often rebooted leaving shadow processes on the server. You can adjust the time that SQL*Net probes for a connection and/or request. If the probe finds a dead connection, the corresponding server process is terminated; this is known as deadman alert. The SQL*Net parameter is sqlnet.expire and is set to the number of minutes between SQL*Net probes for dead connections. You can set this parameter in the sqlnet.ora file located in the $ORACLE_HOME/network/admin directory. The following is an example of the sqlnet.expire option.

```
#########################################
# Filename: sqlnet.ora                  #
#########################################
AUTOMATIC_IPC = OFF
SQLNET.EXPIRE_TIME = 30
```

5.15.3 NETWORKING TRACING

Ensure that SQL*Net tracing is disabled both on the client and the server if you are not experiencing any problems and are not trying to debug a SQL*Net issue. Enabling tracing can cause SQL*Net's performance to degrade due to the overhead of the trace calls on the client and server. To determine if tracing is enabled, examine the sqlnet.ora and listener.ora files in the $ORACLE_HOME/network/admin directory.

5.15.4 PRESPAWNING SERVER PROCESSES

The SQL*Net V2 listener listens on a given port (this is specified in the listener.ora file in the $ORACLE_HOME/network/admin directory). Once a request for a connection comes across the port, the SQL*Net V2 listener (`tnslsnr LISTENER -inherit`) spawns an Oracle process if running in a dedicated server mode, and this new process becomes the dedicated server process for the user (shadow process). The shadow process is also referred to as the dedicated server process. The shadow process communicates with the user (client). The shadow process (acting on behalf of the client) attaches to the SGA and executes the client statements. In a dedicated server mode, each time a user connects to the Oracle Server, a shadow process is created. This can be verified by issuing the `ps -ef | grep LOCAL` command on the server if running SQL*Net V2 or Net8. For example, the following is an example of the `ps` command to list the shadow processes:

```
myhost> ps -ef | grep LOCAL

OWNER      PID    PPID          TIME COMMAND

oracle     25145     1       0:00 oracleSPROD (LOCAL=NO)
```

This example shows a shadow process with `LOCAL=NO`. This means that the connection is a remote connection (from a client or another server).

A new feature of SQL*Net V2.1 (with Oracle 7.1) provides the ability to prespawn connections to the Oracle Server, thereby reducing the user connection time by eliminating the need for the V2 listener to spawn a process for each user connection at connection time. A specified number of prespawned processes can be created, allowing users to attach to these shadow processes immediately.

To configure prespawned processes, set the `PRESPAWN_MAX` parameter in the `listener.ora` file to the maximum number of prespawned servers you want created. You can also set the `POOL_SIZE` parameter in the `listener.ora` file to the number of idle prespawned server processes that the listener should maintain. The `TIMEOUT` parameter specifies the period of time that an idle prespawned server process waits before termination. Without prespawning connection processes, a shadow process is created for each connection, and the shadow process terminates after the user disconnects from the Oracle Server. Setting the `TIMEOUT` parameter can keep a shadow processes active for a specified period of time. If your system has a large number of users constantly connecting and disconnecting (which is very typical in an OLTP application), you may increase performance by prespawning connections, thereby reducing the user connection time.

5.15.5 CONNECTION POOLING

Net8 provides a feature known as connection pooling which maximizes the amount of physical connections to a multithreaded server (MTS) by utilizing idle sessions. Connection pooling allows a dispatcher's set of connections to be shared among client processes. Connection pooling helps maximize the utilization of resources. In order to enable connection pooling, you need to set the `POOL` option of the `init.ora` parameter `mts_dispatchers`. The following example enables connection pooling:

```
mts_dispatchers="(PROTOCOL=TCP)(DISPATCHERS=5)(POOL=ON)"
```

You can also specify whether connection pooling should be enabled for either incoming or outgoing connections or both. You can also specify the timeout (in ticks) for connection pooling for both incoming and outgoing connections. In addition, you can also specify the length of a tick in seconds by using the TICKS option of the init.ora parameter mts_dispatchers. Connections that have been idle for a set period of time can then be reused. Once the idle connection becomes active again, the connection is reestablished with the dispatcher. The following example enables connection pooling for both incoming and outgoing connections and specifies a timeout of 10 for incoming connections, and a timeout of 20 for outgoing connections:

```
mts_dispatchers="(PROTOCOL=TCP)(DISPATCHERS=5)(POOL=ON)  \
                (IN=10)(OUT=20)"
```

Connection pooling is useful for environments with a large number of interactive users whereby users spend more time analyzing the results than submitting requests. Connection pooling effectively increases concurrency and maximizes server utilization. You should also monitor the v$dispatcher and v$queue views to determine if contention for dispatchers or shared server processes is occurring.

5.15.6 CONNECTION MANAGER

Connection Manager is a utility that provides the ability to administer network access, multiplex client sessions, and support multiple protocols. The Oracle Connection Manager replaces the Oracle Multiprotocol Interchange used with SQL*Net V2. You can use the Connection Manager to establish filters and restrictions on access. Connection Manager functions in a manner similar to a router. Connection Manager receives a connection request, negotiates the protocol, and routes the request appropriately. The Connection Manager is invoked and shut down through the Connection Manager Control Utility (cmctl), and is configured via the Connection Manager configuration file (cman.ora). For more information on configuring the Connection Manager, refer to the *Oracle Net8 Administrator's Guide*.

Connection Concentration is a feature of the Oracle Connection Manager that allows multiple client sessions to be multiplexed over a single transport. Connection Concentration reduces the number of server endpoints for incoming connection requests, thus allowing more server sessions. Connection Concentration maximizes network resource utilization by increasing the number of sessions over a fixed number of physical ports. Connection concentration is useful for MTS environments where a large number of users require a constant connection. Using Connection Concentration enables thousands of concurrent user connections. To enable Connection Concentration, set the MULTIPLEX option of the init.ora parameter mts_dispatchers as follows:

```
mts_dispatchers="(PROTOCOL=TCP)(DISPATCHERS=5)(MULTIPLEX=ON)"
```

Connection Manager coupled with Connection Concentration allows you to reduce contention for network resources and maximizes system resources. Connection Manager also provides multiprotocol support as well as mechanisms to control access.

5.15.7 NET8 TNS RAW

Net8 provides an option known as TNS RAW that allows Net8 packets to be transmitted without Net8 headers, if possible. In a networked environment, this can help reduce the amount of data transferred. Net8 has also been optimized to issue low-level API protocol calls.

5.15.8 LISTENER LOAD BALANCING

Net8 provides listener load balancing which helps distribute incoming connection requests over multiple listeners so as to not burden a single listener. Each listener registers itself with a service handler. The service handler maintains load statistics and thus allows the listener to be aware of the load. The listener then redirects the connection to the least busy handler. To enable listener load balancing, configure multiple listeners per database.

5.16 RECURSIVE SQL AND TKPROF

You should monitor the number of recursive SQL calls compared to user calls. Recursive calls typically occur due to dynamic storage management or cache misses in the data dictionary or library cache. For example, an INSERT statement may cause recursive SQL in order to allocate additional extents to hold the new rows that are being inserted if sufficient space does not exist. Recursive calls are also generated for the following activities:

❏ data dictionary cache misses.
❏ invocation of database triggers.
❏ Data Definition Language (DDL) statements.
❏ SQL statements executed from within functions, stored procedures, anonymous PL/SQL blocks, and packages.
❏ referential integrity constraints enforcement.

You can use the following query to monitor the rate of recursive SQL.

```
SQL> select name,value
     from v$sysstat
     where name like '%calls%'
     order by name;
```

(continued)

NAME	VALUE
calls to kcmgas	1833
calls to kcmgcs	5692
calls to kcmgrs	122118
recursive calls	**1506658**
user calls	**23437**

In this example, the ratio of `recursive calls` to `user calls` is 1506658 / 23437 = 64:1. This means that each user call on the average required at least 64 recursive calls to complete. Recursive calls can also occur when PL/SQL blocks issue SQL statements that require recursive calls to handle the equivalent of bind and define. To reduce recursive calls, you may have to either redesign the application to group several SQL statements together, or rebuild the objects (tables and indexes) to reduce dynamic storage management. When you rebuild the objects, you can allocate enough space upfront using the storage clause in order to avoid having to extend the object dynamically.

You should also try to minimize the amount of `user calls`. User calls are calls made to the Oracle kernel. The `parse count` is the number of times a SQL statement was parsed. You should try to reduce the number of calls made to the Oracle kernel. By using array processing and PL/SQL blocks to group multiple SQL statements into a single statement or single batch, you can reduce the calls made to the kernel. Calculate the ratio of `parse count` to `user calls` by querying the v$sysstat view as follows:

```
SQL> select name,value
     from v$sysstat
     where name in ('parse count','user calls');
```

NAME	VALUE
user calls	23443
parse count	30549

In this example, the ratio of `user calls` to `parse count` is 23443/30549 ≅ 77 percent. This means that 77 percent of SQL statements translate into kernel user calls. To determine the source of the bottleneck, you can use the `tkprof` and SQL trace option to see if SQL statements are being grouped. You can set the `init.ora` parameter `sql_trace=TRUE`, or issue the following command:

```
SQL> alter session set sql_trace=true;
```

Once a SQL trace file has been taken, you can use the `tkprof` utility to examine the SQL trace file. SQL trace files are placed in the directory specified by the init.ora paramater `user_dump_dest`. The following is a section from a sample output file from `tkprof` run on a SQL trace file.

```
============================================================


UPDATE stock
       SET s_order_cnt = s_order_cnt + 1,
           s_ytd = s_ytd + :ol_quantity,
           s_remote_cnt = s_remote_cnt + :s_remote,
       s_quantity = :s_quantity
WHERE (s_sid = :ls_sid)


call       count    cpu    elapsed   disk   query   current   rows
-------------------------------------------------------------------
Parse          1   0.02      0.00       0       0         0      0
Execute      744   2.69      2.70       0       0      8412   7367
Fetch          0   0.00      0.00       0       0         0      0
-------------------------------------------------------------------
total        745   2.71      2.70       0       0      8412   7367


Misses in library cache during parse: 1
Optimizer goal: CHOOSE
Parsing user id: 20   (prodo)


Rows      Execution Plan
-----------------------------------------------------
   0      UPDATE STATEMENT    GOAL: CHOOSE
   0      UPDATE OF 'STOCK'
7367      TABLE ACCESS (BY USER ROWID) OF 'STOCK'


============================================================
```

Using the `tkprof` utility with the explain plan option, you can analyze the activity and workload required by each SQL statement. In the above example, the SQL statement was not detected in the library cache, and hence a parse and execute was required. Notice that the `cpu` and `elapsed` time-based statistics are being reported. This is because the `init.ora` parameter `timed_statistics=TRUE`. Unless you are testing or gathering statistics, you should set `timed_statistics=FALSE`. Setting it to true incurs the overhead of the Oracle Server constantly performing time system calls. In the above example, the `disk` column statistics are zero (0). This means that the data was found in the buffer cache, and physical disk I/O was not needed to satisfy the statement. By reviewing the `disk` column statistics and the elapsed times thereof, you can determine if I/Os are taking longer than they should. This helps you identify disk I/O contention. Tkprof is an extremely useful tool and can help you pinpoint SQL bottlenecks in an application. If `timed_statistics=TRUE`, `tkprof` reports CPU and elapsed times for the parsing, execution, and fetching phases, as well as total CPU and total elapsed timings. Use `tkprof` and the explain plan to monitor the application periodically. `Tkprof` and the explain plan may help you catch potential performance problems by examining the SQL workload from the trace file.

5.17   TUNING STORAGE CLAUSES

Setting the storage clauses of database objects can help you reduce dynamic storage extension and thus recursive calls. The high-water mark of a table identifies the portion of the table that has been allocated. You should monitor the table to ensure that the table does not contain a lot of holes—meaning that after a large number of deletions, the high-water mark for the table could be causing the table to waste space. In this event, you can re-create and reload the table to reset the high-water mark to a more optimal position. Oracle 7.3 also provides a new command that you can use to deallocate unused space within a table. The following command can be used to free unused space above the table high-water mark.

```
SQL> alter table <table name> deallocate unused;
```

This will not help you deal with the problem of table holes, but it can free unused space, allowing other objects to make use of the space. To deal with the problem of holes, you can re-create the table using either export/import, create table as select, or SQL*Loader to reload the table. Tuning loads and table creations are discussed in Chapter 6.

The `PCTFREE` and `PCTUSED` columns determine the blocking factor of the table. You should always set these parameters explicitly, as the defaults may not be optimal. Using `PCTFREE`, you can specify the amount of space that will be left free in the object for future inserts. `PCTUSED` specifies the percentage amount of space used per data block. Sizing `PCTUSED` and `PCTFREE` appropriately helps reduce the overhead of dynamic space management. If you expect large amounts of growth, set `PCTFREE` to a high value to account for future inserts or updates. Do not size `PCTUSED` and `PCTFREE` so small that dynamic extension is occurring frequently.

The `PCTINCREASE` parameter specifies the growth rate of each subsequent extent following the second extent allocated. The default for `PCTINCREASE` is 50 percent. In most cases, you should set PCTINCREASE to 0 to prevent fragmentation. Setting it to 0 ensures that each extent is of equal size. You should not rely solely on PCTINCREASE to handle object sizing. You should set the INITIAL and NEXT extent sizes appropriately, as well as PCTUSED and PCTFREE to accommodate future inserts and updates.

    If you are designing a new database, using the Oracle Designer/2000 tool can help you with sizing by making use of the volume growth, initial size, and maximum size input data.

5.17.1 THE ONE EXTENT MYTH

Although it is commonly thought that keeping your data in one extent or as few extents as possible increases performance over having many extents, this, however, is not entirely true. The performance problems associated with many extents has to do with the levels of row fragmentation and block packing, not with the number of extents. Furthermore, trying to keep all your table or index data in one extent can be extremely difficult. It is impossible for very large databases on platforms that support only 2 G data files. For example, with a 10 G table, it is not possible to load all the data into one extent. Oracle 7.3 removed the limit placed on the maximum number of extents per object. Therefore, with Oracle 7.3, you can have an unlimited number of extents. Using either the Export/Import, create table as select, or SQL*Loader utilities, try re-creating the object to eliminate fragmentation.

5.18 THE FREE LIST

Contention for the free list can reduce the performance of an application. The free list contains a list of data blocks allocated for a segment's extents and has free space greater than PCTFREE. When you issue an INSERT, Oracle scans the free list for the first available block and uses it if possible. Deletes and updates that result in the number of used blocks being used by the object being less than PCTUSED cause the blocks to be returned to the free list. You can determine if your system is experiencing high contention for the free list by querying the v$waitstat view:

```
SQL> select class,count
     from v$waitstat
     where class='free list';


CLASS           COUNT
_____

free list         33
```

    The following query reports the total requests make for data:

```
SQL> select sum(value)
     from v$sysstat
     where name in
     (`db block gets','consistent gets');

SUM(VALUE)
_____

   5094340
```

In this example, the `v$waitstat` shows that the number of waits for free blocks is 33. You should compare the number of waits for free blocks with the total requests for data. In the previous example, 5,094,340 requests were made for data. The ratio of waits for free blocks to total requests for data is extremely low. If, however, the ratio was higher than 1 percent, you may want to consider increasing the number of free lists to reduce the contention. You should also monitor the statistic `buffer busy waits` by querying the `v$system_event` view. A high number of `buffer busy waits` indicates free list contention. To increase the number of free lists, you need to re-create the table. For example, you can use the following statement (assuming you have sufficient space) to re-create the table:

```
SQL> Create Table neworders
     storage (initial 100M
              next 100M
              pctincrease 0
              freelist groups 10
              freelists 22)
     as select * from orders;

SQL> drop table orders;

SQL> rename neworders to orders;
```

5.19 MONITORING LOCKING

Locking can also cause performance problems by causing processes to wait long times before locks on rows or tables can be obtained. You can use the Lock Monitor in the Enterprise Manager to monitor the users holding locks and types of locks being held. In some cases, the DBA might have to kill user sessions explicitly in order to remove locks on objects. PMON is responsible for cleaning up user processes and for freeing any resources held by the process upon termination of a process. You can also query the `v$lock` and `v$session` views to show the locks that are being held by users. The following queries can be used to show the DDL and DML locks being held by user processes:

```
SQL> select substr(username,1,12) "User",
            substr(owner,1,8) "Owner",
            substr(name,1,15) "Name",
            substr (a.type,1,20) "Type",
            substr (mode_held,1,11) "Mode held"
     from sys.dba_ddl_locks a,
          v$session b
     where (a.session_id=b.sid);


SQL> select substr(username,1,12) "User",
            substr(owner,1,8) "Owner",
            substr(name,1,15) "Name",
            substr (mode_held,1,11) "Mode held"
     from sys.dba_dml_locks a,
          v$session b
     where (a.session_id=b.sid);
```

You need to run the `catblock.sql` script located in the `$ORACLE_`
`HOME/rdbms/admin` directory. The `catblock.sql` script will create various different lock views that will enable you to monitor the locks being held by user processes.
You can also use the `utllockt.sql` (located in `$ORACLE_HOME/rdbms/admin`
directory) to output the current locks being held in tree format.

There is no secret to performance tuning when dealing with locks. The goal of the
application is to avoid exclusive locks (unless absolutely needed), and use the finest level
of locking possible when acquiring locks. The application should also try to minimize
the amount of time that the lock is held. This will allow other processes to obtain the
lock without waiting for long periods of time.

You should also monitor the enqueue statistics from the `v$sysstat` view. Oracle
uses the enqueue lock manager to manage locks. If `enqueue waits` or `enqueue`
`timeouts` is high, you will need to increase the `init.ora` parameter
`enqueue_resources`. The `init.ora` parameter `enqueue_resources` specifies
the number of resources that can be locked concurrently. If `enqueue releases` and
`enqueue requests` are close in value, this means that sufficient enqueue resources
exist. If enqueue requests are much higher than enqueue releases, you need to increase
the value of `enqueue_resources`. You may also need to increase the value of the
`init.ora` parameter `dml_locks` if the statistics show contention for enqueue locks.
The `dml_locks` parameter should be set to the maximum number of users multiplied
by the number of tables being modified in a transaction. For example, if four users are
modifying three tables, then set `dml_locks=12`.

If you are increasing the number of concurrent locks that can be held, you may also
want to consider increasing the `init.ora` parameters `sessions` and `processes`.
Recall that if your Oracle Server is configured to use semaphores, a semaphore will be
used per process. Therefore, if increasing the `init.ora` parameters `sessions` and

processes, you may also need to increase the number of available semaphores. You can increase the number of semaphores by increasing the semaphore kernel parameters. See Chapter 2 for a complete list of the semaphore-related kernel parameters.

5.20 REFERENTIAL INTEGRITY

Oracle7 introduced the concept of stored procedures and database triggers. Stored procedures and triggers can be used to perform many database operations including Referential Integrity (RI). When you design an application, avoid placing the equivalent referential integrity logic in the application itself. Use primary keys and foreign keys to enforce referential integrity at the database level. It increases the performance of the application since the RI is done at the Oracle kernel level rather than at the application level. Handling RI at the application level can reduce performance because of the increased number of SQL calls that are needed to verify parent and child relationships. In a networked environment, this increases network traffic as more SQL calls are sent across to the server from the client. This also increases the number of SQL user calls made to the Oracle kernel.

Triggers can also be used to handle distributed transactions that need to insert or update data in other tables (possibly in other servers) following an insert or delete on a certain table. Again, do not handle distributed transactions in the application. Allow the server to perform the distributed transaction through the use of triggers and stored procedures. This can increase the performance of your OLTP system.

5.20.1 DEFERRED CONSTRAINTS

Oracle8 provides the ability to defer constraint checking upon commit rather than upon each statement. For example, you may have several update or insert statements within a single transaction and then issue a commit. If the constraint is marked as immediate, then the constraint is validated at the end of each statement. If you specify the constraint to be deferrable, you can also choose whether you want the constraint initially deferred or initially immediate. Initially deferred starts the transaction in deferred mode, and initially immediate starts the transaction in non-deferred mode. The following example creates a deferred unique column constraint with the constraint marked as initially deferred:

```
CREATE TABLE dealer
    (dealer_no number(8),
     territory_id number(5),
     dealer_desc varchar2(60),
     dealer_streetno number(8),
     dealer_address varchar2(30),
     dealer_city_id number(8),
     constraint udealer_no unique(dealer_no)
        initially deferred deferrable);
```

You can use the NOVALIDATE option of the enable constraint clause which enables the constraint for future inserts, updates, and deletes but does not check the existing rows in the table. This can be useful for large bulk load situations where you want to load the data in parallel and eliminate the constraint checks at load time. Following the load, you can then scan the table in parallel in order to determine if rows exist which violate the constraints. The following example enables a constraint with the NOVALIDATE option:

```
SQL> alter table dealer enable novalidate
            constraint udealer_no;
```

5.21 DISCRETE TRANSACTIONS

Discrete transactions can increase performance over the standard transactions. Discrete transactions do not generate any undo or rollback information because, in a discrete transaction, the block is not modified until the transaction commits. Redo information is generated but is held in a separate location in memory. Once the transaction commits, the database block changes are applied directly to the block, and the redo information is copied to the redo buffer and written out to the redo log file in the normal manner.

Discrete transactions can increase performance depending on the type of OLTP workload. In some cases, using discrete transactions for small, light transactions increased performance 50 percent.

Discrete transactions have some limitations: A database block is never modified more than once in the same transaction, the new modified data does not need to be seen by the process, and tables containing columns of type LONG are not modified. If your transaction meets these requirements, you may be able to use discrete transactions to increase performance.

Because discrete transactions do not actually modify the data block until the transaction commits, you cannot see the changes of your modification as in a normal transaction. To enable discrete transactions, set the init.ora parameter discrete _transactions_enabled=TRUE and call the procedure DBMS_TRANSACTION .begin_discrete_transaction from your transaction to indicate that your transaction is a discrete transaction.

Discrete transactions can increase performance by minimizing rollback and redo buffer contention. The discrete transactions feature is ideal for lightweight, short-lived transactions that can live with the restrictions of the discrete transaction.

5.22 HASH CLUSTER

If you have a transaction table that is maintained by a primary or unique key, you can increase the performance of transactions against this table by using a hash cluster key. A hash cluster key uses an internal hash function or the unique key itself as the hash function to locate records. This reduces the number of I/Os needed to locate rows.

In a typical unique index scan, the branch blocks and leaf blocks of the index are searched to find the index data block containing the unique key. Then, the `rowid` stored in the index data block is used to access the row of the table. For a unique scan, this often translates into two or three physical I/Os to locate the row. For a hash cluster key, the row can often be found with one I/O using the hash function to locate the row. Hash tables cannot be loaded in direct path using SQL*Loader. However, for a transaction-based system, using a hash cluster key on the table for the primary key can increase performance. You should make sure you configure the `SIZE` parameter and the number of `HASHKEYS` appropriately; otherwise many more I/Os will be required to locate the row. For more information on creating hash cluster keys, refer to the *SQL Reference Manual for the Oracle Server*.

5.23 ORACLE PARALLEL SERVER (OPS)

Oracle8 integrated the Distributed Lock Manager (DLM) into the Oracle8 DBMS kernel. This improves administration and performance as well as provides a consistent and portable OPS implementation. In addition to the incorporation of the DLM, Oracle8 OPS also provides the Application Fail-Over mechanism which maintains a user connection as long as at least one instance in the OPS environment remains available. Oracle8 provides major enhancements to OPS in the areas of administration, performance, and reliability. Oracle is committed to OPS, and future releases of Oracle8 will include significant enhancements to administration, scalability, performance, and reliability.

The performance of OPS is also highly dependent on the configuration of the interconnect between nodes in the OPS cluster. Hardware vendors continue to improve the interconnect technology by providing low-latency, high-bandwidth interconnects. As interconnect technology continues to improve, more nodes can be added to the cluster in order to increase reliability and performance.

5.24 DATABASE DESIGN

If all the previous recommendations fail to increase performance, you should consider revisiting the database design. Database design deserves a text on its own. However, for an OLTP system, databases tend to be highly normalized. The logic is that joins have a small selectivity and usually return a single row or a small number of rows. Normalizing a database for an OLTP system also helps speed up inserts, updates, selects, and deletes. Since the data is stored in multiple tables—and joins are needed to bring the data together—inserts, updates, deletes, and selects can be executed in parallel on the underlying tables. Denormalizing the database causes longer row lengths which can slow down

OLTP SQL operations that need to insert, update, delete, or select a row (or set of rows) extremely quickly.

Denormalization or star-diagram designs are usually done on Decision Support Systems (DSS), where huge amounts of data are scanned and aggregated. In the case of a DSS, joins can reduce performance by an order of magnitude. Oracle 7.3 and Oracle8 provide additional enhancements for DSS systems that allow large-scale complex queries and joins to operate in parallel, thereby reducing the elapsed time. The database design is crucial to system performance, and you should spend a great deal of time researching the design and reviewing it with your company's application staff and database staff. It is also a good idea to review your design with other database specialists and/or consultants. A good design will help foster a high-performance system.

TUNING A DECISION-SUPPORT SYSTEM (DSS)

This chapter offers recommendations on performance tuning for a Decision-Support System (DSS). This chapter assumes that you are familiar with the basic concepts of the Oracle Server as well as the background processes associated with it. Data warehousing has become extremely popular. In the past, companies mastered the art of processing operational data through the use of transaction systems. Now, those same companies are trying to analyze their operational data using complex models to help them predict customer buying power, loyalty, market share, purchase habits, as well as performing other marketing-related studies that help them to better understand their customers and the market. DSS workloads are quite different than OLTP workloads. In an OLTP environment, small and short-lived transactions consist of inserts, updates, and deletes as new data is received and processed. In an OLTP environment, there are typically many concurrent users, each issuing many light transactions. In a DSS environment, there are fewer users than in an average OLTP system. The DSS users submit much more complex and resource-intensive transactions (queries).

6.1   THE DATA WAREHOUSE

A data warehouse, as defined by the father of data warehousing, Bill Inmon, is a subject-oriented, integrated, time-variant, nonvolatile collection of data used in support of management decisions. Generally, data warehouses are built by extracting and aggregating data from the operational transactional database systems. Figure 6.1 illustrates the concept of a data warehouse.

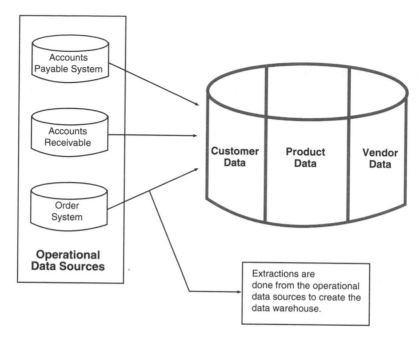

FIGURE 6.1 Data warehousing.

In Figure 6.1, data is extracted from the operational database systems to create the data warehouse. Typically, the data extracted is aggregated by specific metrics such as time or geography. On-Line Analytical Processing (OLAP), as coined by Dr. Codd who developed the relational algebra and the relational calculus, was intended to provide analytical processing and data warehousing technology on-line. The on-line piece of OLAP was meant to indicate that complex analytical processing should occur in almost the same time as OLTP systems can process a transaction. The reality of the situation is that not only is OLAP possible, but also that Oracle and hardware vendors such as Sun, HP, and Sequent have released products that push the limits of parallel processing technology. Oracle7 and Oracle8 provide features that enable customer sites to build large-scale data warehouses, and achieve unparalleled performance. The hardware vendors are also enhancing the hardware systems and operating systems constantly, thus bringing to market larger bus bandwidths, faster processors, enhanced disk I/O subsystems, and larger memory configurations. The disk I/O subsystems have been improved to sustain many more I/Os per second (IOPS). The Sun Ultra Servers such as the Enterprise 10000 and the Sequent NUMA-Q systems are excellent examples of the awesome computing power that is available on the market today. The Oracle DBMS is tailored to take advantage of the specific platforms, providing near linear scalability.

The purpose of this chapter is to offer recommendations based on my personal experiences of building large-scale data warehousing systems. The material presented in the previous chapters as well as in this chapter, will clearly help you to build a high-performance, large-scale data warehouse.

6.2   REQUIREMENTS FOR A DATA WAREHOUSE

A data warehouse is an expansion of a DSS. Traditionally, DSSs were small-scale, summarized databases of operational data that did not permit many permutations of predicate-based analysis. Because the DSS was presummarized, only certain queries could be executed. A data warehouse enhances the traditional DSS by combining the power of large-scale distributed computing and parallel-aware database management systems. This enables a data warehouse to be a vast collection of data in which the complex analysis is done on-line. The data is provided in its raw form and allows many different types of queries, as opposed to the traditional summarized DSS. In this chapter, I use the terms *data warehousing* and *DSS* synonymously. I use the terms synonymously because although data warehousing and OLAP have revolutionized DSS systems, the concept of a data warehouse and a DSS remains the same: *making better decisions faster.*[1]

    Enabling a business analyst to make better decisions faster requires three main components: recent and accurate data, a flexible database design, and a highly parallel hardware and software server environment. Recent and accurate data are needed to make an intelligent decision. Your decision is only as good as the data you use to make the decision. It is also important that the data be recent, so you can make the best decision based on the most recent information. The flexible database design helps you to execute the different types of complex queries in a relatively straightforward manner. The parallel software and hardware help you expedite the processing of your analytical query by breaking down larger tasks into smaller tasks that execute in parallel.

6.3   DSS DATABASE DESIGN

As mentioned in the previous chapter, database design techniques deserve their own text. There are available many data warehousing database design texts that discuss different design methods such as the star schema design. Designing a database requires detailed knowledge of the business rules as well as a firm understanding of end-user requirements. It is important that the database that is designed meet the requirements of end users by enabling them to satisfy their queries to business questions using the database schema provided. Whether you use a relational database design or star schema approach, the important thing is that the DSS should enable the business analyst to get answers to questions quickly. Usually, DSS database designs are somewhat de-normalized in order to reduce the amount of joins needed to gather data.

---

1. Sun Microsystems Computer Corporation. *Data Warehousing White Paper.* February 1995, p.1.

6.4   TUNING I/O

By now, you are probably saying that the subject of tuning I/O has been beaten to death. However, I cannot emphasize enough the importance of tuning I/O. This is extremely critical in a DSS environment. If your I/O subsystem is not tuned properly, you will not be able to achieve good performance. DSS systems typically involve large, complex queries that perform full-table scans and sort large amounts of data. If your I/O system is not tuned properly, loads and queries may take a much longer time. Follow the guidelines discussed in Chapter 3 to tune I/O. Use the I/O monitoring utilities to ensure that I/O is being properly balanced. For optimal performance, use a database block size of 16K (available in 7.3 and above), and use the guidelines from Section 3.4 to optimally select the stripe width. Section 3.15 offers tips on tuning the value of `db_file_multilblock_read_count`. Optimally setting `db_file_multilblock_read_count` helps reduce the amount of time needed to perform a full-table scan.

6.5   SORTING

The Oracle Server uses the `init.ora` parameter `sort_area_size` to specify the size of in-memory sorts. The `sort_area_size`, specified in bytes, allocates the specified amount of memory to be used for a sort. The `sort_area_size` is part of the PGA (Program Global Area). Once the sort is complete and all that remains is to fetch the rows, the sort memory is released down to the size specified by the `init.ora` parameter `sort_area_retained_size`. The `sort_area_retained_size` specifies the maximum amount of PGA memory (in bytes) to retain following a sort. Once the last row is fetched from the sort space, the memory is freed back to the PGA, not to the Operating System (OS). The `init.ora` parameter `sort_read_fac` specifies the ratio of the amount of time needed to read a single database block to the block transfer rate. The formula for `sort_read_fac` is as follows:

$$
\text{sort\_read\_fac} = \frac{(\text{avg.seek time} + \text{avg. latency time} + \text{block transfer time})}{(\text{block transfer time})}
$$

To set `sort_read_fac` properly, obtain the disk seek time, latency time, and block transfer time values for your specific disk I/O subsystem. This helps maximize disk sorting on your platform. When a sort requires more than `sort_area_size`, the sort is done on disk using temporary tablespace extents. There is no multiple allocation of `sort_area_size`. For large sorts, and if memory is plentiful on your system, you may try increasing the value of `sort_area_size`. This helps increase the performance of sorts by performing the sort in memory (assuming the sort_area_size is large enough). You can monitor the amount of in-memory sorts versus disk sorts by querying the v$sysstat view:

```
SQL> select name,value
       from v$sysstat
       where name like '%sort%'
```

NAME	VALUE
sorts (memory)	7003
sorts (disk)	54
sorts (rows)	163488

In this example, the number of sorts done in memory and on disk are reported, as well as the total number of rows sorted. Each sort to disk requires sort_area_size memory since the sort_area_size is filled first, and anything beyond that is sorted on disk. For optimal performance, set sort_area_size so that the ratio of disk sorts to memory sorts is extremely low. Use caution when you increase sort_area_size because this can increase paging and possibly cause swapping if it is set too large.

6.5.1   DIRECT SORT WRITES

Oracle 7.2 and Oracle 7.3 provide additional enhancements for large-scale sorts that are primarily performed on disk, such as large DSS queries involving order by, or sort-merge joins. The init.ora parameter sort_direct_writes, originally introduced in Oracle 7.2 and expanded in Oracle 7.3, specifies whether sorts are to be performed directly to disk, thereby reducing the SGA overhead of first writing the temporary sort segment to the cache and then flushing out the sorted block to disk. When set to true, the sort_direct_writes parameter allocates additional buffers in memory and writes the buffers directly to disk. When sort_direct_writes=false, direct sort writes to disk are disabled, and sort blocks are written to the cache in the usual manner. Oracle 7.3 enables another setting for sort_direct_writes. If sort_direct_writes=auto, Oracle chooses a direct write sort to disk if the sort_area_size is at least ten times greater than the direct write buffer size. If sort_direct_writes=auto, sort_write_buffer_size and sort_write_buffers are configured automatically and override any user setting. The sort_write_buffer_size parameter is the size of the direct write sort buffer. The default is 32K. You can set the value of sort_write_buffer_size to the <stripe interleave size> × <number of distinct members in the stripe> for optimal performance. For instance, if your stripe interleave is 64K, and your temporary tablespace data files are striped across six different disks, set sort_write_buffer_size=384 K. This allows sort disk writes to the temporary tablespace to proceed in parallel since the temporary tablespace is striped. The sort_write_buffers parameter specifies the number of sort buffers to use when sort_direct_writes=true. Using direct sorts on queries that require large sorts can increase performance significantly. Figure 6.2 illustrates the direct write sorts.

Although direct sorts can increase performance for DSS systems, it is important to note that memory requirements may increase when using direct sorts. When sort_direct_writes=auto, Oracle sets the value of sort_write_buffer_size and sort_write_buffers automatically. When sort_direct_writes=auto, the memory for the direct write buffers is taken from the sort area. Therefore, when sort_direct_writes=auto, the total amount of memory used for sorting is still sort_area_size. When sort_direct_writes=true, the memory allocated for direct write sorts is

```
(sort_write_buffers *
 sort_write_buffer_size) +
 sort_area_size
```

When sort_direct_writes=true, the write buffers are allocated in addition to the sort_area_size. Hence, make sure that your system has sufficient memory before you increase the value of sort_area_size or you enable direct write sorts. Increasing sort_area_size or setting sort_direct_writes=true can increase paging and possibly cause swapping

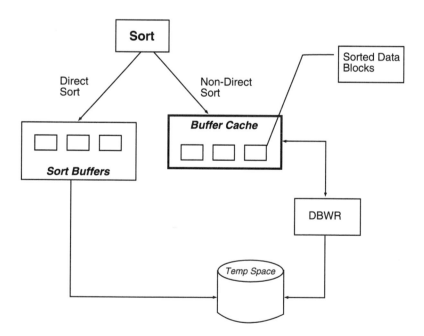

FIGURE 6.2   Direct write sorts.

if careful effort is not taken to ensure that sufficient memory exists. If your sorts are primarily small, setting `sort_direct_writes=true` will decrease performance. Setting `sort_direct_writes=AUTO` (7.3) allows small sorts to sort in memory and large sorts to use the direct write option. If you are using 7.2, you will need to set `sort_direct_writes` in accordance with your workload. If no sorts are being done (or the sorts are small enough to fit in `sort_area_size`), set `sort_direct_writes=false`. If, however, you are doing a lot of large sorts and sort-merge joins, set `sort_direct_writes=true` in your 7.2 Server.

It is important to note that when you use parallel query to parallelize sorts, each parallel query slave allocates a separate `sort_area_size`. For example, if ten parallel query slaves are parallelizing a sort (meaning the query specified a degree of parallelism of 10), and `sort_area_size=5M`, a total of 50 M may be allocated for the sort. Thus, you should be careful because memory can be eaten up quickly if a high degree of a parallelism is selected.

6.5.2 IDENTIFYING SORT USERS

Often it becomes necessary to identify the users performing sorts. This helps identify the particular sessions that may be issuing resource-intensive sorts. You can also determine whether an in-memory or disk sort is being performed. The following query lists the users performing sorts as well as the type of sort:

```
SQL> select   vs.username,
              vs.osuser,
              vsn.name,
              vss.value
     from     v$session vs,
              v$sesstat vss,
              v$statname vsn
     where    (vss.statistic#=vsn.statistic#) AND
              (vs.sid = vss.sid) AND
              (vsn.name like '%sort%')
     order by 2,3;
```

In Oracle8, you can use the `v$sort_usage` view to identify the users of temporary sort extents. The `v$sort_usage` view provides sort usage statistics such as the user of the temporary extent, tablespace name, and the number of blocks and extents. The following is an example query which reports sort usage information:

```
SQL>   select user,
              tablespace,
              contents,
              blocks,
              extents
       from v$sort_usage
       order by user;
```

6.6   THE TEMPORARY TABLESPACE

Oracle uses temporary tablespaces to perform sorts that cannot entirely be sorted in memory from operations such as queries that contain an order by clause, index create statements, and joins. DSS queries can be very complex, and can require a large temporary tablespace to process sorts and joins. When tuning I/O on a DSS system, try to keep temporary tablespace data files separate from data files and redo log files. In a DSS system, consider the temporary tablespace as critical as your redo log files in an OLTP system. In a DSS database, redo activity is minimal since the database is primarily read-only. For this reason, you must stripe the temporary tablespace at least as good, if not better, than the Oracle redo logs in an OLTP system. This improves the performance of queries requiring temporary tablespace extents by minimizing I/O wait time.

Sun offers the Zone Bit Recording (ZBR) technology on its disk drives. ZBR causes the outermost cylinders of the disk to be more efficiently utilized than the inner cylinders on the disk. Therefore, to take advantage of ZBR technology on Sun, configure the temporary tablespace data files by using the `format` utility (or `fmthard` utility) to partition the outer cylinders for the temporary tablespace partitions. Then, if you are using ODS, build a stripe by combining the outer partitions (typically slice 6 or slice 7—s6 or s7) on different disks from different controllers to form the metadevice. Then create the temporary tablespace using the metadevice. This increases the performance of sorts when sort extents are written to disk.

6.6.1   TEMPORARY TABLESPACES IN ORACLE 7.3

Oracle 7.3 allows you to create temporary tablespaces in addition to the permanent tablespaces. Temporary tablespaces reduce the storage management overhead since once extents are allocated, they are reused when other processes need temporary extents. This can help DSS workloads by reducing the amount of storage management performed in order to allocate and free temporary tablespace extents for sorting. To make use of this feature, use the alter tablespace command to mark your tablespaces as temporary. For example,

```
SQL> alter tablespace ts_temp temporary;
```

You can also mark a tablespace as temporary in the create tablespace command. To determine if a tablespace is permanent or temporary, query the `dba_tablespaces` view. For example,

```
SQL> select tablespace_name,
            contents,
            status
     from dba_tablespaces
     order by tablespace_name;
```

```
TABLESPACE_NAME                    CONTENTS  STATUS
```

TABLESPACE_NAME	CONTENTS	STATUS
RBS	PERMANENT	ONLINE
SYSTEM	PERMANENT	ONLINE
TEMP	PERMANENT	ONLINE
TOOLS	PERMANENT	ONLINE
TS_TEMP	TEMPORARY	ONLINE
USERS	PERMANENT	ONLINE

You can also query the `v$sort_segment` view to obtain sort segment information for sorts to temporary tablespaces. The `v$sort_segment` view provides statistics such as the number of current users and total number of extents for a given sort segment as well as the number of extents allocated to sorts.

6.7   BITMAP INDEXES

Oracle 7.3 introduced the bitmap index option in addition to the B*-Tree indexes. You can use bitmapped indexes in a DSS database to increase the performance of queries. Bitmap indexes are ideal for low cardinality columns such as gender, marital status, or account status. Each entry in a bitmap corresponds to a row. Table 6.1 is an example of a bitmap corresponding to the account data.

TABLE 6.1   Example bitmap corresponding to account data

ACCOUNT #	ACCOUNT STATUS	DISTRICT	SERVICE LEVEL
7344	Active	West	Gold
8134	Closed	Central	Silver
8332	Active	East	Gold
8564	Active	East	Bronze
9123	Review	West	Silver

Status='Active'	Status='Closed'	Status='Review'
1	0	0
0	1	0
1	0	0
1	0	0
0	0	1

Suppose that a business analyst wants to know how many active customer accounts in the East or West district maintain a gold service level. The SQL query looks as follows:

```
SQL> SELECT count(*)
        FROM account
        WHERE ((status='Active') and
               (district in ('East','West')) and
               (service = 'Gold'));
```

Using the bitmap index option on these low-cardinality data columns, the optimizer logically combines the bitmaps from the different columns and returns the count. Table 6.2 illustrates the bitmaps used to compute the count.

TABLE 6.2 Boolean operations on bitmap indexes

STATUS='ACTIVE'		DISTRICT='EAST'		DISTRICT='WEST'		SERVICE='GOLD'		
1		0		1		1		1
0	AND	0	OR	0	AND	0	=	0
1		1		0		1		1
1		1		0		0		0
0		0		1		0		0

In Table 6.2, the optimizer combines the bitmaps of the different columns using the logical Boolean operators, and computes the count for the query. Bitmap indexes are substantially faster than having to scan large numbers of rows using the traditional B*-tree index. You can use bitmap indexes to increase performance for DSS queries with the following characteristics: The query contains multiple predicates in the WHERE clause of low-cardinality columns, the query selects a large number of rows, and the tables involved in the queries are relatively large. Using bitmap indexes to index low to medium cardinality data can increase performance of complex DSS queries significantly.

Traditionally, in order to improve the performance of queries, DBAs created multiple concatenated indexes to handle the different types of queries. However, this not only requires substantial disk space, it also requires the DBA either to index every combination of the concatenated columns or to force queries to use a certain index by always providing certain columns.

For example, suppose an index is created on the above account table with a B*-tree index of Account (Status, District, Service). If a query contains all three columns as predicates, then the index can be used. However, suppose the query only specifies District in the WHERE clause. In this case, the index is not used since the leading column of the index is not specified in the WHERE clause of the query. Multiple single-column bitmap indexes solve this classic dilemma by allowing multiple combinations of the different columns.

A bitmap index on a low-cardinality column typically (this is an estimate of course) consumes one-fourth the disk space of an equivalent B*-tree index. B*-tree indexes are great for high-cardinality data such as unique columns or columns where the selectivity per distinct value is low. Therefore, you should not use bitmap indexes on unique columns, or where a B*-tree index is more suitable. Also, because bitmap indexes are designed for use within data warehousing systems, performance can degrade if you use bitmap indexes within OLTP applications that frequently modify the data. An entry in a B*-tree index contains a single row. The single row is made up of its `rowid`, as well as the column(s) of the index. Hence, when an index entry in a B*-tree is locked, the row is locked. A bitmap index entry can consist of a range of `rowids`. Therefore, when locking a bitmap index entry, the entire range of `rowids` is locked. This can have an adverse affect on concurrency because a larger number of rows are locked, possibly preventing other concurrent users from obtaining locks.

The use of bitmap indexes is not recommended within an OLTP application. However, if you are running a mixed environment (OLTP and DSS on the same database), you may want to consider using bitmap indexes to speed up the DSS queries. If your bitmap indexes are updated frequently, make sure you tune the `sort_area_size` appropriately to increase the performance of the updates and inserts on the bitmap index. Follow the recommendations made in Section 6.5 to tune the `sort_area_size` appropriately.

To create a bitmap index, use the `BITMAP` keyword in the `create index` command. For example,

```
SQL> create bitmap index bstatus on Account (status);
```

You can use all the standard index options including the related index storage options for the exception of the `NOSORT` index create option. Bitmap indexes can consist of multiple concatenated columns. To enable bitmap indexes, the `init.ora` parameter `compatible` must be set to 7.3.2 or higher. The standard index object views such as `DBA_INDEXES` or `USER_INDEXES` list bitmap indexes as well as B*-tree indexes. Bitmap indexes have their `UNIQUENESS` column in the `DBA_INDEXES` or `USER_INDEXES` view set to `BITMAP`.

As discussed in Chapter 4, the `INDEX_COMBINE` hint was introduced in version 7.3 to utilize bitmap indexes. You can also use the `INDEX` hint with `BITMAP` indexes. The `INDEX_COMBINE` hint specifies the bitmap indexes that are to be combined when combining Boolean operations on bitmap indexes in a query. The syntax of the `INDEX_COMBINE` hint is `INDEX_COMBINE` (table index1 index2 index3 . . .). If the `INDEX_COMBINE` hint is specified without any arguments, the CBO chooses the Boolean combination of bitmap indexes on the table that is being processed with the best cost.

New `init.ora` parameters—`create_bitmap_area_size`, `bitmap_merge_area_size`, `v733_plans_enabled`—that deal with bitmap indexes were introduced in Oracle 7.3. The `init.ora` parameter `create_bitmap _area_size` specifies the amount of memory that is allocated for creating a bitmap index. The default is 8 M. However, if your bitmap index has a high cardinality, you can increase `create_bitmap_area_size` to speed up the index creation. Conversely, if your bitmap index columns have a very low cardinality, you can reduce the value of `create_bitmap_area_size` since a smaller amount of memory is required. You can alter the value of `create_bitmap_area_size` at the session level as well as at the instance level. The `bitmap_merge_area_size` specifies the amount of memory used to merge bitmaps. Increasing the value of `bitmap_merge_area_size` over the default of 1 M can increase performance of large sorts because the bitmaps must be sorted before the merge is performed. The Oracle7.3 `init.ora` parameter `v733_plans_enabled=TRUE` causes bitmap indexes to be considered on tables with regular B*-tree indexes and at least one bitmap index. Setting `v733_plans_enabled=FALSE` (the default) disables this option.

Bitmap indexes also appear in an explain plan. The explain plan shows the `BITMAP` keyword followed by the bitmap operation such as `BITMAP CONVERSION`, `BITMAP OR`, `BITMAP MINUS`, `BITMAP INDEX`, or `BITMAP MERGE`. If you use bitmap indexes, you should perform an explain plan on the query to ensure that the bitmap index is being used. If the explain plan does not show that the bitmap index is being used, then rewrite the query using the `INDEX` and/or `INDEX_COMBINE` hint and regenerate the explain plan to confirm that the hint is being accepted.

Oracle8 provides the ability to consider a bitmap index access plan even if the table only has B*-tree indexes. The `init.ora` parameter `b_tree_bitmap_plans=TRUE` enables the optimizer to consider a bitmap access path on a table that only has regular B*-tree indexes. The rowid entries for the index are converted to bitmaps and then the various Boolean operations can be applied to the bitmaps. The explain plan shows the `BITMAP CONVERSION FROM ROWIDS` if the optimizer chooses to convert the index rowid entries to bitmaps. This feature can increase the performance of queries that combine low-cardinality criteria with highly selective predicates.

6.8 TUNING QUERIES

In a DSS environment, queries are often complex and run for a much longer period of time than a traditional OLTP query. In some cases, DSS queries can consume a tremendous amount of CPU, sort space, and disk I/O resources. When you tune a DSS query, tune by selectivity. For example, using the `ORDERED` hint, you can specify the join order of the query and force the table that causes the highest selectivity to appear first. By using the `ORDERED` hint, you can use the table that reduces the selectivity the most first in order to cause a reduction in the selectivity before it is joined to the other tables.

6.8.1 THE `STAR` AND `STAR_TRANSFORMATION` HINTS

Oracle 7.2 allows the use of the `STAR` hint. The `STAR` hint causes a star schema to be used. A star schema consists of a single fact table and multiple dimension tables. For example, the fact table may contain all the customer data (facts about customers). A dimension table could consist of dimensions such as time or geography. The dimension tables are often small tables, and the fact table is usually very large for DSS systems. The star hint causes a Cartesian product to be performed on the smaller dimension tables, and the result of the Cartesian product join is then joined to the fact table via a nested loop. This is extremely efficient since the fact table usually contains a concatenated index on the primary key that consists of the foreign key columns used to join to the dimension tables. The logic behind a star query is that the processing of the smaller dimension tables will likely first cause a large reduction in the selectivity of the fact table and thereby reduce the overall elapsed time of the query. To use the star method, you can use the `STAR` hint explicitly (`select /*+ STAR */`) or equivalently simulate the star plan by utilizing the `ORDERED` hint along with the `USE_NL` hint.

Oracle8 provides an alternate method for executing star queries known as the star transformation method. The traditional method for executing star queries is to perform a Cartesian product on the dimension tables and then join the result via a nested loop index join to the fact table. The Cartesian method is ideal for schemas with a dense fact table and a small number of dimensions. The star transformation approach is more suitable for situations where the fact table is large and there are a large number of dimensions. The star transformation method essentially transforms the star query into subqueries using bitmap index access paths on the individual constraints without the need of performing a Cartesian product and requiring a concatenated index on the fact table. The various bitmap indexes can then be merged together to complete the query. To enable star transformations you can use the `STAR_TRANSFORMATION` hint or set the Oracle8 `init.ora` parameter `star_transformation_enabled=TRUE`.

6.8.2 ANTI-JOIN

Another feature of Oracle 7.3 is the anti-join. The anti-join can be used with the `NOT IN` subselect query. The anti-join, instead of returning the rows that satisfy the join predicate, returns the rows that do not satisfy the join predicate, as is the case with the `NOT IN` subselect. The anti-join also enables a hash join or merge-join to be performed, which is much more efficient than the traditional nested loop join. You can use the anti-join feature by using the `HASH_AJ` or `MERGE_AJ` hints in the nested subselect portion of the query, or by setting the `init.ora` parameter `always_anti_join=MERGE`, or `always_anti_join=HASH`. The default setting is `always_anti_join=NESTED _LOOPS`. Using the anti-join feature can increase the performance of `NOT IN` subselect queries by utilizing a hash or merge join in place of the nested loop join.

6.8.3 SEMI-JOIN

Oracle 8.0.4 provides the ability to perform a semi-join to increase the performance of certain queries. The `USE_SEMI, HASH_SJ`, and `MERGE_SJ` hints allow you to specify the use of a semi-join, and whether to use a hash semi-join or merge semi-join, respectively. A semi-join can help improve the performance of certain `EXISTS` subqueries. A semi-join returns the rows that satisfy an `EXISTS` subquery and avoids the duplication of rows from the left side of the predicate when the subquery criteria can be satisfied by multiple rows on the right side. You can specify the HASH_SJ or MERGE_SJ hint in your query to use a hash or merge semi-join as opposed to using a nested loop join which is the default for EXISTS subqueries. In order to enable the optimizer to consider semi-join access paths, set the init.ora parameter always_semi_join=HASH or always_semi_join=MERGE.

6.8.4 HISTOGRAMS

Another feature of Oracle 7.3 is the enhanced histogram option. The CBO works well for uniformly distributed data. For nonuniformly distributed data, the execution plan chosen by the CBO may not be optimal. For this reason, Oracle provides for the use of histograms whereby the table column is analyzed and placed into height-balanced buckets. Each height-balanced bucket has the same height. When the data is highly skewed, height-balanced histograms can increase the performance of queries.

The height-balanced histograms enable the CBO to determine the selectivity of the query more effectively by knowing which buckets the predicates of the query affect. Using a histogram on data that is highly skewed can increase the performance of queries. To generate a histogram, you can use the following example:

```
SQL> analyze table <table name>
       compute statistics for columns
       <column name> SIZE <number of buckets>;
```

Make sure you choose the appropriate number of buckets (or bands) so that the effectiveness of the histogram is maximized. A general rule of thumb is to choose the number of buckets greater than the number of distinct values that occur frequently. Keep in mind that histograms are data distribution dependent. If the distribution of the data changes frequently, the histogram may not be useful unless recomputed frequently. You can query the USER_HISTOGRAMS and USER_TAB_COLUMNS views to obtain histogram and column-level statistics.

6.8.5 MERGE-JOINS

In a DSS system, full-table scans are extremely common, and tables are often joined and aggregated. Using the parallel query and the sort-merge join can increase the performance over a nested loop join when a large number of rows are being joined. A merge sort has an order of NlogN, where N is the number of rows being sorted. The Sort-Merge Join (SMJ) can be significantly faster than a nested loop join because two sorted lists can be merged into a sorted list using no more than (M + N - 1) comparisons, where N is the number of elements in table 1 being merged with M number of elements in table 2.[2] The parallel query option can also be used to parallelize the SMJ. Recall that an

---

2. Rosen, Kenneth H. *Discrete Mathematics and Its Applications*. Random House, 1988, p. 484.

SMJ uses both interparallelism and intraparallelism. This not only means that the table scan is parallelized, but the join and sort are also parallelized. Use the USE_MERGE hint in conjunction with the PARALLEL hint to parallelize large table joins. Nested loop joins are best used for small tables, or tables that are joined on indexes with good selectivity. Sort-merge joins work well for large joins that scan a large number of rows. An SMJ is only possible on an equi-join. An SMJ cannot be used on an outer join. Therefore, if your query contains outer joins, you may have to rewrite the query in the form of an equi-join to utilize an SMJ.

6.8.6 HASH JOINS

Yet another feature of Oracle 7.3 is the hash join. Hash joins can be extremely efficient when joining large tables using equi-joins. Oracle processes a hash join by performing a full-table scan on each of the tables. Then, each table is split into as many partitions as possible based on the amount of available memory. The amount of available memory is specified by the init.ora parameter hash_area_size. Partitions that do not fit into the amount of available memory are written to disk. Oracle then builds a hash table from one of the partitions, and uses the partition from the other table to search the hash table. The hash technique allows smaller partitions to build the hash table, and then the larger partitions are used to probe the hash table to determine a match. To enable the hash join option, set the init.ora parameter hash_join_enabled=true. You can also set hash_join_enabled=TRUE by using the alter session command. The init.ora parameter hash_multi-block_io_count specifies the number of blocks read and written simultaneously during a hash join. You can set hash_multiblock_io_count through the init.ora parameter file or by using the alter session command. You can increase the value of hash_multiblock_io_count if your data files are well distributed. This parameter also controls the number of partitions that the data is divided into during the hash join. When tuning hash_multiblock_io_count, ensure that the following formula remains true:

```
R / M <= Po2 (M/C)

        R = size of the left input to the join
        M = hash_area_size * 0.9
Po2 (n) = largest power of 2 smaller than n
        C = (hash_multiblock_io_count * db_block_size)
```

Hash joins can increase performance of DSS queries by subdividing the data into smaller partitions and using a hash table to join the pairs. You can also use the USE_HASH hint in your SQL statements to explicitly force the use of a hash join. If using the USE_HASH hint, you should also perform an explain plan on the SQL statement to ensure that a hash join is being performed.

6.8.7   ORACLE8 OPTIMIZER ENHANCEMENTS

Oracle8 introduced major enhancements to the Oracle optimizer for complex data warehousing queries. Several new init.ora parameters and hints were added. Oracle 8.0.4 even further enhances the optimizer. A new Oracle 8.0.4 `init.ora` parameter `optimizer_features_enable` allows you to control the optimizer behavior by specifying the version number to be considered for optimizer features. For example, setting `optimizer_features_enable=8.0.4` enables the new optimizer features such as pushing join predicates, complex view merging, fast full scans, and B*-tree bitmap plans.

Oracle8 provides a method to improve the execution timings of distributed join queries by specifying the driving site for the join. The `DRIVING_SITE` hint allows you to specify the driving table with the goal of reducing the amount of work needed by selecting the most selective table as the driving table. The `DRIVING_SITE` hint is useful for tuning distributed join queries that often join local tables with large-size remote database tables. The `DRIVING_SITE` hint allows you to choose the driving table that makes the most sense, thereby reducing the data transmission and join workload.

The `PUSH_PRED` and `NO_PUSH_PRED` hints, added in 8.0.4, allow the optimizer to push the individual join predicates down into the view when the query involves a view with multiple base tables on the right side of an outer join. This enables more efficient execution plans by transforming hash joins into nested loops and full-table scans into index scans. The `NO_PUSH_PRED` hint prevents the join predicates from being pushed into the view. To enable the optimizer to consider pushing the join predicates, set the `init.ora` parameter `push_join_predicate=TRUE`.

The `MERGE` and `NO_MERGE` hints, added in 8.0.4, control whether or not a complex view or subquery within a query is evaluated prior to the surrounding query. The `NO_MERGE` hint causes the optimizer not to merge the view. The `init.ora` parameter `complex_view_merging=TRUE` enables the optimizer to consider merging the views.

Oracle8 release 8.0.5 provides new `init.ora` parameters that help influence the behavior of the optimizer when considering index and nested loop join access paths. The `init.ora` parameter `optimizer_index_cost_adj` specifies the optimizer cost adjustment factor for an index access path. Values for `optimizer_index_cost_adj` can range from 1 to 10,000. The value of `optimizer_index_cost_adj` (other than the default of 100) adjusts the index access path cost at the specified percentage of the regular cost. For example, if `optimizer_index_cost_adj=50`, the optimizer considers an index access path to be half as expensive as the ordinary cost. The `optimizer_index_cost_adj` parameter can be used to tune the performance of queries in which the optimizer is either favoring index access paths or not considering index access paths often enough.

The `init.ora` parameter `optimizer_index_caching`, added in Oracle8 release 8.0.5, provides the ability to influence the decision of the optimizer when choosing between nested loop joins and other join methods such as a hash join. The cost of a nested loop join in which an index is used to access the inner table much depends on the caching of that index in the buffer cache. The degree to which the index is cached relies on such factors as user block access patterns as well as the load on the system. These factors are not predictable by the optimizer. The `init.ora` parameter `optimizer_index_caching` can be used to reduce the cost of a nested loop join thereby making the optimizer more likely to choose a nested loop join over a hash join or sort-merge join. You can set `optimizer_index_caching` to a value between 0 and 100. A value of zero for `optimizer_index_caching` results in the traditional behavior of the optimizer. A higher value for `optimizer_index_caching` reduces the cost of a nested loop join by assuming that the percentage of index blocks specified by `optimizer_index_caching` are in the cache.

6.8.8 PARALLELIZING THE DISTINCT

Queries that perform a count of a distinct column can be rewritten to improve parallel processing. For example, consider the following query:

```
select count(distinct acct_id)
from ACCOUNT;
```

This query returns a count of the number of distinct account IDs in the ACCOUNT table. The scan of the ACCOUNT table can be parallelized, however, the distinct portion causes the final sort group by operation (distinct) to be serialized. The query can be rewritten in the form of a subquery which translates into a view operation. This allows both the subquery and the sort operation to be performed in parallel. The following is a rewrite of the above query which improves parallel query execution:

```
select count(*)
from (select acct_id from ACCOUNT group by acct_id);
```

Tuning SQL is often the effort of rewriting the SQL to either do less work or improve the parallelization factor of the query. In any case, it is important that you spend a great deal of time tuning the application SQL statements. Poorly written SQL can cause a great deal of contention resulting in long execution times.

6.8.9 UPDATABLE JOIN VIEWS

Oracle 7.3 enables you to update joined views that are joined on a primary key. This feature can be useful for applications that needed to update joined views but had to manually code the update against the individual tables in releases prior to 7.3. You can use this feature to reduce overall SQL calls by making one update to the view, rather than several updates to the individual tables making up the view.

6.8.10 FAST FULL INDEX SCAN

The fast full scan index feature provides the ability to perform a parallel multiblock index scan. The fast full index scan is available in Oracle7 release 7.3.3 and Oracle8. A fast full scan is useful when the columns of the index contain all the data needed to satisfy the query. In such a case, scanning the table data is not necessary. A fast full scan requires at least one of the columns in the index key to have the NOT NULL constraint. A fast full scan can be parallelized and it uses multiblock reads similar to a full-table scan. A fast full scan can reduce the amount of I/O needed to complete a query. For example, consider an index on a SALES table of 200 G in size containing two columns, week_no and sale_no. Assume the index is approximately 5 G in size. A query that needed to count the number of sales for weeks after week 10 could utilize a fast full scan as opposed to scanning the entire table. This results in scanning 5 G of data versus scanning 200 G of data. This helps increase the performance of the query by substantially reducing the amount of I/O needed to complete the query. The following is an example of a query and its explain plan showing the use of a fast full index scan:

```
SQL> select /*+ INDEX_FFS (s SALES_WKIDX)
               PARALLEL_INDEX (s,SALES_WKIDX,10) */
       count(*)
       from sales s
       where (s.week_no > 10);
```

ID	EXPLAIN_PLAN	POSITION
0	SELECT STATEMENT	1
1	SORT AGGREGATE	1
2	INDEX FAST FULL SCAN SALES_WKIDX	1
	:Q64000 PARALLEL_TO_SERIAL	

This explain plan shows that a fast full scan is being used and that the fast full scan is being parallelized. To enable the use of the fast full scan feature, set the Oracle8 init.ora parameter fast_full_scan_enabled=TRUE. You can also use the INDEX_FFS and the PARALLEL_INDEX hints to specify the use of a fast full scan and specify the degree of parallelism to be used in the fast full scan. The syntax of the INDEX_FFS and PARALLEL_INDEX hints are INDEX_FFS (table index) and PARALLEL_INDEX (table index tdegree idegree), respectively. The value of tdegree refers to the degree of parallelism to be used on the table, and the value of idegree refers to the degree of cross-instance parallelism. You should also analyze the index to help ensure that the optimizer is able to choose a fast full scan.

6.9 PARTITIONING

Partitioning is the ability to subdivide large tables and indexes into smaller components known as partitions. This allows you to manage the individual partitions rather than the entire table. The Oracle optimizer intelligently employs partition pruning in order to identify the particular partitions needed for a given SQL operation. This avoids having to perform a full-table or full-index scan, thus reducing the amount of work needed to complete the SQL operation.

Oracle 7.3 provides the ability to partition tables by creating a view on the individual tables. The optimizer intelligently decides which tables are needed when processing the predicates of the query on the view. This technique is known as partition views. Partition views was the first phase in providing partitioning capabilities, and Oracle8 expanded the partitioning capabilities by providing the ability to partition a single table based on a partition key. The Oracle8 partitioning feature is a major breakthrough in data warehousing technology and can significantly reduce the amount of I/O needed to process complex queries. The optimizer identifies the partitions of interest based on the partition key range and then scans the relevant partitions. The partitioning capabilities provided in Oracle8 massively improves the performance and manageability of large-scale data warehouses.

6.9.1 PARTITION VIEWS

Partition views are implemented as a view consisting of the `UNION ALL` set operator. Queries are then executed against the view rather than the underlying tables. Based on the predicates specified in the query against the view, the optimizer determines which tables are needed to satisfy the query. In addition, the subqueries that make up the view can also be parallelized. For example, consider the following query:

```
SELECT account_number
FROM ACCOUNT_95
UNION ALL
SELECT account_number
FROM ACCOUNT_96;
```

The CBO parallelizes the individual subqueries because both translate into full-table scans. When each full-table scan is completed, the rows are returned. The same holds true for the `INTERSECT` operation with the exception that, following the full-table scan, a sort is required to return the rows in common. Because the set operators are parallelized, you can use partition views in Oracle to achieve high performance when you need to query from different tables. For example, suppose you created a view on account tables in which an account table existed for each sales quarter per year. If you wanted to return the accounts that purchased a certain amount in each quarter, the equivalent join query could be rather complex and large. However, you can use a partition view, meaning that the view consists of multiple tables partitioned. This improves the performance of the query because each partition can be parallelized. Also, the CBO will not scan partitions that are not used in the query. For example, consider the view and query in Figure 6.3.

In Figure 6.3, because the query does not require any data from the `ACCOUNT_Q296` and `ACCOUNT_Q496` tables, the CBO does not involve the tables in the query. This reduces processing time significantly and increases the performance of the query. To enable partitioned views, set the `init.ora` parameter

```
┌─────────────────────────────────────────────────────────────────────────┐
│  ┌──────────────────┐ ┌──────────────────┐ ┌──────────────────┐ ┌──────────────────┐
│  │ ACCOUNT_Q196     │ │ ACCOUNT_Q296     │ │ ACCOUNT_Q396     │ │ ACCOUNT_Q496     │
│  │ Table            │ │ Table            │ │ Table            │ │ Table            │
│  └──────────────────┘ └──────────────────┘ └──────────────────┘ └──────────────────┘
│
│  VACCOUNT VIEW
└─────────────────────────────────────────────────────────────────────────┘
```

```
SELECT count(*)
from VACCOUNT
WHERE PERIOD IN ('Q196','Q396');
```

FIGURE 6.3   Partition view and query.

`partition_view_enabled=TRUE`. Partitioned views allow you to divide a single large table into smaller tables, thus allowing operations such as loads, index creation, deletes, updates, backups, and restores to be performed at the individual partition level (underlying tables), as opposed to a single, large table.

Partition views represented the first phase in providing partitioning functionality in Oracle. In Oracle8, the partitioning option extends by far the partitioning functionality by providing the ability to partition individual tables and indexes. The performance of partition views seems to drop off as more underlying tables are added to the view. The practical limit highly depends on the sizes of the underlying tables in the view and the degree of parallelism. If you are currently using partition views, I highly recommend that you migrate to Oracle8 and utilize the partitioning option. Oracle8 partitioning scales extremely well for large size tables and has demonstrated superior performance with large numbers of partitions such as several thousand partitions.

6.9.2 PARTITION TABLES

The partitioning option of Oracle8 enables you to apportion a very large table into smaller sections known as partitions. Each section represents a range of the partition key. The current technique used to partition tables in Oracle 8.0 is via a partition range. Oracle8 table partitioning can be useful for both OLTP and data warehousing systems. In a partitioned table, each partition is independent of each other. This allows you to load and perform DML operations at the individual partition. Partition independence also increases availability since the inability to access a partition due to media failure does not affect the other available partitions. Furthermore, by storing each partition in a separate tablespace, backup and restores can be performed at the partition level. This improves backup administration and helps reduce media recovery time. Figure 6.4 is an example of a sales table partitioned by week range.

The following is the corresponding SQL needed to create the sales table partitioned by the sales week range:

```
CREATE TABLE sales
       (week_no     number(2) not null,
        sale_no     NUMBER(8) not null,
        sale_date   date not null,
        sale_amount number(10,2) not null,
        customer_id number(8) not null)
   pctfree 10
   pctused 90
   initrans 10
   storage (initial 1M next 1M pctincrease 0)
   parallel (degree 20 instances 1)
   PARTITION BY RANGE (week_no)
    (PARTITION sales_w1 VALUES LESS THAN (11)
       TABLESPACE tssw1,
     PARTITION sales_w2 VALUES LESS THAN (21)
       TABLESPACE tssw2,
     PARTITION sales_w3 VALUES LESS THAN (31)
       TABLESPACE tssw3);
```

The above create table statement creates a sales table with three partitions partitioned by week range. Inserting a record with week_no=10 causes the row to be inserted into the first partition (w1). Inserting a record with week_no=25 causes the row to be inserted into the last partition (w3) since 25 is larger than 21 but less than 31. If trying to insert a record where week_no > 31, the insert will fail because 31 is higher than the partition bound for the highest partition. You can use the MAXVALUE keyword in the partition bound value as the last partition (highest partition) to define a partition that holds records with partition key values larger than the bounds defined.

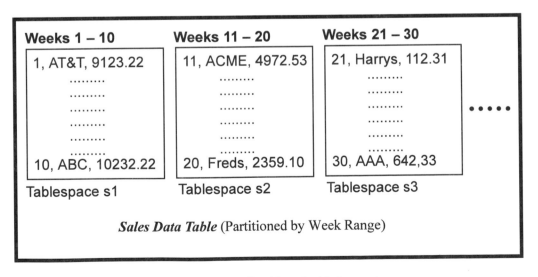

FIGURE 6.4 Partitioned table by week range.

6.9.3   DETERMINING THE PARTITION KEY

In order to maximize the benefits of partitioning, it is crucial that you optimally choose the partition key. The strategy behind selecting the columns that make up the partition key should consider the selectivity of queries and DML statements, partition and tablespace sizing, hot partitions versus seldom accessed partitions, and equi-partitioning versus activity-based partitioning. The partition key is a key factor in the selectivity of queries. If the partition key is too broad or conversely too specific, queries may require more I/O than is necessary by either having to scan a very large partition or scan too many partitions. If certain partitions are accessed much more frequently than others, a uniformly distributed partition key may not be ideal. Date column ranges are also often used in the partition key. Primary keys alone should not be used as partition keys because this translates into having a single row per partition. You may also choose to partition a table based on a date range which may result in certain partitions being more active (recent data) than other partitions (older data).

Two tables or indexes are equi-partitioned when they have identical logical partitioning attributes. Equi-partitioning requires objects to have the same number of partitions as well as the same VALUES LESS THAN boundaries. For example, consider an ACCOUNT table partitioned by ACCOUNT_ID in ranges of 1000 where the first 1000 accounts are stored in the first partition, the second set of 1000 accounts are stored in the second partition, and so on. Then consider an index ACCOUNT_ID_INDEX on the ACCOUNT_ID column of the ACCOUNT table which is also range partitioned on the same boundaries as the ACCOUNT table. This is an example of equi-partitioning. Equi-partitioning tends to improve query performance and optimizer execution plans. It also improves partition administration in the case where partitions need to be split or migrated.

Choosing the partition key that makes the most sense requires that you study in detail the data model, user access frequency, data distribution, data volumes and growth forecasts, performance requirements, tablespace sizing, and database administration requirements. Analyzing these items allows you to have a better understanding of your partitioning needs, subsequently resulting in an optimal choice for a partition key. Whether your focus is performance or administration, you need to spend a fair amount of time in the analysis phase before choosing the partition key.

6.9.4   MANIUPLATING PARTITIONS

There are many different commands that can be used to manipulate or administer partitions. You can move a partition from one tablespace to another using the MOVE PARTITION option of the ALTER TABLE command. You can also rename a partition using the RENAME PARTITION option of the ALTER TABLE or ALTER INDEX command. The MODIFY PARTITION option of the ALTER TABLE or ALTER INDEX command allows you to modify partition attributes such as nologging or storage parameters. The TRUNCATE PARTITION and DROP PARTITION options of the ALTER TABLE command allow you to truncate the rows from a partition and drop the partition from the partitioned table, respectively. You can also drop a partition from a partitioned index using the `ALTER INDEX DROP PARTITION` command.

The `SPLIT PARTITION` option of the `ALTER TABLE` or `ALTER INDEX` command allows you to create two new partitions from an existing partition by specifying the new partition boundaries. The existing partition is then discarded. The `SPLIT PARTITION` option is useful for situations where a single partition has grown too large or you need to redistribute data on disk to improve I/O performance.

The `EXCHANGE PARTITION` option of the `ALTER TABLE` command converts a partition to a nonpartitioned table and a table to a partition of a partitioned table by exchanging their data, and optionally, index segments. The `EXCHANGE PARTITION` option is useful for situations where an application that was previously using nonpartitioned tables would like to switch to partitioned tables. This can also be useful for migrating from partition views (7.3) to Oracle8 table partitions.

The `ADD PARTITION` option of the `ALTER TABLE` command is used to add a partition to the high end of the table. The `ADD PARTITION` option may be useful for scenarios of historical data where new partitions are added at certain periods of time. If you need to add a partition to the middle or beginning of the partitioned table, use the `SPLIT PARTITION` option.

The `REBUILD PARTITION` option of the `ALTER INDEX` command allows you to rebuild a partition of a partitioned index. Rebuilding a section of the index is beneficial as opposed to rebuilding the entire index. For example, you may determine that certain partitions of the partitioned index are very hot as compared to other partitions of the partitioned index. In such a case, the `REBUILD PARTITION` option can be used to migrate the index partition to another tablespace on another set of disks in order to improve I/O throughput.

Oracle8 provides various different options and techniques to administer partitions. This wide variety of partition commands fosters a flexible environment when using partitions. As partitioned objects continue to grow in size and partition access frequency increases, the ability to migrate or split a partition becomes more vital. Partitioned tables and indexes help improve availability, administration, manageability, and performance.

6.9.5 PARTITION INDEXES

There are several types of indexes such as nonpartitioned, global prefixed, local prefixed, and local nonprefixed indexes. Global nonprefixed indexes are not supported by Oracle. The variety of index types allows you to choose the most appropriate index type based on such factors as availability, performance, and manageability. Partitioned indexes are constructed as separate B*-tree structures. A nonpartitioned index is simply a traditional Oracle B*-tree index. A prefixed index has the leftmost columns of the index based on the same columns as the partition key. A unique prefix index requires access to only one index partition in order to retrieve the data when accessing only one row from a DML statement. A nonunique prefixed index where only part of the partition key is provided in the `WHERE` clause requires that all partitions be scanned. If, however, all the columns that makeup the partition key are specified in the `WHERE` clause, then only one index partition is accessed. The columns of a nonprefixed index are not based on the same columns as the partition key. A nonprefixed index is range-based partitioned; however, each B*-tree section of each partition is based on the nonprefixed column(s). In order to guarantee uniqueness, the unique nonprefix index must include the partition key as part of the index key. Unique nonprefixed indexes require only one index partition to retrieve the row when accessing only one row via a DML statement. Conversely, a nonunique nonprefixed index must scan all partitions in order to retrieve the row.

The keys in a particular index partition of a global index may refer to rows stored in more than one partition of the underlying table. A global index is created with the GLOBAL attribute of the CREATE INDEX statement and is typically not equi-partitioned with the underlying table. If the global index is equi-partitioned, Oracle does not automatically maintain the equi-partitioning. The optimizer is also not aware of equi-partitioned global indexes and thus cannot eliminate partitions from execution plans. For this reason, equi-partitioned indexes should be created as local indexes. A global index can be unique or nonunique. The highest partition of a global index must be able to hold the maximum value of the indexed columns for the underlying table.

In a local index, all rows in a table partition have a corresponding index entry in the index partition. Hence, a local index is equi-partitioned with the underlying partitioned table. A local index is created by specifying the LOCAL attribute in the CREATE INDEX statement. Local indexes increase availability by ensuring that partition maintenance operations provide partition independence. For example, you could be loading several partitions while concurrent DML statements are occurring on other partitions. Oracle can also generate more efficient plans by taking advantage of the fact that the table and index are equi-partitioned.

6.9.5.1   Local Prefixed Index

A local prefixed index has its partition key based on the leftmost column(s) of the index. For Massively Parallel Processing (MPP) environments, local prefixed indexes provide good data locality. Local prefixed indexes can be unique or nonunique. The following is an example of a local prefixed index that assumes the table is partitioned on the week_no column:

```
SQL> create index sales_lpidx
     on sales (week_no,customer_id)
     local
       (partition w1 tablespace ixw1,
        partition w2 tablespace ixw2,
        partition w3 tablespace ixw3,
        partition w4 tablespace ixw4);
```

Local prefixed indexes tend to offer the best performance, availability, and manageability. The fact that a local prefixed index is equi-partitioned with the underlying table improves the query plan execution by employing partition pruning. For example, a query that specified the values of week_no and customer_id can take advantage of partition pruning by eliminating the partitions containing weeks other than the ones specified. This improves query performance and reduces the amount of scans needed to execute the query.

6.9.5.2 Local Nonprefixed Index

A local nonprefixed index has its partition key based on something else other than the leftmost column(s) of the index. A local nonprefixed index can be nonunique and can only be unique if the partition key is a subset of the index key. Local nonprefixed indexes are useful in situations where fast access is needed and queries are based on a column which is not part of the partition key of the table. The following is an example of a local nonprefixed index that assumes the table is partitioned on the week_no column:

```
SQL> create index sales_lnpidx
     on sales (sale_no)
     local
     (partition w1 tablespace ixw1,
      partition w2 tablespace ixw2,
      partition w3 tablespace ixw3,
      partition w4 tablespace ixw4);
```

It is generally more expensive to scan a nonprefixed index than to scan a prefixed index. Oracle must apply a predicate involving the index columns to all index partitions for a nonprefixed index in order to perform a single key lookup or index range scan. An index range scan also causes Oracle to combine information from other index partitions. Local nonprefixed indexes reduce the degree of partition independence since DML statements using the keys of local nonprefixed indexes results in the probe of all index partitions. However, several index partitions in a local nonprefixed index can be scanned in parallel in cases where queries specify a range on the index key, thus increasing overall performance.

6.9.5.3 Global Prefixed Index

A global prefixed index is partitioned on a left prefix of the columns of the index. Global prefixed indexes are generally not equi-partitioned with the underlying table. In a global prefix index, Oracle maintains only the index structures, and not the partitions themselves. Global indexes increase administration complexity due to the fact that they do not maintain partition independence. As such, operations such as SPLIT, MOVE, DROP, TRUNCATE, or point in time recovery affect all partitions. The following is an example of a global prefixed index:

```
create index sales_gpidx
   on sales (week_no,customer_id)
global
partition by range (week_no)
  (partition w1 values less than (25),
   partition w2 values less than (maxvalue));
```

Global prefixed indexes minimize the number of index probes, thereby increasing performance. Global prefixed indexes are generally more difficult to manage, and the database administrator is responsible for maintaining the partitioning of the global prefixed index. All corresponding entries in a global prefixed index must be restored to the same point in time when recovering the underlying table partition to a point in time. The only way to recover a global prefixed index is to re-create the index since the index entries may be dispersed across all the partitions of the index which may be combined with index entries from other partitions that are not being restored.

6.9.6   PARTITION PRUNING AND THE EXPLAIN PLAN

The Oracle8 optimizer determines which partitions are needed to satisfy the DML statement based on the predicates specified. Partition pruning can significantly reduce the amount of I/O needed as well as reduce the overall work needed to complete the DML statement. For example, a query might require a hash join and then a sort for a complex join with an order by clause. Without partition pruning, the query might require full-table scans on the tables in the join clause. If the tables listed in the join clause are large in size, the query may take a long time to complete due to the amount of I/O needed as well as the time needed to sort the data. By utilizing partition pruning, the optimizer identifies only those partitions needed to satisfy the query predicates. For example, consider the following query on a partitioned table:

```
SQL> select count(*)
        from sales
        where (week_no between 1 and 15);
```

The explain plan for the above query looks as follows:

ID	EXPLAIN_PLAN	POSITION
0	SELECT STATEMENT	1
1	SORT AGGREGATE	1
2	PARTITION CONCATENATED :Q25000	
	PARALLEL_COMBINED_WITH_PARENT NUMBER(1) NUMBER(2)	1
3	TABLE ACCESS FULL SALES :Q25000	
	PARALLEL_TO_SERIAL NUMBER(1) NUMBER(2)	1

This explain plan shows that the optimizer is employing partition pruning. The PARTITION CONCATENATED operation indicates that more than one partition is involved and that the results from the multiple partition scans will be concatenated. If only one partition were being accessed, there would not be a PARTITION CONCATENDATED operation. Instead, the PARTITION_START and PARTITION_STOP columns would show the same partition being accessed (PARTITION SINGLE). The explain plan table columns PARTITION_START and PARTITION_STOP show the partitions being used. The explain plan above shows the values NUMBER(1) and NUMBER(2) for the columns PARTITION_START and PARTITION_STOP, respectively. This means that partition 1 and partition 2 are needed to satisfy the query. In addition, the explain plan also shows that the query is being parallelized.

The following is another example of an explain plan illustrating partition pruning using an update statement:

```
SQL> update sales_pending
         set sale_amount = sale_amount - (0.10*sale_amount)
     where (week_no between 21 and 30);
```

ID	EXPLAIN_PLAN	POSITION
0	UPDATE STATEMENT	1
1	UPDATE SALES_PENDING	1
2	TABLE ACCESS FULL SALES_PENDING :Q33000	1
	PARALLEL_TO_SERIAL NUMBER(3) NUMBER(3)	

This update statement is used to offer a 10 percent discount on sales still pending for the weeks 21 through 30. The corresponding explain plan shows that partition 3 is being used, and the explain plan also shows that the table access is being parallelized.

Using the explain plan utility, you can determine whether or not a query is employing partition pruning. Furthermore, you can determine which partitions are involved in the SQL operation. You should perform an explain plan on your SQL statements to ensure that partition pruning is being utilized. The explain plan data helps you understand the execution path of your SQL statements. By using the explain plan utility, you can take steps to improve execution times should you determine that the plan being generated is suboptimal. You may have to regenerate table and partition statistics, or rewrite the SQL statement.

6.9.7 PARTITION EXTENDED TABLE NAMES

You can also explicitly specify the name of the partition to be used in a SELECT, INSERT, UPDATE, or DELETE SQL statement. This allows you to view an individual partition as a separate table. If you choose to use partition extended table names, you should use a view in order to insulate the application from the specifics of this SQL extension. In addition, using a view avoids having to hard-code partition names inside the application. The following is an example of explicitly specifying the partition name as part of the SELECT statement:

```
select count(*)
from sales partition (w1)
where (week_no <= 10);
```

The use of views in conjunction with partition extended table names can also help build partition-level security. By building a view against a select statement that uses the partition extended table name feature, you can then grant or revoke privileges to the view to and from other users or roles. This is useful for situations where certain users' access should be restricted to certain partitions within the entire table.

6.9.8 PARTITION TABLESPACE OPTIMIZATION

The beauty of Oracle8 partitioning is that it allows you to spread your tables and indexes across different tablespaces. This not only allows you to achieve high I/O throughput by distributing your tablespace data files across different disks and controllers, it also allows you to partition by frequency of access. For example, certain partitions of a partitioned table may seldom be accessed because they represent archive or historical data. You may also have certain partitions that are not updated in which case you can employ read-only tablespaces for such partitions. It is important that you lay out your table data and partitions appropriately so as to minimize I/O contention and separate partitions and tablespaces by criteria such as workload, administration requirements, availability, and performance requirements. You may have to stripe certain frequently accessed (very hot) partitions across more disks and controllers more than other infrequently accessed partitions. For example, a frequently accessed partition may be striped across 20 disks with a small stripe interleave while a partition that is seldom accessed may be striped only across 2 disks with a larger stripe interleave. It is vital that you consider the many different factors such as workload, performance, manageability, access frequency, type of access, availability, data distribution, and level of concurrency when planning and sizing table and index partitions. You should also monitor I/O utilization using the Oracle Enterprise Manager as well as the server utilities such as `sar` or `iostat` to determine if I/O contention is occurring. If I/O contention is occurring, you may have to split or move partitions in order to redistribute data.

6.9.9 GATHERING STATISTICS AT THE PARTITION LEVEL

Oracle8 allows you to gather statistics at the partition level for a table and index. This helps you parallelize statistics gathering for very large tables and indexes. By choosing a reasonable sampling size per partition, you can estimate statistics at the partition level if the partitions are too big to perform a compute statistics. For example,

```
SQL> analyze table sales partition (sales_w1)
        estimate statistics sample 5000 rows;
```

Gathering statistics at the partition level improves the performance and manageability of statistics gathering. You should compute or estimate statistics at the partition level so that the optimizer can produce intelligent execution plans. Without statistics, it is difficult for the optimizer to generate efficient execution plans since the default estimates may not be optimal. You can reduce the time it takes to gather statistics by submitting multiple analyze statements in parallel, each against different partitions.

6.9.10 PARTITION CATALOG TABLES

There are various new Oracle8 catalog views that provide information on partitions such as partition ranges, statistics, storage information, and number of partitions. The following are the catalog views pertaining to partitions:

- ALL_IND_PARTITIONS
- ALL_PART_COL_STATISTICS
- ALL_PART_HISTOGRAMS
- ALL_PART_INDEXES
- ALL_PART_KEY_COLUMNS
- ALL_PART_TABLES
- ALL_TAB_PARTITIONS
- DBA_IND_PARTITIONS
- DBA_PART_COL_STATISTICS
- DBA_PART_HISTOGRAMS
- DBA_PART_INDEXES
- DBA_PART_KEY_COLUMNS
- DBA_PART_TABLES
- DBA_TAB_PARTITIONS
- LOADER_PART_INFO
- USER_IND_PARTITIONS
- USER_PART_COL_STATISTICS
- USER_PART_HISTOGRAMS
- USER_PART_INDEXES
- USER_PART_KEY_COLUMNS
- USER_PART_TABLES
- USER_TAB_PARTITIONS

For more information on the above views and other catalog views, refer to the *Oracle8 Reference Release 8.0 Manual.*

6.10 LOADING DATA

Loads are often performed in a DSS environment to refresh data. SQL*Loader with the parallel option can reduce the time it takes to load a large table by loading the table in parallel. Do not confuse the parallel query option with the parallel load option. Parallel load does not use query slaves to parallelize the load. Parallel load removes the exclusive lock held on the table, enabling multiple processes to insert into the same table. Each parallel load session loads the data into temporary table extents and then merges the temporary table extents upon completion. You can verify the existence of the temporary table extents by querying the DBA_EXTENTS view setting segment_type='TEMPO-RARY' while a parallel load is running.

6.10.1 DIRECT PATH LOADS

As of Oracle7, release 7.1, the SQL*Loader utility provides a parallel load feature. The parallel load feature, along with the direct path option, can load large amounts of data in a relatively small period of time. The direct load option of SQL*Loader bypasses the Oracle SGA by writing directly to disk and updates the high-water mark of the table. You can obtain high I/O throughput during loads by using raw devices, striping, and a volume manager. The parallel load feature enables multiple loads to proceed in parallel on the same table. Without the `parallel=true` SQL*Loader option, an exclusive lock is placed on the table until the SQL*Loader session completes. By parallelizing the load process, you can reduce the amount of time it takes to load a table. You can also use the `FILE` option of SQL*Loader. The `FILE` option enables you to specify which database file Oracle will allocate extents from for the load. Using the `FILE` option, you can achieve high throughput by spreading the data across different files and different disk drives. If you are using SQL*Loader direct path, you may want to decrease the size of the SGA temporarily to enable more memory to be dedicated to the load processes. Because direct load bypasses the SGA, a large SGA is not needed.

6.10.2 CONVENTIONAL PATH LOADS

If you use the conventional load option of SQL*Loader, you can make use of the `bindsize` parameter. SQL*Loader uses the SQL array interface option, and `bindsize` specifies, in bytes, the size of the array for each insert. A larger number of rows can be inserted at each time by increasing the `bindsize`. SQL*Loader reads the number of rows that fit into the `bindsize` array and then performs an array insert of the bind array. This reduces the number of SQL calls between the SQL*Loader process and the Oracle Server. It can also pseudo-parallelize the load process by allowing the Oracle Server to insert the bind array while SQL*Loader reads continue to populate the bind array for the next insert. Increasing the bind array maximizes CPU utilization and minimizes I/O wait time. Of course, when you size the bind array, be careful to size it accordingly so that sufficient memory is available for the size of the bind array, and paging and swapping do not occur. If you load through the conventional path, the SGA should be optimally sized so as to accommodate the bind array inserts into the SGA. Please refer to the *Oracle7 Server Utilities Guide* or the *Oracle8 Utilities Release 8.0 Guide* for more information on the SQL*Loader utility.

6.10.3 PARTITION LOADS

In Oracle8, you can load data at the partition level. By specifying the name of the partition in the SQL*Loader control file, you can invoke concurrent loads, each loading a separate partition. The following is an example SQL*Loader control file that specifies the name of the partition:

```
— Parallel, direct-path load at the partition level..
— Unrecoverable option used to speed up the load..
—
OPTIONS (DIRECT = TRUE, PARALLEL = TRUE)
UNRECOVERABLE
LOAD DATA
INFILE 'sales.dat'
APPEND
INTO TABLE sales partition (sales_w1)
APPEND
FIELDS TERMINATED BY ',' OPTIONALLY ENCLOSED BY '"'
(
    week_no                integer external,
    sale_no                integer external,
    sale_date              date "MM/DD/YY",
    sale_amount            integer external,
    customer_id            integer external
)
```

This control file example specifies the name of the table partition following the partition clause. The control file also specifies a direct path and parallel load. Loading at the partition level allows you to achieve a high degree of parallelism. By optimally distributing the partition tablespaces, you can reduce the amount of time needed to load the entire table by loading concurrently at the partition level. In order to achieve a high throughput load, it is important that the data files of the underlying table partitions be distributed so as to minimize I/O contention. In an optimal situation with no I/O contention nor resource contention (processor and memory), the time needed to load all the partitions (in parallel) should be roughly near the time it takes to load a single partition. Monitor I/O utilization during the load in order to ensure I/O is being distributed and to determine if I/O contention is occurring.

6.10.4 FIXED FIELD LOADS

Another technique you can use to increase the performance of SQL*Loader loads is through the use of fixed-length fields in the SQL*Loader control file. By using fixed-length columns, as opposed to variable-length fields delimited by a delimiter, you will reduce SQL*Loader parsing. When using variable delimited fields, SQL*Loader spends a considerable amount of time parsing the records by setting the start position and the length of each field for the data records. By using fixed-length record fields in the SQL*Loader control file, parsing time can be reduced significantly and you can increase the performance of the load.

6.10.5 UNRECOVERABLE OPTION

The UNRECOVERABLE option can be used with a direct path load to request that the load data not be logged. Instead, invalidation redo is generated. This helps increase load performance. However, you need to consider media recovery when using the UNRECOVERABLE option since the load data blocks cannot be recovered. You should backup the table following the load to ensure that you will be able to recover the table data should media recovery be necessary.

6.10.6   LOADING THROUGH NFS

When running parallel loads, it is critical that I/O be distributed. Try to place the input files on a striped file system separate from the Oracle data and redo log files. This minimizes I/O contention and thus increases the performance of the load. When loading from a remote file system staging area (not local to the database server), either load from the machine that contains the file system using SQL*Net or Net8, or NFS-mount the file system on the database server and run a local load. As far as Oracle is concerned, it has no idea that the input data is NFS-mounted; this is handled by the OS. NFS tends to have a higher throughput than SQL*Net or Net8 and can therefore reduce the time it takes to load the data. To increase the load performance over an NFS link, you may want to consider setting up a dedicated connection between the database server and file system staging area server using a dedicated Ethernet connection or even a fiber connection. This reduces network contention and may reduce the length that the packet must travel if the dedicated connection is directly connected between one server and another (bypassing routers and other network segments).

By tuning loads appropriately, you can achieve a very fast high-throughput load. In my experience, I have been able to concurrently load 10-G tables on highly tuned servers in less than 30 minutes by starting multiple loads and distributing I/O as optimally as possible. In Oracle8, load throughput can be increased by loading at the table partition level. This allows you to sustain more concurrent loads by making sure that each load at the partition level loads a small subset of the data. You should also divide your input data streams (SQL*Loader input data files) into partitions, thus allowing each input data stream to map to an Oracle table partition.

6.11   BUILDING INDEXES

In addition to loading data in parallel, you can also create indexes in parallel and reduce the time it takes to build an index. Oracle 7.1 introduced the parallel index creation option, and Oracle 7.2 introduced the unrecoverable option, further increasing performance. Oracle 7.3 introduced the alter index rebuild option that allows an index to be rebuilt using the existing index. In Oracle8, you can rebuild an index at the partition level. To create indexes in parallel, you can use the following example:

```
SQL> Create Index ACCOUNT_INDEX on Account (ACCOUNT_NO)
     unrecoverable          *** Oracle7
     nologging              *** Oracle8
     parallel (degree 4)
     storage (.......);
```

In this example, the ACCOUNT_INDEX is created in parallel using a degree of parallelism of four. The Oracle7 unrecoverable keyword indicates that no redo information will be generated for this index creation. The equivalent to unrecoverable in Oracle8 is nologging. The unrecoverable (Oracle7) or nologging (Oracle8) keyword means that the index cannot be recovered using the redo log files or archived redo log files. However, it can speed up the creation of the index tangibly if redo is a bottleneck on your server. Be careful when choosing the degree of parallelism. Although a degree of parallelism of four is selected, eight slave processes actually will be spawned. Four of the slaves will scan the table gathering the ACCOUNT_NO columns, and four of the slaves will perform the sorting of the ACCOUNT_NO columns. Again, this demonstrates the use of inter-parallelism. Be careful not to choose a high degree of parallelism; otherwise too many processes will be spawned, and the high degree of parallelism may have a negative effect.

6.12 BUILDING TABLES

In a DSS environment, tables are often created for the purpose of aggregation or analysis. The tables are often dropped and re-created in order to refresh the data. Building a large table without parallelism can take a long time. Oracle 7.2 provides the parallel table creation option that allows not only the underlying query to be parallelized, but the table creation itself is also parallelized. To create a table in parallel, you can use the following example:

```
SQL> Create Table ORDERS_PER_STATE
     nologging
     parallel (degree 4)
     AS SELECT /*+ ORDERED
                    FULL (A)
                    FULL (O)
                    PARALLEL (A,4)
                    PARALLEL (O,4)
                    USE_HASH (A O) */
          A.STATE_ID,
          count(*) SALES_COUNT
       FROM ACCOUNT A,
            ORDERS O
       WHERE  (A.ACCOUNT_NO=O.ACCOUNT_NO)
       GROUP BY A.STATE_ID;
```

In this example, the ORDERS_PER_STATE table is created in parallel by using a degree of parallelism of four. Both the subselect query and the table creation are parallelized. The nologging keyword (unrecoverable in Oracle7) also can be used with table creations as well as with index creations to eliminate the redo for the table creation. However, keep in mind that using the nologging (or unrecoverable) option prevents you from being able to recover the table through the redo log files or archived redo log files. The performance increase offered by the `nologging` option can make dealing with the recoverability issue worthwhile. Following the completion of the table create statement, you should make a backup of the table in the event of a media failure. Choosing the appropriate degree of parallelism can help minimize the time needed to create the table.

In a data warehousing environment, it is often necessary to refresh table data. This can be done in many different ways. If there are a small number of rows that need to be refreshed, an update statement can be used to update the table. However, if dealing with a large amount of rows, a Create Table as Select (CTAS) statement is much faster than an update statement. The CTAS operation can be parallelized even on nonpartitioned tables. If you are using update statements to refresh tables in a data warehousing environment, you may want to consider using a CTAS statement in place of the update to re-create the table. When updating a large number of rows, a CTAS statement outperforms an equivalent update statement.

6.13 PARALLEL STORAGE

When you load, index, or create tables in parallel, recall that each slave allocates an initial extent followed by next extents if needed. This means that if you load a table in parallel with `INITIAL` extent size set to 100 M, and five parallel loads are running simultaneously on the table, 500 M (5 × 100 M) in initial extents are allocated. Therefore, make sure you have enough space for the parallel load, index, or table create.

You should also make sure that your data file extents are distributed and sized properly so as to avoid disk contention and fragmentation. You can use the `FILE` option of SQL*Loader to specify from which data files Oracle will allocate extents. This allows you to distribute your data across different data files and different disks. When building or loading indexes and tables in parallel, it is essential that you optimally size and distribute the Oracle data files in order to maintain high I/O throughput.

6.14 DEGREE OF PARALLELISM

The degree of parallelism you choose is highly dependent on your system configuration. The number of processors, level of I/O distribution, and the amount of available memory all contribute to the optimal selection of the degree of parallelism. You should balance the degree of parallelism with the number of on-line available processors, and the degree of striping. For example, if your data is spread across only two disk drives and you have ten processors, starting up ten slaves to scan the table (data) will likely saturate the two disks and cause high I/O wait times.

You should balance I/O with available processors when selecting the degree of parallelism. Also, if for example, you are trying to parallelize a query that consists of a large hash join, and the tables' data files are striped across five different disks and controllers, and the temporary tablespace is also stripped across five different disks and controllers (different disks and controllers than the tables), and you have ten processors, choosing a degree of parallelism of five is optimal. Recall that a parallel query using a hash join utilizes both inter- and intraparallelism. In this case, a degree of parallelism of five will actually spawn ten query slaves—five of the slaves will attack the table (scanning the table) in parallel, and five slaves will perform the join. For a large hash join, the data blocks may be written out to the temporary tablespace. If so, the five scan slaves and the five join slaves will experience minimal contention since the data files and temporary tablespace files are separated. Use `sar` `-u` and `sar` `-d` to monitor processor and disk I/O utilization to help you choose the most effective degree of parallelism.

6.15 PARALLEL QUERY AND THE 9/13 RULE

The Parallel Query Option (PQO) uses a 9/13 rule when it parallelizes queries. First, PQO (when used) converts the base user shadow process into the Query Coordinator (QC). The QC then spawns the number of query slaves needed. If slaves are already available, then the QC uses the available slaves. The QC is responsible for partitioning the work among the parallel query slave processes, managing the workload among the parallel query slaves, and returning the results of the query back to the client. The QC divides the total number of blocks occupied by the table by the number of parallel query slaves assigned to the query, rounding up when necessary. The QC then further subdivides each partition into thirteenths. Each partition is divided into three subpartitions: one 9/13, one 3/13, and the last partition of 1/13.

For example, suppose a query is submitted with a degree of parallelism of four. The QC divides the table being scanned into four equal-size partitions (rounding may be necessary, causing the partitions to be near in size). Figure 6.5 shows the query coordinator and the four query slaves.

FIGURE 6.5   The query coordinator and the parallel query slaves.

Then the QC further subdivides each of the four partitions into three subpartitions of 9/13, 3/13, and 1/13 in size. Then, the QC assigns each slave a 9/13 partition to scan. As each slave finishes its 9/13 partition, the QC then assigns the 3/13 partition on a first-come, first-serve basis. The first slave to finish the 9/13 scan, receives a 3/13 partition to scan until all scans of the 3/13 partitions are completed. Then, the QC distributes the remaining 1/13 partitions to the slaves also on a first-come, first-serve basis. The 9/13 technique minimizes the effects of uneven data distribution. Even if all the data for a table is located in one or a few areas, the workload of the parallel query slaves will still be distributed. For example, suppose a parallel query with a degree of parallelism of four is executed on a table that has most of the data centered in one area. Some of the slaves likely will finish their 9/13 partition quickly because not much data is located in the partitions. However, one of the slaves will be quite busy scanning the first 9/13 partition because all the data is concentrated in one area. However, because the other slaves returned quickly, they now can start to receive the 3/13 partitions that contain the bulk of the data. This will help keep all the slaves busy until all the partitions are scanned. Therefore, it is apparent that distributing your I/O and data can help maximize the performance of parallel query.

6.16 MAXIMIZING PARALLEL QUERY PERFORMANCE

The parallel query option provides an extremely fast mechanism to perform large table scans, sorts, joins, and index builds. To maximize the performance of the parallel query option, it is important that your I/O be tuned so that each parallel query slave receives an equal amount of work. This prevents an uneven distribution in which some slaves are scanning large partitions, and other slaves are scanning much smaller partitions. When you build large tables, try to size each table extent near in size. Doing so will ensure that partition sizes are evenly distributed to each parallel query slave. This allows a parallel query slave to complete its work in roughly the same amount of time as the other slaves. However, this is highly dependent on the level of striping and data distribution. You can maximize the performance of the parallel query option by distributing and striping the Oracle data files evenly and by sizing object extents equally to prevent an uneven parallel query workload.

6.16.1 CONFIGURING THE NUMBER OF PARALLEL SLAVES

The `init.ora` parameters `parallel_min_servers`, `parallel_max_servers`, and `parallel_server_idle_time` specify the minimum number of parallel query slaves started upon instance startup, the maximum number of query slaves that can be started, and the period of time that a parallel query slave can be idle (in minutes) before it is shut down, respectively. To reduce startup time overhead, set `parallel_min_servers` to the number of parallel query slaves that will be used in the DSS system. Ensure that your system has sufficient memory to handle the parallel query slave processes. The `init.ora` parameter `optimizer_percent_parallel` specifies the amount of parallelism to be used in computing CBO cost estimates. A value of 0 means that the objects' degree of parallelism is not considered when computing the cost. A value of 100 means that the objects' degree of parallelism is used when computing the cost of a full-table scan. The init.ora parameter `parallel_min_percent` specifies the minimum number of query slaves that must be available to execute a parallel query. For example, if set to 50 (i.e., 50%), and a parallel query with a degree of parallelism of ten is specified, at least five slaves must be available. If not, the query terminates, and an error is returned.

6.16.2 CONTENTION FOR THE PARALLEL QUERY SLAVES

To determine if your system is experiencing contention for parallel query slaves, you can query the `v$pq_sysstat` view as follows:

```
SQL> select *
          from v$pq_sysstat
          order by statistic

     STATISTIC                    VALUE
     _____

     DFO Trees                       24
     DML Initiated                    1
     Distr Msgs Recv'd                0
     Distr Msgs Sent                  0
     Local Msgs Recv'd              810
     Local Msgs Sent                681
     Queries Initiated               22
     Server Sessions                 60
     Servers Busy                     3
     Servers Cleaned Up               0
     Servers Highwater               17
     Servers Idle                     5
     Servers Shutdown                58
     Servers Started                 66
     Sessions Active                  1
```

These statistics show minimal contention for query slaves since `Servers Busy` is three. If `Servers Busy` were high, you would need to increase the value of `parallel_max_servers`. If increasing `parallel_max_servers`, you may also have to increase the amount of concurrent processes (`MAXUP`) per user, as well as the total number of processes (`NPROC`) in the operating system kernel. Refer to Chapter 2 for specific information on increasing the OS process kernel limits. You should also monitor the views `v$pq_sesstat` and `v$pq_slave`. The `v$pq_sesstat` view provides parallel query statistics at the session level while parallel queries are in progress. The `v$pq_slave` view provides statistics such as processor utilization and messaging statistics at the parallel query slave level. The `v$pq_slave` can help you determine if certain slaves are busier than others.

6.16.3   TUNING THE MESSAGE POOL

When interparallelism is used such as a hash join between two tables whereby one set of slaves is scanning the data while another set of slaves is consuming the data and processing the hash join, messages are sent between the slaves during parallel execution. The Oracle8 init.ora parameters `parallel_min_message_pool`, and `parallel_execution_message_size` (added in 8.0.4) specify the size of the minimum amount of memory allocated at startup time from the shared pool to be used for parallel execution messages and the size of each message, respectively. When `parallel_min_servers` is greater than zero, explicitly setting `parallel_min_message_pool` improves performance since memory is allocated in a contiguous section. Before setting `parallel_min_message_pool`, you should review the statistics from the `v$pq_sysstat` view. The `v$pq_sysstat` view reports the number of messages sent and received both local and distributed messages. This gives you an idea as to the amount of message pool memory that will be required based on your workload. Also, be careful not to set `parallel_min_message_pool` so high that a memory shortage occurs in the shared pool.

   The `parallel_execution_message_size` parameter specifies the size of the message used during parallel execution. The default is 2148 bytes. The default is sufficient for most applications, however, if there is a high amount of messaging occurring, increasing the parameter from its default can improve parallel execution performance. For data warehousing systems that heavily utilize parallel query and parallel execution messaging, setting `parallel_execution_message_size=8192` or `parallel _execution_message_size=16384` results in performance gains of 15–20 percent. A larger message size results in more data being passed in a fewer number of messages. A larger setting for `parallel_execution_message_size` requires more memory for the message pool since the messages are of larger size. Therefore, if increasing the value of the parameter `parallel_execution_message_size`, you may also need to adjust the size of the message pool (`parallel_min_message_pool`) and the size of the shared pool (`shared_pool_size`). Measure the performance gains of your system when adjusting the size of `parallel_execution_message_size` to determine the optimal setting for your environment.

6.16.4   PARALLEL QUERY OPTIMIZATIONS

Oracle8 release 8.0.4 enhances the performance and scalability of parallel query. The performance of parallel query is dependent on many different factors, one of which is the degree of parallelism. Typically, the degree of parallelism is tuned for a single user or a few users. When the number of users increases, contention surfaces and the performance of parallel query degrades. A new init.ora parameter `parallel_ adaptive_multi_user` provides a mechanism to tune parallel query for multi-user environments. If `parallel_adaptive_multi_user=TRUE`, the degree of parallelism is automatically reduced based on the current number of active parallel query users. This uses an adaptive algorithm to reduce the amount of parallelism based on the degree of parallelism specified by the table or hint divided by the total number of parallel query users. The adaptive algorithm assumes that the degree of parallelism has been tuned for a single-user environment.

Another parallel query enhancement of Oracle8 release 8.0.4 is the ability to improve the performance of hash and merge-joins when a result set of a very large table is being joined with a result set of a very small table. The `init.ora` parameter `parallel_broadcast_enabled`, when set to TRUE, causes the optimizer to broadcast via a single table queue the row sources of the small result set to each of the parallel query slaves that are processing the rows of the large set. This improves the performance of the join.

6.17 PARALLEL DML

Oracle8 provides the ability to parallelize DML statements such as inserts, updates, and deletes. This helps improve the performance of DML operations in data warehousing environments where data needs to be updated or deleted from large size tables. You can specify the degree of parallelism via a hint or by setting the degree of parallelism at the table level via the `CREATE` or `ALTER TABLE` commands. Parallel DML avoids the traditional technique of parallelizing updates, deletes, and inserts by establishing multiple sessions with each session specifying a range of key values. Parallel DML allows you to submit a single DML statement within a single transaction and have the DML statement automatically parallelized. In an Oracle Parallel Server (OPS) environment, parallel DML affinity is managed by the Oracle server. Oracle employs a partition to device mapping to allocate parallel slave processes to a specific partition, thus allowing OPS to utilize resources across multiple instances. Parallel DML does not require user knowledge of data (partition) affinity distribution.

Parallel insert uses a direct-load insert, meaning that the data is inserted into new blocks and then merged with the table. This is similar to the way SQL*Loader direct path works. The `APPEND` hint is the default behavior for direct-load insert which means that new blocks are appended to the table. The `APPEND` hint causes more space to be used but results in a faster insert operation. You can use the `NOAPPEND` hint to override the default `APPEND` mode. The `NOAPPEND` hint causes the default storage management algorithm to be utilized to hold the new rows to be inserted. The following is an example of a parallel insert direct-load statement:

```
SQL> insert /*+ APPEND PARALLEL (tsales,4) */
          into tsales
      select /*+ FULL (s) PARALLEL (s,4) */
          * from sales s;
```

The following is the explain plan for the above parallel insert statement. The explain plan shows that both the insert and the select operations are being parallelized.

ID	EXPLAIN_PLAN	POSITION
0	INSERT STATEMENT	1
1	PARTITION CONCATENATED :Q53000	1
	PARALLEL_COMBINED_WITH_PARENT NUMBER(1) NUMBER(4)	
2	TABLE ACCESS FULL SALES :Q53000	1
	PARALLEL_TO_SERIAL NUMBER(1) NUMBER(4)	

You can also use parallel DML to parallelize update and delete statements. However, parallelizing update and delete statements requires that the tables be partitioned. The parallelism for delete and update statements is done at the partition level. Therefore, there is no advantage in specifying a degree of parallelism higher than the number of partitions. The following is an example of a parallel delete and a parallel update statement:

```
SQL> update /*+ PARALLEL (sales,4) */
     sales
     set sale_no=sale_no + 1000
     where (week_no <= 21);

SQL> delete /*+ PARALLEL (sales,4) */
     sales
     where (week_no between 1 and 40);
```

To explicitly enable parallel DML at the session level, you must issue the following statement as the first statement in the transaction:

```
SQL> alter session enable parallel dml;
```

You can also explicitly disable parallel DML at the session level by issuing the following command:

```
SQL> alter session disable parallel dml;
```

In Oracle8 release 8.0.3, the use of parallel DML required you to issue either a commit or rollback following the parallel DML statement within your transaction. No other statements could be issued following a parallel DML statement except for either a rollback or commit. In 8.0.4, you can issue multiple parallel DML, serial DML, or other query operations within a transaction following a parallel DML statement. The only caveat is that you cannot access the same table in the same transaction after modifying it in parallel. In addition, 8.0.4 now maintains local and global indexes during parallel insert operations.

Oracle8 parallel DML is extremely useful for reducing the time it takes to modify large tables. In addition to distributing file I/O, you should also size and distribute your rollback segments appropriately. Each parallel slave transaction can be assigned to different rollback segments and this is likely given the fact that Oracle will attempt to load balance when assigning transactions to rollback segments. Therefore it is important that you have a sufficient number of rollback segments so as to minimize parallel slave transaction contention for rollback segments. You should also make sure that the rollback segments are sized properly since long-running transactions may require a large amount of rollback segment space. Also, rollback segments should be equal in size when using parallel DML since you cannot be certain which rollback segments get assigned to which parallel slave transactions. If they are not equal in size, certain parallel slave transactions may have enough space in their assigned rollback segment while other rollback segments may not. The statistic DML Initiated from the v$pq_sysstat view reports the number of DML statements that were initiated. The statistic DML Parallelized from the v$pq_sesstat view reports the number of DML statements parallelized within the session. You can monitor these statistics to determine the amount of parallel DML activity on your system.

In choosing the degree of parallelism for parallel DML operations, you should consider the degree of data distribution, number of processors, amount of available memory, number of disks and controllers, and amount of concurrency of other users performing parallel query or parallel DML operations. For parallel update or delete operations, you should constrain the degree of parallelism by the total number of partitions. Monitor disk, processor, memory, rollback segment, and parallel slave utilization to determine the optimal degrees of parallelism. Use the guidelines presented in Section 6.14 to help determine the optimal degree of parallelism.

6.18 INDEX ONLY TABLES

Oracle8 provides the ability to create index only tables. An index only table has all the table data stored in the index. In data warehousing environments, a DBA often creates many indexes to improve query plan execution so as to avoid full-table scans. However, this can be expensive in terms of the disk storage space required to hold both the table and the additional indexes. The index only table allows you to build a table of the index, meaning that you do not need to store all the table data. This conserves space and improves the performance of DML operations such as inserts, deletes, and updates because only the index needs to be updated. Index only tables store the data as a standard Oracle B*-tree index. Index only tables are useful for data warehousing and OLAP environments, information retrieval applications, and spatial and GIS applications.

To create an index only table, you simply need to add the ORGANIZATION INDEX clause to the CREATE TABLE statement. For example,

```
SQL>   create table bookindex
          (book_id number(8),
           book_title varchar2(30),
           author_name varchar2(30),
           book_description varchar2(2000),
           constraint bookindex_pk
             primary key (book_id))
           organization index
           tablespace tsbook
           pctthreshold 20
           overflow tablespace tsbook_overflow;
```

In this example, an index only table is created to store information on books. The primary key for the table is the book_id column. The PCTTHRESHOLD option allows you to specify an overflow area. In this example, for the rows that are larger than 20 percent of the block size, the nonkey columns of those rows will be stored in the overflow tablespace (tsbook_overflow). The overflow area option is useful for situations where large rows are resulting in slow full-index scans. When an overflow area is specified, the index contains only the key value and a pointer to the columns in the overflow area. The IOT_TYPE column of the USER_TABLES view has a value of IOT for index only tables and is set to NULL for all other tables. You can use standard DML operations, direct path insert, SQL*Loader, Export, and Import on index only tables.

6.19 REVERSE KEY INDEXES

Oracle8 provides the ability to create reverse key indexes. Reverse key indexes reverse the bytes of each indexed column for the exception of rowid and still maintain the column order. Reverse key indexes are useful for Oracle Parallel Server (OPS) environments. In an OPS environment, modifications to indexes are focused on a small set of leaf blocks. Reversing the keys of the index allows insertions to be distributed across all the leaf keys in the index. Reverse key indexes prevent queries from performing an index range scan since lexically adjacent keys are not stored next to each other. Reverse key indexes can also be used in situations where users insert ascending values and delete lower values from the table, thus helping to prevent skewed indexes. To create a reverse key index, simply add the keyword REVERSE to the CREATE INDEX statement. For example,

```
SQL> create index tsales_index
        on tsales (week_no,sale_no)
     reverse;
```

6.20 REDUCING LOCKS

DSS databases tend to be primarily read-only. Therefore, reducing the number of dml_locks can help increase performance. The init.ora parameter dml_locks specifies the maximum number of dml_locks. You can increase performance by disabling enqueues, thereby setting dml_locks=0. However, if dml_locks=0, you cannot issue the following statements DROP TABLE, CREATE INDEX, or explicit lock statements such as LOCK TABLE IN EXCLUSIVE MODE. If your DSS is fully configured, no new tables or indexes will be created, and no locks statements will be explicitly issued, set dml_locks=0 to increase performance.

6.21   INTER-NODE PARALLEL QUERY

Oracle Parallel Server 7.3 introduced the Internode Parallel Query (IPQ) feature. IPQ enables multiple nodes in the parallel server cluster to each execute a query in parallel. This means not only that a query can be executed in parallel on a single node, but also that the query can be executed in parallel across several nodes. This helps make use of all the nodes' processors and disks by distributing the workload across the nodes. To enable IPQ, set the Oracle7 `init.ora` parameter `use_internode_pqo=TRUE`. For example, if each node in the cluster has six processors and the table is very large, you can distribute the query by allowing six slaves to be created on each node. This is much faster than having only six slaves execute on only one machine. Oracle Parallel Server (OPS) handles the creation of the IPQ slaves as well as the communication among the IPQ slaves.

In Oracle8, the `init.ora` parameter `use_internode_pqo` has been made obsolete. However, you can achieve the same result by setting the value of `INSTANCES` in the parallel settings for the table or index. You can also specify the value of `INSTANCES` via the `PARALLEL` hint. The syntax for the `PARALLEL` hint is `PARALLEL` (table *tdegree idegree*). The *tdegree* is the degree of parallelism used for the table, and the *idegree* is the degree of parallelism used across the instances. The following is an example of setting the value of `INSTANCES`:

```
SQL> alter table customer parallel (degree 10 instances 4);
```

In this example, a degree of parallelism for the table is set to ten, and the degree of parallelism across the instances is set to four. You can also set the value of the `init.ora` parameter `parallel_default_max_instances` which specifies the default degree of parallelism to be used for cross-instance parallelism. The setting for `parallel_default_max_instances` is used if the value of `INSTANCES` in the parallel settings for the table or index is set to the keyword `DEFAULT`.

6.22   SINGLE-TASK PROCESSES

By default, Oracle processes are two-task, meaning that a shadow process is spawned on the database server (via the SQL*Net or Net8 listener) for the client process, such as SQL*Plus, or Developer/2000. The shadow process communicates to the Oracle Server and processes the client request. For a client program such as Export, Import, or SQL*Loader, this can increase the amount of communication between the client process and the shadow process. Figure 6.6 illustrates the two-task and single-task architecture.

In the two-task architecture, a shadow process is created, and the client and shadow process communicate via SQL*Net or Net8. SQL*Net and Net8 use a secured RPC method of communication. The shadow process protects against an unstable application

FIGURE 6.6   Two-task and single-task architecture.

by separating the application from the Oracle shadow process and server code. In a single-task environment, the Oracle Server code is linked in with the application thereby reducing the number of messages and amount of communication between the application and the server process. However, because single-task programs link the Oracle Server code in with the application, the application either needs to be a set-uid program (set-uid of the Oracle software owner), or the executable needs to be owned by the Oracle software owner so that it can attach to the SGA. Single-task programs are dangerous and are not recommended because an unstable application can cause the Oracle Server to crash.

You can use single-task with programs such as SQL*Loader, and Export/Import to increase the performance of loads and/or exports/imports. To link single-task use the make file provided by Oracle ($ORACLE_HOME/rdbms/lib). For Oracle 7.2 and below, use the oracle.mk file. For Oracle 7.3 and above, use the ins_rdbms.mk make file to link the server executables as single-task. For loads, linking single-task can increase performance since in two-task mode huge amounts of data are being passed from the SQL*Loader application to the shadow process during a large table load. Single-task reduces this overhead by combining the server process and the application process into one process. For example, to link SQL*Loader single-task in Oracle 7.3 or Oracle8, issue the following make command:

```
myhost{oracle}-> cd $ORACLE_HOME/rdbms/lib
myhost{oracle}-> make -f ins_rdbms.mk sqlldrst
```

After the executable sqlldrst is successfully built, you can then use the executable sqlldrst to perform your loads.

MEDIA RECOVERY

As databases continue to grow in size, the task of backing up the database can become tedious and time consuming. There are many customer sites running hundreds of gigabyte- and terabyte-size databases in production. Backing up a very large database of several hundred gigabytes or even a terabyte is an enormous task that requires careful thought and precision planning. The slightest mistake can invalidate an entire backup. Not only are the logistics of backing up a very large database an issue, attaining a reasonable level of performance is also an issue that warrants legitimate concern. In some cases, backups that run slowly may still fit within the backup service time window. However, if you have to backup a 300 G database and the system can only be down for a few hours, performance of the backup is critical. In many production sites, the database server must be available seven days a week, 24 hours a day with no down time. In this chapter, I offer recommendations based on my personal experience backing up and restoring large databases.

7.1 THE SYSTEM IS DOWN

If your system becomes unavailable due to some sort of hardware or software failure, it is important that you execute your recovery efforts carefully and thoroughly. First and foremost, do not panic. This will only make matters worse by possibly disrupting the proper sequence of events needed to recover the system. It is important that you study the situation in complete detail to determine the cause of the failure, the effects of the failure, and the set of possible solutions to the problem of recovering the system in the most efficient manner. Do not start by executing media recovery commands and scripts before you understand completely what happened, and what sections were affected.

When you deal with a down system, it is important that you work in a coordinated environment. You need to coordinate your efforts with the system administrator, database administrator, and network administrator. The system administrator is responsible for administrating the hardware and the Operating System (OS). The system administrator is able to brief others on the cause of the failure, and the subsequent effects. The database administrator, after being briefed by the system administrator, knows which sections of the database are affected from the system failure. Finally, the network administrator helps coordinate network backups and restores to ensure that the network is not taken off-line for administration purposes.

Even if your restores are performed locally (on the system itself), you may still need to coordinate your efforts with the network administrator in the event that your commands are being submitted remotely (across the network) from a workstation or another console. If the network is taken off-line for some reason, all your recovery work may be lost. In addition, the system may be left in a state of inconsistency if the restore terminated before successful completion.

It is also important that when backing up a system, you maintain a detailed catalog of the backup, including a list of the files backed up, date and time stamps, size of the files backed up, and type of backup (complete, incremental, etc.). Make sure that backup tapes are kept in a safe and secure area. Also, ensure that each tape is properly labeled. Most mission-critical sites have a tape vault (or a secure area for tapes) as well as a tape management system to catalog tapes.

Restoration of a down system requires precise and attentive steps to bring the system back on-line. Therefore, it is important that at a minimum you follow the recommendations made previously to help ensure a smooth backup and restore. Despite the famous system administration claim *the best backup is the one that never needs to be used,* your system may fail and proper steps need to be taken to ensure that the system and data are restored in the shortest time possible.

7.2 SYSTEM ARCHITECTURE

It is vital that you design a complete system architecture to handle the tasks of backing up and restoring your systems. The architecture needs to consider such things as

- ❑ Amount of data to be backed up per system
- ❑ Service time window for each backup
- ❑ Can the system be taken off-line?
- ❑ Media device data transfer speeds
- ❑ Network data transfer speeds
- ❑ Performance requirements

- ❏ Multiplatform issues
- ❏ Version control system
- ❏ Tape management system
- ❏ Permissions required for the backup and/or restore
- ❏ Off-line and on-line backups
- ❏ Complete, incremental, and cumulative backup
- ❏ Multiple task (scripts) dependencies

The architecture must address issues such as the service time window in which the backup needs to complete, multiplatform issues if a heterogeneous environment of different hardware and software platforms is to be backed up, and the tape management system. Architectural design must be a coordinated effort between database, system, and network administrators, as well as with end users. Working closely with the end users helps administrators to better understand the end users' backup and restore requirements. It also provides end users with a complete understanding of the tasks and subtasks involved when systems are backed up or restored. This informs the end user of the time that is required to perform each task as well as the dependencies between tasks. Often, when a system becomes unavailable, end users contact the system or database administrator constantly during the restoration process and ask, "What is taking so long? Why is the system still down?" Explaining the backup and restore process to the end user completely can help to reduce end users' level of frustration as well as misunderstanding.

You should use a version control system to manage backup and restore scripts as part of the backup and restore architecture. This helps to maintain a repository of the backup and restore scripts as well as any changes that are made to the scripts. Using the version control system helps coordinate system administration efforts, especially in a situation in which multiple system administrators manage the same environment.

In addition to the version control system, you should thoroughly comment all of your backup and restore scripts (line by line). Your scripts may be run by someone other than you, and the comments you make in the scripts can help the person who runs the script to better understand each step. The comments also help you to remember the purpose and the logic underlying the script in the event that future changes are necessary.

7.3 HARDWARE REQUIREMENTS

The design of a complete backup and restore architecture is highly dependent on the hardware configuration of your environment. To backup a very large database, you must have a multiprocessor system with an appropriate number of high-speed backup devices (tape drives). To obtain optimal backup and restore performance, you must configure an appropriate number of backup devices so that backups and restores can proceed in parallel. If your environment consists of very large databases, you must choose the right number of backup devices as well as the right type of backup device, such as an autoloader or jukebox. For large system configurations, you need to implement a backup and recovery system that is fully automated, fast, and reliable. An automated system reduces the tedious manual effort required to load tapes and start backups and/or restores. A fast system enables you to backup and restore large quantities of data in a small period of time. The new backup and recovery systems often multiplex the workload and thereby substantially reduce the time needed to complete the backup and/or restore.

7.4 SELECTING THE BACKUP AND RECOVERY TOOLS

Implementing a complete backup and recovery system requires that you select both the appropriate type of backup system as well as the number of backup devices. For example, trying to backup a 500 G database on a Sun Enterprise 6000 using a single, or even a few, 8-mm 5 G external tape drives is impractical and will take an enormous amount of time. It is critical that you choose the correct number of backup devices in addition to the type of backup system.

Before you select the number of backup devices, you need to obtain a complete set of backup and restore tools for your environment. If you run a heterogeneous environment, you will need a tool that supports multiple platforms. You may also need the capability to perform network-based backups. There are many backup and restore tools available. When you select a tool, try to select it based on the following criteria:

- ❏ Complete backup and restore catalog system
- ❏ Database support (preferably native)
- ❏ Automated (scheduled) backups and restores
- ❏ Ability to schedule events
- ❏ Distributed capabilities
- ❏ Backups and restores are parallelized
- ❏ Supports file systems and raw devices
- ❏ Supports complete, incremental, and cumulative backups
- ❏ Supports on-line and off-line backups
- ❏ Multiplatform support
- ❏ Supports a wide variety of tape media devices
- ❏ Tool maintains a high level of performance
- ❏ Easy to use and easy to configure
- ❏ GUI functionality (browser interface)

Selecting a backup and restore tool based on the above criteria enables you to manage your environment smoothly and flexibly.

The tool should enable you to perform network-based and distributed backups, possibly from one server to another. The tool should parallelize backups and restores. This can make a magnitude of a difference for large databases and large system backups. The tool can significantly reduce the amount of time needed to perform a backup and/or restore by utilizing multiple processors and multiple tape drives. It is also important that the tool you choose supports both file systems and raw devices. Raw devices are commonly used with large databases to achieve a high level of performance. Therefore, the tool must be able to backup and restore both file system-based files as well as raw devices.

The tool should also support the different levels of backup, such as complete, incremental, and cumulative. If you manage a heterogeneous environment, it is also imperative that the tool support multiple platforms. This avoids you having to use many different tools to manage your environment. In fact, choosing a tool that enables you to manage your entire environment from a single console is the ideal choice for a heterogeneous environment. Try to choose a tool that is easy to use and configure. Some tools are extremely complicated and require too much technical knowledge to be implemented. Keep in mind that the backup and restore tool may have to be used by persons other than yourself who may not have as much detailed knowledge of your systems. You should also choose a tool that uses a catalog and thereby enables you to search the catalog quickly without having to scan the entire tape for the existence of a file.

There are several backup and restore tools that you can use to manage your environment. Sun provides the Solstice Backup tool. The Sun Solstice Backup tool is basically a rebundle of the Legato Networker backup product. Legato's Networker product provides a tremendous amount of functionality. In addition, Legato provides an Oracle database module that performs Oracle database backups and restores. EMC provides the Epoch Enterprise Backup tool that also allows you to backup your Oracle databases.

7.5 CONFIGURING AND SIZING THE MEDIA DEVICES

Selection of the backup device type depends on the amount of data you need to backup. For example, purchasing an expensive autoloader or jukebox when you only need to backup less than 1 G is overkill. By the same token, using a few tape drives to backup a several hundred gigabyte database is less than adequate. The most popular backup media device seems to be the Quantum DLT 4700. The DLT 4700 is an autoloader tape backup device that allows up to seven DLT cartridges with each cartridge having a maximum capacity of 20 G (40 G compressed). This allows a single DLT 4700 autoloader to backup 140 G (280 G compressed) of data. The Quantum DLT 4700 uses a single-ended SCSI-2 connection that provides a maximum data transfer rate of 3 M/second. There are other tape backup device vendors that also provide autoloaders and tape libraries. When you select the type of backup device, make sure that tape loads are automatic so that your backup and restore can be automated, thereby eliminating the need for someone to manually load tapes.

It is important that you try to obtain a tape media device with the highest data transfer rate. This increases the performance of your backups and restores. Also, try at least to match the data transfer rate of the tape media system with your disk I/O subsystem. For example, if your disk I/O subsystem has a 20 M/second (fast-wide differential SCSI) maximum data transfer rate, selecting a tape media device of 5 M/second will not enable you to maximize the performance of your I/O subsystem. In this case, you will need to synchronize the disk I/O subsystem transfer rate with the tape media system in order to avoid saturation of the tape media device. Disk I/O subsystems are constantly improving, and as more of the disk I/O subsystem vendors move toward a fiber optic-oriented design, data transfer rates are likely to increase to 100 M/second. Therefore, it is important that the tape media device be synchronized with the disk I/O subsystem so that the utilization of the system is maximized.

In order to choose the optimal number of backup media devices, you need to consider your backup window as well as the data transfer rates of the media devices. For example, suppose the average data transfer rate for a given media device is 10 G/hour. If you need to backup your 400 G database in at most two hours, you will need a minimum of 20 of these media devices, each offering you 10 G/hour. Of course, this assumes that the system can handle this many media devices running concurrently while the 10 G/hour average throughput is maintained. The reality of the situation is that having this many devices on a single system that perform backups simultaneously will more than likely saturate the SCSI bus and the central bus. For this reason, you may need to distribute your backup devices such that the 20 backup devices are distributed evenly across two or three systems rather than a single system. The optimal number of tape media devices that should be attached to a single system depends on the number of available processors on the system. For example, if your system has ten processors, try not to configure or attach more than ten or fifteen tape drives or tape media systems to the system. Backups and restores can be CPU-intensive operations when compression is used. Therefore, to maximize performance and processor utilization, try to balance the number of tape drives with the number of available processors. This helps to avoid CPU saturation and helps prevent backup and restore processes from waiting for long periods of time for an available processor. This also improves the utilization of the tape drive because each processor can service a separate tape drive.

7.6 EXPORT AND THE BUFFER OPTION

You can use the Oracle Export (EXP) utility to export data from an Oracle database, or to perform a backup of the database. You can reduce the amount of time it takes to export the data from the database by using the BUFFER option of the EXP utility. The BUFFER option defines the size (in bytes) of the data array. The array is used to perform an array fetch from the database and allows a larger number of rows to be returned at each fetch. Using the array fetch feature by increasing the value of the BUFFER parameter can reduce the SQL parse and call overhead of the EXP process. It can also increase CPU utilization and I/O throughput. The following is an example of how to use the Export BUFFER option:

```
####################################
#Name: exparray.par
#Sample Export Parameter File
#Using the Array/Buffer Option
#
####################################
USERID=test/test
FULL=N
BUFFER=10485760      # Set Buffer Size to 10MB
FILE=exparray.DMP
TABLES=(ACCOUNT,ORDERS,PARTS)
COMPRESS=N
GRANTS=Y
INDEXES=Y
ROWS=Y
CONSTRAINTS=Y
LOG=exparray.log
```

This Export parameter option file shows the use of the BUFFER option. To use the parameter file, invoke the Export utility and specify the name of the parameter file as follows:

```
myhost> exp parfile=exparray.par
```

If your system has plenty of memory, you can use the BUFFER option to substantially accelerate exports. On the other hand, if your system does not have sufficient memory, or your system experiences memory shortages, setting BUFFER to too a high value can increase paging and possibly cause swapping. On a system that has sufficient free memory, values of 5 M or 10 M are reasonable for the export BUFFER parameter and offer optimal performance for large exports. If you are performing a large export, it is better to execute multiple smaller exports rather than one large export. This helps parallelize the exports and reduces the overall time that is needed to export the database objects. You should monitor the SGA and system memory utilization while running exports to determine if the value you selected for BUFFER is optimal.

7.7 THE DIRECT EXPORT OPTION

Oracle 7.3 offers a new direct export option that enables exports to read the data directly from the database and avoid the evaluation buffer. The direct export option also helps reduce the number of data copies. Figure 7.1 illustrates the difference between the direct export path and the conventional export path.

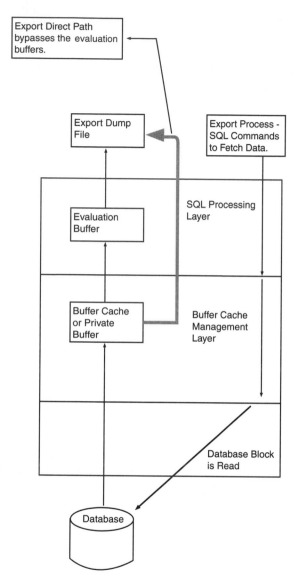

FIGURE 7.1   Direct and conventional export paths.

Figure 7.1 shows the traditional export path as well as the direct path that avoids the evaluation buffer. Avoiding the buffer evaluation enables the export to read from the database directly. This reduces the overhead of the SGA and SQL call interface. To use the direct export option, you must ensure that the `catexp.sql` script has been run on your database. The `catexp.sql` script is located in the `$ORACLE_HOME/rdbms/admin` directory. You can use the direct export option by specifying the

DIRECT=Y option when you invoke the export utility. The following is an example export parameter file that uses the direct export option:

```
######################################
#Name: expdirect.par
#Sample Export Parameter File
#Using the Direct Option
#
######################################
USERID=test/test
FULL=N
DIRECT=Y
FILE=exparray.DMP
TABLES=(ACCOUNT,ORDERS,PARTS)
COMPRESS=N
GRANTS=Y
INDEXES=Y
ROWS=Y
CONSTRAINTS=Y
LOG=exparray.log
```

This example export parameter file shows the direct option being used (DIRECT=Y). Also, because the direct path option avoids the buffer evaluation, the BUFFER parameter has no affect. The BUFFER parameter is used with the conventional path to specify the array fetch size. Exporting large databases with the direct option can increase the performance of the export up to 100 percent.

7.8 IMPORT AND THE BUFFER OPTION

The Oracle Import (IMP) utility is used to import data from an Oracle Export file (using the Oracle Export utility) into the Oracle database. Importing large objects or large files can often take a long period of time. For this reason, you can utilize the BUFFER option to specify the size of the import insert array. You can reduce the amount of time it takes to import the data into the database by using the BUFFER and COMMIT option of the IMP utility. The BUFFER option defines the size (in bytes) of the data array. The array is populated by reading the size of BUFFER bytes from the export file into the array. The import then performs an array insert into the database. You should also use the COM-MIT=Y option to ensure that commits are performed at each array insert. Otherwise, your rollback space requirements will increase as the load continues. This allows a larger number of rows to be inserted at each insert call. To specify the size of the import buffer, you can use the import command to specify the name of an import parameter file. The following is an example of the import BUFFER option using an import parameter file to specify the size of the buffer:

```
####################################
#Name: imparray.par
#Sample Import Parameter File
#Using the Array/Buffer Option
#
####################################
USERID=test/test
FULL=N
BUFFER=10485760        #Set buffer to 10MB
FILE=export.DMP
SHOW=N
TABLES=(ACCOUNT,ORDERS)
IGNORE=Y
GRANTS=Y
INDEXES=Y
COMMIT=Y
ROWS=Y
LOG=imparray.log

myhost> imp parfile=imparray.par
```

Using the array insert feature by increasing the value of the BUFFER parameter can reduce the SQL parse and call overhead of the IMP process. It can also increase CPU utilization and I/O throughput. Importing large export files into the database using a large BUFFER and the COMMIT=Y option have resulted in performance gains of 50–100 percent. To reduce the amount of time needed to import objects, use the BUFFER option and invoke multiple imports to help parallelize the imports. If you have a multiprocessor system with a large amount of memory, starting multiple imports with each import using the BUFFER option can decrease the total import time by parallelizing the imports and using the array insert option.

7.9 EXPORTING AND IMPORTING BY PARTITION

Oracle8 allows you to export and import tables at the partition level. This can be used to parallelize exports and imports by invoking multiple sessions of exports or imports with each processing different partitions. This also helps reduce disk contention assuming each partition is separated from the other in terms of disk data distribution. Exporting at the partition level can also help you deal with the export file size limit. Instead of exporting the entire table, you can export the individual partitions. The following is an example of an export by partition using an export parameter file:

```
####################################
#Name: exppart.par
#Sample Export Parameter File
#Exporting by Partition
#The syntax for exporting by table partition
#is TABLE:PARTITION
####################################
USERID=prod/prod
FULL=N
DIRECT=Y
FILE=exppart.DMP
TABLES=(SALES:SALES_W2)
COMPRESS=N
GRANTS=Y
INDEXES=Y
ROWS=Y
CONSTRAINTS=Y
LOG=exppart.log
```

You can also import by partition by specifying the name of the partition in the TABLES clause. The following is an example of an import by partition:

```
####################################
#Name: imppart.par
#Sample Import Parameter File
#Importing by Partition
#The syntax for importing by partition
#is TABLE:PARTITION
####################################
USERID=prod/prod
FULL=N
FILE=exppart.DMP
TABLES=(SALES:SALES_W2)
IGNORE=Y
GRANTS=Y
INDEXES=Y
ROWS=Y
LOG=imppart.log
```

Importing by partition also allows you to parallelize the import of a large table by invoking multiple sessions of import, each processing a distinct and disjoint partition. The import by partition option is extremely useful for large size tables when used in conjunction with the export by partition option.

7.10   EXPORT/IMPORT AND THE 2 G FILE LIMIT

If you are exporting to a file system-based file, a single file cannot exceed 2 G on most UNIX platforms. Oracle8 release 8.0.4 for HP-UX 10.2 and 11.0 support large files for the Export and Import utilities. The 64-bit releases of Oracle8 also support large files. If your platform does not support large files and you need to export an object larger than 2 G, you can export the object to tape. Therefore when you build export scripts, remember to divide the objects across multiple exports so that no single export dump file exceeds 2 G. Also, if you have a single object that is larger than 2 G, you should use some other technique to backup the object. You should use a backup and restore tool to backup large database objects. You can use the dd utility if your Oracle data files are on raw devices, or use a file system utility to backup the Oracle data files. When you use the dd or file system utility, the database must be shut down if it is running in noarchivelog mode. Backing up large databases using Export and Import is not often possible due to the limitations. For this reason, some sites have elected to use the Oracle7 Enterprise Backup Utility (EBU) or the Oracle8 Recovery Manager (RMAN).

7.11   ORACLE7 ENTERPRISE BACKUP UTILITY (EBU)

The Oracle7 Enterprise Backup Utility (EBU) offers users the ability to backup large databases in parallel. EBU works in conjunction with the tape media management software, such as Legato or Epoch, to parallelize the backup and/or restore. EBU cannot be used to backup an Oracle8 database, and EBU supports only Oracle7 databases. EBU provides the ability to perform hot and cold backups. EBU release 2.2 provides a GUI interface via the Oracle Enterprise Manager (OEM).

EBU uses tape management media software such as the Legato Oracle Database Module to perform the backups and restores of the Oracle database. The Legato Oracle Database Module provides a shared library (libobk.so) that EBU uses to perform the database backups and restores. EBU uses a separate database (other than the database that is being backed up) to store the backup catalog.

EBU enables the database administrator to parallelize backups and restores. If your system has multiple processors and multiple tape drives, you can increase significantly the performance of your backup and restore. EBU can spawn multiple processes to help parallelize the work of the restore or backup. EBU offers two different I/O models, the asynchronous I/O model and the shared memory model. For those model platforms that support both, the user can select either the asynchronous I/O model or the shared memory model by using the EBU parameter use_io_model. You can set use_io_model=AIO to direct EBU to use the asynchronous I/O model, or you can set use_io_model=SHM to employ the EBU shared memory model. Figure 7.2 illustrates the shared memory model architecture of EBU using a degree of parallelism of three.

In Figure 7.2, multiple processes are spawned to parallelize the backup or restore. The ebu is the main control process and spawns the instance manager process (brd).

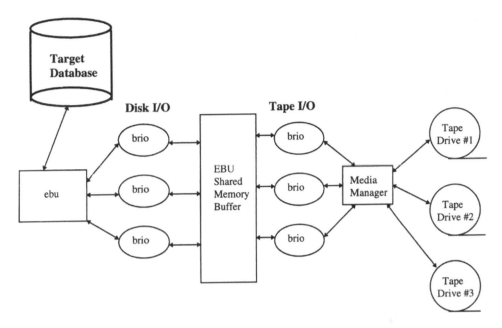

FIGURE 7.2 EBU shared memory model architecture.

The `brio` processes handle the reads and writes of the disk and tape files. Multiple `brio` processes are spawned for each parallel I/O stream.

EBU uses a shared memory buffer to improve the performance of backups and restores. Each disk `brio` process reads the database disk files and writes into the shared memory buffer. The tape `brio` processes then write the contents of the shared memory buffer out to the tape device via the media manager software. You can achieve high throughput backups and restores by tuning the degree of parallelism as well as the size of the shared buffer. EBU provides many parameters that you can set via the EBU parameter file. Table 7.1 shows the main EBU parameters affecting performance.

Each `brio` process allocates the size specified by BUFFER_SIZE for the shared memory buffer. Therefore, the total amount of shared memory allocated can be calculated as follows:

```
Total Shared Memory = (BUFFER_SIZE * db_block_size * NBRIO)
```

NBRIO refers to the number of `brio` processes. To increase the performance of EBU, set `parallel=<number of tape drives>`. This will maximize the performance of the backup and restore by parallelizing the backup and/or restore across all available tape drives. If you have more tape drives than you have processors available, try to set the parallel parameter so that you balance the number of available tape drives with the number of processors.

TABLE 7.1 EBU parameters

PARAMETER	DEFAULT	DESCRIPTION
PARALLEL	1	Degree of parallelism.
DISK_IO_SIZE	16	The number of database blocks read or written per disk I/O.
TAPE_IO_SIZE	32	The number of database blocks read or written per tape I/O.
BUFFER_SIZE	128	Size of the EBU shared memory buffer (specified in database blocks).

The following is an example EBU parameter file:

```
##EBU Sample Parameter File:
backup on-line
db_name="SALES"
oracle_sid="SALES"
tablespace = "ORDERS_TS"
parallel=5
log="/oracle7/obackup/log/obkSALES.log"
buffer_size=16384
tape_io_size=32
disk_io_size=16

## End of EBU Parameter file
```

In this example, a degree of parallelism of five is selected, and the database is backed up on-line (hot backup). The ORDER_TS tablespace is backed up. The output from obackup will be sent to the log file specified in the parameter file (log="/oracle7/oback-up/log/obkSALES.log").

7.11.1 EBU AND COLD BACKUPS

If you are performing a cold backup, meaning the database is shut down prior to starting the backup, you can create a large shared memory buffer. Because the database is shut down, the memory for the SGA and the Oracle database processes can instead be used by EBU. In this case, set BUFFER_SIZE=<db_block_buffers> / (NBRIO). For example, if your db_block_buffers=65536, set BUFFER_SIZE= ((65536) / (NBRIO)). This optimally sizes the total EBU shared memory buffer in accordance with the degree of parallelism. Declaring a large shared memory buffer can increase the performance of EBU. The large shared memory buffer also minimizes wait time between the tape processes and disk processes. A large buffer allows enough space in which tape processes can be writing out buffers to the tape drives, while the disk reader processes can be writing data into the shared memory buffer. The BUFFER_SIZE parameter must be a power of two, and at least equal to the greater of the DISK_IO_SIZE and TAPE_IO_SIZE values.

7.11.2 EBU AND HOT BACKUPS

Performing a hot backup requires that the database be available and in archive log mode. Because the instance is running, the SGA may consume a large portion of the system's physical memory. In addition, database and user processes also may be using additional memory. Therefore, you will need to set BUFFER_SIZE to a much smaller value than the size recommended for a cold backup. If you are performing a hot backup, try to estimate the amount of free memory that is available on the system. This estimate should take into consideration future user connections and processes. Then set BUFFER_SIZE using the following recommendation:

$$\text{BUFFER\_SIZE} = \frac{(\text{amount of free memory} - \text{free pool})}{(\text{NBRIO}) * (\text{db\_block\_size})}$$

The free pool is the amount of memory that should be left free for future processes and/or database connections. Recall that the BUFFER_SIZE parameter must be a power of two. For example, if your system has 2 G of memory, and the existing SGA is 1 G in size, you may consider setting the total EBU shared memory to 128 M or 256 M in order to allow sufficient memory for other user processes. The optimal setting for BUFFER_SIZE is highly dependent on your system configuration and system workload. You should start with the default setting and then continue to tune BUFFER_SIZE until EBU performance is maximized. It is important that you not degrade the performance of the SGA and the user processes when tuning EBU parameters for a hot backup.

7.11.3 DISK AND TAPE I/O SIZES

The defaults for DISK_IO_SIZE and TAPE_IO_SIZE are usually optimal; however, if your disk data files are striped, you can increase the value of DISK_IO_SIZE to allow more database blocks to be processed to disk per I/O. Similarly, if your tape drive system supports high-speed data transfer rates, you can increase the value of TAPE_IO_SIZE to allow more database blocks to be written to tape per I/O. If your database files are striped, you can set DISK_IO_SIZE = (stripe size) + (number of members in the stripe) in order to maximize EBU performance. This allows a single read to utilize all the physical disks in the stripe. For example, if your database block size is 8 K and you have a striped volume that consists of six disks with a stripe size of 64 K, set DISK_IO_SIZE=48 (384 K). The optimal value of TAPE_IO_SIZE depends on the media manager software and tape management system being used. Each media manager software may have its own optimal I/O size for tape I/O operations. In general, you should set `TAPE_IO_SIZE=DISK_IO_SIZE` and tune `DISK_IO_SIZE` such that a single I/O utilizes all the disks in the stripe.

You can also increase backup performance by multiplexing different database files into a single Backup File Set (BPS). Multiplexing effectively integrates the database blocks from multiple database files into a single logical stream. Using the multiplexing feature can help increase disk throughput if each of the multiple database files are striped across different disks. To enable the multiplexing feature, use the EBU parameter `mux` to specify the database files to be multiplexed.

Compression may also reduce the stream throughput by not keeping the tape drives busy. Certain data may be more compressible than other data. In this case, there may be a throughput imbalance between certain tape drives processing files with high-compression ratios versus other tape drives processing files with low-compression ratios. Therefore, try to balance the mix of files in terms of compression ratios so that the overall compression ratio results in a medium-compression ratio.

If your platform supports both the shared memory model and asynchronous I/O model, you can set the parameter `use_io_model=AIO` to direct EBU to use the asynchronous I/O model (AIO). In the asynchronous I/O model, EBU uses the capabilities of the operating system to issue asynchronous I/O to disk. However, some operating systems may not support asynchronous I/O on database files residing on file systems. Irrespective of the I/O model used, the goal is to maximize the disk transfer rates and overall I/O throughput. By tuning the I/O size parameters and the number of I/O processes, you can maximize the performance of EBU as well as the disk and tape I/O throughput.

7.11.4   TUNING EBU PARAMETERS

The performance of EBU depends on the configuration of your database and system. You can achieve a high backup and restore throughput by tuning the database system and EBU appropriately. You should benchmark EBU extensively and continue to tune the parameters until you achieve the best performance. EBU is an excellent utility that can help achieve phenomenal backup and restore rates. On a Sun Ultra Enterprise 6000 server, I have been able to achieve an 85 G per hour backup and restore rate. Some sites have achieved even higher rates by using more backup tape drives, thereby increasing the degree of parallelism. For more information on the Enterprise Backup Utility, refer to the *Oracle7 Enterprise Backup Utility Administrator's Guide*.

7.12   ORACLE8 RECOVERY MANAGER

Oracle8 offers a new utility known as the Recovery Manager (RMAN) to manage database backups. For Oracle8 databases, RMAN replaces the Oracle7 EBU utility. RMAN is a more comprehensive utility and integrates the backup and restore functionality inside the Oracle8 kernel. This not only simplifies the architecture of RMAN, it also allows you to utilize the Oracle Enterprise Manager (OEM) to schedule, perform, and administer database backups. You can think of RMAN as another database service rather than an external component like EBU. RMAN uses a recovery catalog to maintain the repository of information used for managing backup and restore operations. RMAN also supports tertiary storage subsystems such as Epoch, Legato, StorageTek, and HP. RMAN can backup individual tablespaces or data files as well as only changed blocks. RMAN can automate media recovery operations and can generate a log of all backup and restore activities. RMAN can also parallelize backups and restores as well as automatically compress unused blocks. RMAN can be used via the command-line interpreter in interactive mode or via the OEM GUI tool. Figure 7.3 illustrates the architecture of RMAN.

In the RMAN architecture diagram in Figure 7.3, the Media Management Library (MML) is a vendor-supplied API that is used to interface to Oracle. The Oracle server process invokes the MML routines to backup and restore the Oracle database files to media devices managed via the media manager software.

The RMAN recovery catalog should be maintained in a separate database. The `catrman.sql` script located in `$ORACLE_HOME/rdbms/admin` is used to create the RMAN catalog tables and views. The recovery catalog contains information about the data files and archive log backup sets, data file copies, archive redo log files, physical structure of the target database, and named sequences of commands call stored scripts.

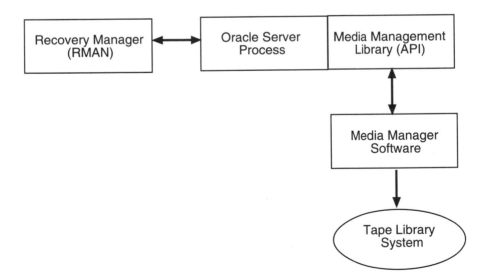

FIGURE 7.3 RMAN architecture.

7.12.1 PARALLELIZING BACKUPS AND RESTORES

RMAN uses two main command options to parallelize backups and restores: channels and files per set. The `channel` control commands specify the degree of parallelism to be used for backup operations and also specify the size of the backup pieces. The `channel` command can be used to specify limits on I/O bandwidth. Each channel establishes a connection to a target database instance and each connection operates on one backup set at a time. If multiple connections are established, than each connection operates on a separate file copy or backup set. Using the `allocate channel` command, you can parallelize your backup operation by configuring multiple channels. The `release channel` command releases the channel and terminates the connection, thus allowing the channel to be reused. The `setlimit channel` command can be used to set the maximum number of kilobytes that the backup command will attempt to write to a backup piece. The `setlimit channel` command allows you to specify the readrate which specifies the number of blocks read per second by a backup or copy command. The `filesperset` option of the backup command specifies the maximum number of files that will be placed in a single backup set. If the number of files to be backed up is greater than `filesperset`, then the backup sets will result in the creation of multiple backup sets. By allocating a channel per device (disk or tape), you can achieve a high-throughput backup. This allows you to parallelize the backup across the different devices. You should also balance the number of active concurrent channels with the number of tape media devices. Too many concurrent channels may cause contention for the tape media devices. The `filesperset` option can also be used to control the degree of multiplexing. Data files within the same backup set are multiplexed and sent as a stream to the tape media device.

You can also utilize I/O slaves to parellelize RMAN reads and writes. The Oracle8 `init.ora` parameters `backup_tape_io_slaves` and `backup_disk_io_slaves` specify whether or not I/O slaves should be used for backups. To enable I/O slaves, set `backup_tape_io_slaves=TRUE` and `backup_disk_io_slaves=<N>` where N refers to the number of slaves per channel. Monitor I/O utilization to determine the optimal number of backup I/O slaves. I/O slaves can be especially useful for situations where asynchronous I/O is either inefficient or not available.

By tuning the number of channels, files per set, and I/O slaves, you can increase the performance of your backup and restore. You should monitor tape drive, disk, and processor utilization in order to choose optimal settings for the number of channels, files per set, and I/O slaves. RMAN provides a tremendous amount of functionality and number of performance features that allow you to effectively manage your database backups while achieving high-backup and restore throughput. Incorporating the recovery management functionality in the Oracle DBMS allows you to utilize the OEM tool to manage your backups. For more information on RMAN, refer to the *Oracle8 Backup and Recovery Guide Release 8.0.*

7.13 PARALLEL RECOVERY

As of release 7.1, the Oracle Server provides the capability to accelerate database recovery time by employing multiple slave processes to parallelize the recovery work. This can reduce significantly the elapsed recovery time by an almost linear factor. In order to take full advantage of the parallel recovery option, the system should have multiple processors and should be configured with well-balanced I/O striped devices (using the volume manager). The degree of parallelism for recovery can be controlled through the `init.ora` parameter `recovery_parallelism`. To minimize the recovery time, set `recovery_parallelism=<number of available processors in the system>`. For example, setting `recovery_parallelism=4` will spawn four processes during the instance or media recovery phase, and each process (slave) will read a different section of the redo files and apply the changes in parallel. The effectiveness of parallel recovery is inherently dependent on the system's I/O distribution. If the redo log files are poorly distributed or are located on one disk or a few disks, spawning many processes to read the same disk will not produce any gains. This simply results in an I/O bottleneck where the traditional synchronous recovery process of one single process performing the recovery probably would be faster. If your system has multiple processors and your redo log files are striped, set `recovery_parallelism` to the number of available processors limited by the degree of the I/O distribution of the redo log files. This helps expedite instance or media recovery.

7.14 STANDBY DATABASE

Oracle 7.3 provides the standby database feature that allows another system to act as a backup system in the event of a failure on the primary system. A standby database is a copy of the primary database on a separate system that is in a constant state of media recovery. If the primary system fails, the standby database can be brought on-line relatively quickly by applying the archive redo logs from the primary database to make the standby database consistent with the primary database prior to the system failure. This allows the standby database to continue serving the user community so as to minimize downtime while the primary database can be recovered. The users can continue using the standby database until the primary system becomes available. Using a standby database can help reduce the amount of down time.

7.15 TABLESPACE POINT-IN-TIME RECOVERY

Oracle8 provides a new feature known as Tablespace Point-in-Time Recovery (TSPITR) which allows a tablespace to be recovered to a point-in-time different from that of the rest of the database. TSPITR is most useful for scenarios such as recovering from a `drop` or `truncate table` statement, recovering a table that has become corrupted, or recovering from an invalid batch job. Oracle8 TSPITR builds on top of the Oracle7 export and import functionality for recovering a subset of the database. Oracle8 TSPITR allows the user to make a copy of the relevant data files of the recovered database referred to as the clone database. The data file copies along with the corresponding data dictionary information are transferred over to the production database. Both the Export and Import utilities support tablespace point-in-time recovery. TSPITR is a complex process, and you should fully understand all the steps required to configure TSPITR. You should also thoroughly test TSPITR to ensure that it is working and the correct steps have been taken to configure and use TSPITR. For more information on TSPITR, refer to the *Oracle8 Backup and Recovery Guide Release 8.0.*

NCA AND OBJECTS

Oracle8 is the database management software for networking computing. Oracle8 and Oracle tools are focused on providing network computing solutions. The goal of network computing is to reduce computing complexity and cost, and improve manageability. Network computing is also centered around open systems and distributed computing. Oracle8 is an object-relational database management system combining the functionality of relational databases with the ability to create and manage complex objects. Release 8.0 of Oracle8 represents the first phase of database object functionality. Future releases of Oracle8 will continue to expand the object functionality such as providing the ability to code stored procedures in Java.

8.1 THE NETWORK COMPUTING ARCHITECTURE

Oracle's Network Computing Architecture (NCA) is a paradigm shift in computing that emphasizes the easy access, power, and stability of distributed computing. For large-scale systems, the traditional two-tier client-server model is insufficient. Large-scale systems that require a high level of performance, interoperability and security require a multi-tier approach that distributes the computing workload across application and database servers. There are several tiers of NCA consisting of thin clients on the client side, such as network computers (NCs), an application server in the middle tier to manage business objects and logic, and a universal data server to manage the objects and their data. Oracle products such as Developer/2000, and Oracle Application Server are examples of NCA-enabled products that allow you to build high-performance distributed sys-

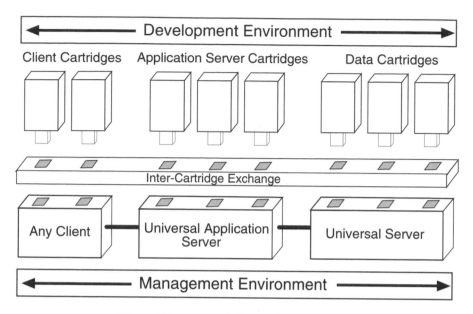

Figure 8.1 Network Computing Architecture.

tems. Figure 8.1 illustrates the Network Computing Architecture. One of the core components of the Network Computing Architecture is the concept of cartridges. In essence, cartridges combine business objects and rules into software components. They consist of applications or application components written in many different languages, such as JAVA, PL/SQL, Perl, or C. The beauty of cartridges is that they take advantage of the CORBA interface, thereby enabling the dynamic expansion and addition of functionality at any of the tiers of the NCA model. It is important that you begin to adopt and utilize the NCA model when designing new applications. The NCA model is centered around the concepts of easy access, open systems, and distributed computing. The cartridges further demonstrate the openness and deployment ease of NCA-based applications.

The NCA model centers around the ability to easily add cartridges to either the database server, application server, or client. The time series, spatial, and image cartridges are examples of database server cartridges in Oracle8. The intercartridge exchange provides a common protocol for information exchange between cartridges. The cartridge model allows you to easily deploy new cartridges that provide new application functionality.

You should also become familiar with CORBA (Common Object Request Broker Architecture) and the IIOP (Internet Inter-ORB Protocol) which is the protocol that CORBA uses to transmit on the Internet as these are fundamental layers in the network computing object model. You can obtain the CORBA/IIOP specification from the Object Management Group (OMG) Web site at www.omg.org.

8.2   ORACLE8 OBJECTS

Oracle8 provides the ability to create object types with member functions. You can then create a table based on the object type. Using object types allows you to encapsulate the supported operations within the object type. This allows application languages such as C++ to encapsulate the data with its methods. SQL, PL/SQL, and the precompilers have been extended to support operations on object types. Although object types can simplify data models and provide an elegant interface to the application developer, it is important that you consider performance when designing and creating object types.

8.2.1   MAP VERSUS THE ORDER METHOD

When creating object types in Oracle8, you can choose to use the MAP or ORDER comparison methods. A MAP method returns the relative position of a record within the order of records within the object. The ORDER method must be called for every two objects being compared. The MAP method is called only once per object. When sorting a set of objects, an ORDER method is called more than the number of times that a MAP method would be called. Scalar value comparisons are very efficiently complemented by the fact that invoking a user-defined function is slower than calling a kernel implemented function; sorting objects using the ORDER method is relatively slow as compared to sorting the mapped scalar values that are returned by the MAP function.

8.2.2   BLOB VERSUS THE BFILE

The BLOB datatype can be used to store unstructured binary data inside the database. The BFILE datatype can be used to store unstructured binary data outside the database, via operating system files. As opposed to BFILE data, the data for a BLOB/CLOB is stored inside the database. BFILE data is stored in an operating system file and is therefore stored external to the database. A user can read and write data to a BLOB or CLOB. However, database access to a BFILE is read-only since the main purpose of a BFILE is to support access to data on read-only devices. A BLOB or CLOB participates in database transactions and is also recoverable. BLOBs and CLOBs maintain all ACID properties. BFILEs maintain integrity by the operating system and through the application. BLOB and CLOB data is backed up along with other database data whereas BFILE data is not backed up. BFILE data is not replicated whereas BLOB and CLOB data is replicated. Future releases of Oracle in which partitioning is supported for LOBs, allows the BLOB and CLOB data to be partitioned. With LOB partitioning capabilities, only the BFILE locator will be partitioned, and not the actual BFILE data. Although BLOBs and BFILEs have relatively similar read performance, it is important that you consider all the different constraints when choosing between a BLOB or a BFILE.

8.2.3   VARRAYS VERSUS NESTED TABLES

Nested tables can be fully manipulated via SQL and PL/SQL whereas manipulating VARRAYS can be done only through PL/SQL or OCI. You cannot access an individual element of a VARRAY within SQL. Nested tables are stored in a storage table with every element mapping to a row in the storage table. VARRAYs, on the other hand, are stored as opaque objects (raw or blob). VARRAYs are a good choice if your application primarily retrieves an entire collection as a value. If the collection is very large and the application needs only a small subset of the collection, then nested tables are more appropriate. Nested tables also allow you to pin the object using REFs in the object cache, thus increasing performance if the application continues to access the object. Inserts on nested tables can consume more time since the insert operation needs to follow the nested operations.

8.2.4   ORACLE8 REFS

An Oracle8 REF can be thought of as a database pointer to an instance of an object in an object table. Collections can contain elements that are REFs to objects that exist in object tables or objects that exist only within the collection. Objects that have significance out-side of the object in which they are contained should generally be made referenceable. For example, employees have significance outside of any specific department to which they may be assigned; therefore they should be referenceable. Also, each department may consist of a large number of employees. Therefore, selective queries on personnel within a department are often typical, thus making a nested table with REFs to employ-ees an optimal solution. VARRAYs and a VARRAY of REFs can be fetched in a single-server round trip. Nested tables can vary in size. Although a nested table can be fetched in a single-server round trip, the amount of data needed to be transferred can result in a large amount. VARRAYs typically generate less network traffic than a nested table.

INSTALLING AND CONFIGURING UNIX FOR OPTIMAL PERFORMANCE

This appendix summarizes installation and configuration tips for the UNIX operating system. It is organized into the following sections:

- ❑ A Corporate Architecture
- ❑ Determining the Type of System
- ❑ Sizing the File Systems
- ❑ Mirroring the Operating System
- ❑ Installing the UNIX Operating System
- ❑ Naming Service
- ❑ Post-Installation Procedures

A.1 A CORPORATE ARCHITECTURE

If you are managing many different UNIX systems, it can be extremely helpful to define a complete UNIX systems architecture such as host name standards, networking standards, security standards, and configuration standards. The architecture will help you to more effectively manage your environment by implementing a consistent set of standards across all the UNIX systems. Defining the UNIX systems architecture must be a coordinated effort among the system, database, and network administrators, as well as the application staff who use these systems to develop applications.

A.2   DETERMINING THE TYPE OF SYSTEM

Before you install the UNIX operating system on your system, you must determine the main purpose of the system. Will the system be a server, a client workstation, an NFS server, and so on? The type of system is important because the system may require extra packages and/or patches. Determining the main purpose of the system will also help during the post-configuration phase.

A.3   SIZING THE FILE SYSTEMS

It is extremely important that you size the file systems appropriately before you install the operating system. If the file systems are not sized properly, you may not have enough space to install certain operating system packages. The root (/) file system is the most critical file system. My recommendation is that you always leave at least 100 M of free space in the root file system to account for kernel rebuilds and kernel patches. Also, use separate file systems for the /(root), /usr, /var, and /opt directories. This helps keep separate the operating system binaries from user software packages and system administration files. The /usr file system typically contains operating system utilities as well as operating system-related applications. The /var file system typically contains patches, E-mail, and system administration log files. The /opt directory typically contains operating system packages. Therefore, separating these directories into separate file systems can help reduce the chances of the /(root) file system from filling up.

A.4   MIRRORING THE OPERATING SYSTEM

Most software and hardware volume managers provide you with the ability to mirror your operating system file systems, such as the /(root), and /usr file systems. Doing so helps reduce system down time should a media failure occur on the /(root), or other operating system file systems. Refer to the volume manager documentation for your platform for specific details on how to set up operating system mirroring. Enabling mirroring helps reduce system downtime and increases the reliability of the system. As always when mirroring, distribute the submirrors across multiple disk drives and controllers so that the members of the mirror are not on the same disk and controller.

A.5   INSTALLING THE UNIX OPERATING SYSTEM

When you install the operating system, try to install it in its entirety upon your system, depending on space. This enables you to utilize any of the system packages easily without having to add the software package later. Installing the entire OS upfront may also help reserve disk space for the operating system which may not be available in the future.

During the installation, make sure that you configure a sufficient amount of swap space. You can also configure and add the swap space following the OS installation by using the swap command. Chapter 3 discusses how to list the current swap devices as well as how to add swap devices.

Following the installation, it is critical that you determine the patches that are needed for your system. Obtain the relevant patches from the appropriate vendor and install the patches. If you are installing a new operating system release, make sure you obtain the recommended patch list from the OS vendor to determine if your system needs the patches.

A.6   NAMING SERVICE

If you plan to manage a medium- to large-size UNIX environment, you should configure a naming service such as NIS (YP) or NIS+. This improves the ease of administration by allowing a root master server to push the namespace maps such as the password, hosts, and services tables. This avoids having to edit these files manually on all the different systems. If your environment consists primarily of Sun Solaris Servers, you should use the NIS+ naming service. HP-UX 11.0 also provides support for NIS+. For more information on configuring YP or NIS+, refer to your platform's system administration documentation.

If you plan to configure a naming service such as YP or NIS+, make sure you configure at least one replica server in the event that the root master server fails. Creation of multiple replica servers on different subnets can increase performance by minimizing the network traffic and distributing the NIS calls to the root master and the replicas.

A.7   POST-INSTALLATION PROCEDURES

After the operating system has been installed and configured successfully, you must make sure that any operating system or kernel patches were also installed successfully. If you are configuring a database or application server, you may need to increase the amount of semaphores in the system. You may also need to increase the maximum amount of shared memory if, for example, you will be configuring a large SGA. You may also need to set kernel process, file size, and memory size limits. After you set the kernel parameters, you must rebuild the kernel and reboot the system for the changes to take effect.

In addition to the kernel parameters, you may also need to alter the security configuration of the system, such as disabling certain `inetd` services. Most system administrators tend to disable finger, remote shell, and other `inetd` services in order to increase the security of the system. You may want to configure a set of post-install scripts. This will enable you to automate the post-install process.

INSTALLING ORACLE FOR OPTIMAL PERFORMANCE

This appendix summarizes installation and configuration tips for the Oracle software. It is organized into the following sections:

- ❏ A Corporate Architecture
- ❏ Determining the Type of System
- ❏ Sizing the File Systems
- ❏ Directories and File Locations
- ❏ Installing the Oracle DBMS
- ❏ Configuring SQL*Net/Net8
- ❏ Post-Installation Procedures

B.1 A CORPORATE ARCHITECTURE

If you plan to manage many different Oracle systems, it can be extremely helpful to define a complete Oracle architecture such as database standards, application standards, security standards, and configuration standards. The architecture will help you manage your environment more effectively by implementing a consistent set of standards across all the Oracle database systems. Defining the Oracle database systems architecture must be a coordinated effort between the operations and application staff.

B.2   DETERMINING THE TYPE OF SYSTEM

Before you install the Oracle software, it is important that you determine the main purpose of the system. Will the server be an application server, or will the server be a DSS or OLTP database server? The type of system is important because not only may the system require different packages and/or patches, the system may also require a different release of Oracle. For example, certain versions of Oracle tools or Oracle Applications may also require a specific release of the Oracle Server. Determining the main purpose of the system also will help during the post-configuration phase.

B.3   SIZING THE FILE SYSTEMS

It is vital that you size the file systems appropriately before you install the Oracle software. If the file systems are not sized properly, you may not have enough space to install the Oracle software packages. I recommend that you create a separate file system dedicated to Oracle software and allocate anywhere from 1 G to 2 G to allow for product upgrades and additional packages. Separate the disks used for the Oracle software file system from other operating system disks to help distribute I/O.

B.4   DIRECTORIES AND FILE LOCATIONS

I recommend that you keep a consistent set of directory names across all the database servers. This will help you to locate trace files and database startup scripts more easily. Create a dbs directory (separate from the $ORACLE_HOME/dbs), and use the following directory structure:

```
../../../dbs/$ORACLE_SID/    — main directory

                  adump    - audit dump destination
                  bdump    - background dump destination
                  cdump    - core dump destination
                  create   - database creation scripts
                  export   - export scripts/files
                  import   - import scripts/files
                  pfiles   - parameter files (init.ora)
                  udump    - user dump destination
```

Use this structure to help you organize files in a consistent manner. This structure also helps organize files for single servers that run multiple databases. Because the directory structure is organized by $ORACLE_SID, each database will have its own directory and set of related subdirectories.

Remember to create at least three control files and place them on separate disks and controllers to minimize the probability of losing a control file. You can generate a control file creation script by issuing the command:

```
SQL> alter database backup controlfile to trace;
```

The trace file then can be edited and used to re-create the database control file if needed.

B.5 INSTALLING THE ORACLE DBMS

When you install the Oracle DBMS, install those options that you have licensed from Oracle. It is a good idea to select the relink option in the installer. This causes products being installed to be relinked on your specific platform. You should also make sure that the Oracle software file system has sufficient space for future upgrades and patches.

Oracle 7.3 provides the new Oracle Installer Version 4. This installer provides a GUI interface that makes the task of installing a great deal easier. I recommend that you use the GUI installer to install the Oracle products. If your system or workstation does not support GUI, you can use the standard character mode installer.

Following the installation, you may need to run the `root.sh` script generated by Oracle that performs post-installation actions as the root user. The `root.sh` file needs to be run as the root superuser account. After the installation completes, review the contents of the root.sh file to determine if you need to execute the `root.sh` script.

B.6 CONFIGURING SQL*NET/NET8

SQL*Net V2 and Net8 provide a tremendous amount of new functionality. SQL*Net V2 and Net8 allow multiple protocol adapters to be used. SQL*Net V2 and Net8 enable you to prespawn connection processes so that user connection time is minimized. Chapter 5 discusses how to tune SQL*Net V2 and Net8.

SQL*Net V2 and Net8 also enable you to configure a name server so that managing SQL*Net V2 and Net8 configuration files can be done from a central server. SQL*Net V2 and Net8 also provide a NIS agent to enable SQL*Net V2or Net8 to work in conjunction with NIS servers.

You will need to configure the `listener.ora`, `sqlnet.ora`, and/or `tnsnames.ora` files after installing SQL*Net V2 or Net8. You can use the Oracle Network Manager tool to administer the SQL*Net V2 configuration files and Net8 Assistant to manage the Net8 configuration files. Using a central name server can help you reduce the manual effort of maintaining the SQL*Net V2 and Net8 configuration files on all the different database servers and clients.

B.7   PASSWORD MANAGEMENT

Oracle8 provides password management services such as account locking, password aging and expire, password history, and password complexity verification. The script `utlpwdmg.sql` located in `$ORACLE_HOME/rdbms/admin` needs to be run in order to enable password management. Using the `CREATE USER` and `ALTER USER` commands, database administrators can lock, unlock, and expire database accounts. Password limits are set up in the user profiles and are always enforced. By using the `CREATE PROFILE` command, the database administrator can establish rules for password aging and password history. Additionally, the DBA can also code his or her own complex PL/SQL function for password verification and then specify the use of the function within the `CREATE PROFILE` or `ALTER PROFILE` statement. Password management is a useful feature and should be used by the DBA to increase the security of the Oracle database.

B.8   POST-INSTALLATION PROCEDURES

After you install the Oracle software, you may need to run the `root.sh` post-configuration script. You may also need to set some new environment variables that are specific to the new version of the Oracle products. You should add the environment variables to the appropriate user startup scripts to ensure that the environment variables are set automatically upon a user login. You should also check with Oracle to determine if you need to install patches for the products you are installing. Oracle generally provides `README` files and installation and configuration documentation that report any required patches. The CD often contains a patches directory with `README` files describing the purpose of each patch.

You may also need to alter the `ksms.s` file (SGA mapping file) and relink the Oracle Server executable if you are configuring a large SGA. If you are configuring a large SGA, you may also need to alter the relevant UNIX kernel parameters. If you install new versions of the Oracle Server and PRO*C, I recommend that you recompile a few of your PRO*C programs to ensure that your applications are working properly. You should also perform a complete set of regression tests on the new software versions in order to ensure that your existing applications are completely functional. The regression tests may also help you resolve problems (if any) with the new versions of the software packages.

REFERENCES

0. Cockcroft, Adrian and Richard Pettit. *Sun Performance and Tuning*, 2nd ed. Englewood Cliffs, NJ: Prentice Hall, 1998.

1. Cockcroft, Adrian. *Sun Performance and Tuning*. Englewood Cliffs, NJ: Prentice Hall, 1995.

2. Date, Chris J. *An Introduction to Database Systems*, 5th ed. Addison-Wesley, 1990.

3. Deitel, Harvey M. *Operating Systems*, 2nd ed. Addision Wesley, 1990.

4. Kulihin, Julia, Mary L. Fox, and Joan Nester. *System Administration for Intel Processors UNIX SVR4.2MP*, Vol. 2, UNIX Press. Englewood Cliffs, NJ: Prentice Hall, 1993.

5. Rosen, Kenneth H. *Discrete Mathematics and Its Applications*. Random House, 1988.

6. *Oracle7 for Sun Performance Tuning Tips. Oracle Corporation*, 1995.

7. *Oracle7 for UNIX Performance Tuning Tips*. Oracle Corporation, 1995.

8. *Oracle7 Server Administrator's Guide*. Oracle Corporation, 1993, 1996.

9. Oracle8 Reference Release 8.0 Manual, Oracle Corporation, 1997.

10. ^tOracle8 Backup and Recovery Guide Release 8.0, Oracle Corporation, 1997.

11. /tOracle8 Administrators Guide Release 8.0, Oracle Corporation, 1997.

12. *Oracle7 Server Concepts Manual*. Oracle Corporation, 1993, 1996.

13. *Oracle8 Concepts Release 8.0 Manual*. Oracle Corporation, 1997.

14. *Oracle7 Server Manager User's Guide*. Oracle Corporation, 1992, 1994, 1995.

15. *Oracle7 Server SQL Reference Manual*. Oracle Corporation, 1992, 1996.

16. *Oracle8 SQL Reference Release 8.0 Manual*. Oracle Corporation, 1997.

17. *Oracle7 Server Tuning Manual. Oracle Corporation*, 1995, 1996.

18. *Oracle8 Tuning Release 8.0, Oracle Corporation*. 1997.

19. *Oracle7 Server Utilities Manual. Oracle Corporation*. 1995, 1996.

20. *Oracle8 Utilities Release 8.0 Manual, Oracle Corporation*. 1997.

21. *Oracle7 Enterprise Manager Performance Monitoring User's Guide*. Oracle Corporation, 1996.

22. *Oracle Net8 Administrator's Guide Release 8.0*. Oracle Corporation, 1997.

23. *Oracle8 PL/SQL User's Guide and Reference Release 8.0*. Oracle Corporation, 1997.

24. *Oracle7 Server Application Developer's Guide*. Oracle Corporation, 1992, 1996.

25. *Oracle8 Application Developer's Guide Release 8.0, Oracle Corporation*. 1997.

26. *Performance Tuning an Application*. SPARCWorks SunPro, Part Number 800-6018-11, Revision A, October 1992.

27. *Programmer's Guide to the Oracle PRO*C/C++ Precompiler*. Oracle Corporation, 1994, 1996.

28. Pro*C/C++ Precompiler Programmer's Guide Release 8.0, Oracle Corporation, 1997.

29. *Symmetry Multiprocessor Architecture Overview*. Sequent Computer Systems, Inc. Part Number 1003-50113-03, 1994.

30. *Solstice DiskSuite Tool 4.0 Users Guide*. SunSoft, Sun Microsystems Computer Corporation. Part Number 802-1724-10, Revision A, March 1995.

31. *Solstice DiskSuite 4.0 Administration Guide*. SunSoft, Sun Microsystems Computer Corpororation.Part Number 802-2422-10, Revision A, March 1995.

32. *Configuration and Capacity Planning for Sun Servers*, 3rd ed. Sun Microsystems Computer Corporation, Technical Product Marketing. Part Number 801-6876-01, Revision A, January 1994.

33. *Data Warehousing White Paper*. Sun Microsystems Computer Corporation, February 1995.

34. *Multithreaded Applications Programming*. SunService Division, Sun Microsystems, Inc. Technical Education Services. Part Number SI-260-02, Revision SunSoft 2.1.

35. *Sun OS 5.X Internals*. SunService Division, Sun Microsystems, Inc. Technical Education Services. Part Number SP-365, Revision B.1, September 1993.

36. *SVM Configuration and Administration Guide*. Sequent Computer Systems, Inc., 1994.

INDEX

Oracle DBA
REFERENCE LIBRARY

Ahmed Alomari,
Lynnwood Brown and
Guy Harrison

1998, Slip Case, 0-13-894742-2

This new three-book set is an unparalleled practical resource for any professional called upon to make the most of Oracle database technology. Includes Oracle and UNIX Performance Tuning, Oracle Database Administration on UNIX Systems, and Oracle SQL High-Performance Tuning.

Developing Oracle Forms Applications

Albert Lulushi

1997, 752pp, paper, 0-13-531229-9

A BOOK/CD-ROM PACKAGE

The best-selling handbook for anyone who wants to use Oracle Forms to build sophisticated client/server database applications.

Oracle Developer/ 2000 Handbook

Michael W. Stowe

1996, 304pp, paper, 0-13-227968-1

A BOOK/DISK PACKAGE

Provides practical experience and examples for developing real-world applications using Oracle's Developer/2000 development tool.

Coming Fall 1998

Oracle8 Database Administration on Windows NT
Lynnwood Brown—0-13-927443-X

Oracle Developer/2000 Forms
Albert Lulushi—0-13-949033-7

Oracle Developer/2000: Client/Server and Web-Site Publishing
Michael Stowe—0-13-918111-3

Keep Up-to-Date with
PH PTR Online!

We strive to stay on the cutting-edge of what's happening in professional computer science and engineering. Here's a bit of what you'll find when you stop by **www.phptr.com**:

@ Special interest areas offering our latest books, book series, software, features of the month, related links and other useful information to help you get the job done.

Deals, deals, deals! Come to our promotions section for the latest bargains offered to you exclusively from our retailers.

$ Need to find a bookstore? Chances are, there's a bookseller near you that carries a broad selection of PTR titles. Locate a Magnet bookstore near you at www.phptr.com.

! What's New at PH PTR? We don't just publish books for the professional community, we're a part of it. Check out our convention schedule, join an author chat, get the latest reviews and press releases on topics of interest to you.

Subscribe Today! Join PH PTR's monthly email newsletter!

Want to be kept up-to-date on your area of interest? Choose a targeted category on our website, and we'll keep you informed of the latest PH PTR products, author events, reviews and conferences in your interest area.

Visit our mailroom to subscribe today! **http://www.phptr.com/mail_lists**

LICENSE AGREEMENT AND LIMITED WARRANTY

READ THE FOLLOWING TERMS AND CONDITIONS CAREFULLY BEFORE OPENING THIS SOFTWARE PACKAGE. THIS LEGAL DOCUMENT IS AN AGREEMENT BETWEEN YOU AND PRENTICE-HALL, INC. (THE "COMPANY"). BY OPENING THIS SEALED SOFTWARE PACKAGE, YOU ARE AGREEING TO BE BOUND BY THESE TERMS AND CONDITIONS. IF YOU DO NOT AGREE WITH THESE TERMS AND CONDITIONS, DO NOT OPEN THE SOFTWARE PACKAGE. PROMPTLY RETURN THE UNOPENED SOFTWARE PACKAGE AND ALL ACCOMPANYING ITEMS TO THE PLACE YOU OBTAINED THEM FOR A FULL REFUND OF ANY SUMS YOU HAVE PAID.

1. **GRANT OF LICENSE:** In consideration of your payment of the license fee, which is part of the price you paid for this product, and your agreement to abide by the terms and conditions of this Agreement, the Company grants to you a nonexclusive right to use and display the copy of the enclosed software program (hereinafter the "SOFTWARE") on a single computer (i.e., with a single CPU) at a single location so long as you comply with the terms of this Agreement. The Company reserves all rights not expressly granted to you under this Agreement.

2. **OWNERSHIP OF SOFTWARE:** You own only the magnetic or physical media (the enclosed disks) on which the SOFTWARE is recorded or fixed, but the Company retains all the rights, title, and ownership to the SOFTWARE recorded on the original disk copy(ies) and all subsequent copies of the SOFTWARE, regardless of the form or media on which the original or other copies may exist. This license is not a sale of the original SOFTWARE or any copy to you.

3. **COPY RESTRICTIONS:** This SOFTWARE and the accompanying printed materials and user manual (the "Documentation") are the subject of copyright. You may not copy the Documentation or the SOFTWARE, except that you may make a single copy of the SOFTWARE for backup or archival purposes only. You may be held legally responsible for any copying or copyright infringement which is caused or encouraged by your failure to abide by the terms of this restriction.

4. **USE RESTRICTIONS:** You may not network the SOFTWARE or otherwise use it on more than one computer or computer terminal at the same time. You may physically transfer the SOFTWARE from one computer to another provided that the SOFTWARE is used on only one computer at a time. You may not distribute copies of the SOFTWARE or Documentation to others. You may not reverse engineer, disassemble, decompile, modify, adapt, translate, or create derivative works based on the SOFTWARE or the Documentation without the prior written consent of the Company.

5. **TRANSFER RESTRICTIONS:** The enclosed SOFTWARE is licensed only to you and may not be transferred to any one else without the prior written consent of the Company. Any unauthorized transfer of the SOFTWARE shall result in the immediate termination of this Agreement.

6. **TERMINATION:** This license is effective until terminated. This license will terminate automatically without notice from the Company and become null and void if you fail to comply with any provisions or limitations of this license. Upon termination, you shall destroy the Documentation and all copies of the SOFTWARE. All provisions of this Agreement as to warranties, limitation of liability, remedies or damages, and our ownership rights shall survive termination.

7. **MISCELLANEOUS:** This Agreement shall be construed in accordance with the laws of the United States of America and the State of New York and shall benefit the Company, its affiliates, and assignees.

8. **LIMITED WARRANTY AND DISCLAIMER OF WARRANTY:** The Company warrants that the SOFTWARE, when properly used in accordance with the Documentation, will operate in substantial conformity with the description of the SOFTWARE set forth in the Documentation. The Company does not warrant that the SOFTWARE will meet your requirements or that the operation of the SOFTWARE will be uninterrupted or error-free. The Company warrants that the media on which the SOFTWARE is delivered shall be free from defects in materials and workmanship under normal use for a period of thirty (30) days from the date of your purchase. Your only remedy and the Company's only obligation under these limited warranties is, at the Company's option, return of the warranted item for a refund of any amounts paid by you or replacement of the item. Any replacement of SOFTWARE or media under the warranties shall not extend the original warranty period. The limited warranty set forth above shall not apply to any SOFTWARE which the Company determines in good faith has been subject to misuse, neglect, improper installation, repair, alteration, or damage by you. EXCEPT FOR THE EXPRESSED WARRANTIES SET FORTH ABOVE, THE COMPANY DISCLAIMS ALL WARRANTIES, EXPRESS OR IMPLIED, INCLUDING WITHOUT LIMITATION, THE IMPLIED WARRANTIES OF MERCHANTABILITY AND FITNESS FOR A PARTICULAR PURPOSE. EXCEPT FOR THE EXPRESS WARRANTY SET FORTH ABOVE, THE COMPANY DOES NOT WARRANT, GUARANTEE, OR MAKE ANY REPRESENTATION REGARDING THE USE OR THE RESULTS OF THE USE OF THE SOFTWARE IN TERMS OF ITS CORRECTNESS, ACCURACY, RELIABILITY, CURRENTNESS, OR OTHERWISE.

IN NO EVENT, SHALL THE COMPANY OR ITS EMPLOYEES, AGENTS, SUPPLIERS, OR CONTRACTORS BE LIABLE FOR ANY INCIDENTAL, INDIRECT, SPECIAL, OR CONSEQUENTIAL DAMAGES ARISING OUT OF OR IN CONNECTION WITH THE LICENSE GRANTED UNDER THIS AGREEMENT, OR FOR LOSS OF USE, LOSS OF DATA, LOSS OF INCOME OR PROFIT, OR OTHER LOSSES, SUSTAINED AS A RESULT OF INJURY TO ANY PERSON, OR LOSS OF OR DAMAGE TO PROPERTY, OR CLAIMS OF THIRD PARTIES, EVEN IF THE COMPANY OR AN AUTHORIZED REPRESENTATIVE OF THE COMPANY HAS BEEN ADVISED OF THE POSSIBILITY OF SUCH DAMAGES. IN NO EVENT SHALL LIABILITY OF THE COMPANY FOR DAMAGES WITH RESPECT TO THE SOFTWARE EXCEED THE AMOUNTS ACTUALLY PAID BY YOU, IF ANY, FOR THE SOFTWARE.

SOME JURISDICTIONS DO NOT ALLOW THE LIMITATION OF IMPLIED WARRANTIES OR LIABILITY FOR INCIDENTAL, INDIRECT, SPECIAL, OR CONSEQUENTIAL DAMAGES, SO THE ABOVE LIMITATIONS MAY NOT ALWAYS APPLY. THE WARRANTIES IN THIS AGREEMENT GIVE YOU SPECIFIC LEGAL RIGHTS AND YOU MAY ALSO HAVE OTHER RIGHTS WHICH VARY IN ACCORDANCE WITH LOCAL LAW.

ACKNOWLEDGMENT
YOU ACKNOWLEDGE THAT YOU HAVE READ THIS AGREEMENT, UNDERSTAND IT, AND AGREE TO BE BOUND BY ITS TERMS AND CONDITIONS. YOU ALSO AGREE THAT THIS AGREEMENT IS THE COMPLETE AND EXCLUSIVE STATEMENT OF THE AGREEMENT BETWEEN YOU AND THE COMPANY AND SUPERSEDES ALL PROPOSALS OR PRIOR AGREEMENTS, ORAL, OR WRITTEN, AND ANY OTHER COMMUNICATIONS BETWEEN YOU AND THE COMPANY OR ANY REPRESENTATIVE OF THE COMPANY RELATING TO THE SUBJECT MATTER OF THIS AGREEMENT.

Should you have any questions concerning this Agreement or if you wish to contact the Company for any reason, please contact in writing at the address below.
Robin Short
Prentice Hall PTR
One Lake Street
Upper Saddle River, New Jersey 07458

CONTENTS

The CD included with this book includes white papers, utilities, and scripts. The CD is intended to complement the book by offering additional information such as architecture white papers, product features, and performance tuning tips. The CD also includes SQL scripts that can be used to monitor database performance.

SYSTEM REQUIREMENTS

The file types are noted in each README file per section. You may need a PostScript Viewer (.ps files) such as pageview on Solaris, a browser (.html files), Acrobat Reader (.pdf files), Microsoft PowerPoint (.ppt files), Microsoft Word (.doc files), and a text editor (.txt or .sql files). The CD is organized into the following directories:

hp: HP white papers and bulletins

nca: Network Computing Architecture white papers

oracle: Oracle white papers

scripts: Performance monitoring scripts (SQL)

sequent: Sequent white papers and utilities

sun: Sun white papers, bulletins, and scripts

veritas: Veritas white papers

TECHNICAL SUPPORT

The CD does not include software. Therefore, technical support is not provided by Prentice Hall nor the author. If, however, you feel that your CD is damaged, please contact Prentice Hall for a replacement: disc_exchange@prenhall.com.